Releasing Pain

Releasing Pain

Introducing the Rapid Release Progressive Flexibility Program

Innovative Exercises for
Physical Rehabilitation and Pain Management

Nancy Griggs PT
Illustrated by Jeff Griggs

Intriguing New Perspectives Reveal how Diverse Diagnoses have More in Common than You Could ever Imagine... and How the Eyes Effect them All!

Copyright © 2018 by Nancy Griggs PT.

Library of Congress Control Number: 2017916256
ISBN: Hardcover 978-1-5434-5986-9
Softcover 978-1-5434-5987-6
eBook 978-1-5434-5988-3

All rights reserved. No part of this book may be reproduced or transmitted in any form or by any means, electronic or mechanical, including photocopying, recording, or by any information storage and retrieval system, without permission in writing from the copyright owner.

This publication provides recommendations and ideas for rehabilitation and pain management. All efforts have been made to ensure the accuracy of the information contained in this book. Consultation with a qualified medical professional prior to beginning any new exercise or health program is advised. The author and publisher of this material are not responsible in any manner whatsoever for any injury or adverse effects that may occur through following the instructions contained in this material.

Courses to train health care providers for continuing education purposes are available through the author. Information can be obtained on the website releasingpainnancy.com.

Print information available on the last page.

Rev. date: 09/07/2018

To order additional copies of this book, contact:
Xlibris
1-888-795-4274
www.Xlibris.com
Orders@Xlibris.com

Contents

Chapter 1 *Releasing* Pain 1

Chapter 2 What Is *Rapid Release?* 15

Chapter 3 *Rapid Release*— Better Than Stretching! 65
                Contraindications and Precautions 69

Chapter 4 Answering Your Questions . . . Helping Yourself 113

Chapter 5 Examples of Effectiveness 147
                Releasing Knee Pain 154
                Releasing Hip Pain 181
                Releasing Balance Dysfunction 202
                Releasing Ankle Dysfunction 221
                Releasing Low Back Pain 225
                Releasing Neck Pain 288
                Releasing Shoulder Pain 313
                Releasing Headaches 347
                Releasing TMJ Pain 354
                Releasing the Elderly 360
                Releasing Pain during Hospitalization 371

Chapter 6 Why Does It Work? 387

Chapter 7 Putting It All Together 445

Acknowledgements

Thanks to my brother, Jeff, who patiently helped me with a seemingly never ending list of illustrations without ever complaining.

And, to my many patients. This book could not be a source of encouragement for others if you had not put in the effort to validate the effectiveness of this method.

Foreword

"*Rapid Release* is an exciting and innovative approach to the rehabilitation of recovering patients. I have had the pleasure of witnessing the success of this therapy for my injured patients. Nancy's ideas and theories regarding the possible prevention of the long term effects of traumatic injury are insightful and thought provoking."

Thomas R. Howdieshell, MD
Professor of Surgery
Trauma/Surgical Critical Care
Department of Surgery
University of New Mexico HSC
Albuquerque, New Mexico

"I have watched Nancy use her techniques to improve patient outcomes in many different settings for several years now. Her understanding of how posture and positioning effect patient care provides an excellent opportunity to improve collaboration of care between therapists and nursing. I look forward to working with her to make improvements in our treatment practices for the good of our patients. This book will be an essential tool to help us do that!"

Kathy Lopez-Bushnell APRN, EdD, MPH, MSN
Director of Nursing Research
University of New Mexico Hospital

"Everyone should have *The Rapid Release Progressive Flexibility Program* in their physical therapy toolbox. Rapid Release is not just a 'program,' but a mindset, to look at the total patient with past traumatic injury and limitations of mobility and pain affecting the whole body. I have used this method with patients and it *is* progressive with the ability to jump into lymph drainage and improved mobility after releasing total body fascial restrictions. If one finds something that works, use it and let your clients benefit!"

Amanda Cannady PT CLT LANA

"I have clinically found that Nancy's *Rapid Release* program is very effective in promoting correct postural alignment, increasing range of motion and decreasing pain, which ultimately leads to increased functional mobility and improved emotional state of patients. I feel this program can be applied to a variety of patient populations in all settings of physical therapy."

Christina Munoz, DPT
Supervisor Rehabilitation Services
University of New Mexico Hospital

"*Rapid Release* is a fabulous approach to improving one's structural alignment and kinesthetic behaviors with simple movements designed specifically to access fascial planes and previous traumas within the body. These techniques can help influence both physical and emotional patterns, promoting a holistic reduction of dysfunction on many levels."

Patricia Marie Hubard MOTR/L CLT LMT

"My experience with *Rapid Release* is that the eye movement exercises were able to access the fascial connections to deep core musculature in my back and achieve the release of tension that - for me - has been present for years. By massaging the muscles under my tongue, I experienced a release of the "complimentary" psoas musculature, which has been a chronic problem as well. That, to me, is just amazing!"

Julie Cleveland, PT

"Nancy's approach offers a gentle option to improve posture, increase range of motion, and decrease pain. This is a wonderful alternative for any individual for whom the traditional approach to Physical Therapy is not working."

Alexa Allen, OT, MOTR/L

Preface

The practice of physical therapy is more than the application of science to rehabilitation. It is also an art. An artist must first understand the properties and characteristics of his paints, brushes, and canvas. Years of practice help him refine the methods and techniques of his craft. The blending of his knowledge and tools with his vision and message yield the ultimate artistic expression.

The exercise program I will introduce in this text is a similar expression. My formal education as a physical therapist was completed at the University of New Mexico in 1977. The combination of the academic training and lessons I have learned from personal injury has been polished by hundreds of hours spent with my patients. This has resulted in a new method of rehabilitation.

The beginnings of the **Rapid Release Progressive Flexibility Program** occurred in March of 1982. I was on my way to work when my car hit black ice on a winding mountain road. I was next seen at the bottom of a forty-foot ravine. When I finally arrived at the hospital as a patient rather than an employee, X-rays revealed a compression burst fracture of the third lumbar vertebra in my lower back. The next day, my complete lumbar spine was fused together with two steel rods and multiple metal screws. My surgery went very well, but when the cast came off six months later, I was left with a permanent deformity of my lower back and a very unusual gait pattern. As I would learn years later, the normal amount of lordosis, or "sway back," a person should have measures thirty degrees on X-ray. My X-rays revealed the curve of my lower back was forty-two degrees, but in the opposite direction. I had a seventy-two-degree shift in the alignment of my spine. As you can see from my X-rays, my posture was hugely distorted.

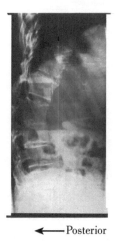 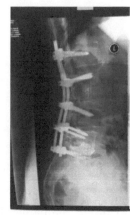

- Left: Spine prior to 2004 reconstruction (Original hardware removed in 1984)
- Right: Spine after 2004 reconstruction

⟵ Posterior   Anterior ⟶

After my cast was removed, my roommate from physical therapy school suggested I see the massage therapist at her clinic. The longer I live, the more I know she gave me some of the best advice I would ever receive. I was more than a little surprised by the *extreme discomfort* I experienced in response to the therapist's very light touch, and it covered my entire body. I was unaware of this hidden pain buried in the soft tissues of my body prior to that first massage. Over the course of the next month, I received three full body massages per week. As the discomfort lessened during the treatments, my gait became more normal, and my tolerance for activity also improved.

Surgically removing my original hardware in 1984 eased the discomfort I experienced at the end of one rod. I took the next eight years off from work after my accident to have my three daughters. During this time I managed my pain by walking, stretching and receiving regular chiropractic adjustments.

I returned to work as a physical therapist in 1992. I took courses in neuromuscular therapy and craniosacral therapy to meet the continuing education requirements I needed to maintain my physical therapy license. **Neuromuscular therapy** is a specific massage technique that teaches the therapist how to examine and treat each muscle of the body from the origin of the muscle to its insertion. **Craniosacral therapy** teaches the therapist how to release soft tissue restrictions along the spine as well as around and beneath the skull. These two therapies form the foundation from which I continue to practice. As I applied these therapies to my own body and to my patients, I gained valuable insights into soft tissue dysfunction I would not have learned apart from my own injury.

The **Rapid Release Progressive Flexibility Program** *is a way to mobilize these tissues with movement.* The classroom of my body has given me an understanding of pain I never received in an academic classroom. Listening to and observing my patients showed me that, regardless of their current complaint, *we all have far more in common than I ever imagined.*

In the fall of 2000, the rheumatology department at the hospital where I was working asked for help in caring for their fibromyalgia patients. I was hopeful my manual skills would help this population, so I volunteered to try. I checked out a book about fibromyalgia from the hospital library to get additional ideas for treating this condition. The most important suggestion I found in the book was to exercise these patients in supine, or flat on their back. The book explained that supine should be the most comfortable position for exercise because it is the position in which the body becomes the most weightless. The effects of gravity on movement are the least when the body is positioned in supine. What I soon learned, however, was most of these patients were most *uncomfortable* in supine. I also noted how distorted their cervical, or neck, posture was in this position. It was either very difficult or impossible for them to independently position their neck in correct alignment. Most of my patients tilted their head back so their chin was pointing toward the ceiling to some extent.

In an effort to implement the suggestion of supine positioning for exercise, I began to first provide as much compensation as was needed to correct the posture of the cervical spine. I would also provide compensation under their knees to ease any lower back pain without deviating from a position of correct posture any more than necessary. The exercises I gave to each patient were specifically directed to the area of their primary pain complaint. If they were referred to therapy for shoulder pain, I gave them exercises for their shoulder. If their complaint was knee pain, I gave them exercises for their knee. The only difference was they were doing their exercises lying down on their back as opposed to sitting or standing.

In the spring of 2001, I decided to try some of the suggestions I had been giving to a woman I was treating for lower back and hip pain on myself. I had completed some work in my backyard that required hours of forward bending at the waist. When I completed my work, the tension in my lower back made standing straight virtually impossible. As I lay down in the grass and started to do some very basic active range-of-motion exercises, I sensed how my body wanted to respond to each movement. I followed the leads my body gave me and was soon aware the movements released tension in each other as I alternated them. After only five to ten minutes of very non-strenuous exercise, I was able to stand straighter and was more flexible and buoyant in my legs.

Once I became familiar with the movement patterns for my lower body, I wondered if the same types of alternating movements would be effective for the neck. As it turned out, the exercises not only helped my neck but also promoted even *greater* flexibility in my lower body. Exercises for the upper body were next to fall into place. Then one day I randomly started the eye exercises with a patient suffering from cervical pain. *I continue to be amazed daily at the help so many people receive by doing these very simple eye exercises.* This book will show you how to use this series of exercises to help you with your problem.

I had no idea what would become of this exercise program that day in my backyard. The past eighteen years have been a remarkable journey of revelation and discovery for me. *What I appreciate most* about this program is the fact that it is so safe. **Rapid Release** provides a new entry level to exercise for those who have an obvious need for exercise but have not found a form of exercise they can tolerate. Because it is intended to be used within a pain-free range of motion, there are virtually no contraindications. Caution should be used, however, by those who are extremely frail and/or elderly. Other precautions are explained on pages 69-71.

The things I most enjoy about the program are its simplicity and versatility. Within eighteen months of its completion, I realized these exercises could benefit every type of patient I saw. It is a postural balancing program, so it is helpful and relaxing even for individuals who do not have pain. When pain *is* present, it does not matter whether it is chronic or acute. It is particularly good for post-motor vehicle accident, falls, or fibromyalgia, where there can be multiple pain sites. I have used it equally as well for diverse orthopedic referrals, preoperatively or postoperatively, including rotator cuff tears or total knee replacements, which *appear* to be more localized and straightforward. These exercises have helped with balance disorders, vertigo, and migraine headaches as well as more involved neurological conditions, such as cerebral palsy, Parkinson's disease, multiple sclerosis, and post CVA (cerebrovascular accident), or stroke. Even individuals who are highly athletic and exercise regularly have experienced the positive effects of these exercises. I have used them in a variety of settings, including outpatient clinics, skilled nursing facilities, home health, hospitals, my private office, and my mother's living room floor. All age groups have responded surprisingly well whether they be adolescents or the elderly in their eighties and nineties. **Rapid Release** is easy to teach and easy to learn.

The comprehensive exercise program I present in this text is a noninvasive therapeutic approach to pain management that can be used to supplement or enhance existing techniques. My ideas resonate with several other theories and concepts that have been documented for decades. What is different is how the ideas are packaged and applied. This program is my offering to those who are looking for help with their unresolved pain issues. It is a new tool for the health-care providers' toolbox to help make their job easier while they continue to provide the best possible care for their patients.

I have included more than seven dozen case examples in this book to help you understand how this treatment approach can help **you**. Each case example represents a common situation or diagnosis. As you read the patients' history and their response to treatment, my hope is for you to be encouraged about the possibility for your own improvement. Until now, I have worked alone with each one of my patients. No one, except an occasional family member, close friend, student, or curious therapist, has been with me to share the fun I have had as I have seen my patients remarkably respond to these very simple movements. You are now invited to share some very surprising and rewarding moments. Forty-five testimonial letters from a few of my patients will validate the results you may achieve with this method.

The majority of you who implement these exercises will experience some degree of success by doing these exercises. I tracked the outcomes of one hundred consecutive patients in 2014. These patients had nothing in common, except they all received this exercise program as the foundation of their therapy. Fifty-eight percent reached all their functional and pain goals. Another seventeen percent partially reached their goals. The final twenty-five percent were not helped by this method. If you are a "patient," this method offers you a seventy-five percent chance to feel and function better. If you are a therapist, these concepts will provide you an option for patients who are not responding to traditional therapy.

The more I implement this program, the more I feel like the blessed recipient of it than the developer of it. It has given me such great joy to watch people improve by doing these very simple exercises. I am excited the time has finally come for me to share them with you. I hope you will be encouraged by the following letter written by a personal friend of mine. She brought her daughter to me for help, but later learned the exercises were good for her and her husband too. Maybe this sort of thing will happen in your home as well.

> *Dear Nancy,*
>
> *We want you to know how much we appreciate what your rehabilitative exercises did for our family. When we came to you, we were out of options. Our daughter, who was ten years old at the time, had suffered a horseback riding accident two years prior to our initial visit. We were under the care of a well respected chiropractor, but we were making very slow progress. The chiropractic care brought our daughter temporary relief, but we were praying for more than that!*
>
> *During the two years after the riding accident, our daughter could no longer enjoy bike rides, swimming, archery, or softball—and she had been a pretty good little pitcher too! If she did a little too much, she would sometimes cry when the tightness and sharp pains would grab her upper back. We tried so hard to avoid any over exertion that would send us back to the chiropractor for adjustments and electrotherapy. And because of her reduced activity, she put on weight. It broke our hearts to see her endure so much pain!*
>
> *When I heard that your program was having such tremendous success, we had to try it. After meeting with you one time, we began doing the exercises like you showed us. They were simple and easy! I could tell her body alignment improved*

after the first time she did them. And she experienced immediate relaxation. Within a few days, she noticed she was enjoying a larger range of motion. After two weeks, we knew she was going to have a complete recovery! We kept doing the exercises for two months, even though she seemed to be completely better after the first month.

Today our daughter continues to be pain-free, without any recurring symptoms of trauma. My husband and I have used the same exercises to achieve relief from back pain too. We used to be regulars at the chiropractic clinic, but we have not been back now for a long time.

We are so happy you are publishing this book! We know God is going to bless many people through this! We thank Him for sending you our way.

Chapter 1

Releasing Pain

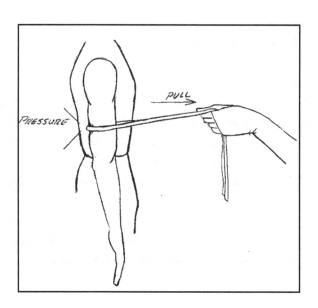

It is the job of the physical therapist to help their client recover from functional deficits. Lingering pain following injury or surgery is often a prohibitive factor to the rehabilitation process. Most people have experienced the inability to function at their best capacity when their back is hurting or their head is pounding. Everyone knows what a bother pain can be. "No pain, no gain" is the mantra of many in their attempt to overcome their pain, only to find that provoking pain begets *even more pain*.

I am convinced the pain we visit our doctors about is a symptom of a more extensive scenario. I believe any trauma we sustain to our body stays with us to some degree until it is intentionally addressed. I also believe a progressive tension develops in the body after an unresolved trauma, which provokes an increased pressure in the body. This pressure can and will manifest itself through a variety of symptoms. The key to **resolving** the obvious and the immediate pain complaint is to release the tension to relieve the pressure. The key to **preventing** future pain and a variety of other problems is also to release the tension to relieve the pressure. I am hopeful the case examples I present in this book will make a case for an early comprehensive intervention following traumatic injury. I believe the possibility of providing an intentional new avenue of preventive care is an attainable reality.

It is controversial to assume past physical trauma will create problems later in life. Many people would doubt a motor vehicle accident or a fall several years ago, or even months ago, could be the source of a current pain complaint. If the trauma occurred *decades* ago, it would certainly be disregarded by many people. I, on the other hand, believe the overwhelming majority of our problems *can* and *do* extend back to these traumatic events in our past. It is my hope the common thread of past traumatic injury coursing through the case examples I will present will motivate us to consider new holistic plans of care following traumatic injury.

Let me use an illustration to validate my point. My dad loved to get a great deal on a car. At one point in his life, Dad met a guy who restored damaged vehicles and sold them at the car auction. Dad enjoyed nothing more than getting a top-of-the-line vehicle at an unheard-of low price. There are many people who would never consider buying a restored vehicle. If you ask them why, they would probably tell you it is because *they are afraid of the unseen damage*. They don't know what problem(s) might surface in the future that are not so obvious today. We are very quick to acknowledge the damage impact and force can have on steel and metal. We disregard the fact that the same impact and force that mangled the car can and will have a lasting effect on the flesh, bones, and soft tissue that drove the very same vehicle.

Acknowledging the lasting effect(s) of a previous trauma helps make sense of the mysterious and the frustrating. Quite often, physical problems spontaneously appear in an individual's body. They are unable to recall any particular injury to the area that is now painful or dysfunctional, but the pain they perceive is very real. The sequence of events that tend to follow is, unfortunately, very common. Initially, resting the part or cutting back on certain activities is tried, along with topical creams and heat or cold applications as a remedy for the pain. If the person next tries over-the-counter or prescription medications unsuccessfully, the situation becomes somewhat worrisome and frustrating. Discouragement develops if tests such as X-rays and MRIs are completed and return normal. So far, there is no explanation for this curious pain, much less a solution. Depending on the intensity of the pain and the degree to which it is changing the person's lifestyle, some people are on the verge of hopelessness.

Acknowledging the theory that a previous trauma has lasting effects on the body gives us hope for understanding the current problem. As we begin to consider the effects of *force, tension, and pressure* on and within the body, we are given a new perspective on what we previously perceived as inexplicable. Addressing the problem now has some very practical solutions. New treatment options can be considered that otherwise would not have been thought of. The process of preventing future complications can also begin.

Force

Anytime I must learn something new, I do best if I have a clear definition of my terms. So I will begin there for you. All trauma begins with an impact that generates *force*. By definition, "a force has acted on a system anytime there is a change in the state of that system; a force may be understood by the effects it produces: deformation, movement, heat, or friction."[1] A force either pushes or pulls on an object. The vector of the force describes its magnitude and direction. There are two basic classes of force. "Contact forces act on an object by touching it at a specific point. Long-range forces act on an object without making physical contact. Magnets and gravity demonstrate long-range force. You have undoubtedly held a magnet over a paper clip and watched it leap up to the magnet. Or, seen your coffee cup fall to the ground if you release your grasp."[2] **Motor vehicle accidents and falls involve both types of force.**

Even contact force can cause far-reaching effects. For example, when a person slips on ice and falls back onto their buttocks, a force enters their body at the site of impact. There may or may not be visible bruising or soreness. This energy will proceed through the body toward its final destination. If the force is electricity, it leaves a larger wound at the point of exit than at the point of entrance. The force generated by the impact will not leave a visible exit wound, except in the instance of a compound fracture; instead, the force *settles* in the body somewhere, doing more damage where it settles than where it enters. The damage the force generated by the impact is often *invisible* unlike the damage from electricity, which is *visible*. The damage done by the force generated from an impact can enter the body from any direction and varying magnitudes. Understanding the mechanism of injury is always helpful in making practical sense of current pain complaints.

We have all witnessed the rippling effect of a rock being thrown into a body of water. This demonstrates how areas other than the point of contact are affected by and absorb the impact and force generated by the rock hitting the water. On a much larger scale, none of us will ever forget the sight of the World Trade Center collapsing after being struck at a very specific location on the building. The force of the impact traveled throughout the entire building, weakening it at every level. In the same way,

---

CHAPTER 1

[1] Knight, Randall D., Jones, Brian, and Field, Stuart, *College Physics: A Strategic Approach*, Second Edition (Pearson Education, Inc., publishing as Addison-Wesley, 2010), p. 105.
[2] Knight, Randall D., Jones, Brian, and Field, Stuart, *College Physics: A Strategic Approach*, Second Edition (Pearson Education, Inc., publishing as Addison-Wesley, 2010), p. 105.

the force of the impact generated by a motor vehicle accident or a fall will be absorbed *directly* and *indirectly*. The damage it does can be obvious, but the damage often occurs at the site where it settles unrecognized. This explains why a person who recalls no injury to their neck may experience neck pain at some time following a fall onto their tailbone.

Osteopathy is a system of medical practice based on a theory that diseases are chiefly due to loss of structural integrity, which can be restored by manipulation and massage of the bones, joints, and muscles. The presence of whole-body dysfunction and the need to treat a person holistically is at the premise of their practice. As stated, "Lesions, or damaged areas, occur not only locally at the point of contact, but also at distant sites as a result of shock waves or similar phenomena. A global lesion is far removed from the symptom. It reflects the belief that nothing is isolated in a living organism and that all structures and processes are inter-dependent. Clinically, this concept leads us to treat people instead of symptoms, and to look at the entire person and his bodily structure instead of simply the place that hurts. The concept of the global lesion is at the foundation of osteopathy."[3]

As the body absorbs the force of any impact, whether it be the result of a collision or fall, it will stress all different types of tissue. For the purpose of this text, we will consider its effect on the *fascia* of the body. Fascia is comprised of layers and layers of connective tissue within the body that virtually holds everything together. When the skin is removed from a piece of chicken, the fascia is easily seen as the sheer membrane overlying the muscle. But fascia is not only present where it interfaces with muscle. Fascia is the connective tissue matrix that holds everything in its place, literally connecting anything in the body to everything else. Instead of "wrapping up" a muscle to separate it from other structures, fascia acts like a spiderweb to "connect" each structure in the body to its neighbor. In my experience, restricted fascia has made me feel as if I was "wrapped up too tightly" on the inside. One patient told me her skin did not feel like it was big enough for her body.

---

[3] Barral, Jean-Pierre and Croibier, Alain, *Trauma - An Osteopathic Approach* (Eastland Press, 1999), p. 11.

In its healthy state, fascia is a connective tissue "fabric" that distributes mechanical forces in the body. The shape of the fascial tissue is the result of tension and compressive forces in the area. This form can be altered by strain or stress. "While muscle is designed to contract and relax either slowly or quickly, fascia is not. Muscle is elastic, but fascia is plastic. When muscle is stretched, it will attempt to recoil back to its resting length. When fascia is quickly stretched, it can tear. If the stretch is applied slowly enough, it will deform plastically: it will change its length and retain the change."[4] Fascia can become stronger and denser in response to stress and strain. The best analogy I can give from personal experience to describe what areas of increased fascial density feel like is "my insides have been starched." Comparing the injured fascial web to phyllo dough that has become baklava is another helpful word picture.

Because fascia is literally *everywhere* in our body, it can affect *everything*. Imagine how difficult it would be to enjoy a workout of running or weight lifting if you wrapped yourself up in plastic wrap prior to exercising. So it is with a person whose motion and function are restricted by tight fascia. Imagine yourself wearing a piece of clothing that fits you nicely and hangs comfortably on your body, but the lining of the garment is one or two sizes too small. Even though everything seems fine from the outside, you feel uncomfortable. So it can be with the fascia. There may or may not be any external evidence to the effect(s) it is having on the inside of the body.

Body workers and massage therapists have long said "The body has memory." Examining the body for fascial restrictions enables us to "see the memory" trapped in the body in the form of damaged fascia. There are currently no ways available on a large scale to objectively evaluate the condition of the fascial system, so it can often be overlooked or forgotten. The tone or the tension of the fascia can be palpated and treated, however, through the hands of another person, which brings us to consider tension.

---

[4] Myers, Thomas W., *Anatomy Trains Myofascial Meridians for Manual and Movement Therapists*, Third Edition (Churchill Livingstone Elsevier, 2014), p. 22.

Tension

Our bodies basically function like an elaborate pulley system. When all the muscles, or pulleys, are balanced and harmoniously exerting the correct amount of tension among themselves, the system functions efficiently. We have all experienced those times, however, when one area is tighter than another. We feel the discomfort of "being out of balance." If the imbalance is significant enough, it will visually manifest itself as postural distortions or gait discrepancies. The pulleys may be imbalanced enough to make standing still or walking a straight line difficult. If this loss of equilibrium provokes an actual fall, whether from tripping while walking or during a sporting event, the result is a pulley system sprained and/or strained further out of balance. No one has ever fallen while maintaining a perfect posture. This opens the door for a painful tension to develop, alerting us to our body's need for correction. As we consider how tension relates to pain, there are three things to keep in mind.

First of all, adverse tension in a muscle does not always limit movement. It is possible to have a great range of motion but still experience pain in a certain muscle when it is used or palpated. This is because a *section* of the muscle may be tight, but the area of tension is not actually large enough to hinder the overall motion. These areas of increased tone are referred to as *trigger points*. They are painful because the tension is significant enough to hinder blood flow to the area. While trigger points may hinder muscle lengthening, they do not always do so. Trigger points can cause pain locally, or they can refer pain to other areas as well.

Second, if the range of motion *is* hindered in a particular direction, it is not necessarily the result of excessive tension in an opposing muscle group. The restriction may be the result of tightness within the muscle working to produce the motion instead. For example, if I cannot fully straighten my knee, it would be logical for me to suspect the muscle that bends my knee is too tight, which then prevents the knee from completely straightening. What may actually be limiting the motion instead are the trigger point areas within the muscle that straightens my knee. These areas prevent the complete muscle from contracting, and range of motion is limited. This is, in part, why stretching or strengthening only the areas of obvious deficits in our bodies will not produce the movement we are striving for. If you reconsider the body as a pulley system, it is easy to understand you cannot an adjustment on one side without affecting the other. Any time there obvious problem, it is safe to say there is a secondary problem close by that may not be quite as obvious.

The third way tension affects the body relates to pain perception. It is not only a little more surprising, but also easy to understand. The best way to explain this point is through another illustration. If I stood in *front* of you and tied a rope around your arm and then pulled on the rope, you would feel the discomfort from the pull in the *back* of the arm. In an effort to reduce the discomfort, I could rub the back of your arm or heat it repeatedly, but neither of these things would help as much as if I just *released* my pull from the front. The primary source of pain in an area frequently can be found as adverse tension on the *opposite* side of the body.

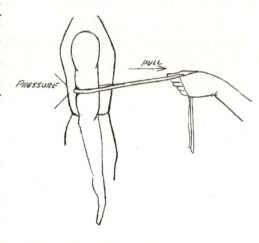

The best and most common example of this is **lower back pain** and the muscle that flexes, or bends, the hip. The psoas (so-as) muscle attaches to the anterior, or front, side of the vertebrae, or bones in the lower back. The muscle passes through the abdomen to reach its point of insertion at the top of the femur, or the long bone in the thigh. When this muscle becomes too tight, which it often does with prolonged sitting, it exerts a pull on the vertebrae in the lower back. **The pain or tightness is felt in the lower back, but it is best resolved by releasing the pull from the front of the body in the abdomen.**

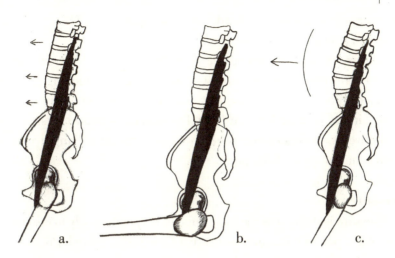

a. Normal length of the psoas muscle in standing.
b. The lower half of the psoas becomes shortened during prolonged sitting.
c. When the psoas is required to lengthen during standing, the upper half of the muscle must pull the vertebrae of the lower back forward to compensate for the overall length that has been lost to tightness in the lower half of the muscle.

The effect is the same if I pull on the front of your shirt to make it pull tightly across your lower back. This is why applying heat or cold directly to the low back is only partially and/or temporarily effective in relieving lower back pain. While it is okay to treat the symptoms directly, more pain relief will be realized if you do not neglect the source of the discomfort by applying heat or cold to your abdomen. **Decrease the pain in your back by treating the tension in the front—in the abdomen.**

In the same way, discomfort in our upper bodies or torso is often the result of a downward pull from the tight fascia in the lower body and/or lower extremities. If I applied a downward pull on the hem of your shirt, you would experience the pressure and tension from the pull across the top of your shoulders. That same pressure would be relieved by interrupting the pull on the hem of the shirt. Because the fascia is a continuous sheath covering the entire body, it actually acts more like a hooded bodysuit than just a shirt. As you visualize this example, it is easy to see how tension in the lower body can affect the head, neck, and upper torso. Or, tension from above can also affect an area below.

Adverse tension in the body can develop in several different ways. It can be the result of a sedentary lifestyle or prolonged positioning that is not corrected with regular stretching. It may be the result of a very direct or indirect injury or trauma. Regardless of the cause, increased tension in the connective tissue creates increased pressure on the underlying structures, which brings us to my final point.

Pressure

Pressure is defined as the force applied perpendicularly to the surface of an object per unit area over which that force is distributed. Pressure is a pushing force. Tension is a pulling force. What I have observed clinically is that increased fascial tension applies pressure on whatever lies beneath it as it pulls across the underlying structure. Because the fascial web is continuous from the feet to the head, and even inside the head, I have seen how increasing tension by dorsiflexing the foot, or pulling the toes towards the nose, can increase the pressure in a person's head, or lifting their arm can increase the pressure in their head. What I see most commonly can best be illustrated by thinking about the body as if it is a rectangular water balloon.

The body is largely comprised of water. "Normal values for total body water expressed as a total body weight will vary between 45 percent and 75 percent. The total body water can be divided into two major fluid compartments. Thirty-four percent of this fluid is in the extracellular compartment consisting primarily of the plasma found in blood vessels and in the interstitial fluid that surrounds the cells. Lymph, cerebrospinal fluid, joint fluids, and humors of the eye are, also, considered extracellular fluid. The remaining sixty-six percent is intracellular fluid which is the water found inside the cells."[5]

What I began to notice very early in the application of this program to my treatments was *areas of pain or joint stiffness were best relieved by movement at the opposite end of the body from the symptoms.* The tension

---

[5] Patton, Kevin T., PhD and Thibodeau, Gary, A., PhD, *Anatomy and Physiology*, Seventh Edition, (Mosby Elsevier, 2010), p. 980.

in the lower body increased pressure and/or provoked symptoms above. When the tension was released in the lower body, the symptoms resolved in the upper body, neck, and/or head. The same principles applied to tension above and symptoms below. When it came to symptoms more in the middle, like shoulder pain, the tension needed to be released above *and* below.

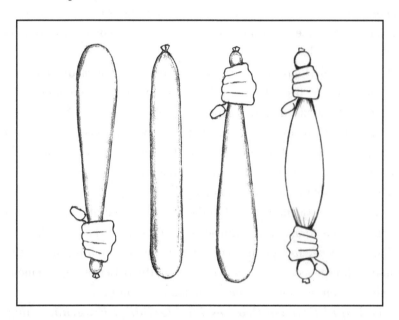

So how does this affect treatment?

Opening my eyes to this concept has completely turned my treatment techniques upside down. I mean this *quite literally*. I usually get my best results by treating the opposite end of the body from the symptoms. To say this approach is "unorthodox" in the world of physical therapy is an understatement. I am hopeful the observations, ideas, and concepts I present in this text will help us approach rehab more holistically through the conventional vehicle of exercise, but with a new intention.

Understanding these concepts has shown me how to be more thorough in my caregiving. I now have reasons to look elsewhere for contributing factors to a problem or even for the cause. I have options to consider that almost always provide solutions for even the toughest conditions. Most of the stubborn symptoms lingering in the shoulders, upper back, head, or neck can be resolved by thoroughly addressing the lower body. Greater success is achieved in the lower back and legs as the eyes, head, and neck are treated. Neither my patients nor I have to settle for unsatisfactory results.

Understanding how one end of the spine, or one area of the body, influences the opposite end of the spine, or another area of the body, has specific implications for potential rehab outcomes. I believe our best results will come when the spine is treated as one continuous unit. We should not separate our treatments of the cervical and lumbar spine, or of the neck and the lower back.

Unfortunately, there is no current way to objectively measure or evaluate the integrity of the fascial system. Decreased range of motion, decreased function, and increased pain are indicators of its condition. Any one or all three of these symptoms may be present when the fascia is not healthy and functioning efficiently. Improvements in the fascia will manifest themselves as increased range of motion, improved function, and decreased pain.

Regardless of the fact that radiographic imaging is not available to the majority to objectify changes within the fascial system, it can be assessed through the palpation skills of anyone trained to do so. Fascia will release tension in response to light touch or gentle manual stretching. While these manual techniques can be effective, much of the patient's improvement is dependent upon the intervention of the manual therapist.

The **Rapid Release Progressive Flexibility Program** is unique from other forms of exercise because of its apparent effect on the fascia as it is engaged through gentle movement from a position of correct alignment. It is a home exercise program that allows the patient to take an active part in their healing. Gently moving the soft tissue prepares it for the treatment it receives from the therapist. Time previously spent during the therapy session to *initiate* change in the tissues is used instead to *advance* further release and flexibility. The therapist is able to focus treatment time on stubborn areas of connective tissue restriction that have not changed in response to exercise. The positioning the patient uses to complete the exercises helps the therapist identify the source of the problem, which is not usually in the same place as the patient's primary complaint. This partnership between the therapist and the patient translates into quicker recovery and improved pain relief for the patient.

When I take a history from my patients, I want to know about *any* motor vehicle accident, fall, or trauma that has occurred at *any* time in their lives. As I collected data on three separate occasions from a total of 450 new patient evaluations, an average of 96 percent* of those patients had some episode of significant trauma in their lives in the form of a motor vehicle accident, fall, or both. From that group, the trauma for 88 percent of them occurred more than three to five years ago. For many of those patients, the trauma was identified as a specific incident that occurred even several decades ago. My palpation evaluation usually uncovers a *pattern of dysfunction* in addition to localized pain or dysfunction. I could have treated these patients locally at the site of the primary complaint, but I believe *I managed my patient's care better by treating them as a whole person.*

I believe most of the aches and pains we suffer with on a daily basis could be prevented by early comprehensive treatment of the soft tissue following any type of traumatic injury. **The *Rapid Release Progressive Flexibility Program* is one way to do just that.**

---

* This 4 percent might be less if people's memories were better. I worked with one woman who came to therapy for lower back pain. She had no recollection of any trauma to her body at the time of her initial evaluation. Almost a full month into her treatment, she remembered the time she fell down twenty-five marble steps on her tailbone. She was bedridden for three weeks. This is an extreme example of a forgotten trauma. Less serious accidents than this have happened to others that were still significant enough to contribute potentially to future problems.

Chapter 2

What Is *Rapid Release?*

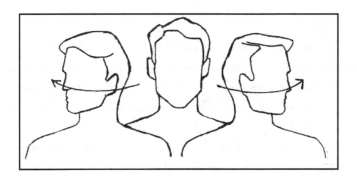

Rapid Release is an active range-of-motion exercise program that promotes flexibility more effectively than conventional stretching. This is accomplished by addressing restrictions throughout the complete full body fascial system. The purpose of the exercises is to restore good posture and function by lengthening the soft tissues. How this is done is explained on p. 17-37. The exercises used in this program are illustrated in chapter 3. **Moving the body from a position of correct alignment is very important to the success of this method.**

The exercises are done in *four sections of the body*:

1. the lower extremities and the pelvis
2. the upper extremities and the scapula, or shoulder blades
3. the neck and the occiput, or the base of the head
4. the eyes

Improved functional mobility is achieved by first improving the quality of movement in each section and then adding them together. *We are the sum of our parts.*

Multiple *pairs of movements* are done within each section to release tension in that section as the motions are alternated. As flexibility improves in each section, one section helps relax tension in *another section*. For example, a certain degree of flexibility can be achieved by doing the exercises for the head and neck. If the lower body exercises are then done and release tension in the lower back, the head and neck may release even more tension, even though no additional exercises have been done directly in that area. *Lengthening* the soft tissues of the entire body is the purpose of the exercises. When ***Rapid Release*** is done in its entirety, maximum flexibility is achieved secondary to the thoroughness of the approach.

The ***Rapid Release*** exercise program is unique from other forms of exercise in five different ways. These differences include the position of the body, the position of the head and neck, the type and quality of the motion, the manner of exercise progression, and the theory behind its effectiveness.

1. The Position of the Body

• Correct supine alignment •

All the exercises from the original program are done in the *supine*, or flat on your back, position. The illustration above represents the **correct alignment** of the body in the supine position, which is referred to as the 0 (or zero) position throughout this exercise program and on the exercise flow chart on p. 98. There are *positional variations and supplemental exercises* to the basic program that will be explained after the original program design has been thoroughly explained. Pay special attention to the Seated Worker series on pages 74-76. I now use this version of the program to begin the exercises for most of my patients.

The first step in the program is to assess the alignment and the comfort of your body in the supine position. The best place to do this is on the floor if you are able to get up and down from the floor without injuring yourself. A hard surface will expose any and all connective tissue discrepancies. It is acceptable to lie down on a carpeted floor or put a blanket down to cushion the floor if your floor is tile or wood. If lying down on the floor is not an option for you, lie down on your bed. Be aware, however, that the softer the surface you lie down on, the less likely you will be engaging all the soft tissue restrictions in your body.

Notice the position of your body in relation to the surface you lie down on. If you are on the floor, be sure your body is parallel with the side of the couch, for example, or with a wall. If you are on a bed, align your body parallel to the edge of the bed. It is not uncommon for those I evaluate to position their feet in the right or left corner of the treatment table with their torso and/or head on the opposite side of the table. In other words, the body is positioned at an angle in respect to the surface it is on. When the position is corrected with the feet directly under the pelvis, which is directly under the neck and shoulders, the person is now in correct alignment. Another common error is for the person to lie down with his or her legs and pelvis centered on the surface, but he or she side bends his or her upper body at the waist. Interestingly, many people feel crooked once their alignment has been corrected. This is an excellent example of how abnormal fascial tension can distort our proprioception, or the way the body perceives where it is in space. **Completing the exercises from this foundational position of correct alignment is the beginning of restoring balance and symmetry to your body.**

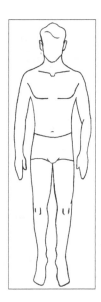
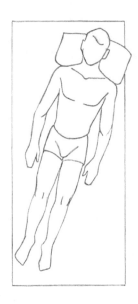
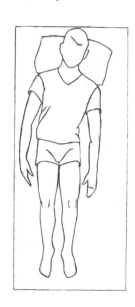

It is important to make as many skeletal corrections as needed to restore balance and symmetry in this position before beginning the exercises. In other words, be sure you are lying down straight. This retrains neuromuscular components to function from positions of correct alignment during movement. The single most common discrepancy is usually noticed in the position of the pelvis. If you have a tendency to weight bear on one side of your buttocks more than another while you are lying down, this should be corrected as much as possible as it indicates a rotation of the pelvis. If this or other discrepancies, such as uneven shoulders or a tilt or rotation of the head, have been present long enough, you will not initially notice them because the position will feel "normal." It is helpful to ask a friend or family member to observe your posture to help make necessary corrections. Through increased awareness, you will soon be able to make these necessary adjustments yourself.

Being in the supine position is the closest you will ever come to being *weightless* while you are experiencing the effects of gravity on your body. When external stress is eliminated from the body as much as possible by using this positioning, the body *should* experience maximum comfort and freedom of motion. Most people, however, are not only uncomfortable in this position, but it is also their least favorite position. If the discomfort is mild to moderate initially, most people will change their position within a very short time to accommodate their increasing discomfort. It is reasonable to conclude some changes need to be made if the position that should be the most easily tolerated is actually one of the most uncomfortable.

Posture is the foundation for movement. Any compensations you must make in your body to increase your tolerance for correct alignment are indicators of areas in need of correction. If you do not correct the foundational problem(s), how can you expect to achieve maximum success in addressing the more extenuating issues? For many, the first goal to achieve in this exercise program is to tolerate the supine position without any postural compensation.

So how is this accomplished? This is a process for most people. I will explain how to systematically modify the supine position in the beginning to reduce the strain on the soft tissue while you lie on your back. As the strain is passively taken off the body, it may be able to relax for the first time in many years. The soft tissue then has the freedom to lengthen in response to gentle active movement.

Full Body Alignment

Once you are aligned correctly on your back, notice which areas are uncomfortable in your body. Most of the time, there is a tension, an ache, or a sense of pressure in the lower back. There may also be some discomfort in the neck and shoulders, which will be discussed later. Typically, a person will bend at the hips and knees so the feet are flat on the floor to resolve the discomfort in the lower back. *This position usually overcompensates for the discomfort and is an unacceptable method of compensation.*

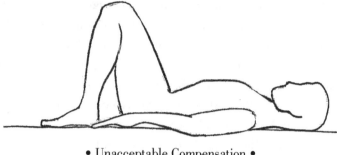

• Unacceptable Compensation •

Most people assume this position instinctively, but others have been advised by a health-care professional or exercise trainer to use this position to alleviate low back discomfort. While this advice was surely given with the best of intentions, it should only be used for short periods. *Do not use this position habitually, or at all if possible, because it ultimately reinforces the problem that is often creating the discomfort in the first place.* **There is a better way.**

As we discussed earlier, lower back pain is often the result of adverse tension in the psoas muscle. When a person lies on his or her back and bends at the hips, the psoas is put on slack, which decreases the strain on the lower back. It is important to understand the lower back feels better because *the tension in the psoas has been accommodated, but nothing has been corrected.* This type of positioning accomplishes the same thing a parent does when they give their screaming child the candy he or she is crying for. The immediate resolution of the problem provides temporary relief, but ultimately, a greater problem is being perpetuated.

I allow my patients to accommodate for psoas tension as well, but I encourage them to alleviate the strain on the muscle at the end that attaches to the spine rather than the leg by positioning themselves on some degree of **an upper body wedge**. The distal end of the muscle on the leg, which is often the more tense end, is lengthened. *This position of accommodation is acceptable because it is not to be used habitually to manage pain; instead, it becomes the beginning position used to do the exercises in supine.* As the body releases the fascial tension and becomes more flexible, the size of the wedge is reduced. The use of the wedge will be explained in greater detail later in this chapter.

One, two, or three pillows under the knees may be needed in addition to the wedge initially.

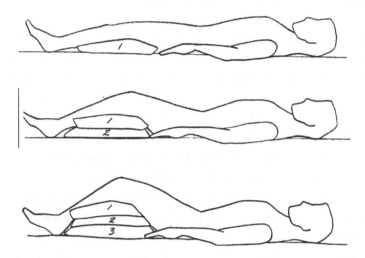

I would rather my patients start with a larger upper body wedge and omit the pillows under their knees if this enables them to lie comfortably with their hips more lengthened.

• Greater Upper Body Compensation
with Leg Lengthening •

The final goal is to tolerate flat supine without any compensation under the upper body, head, and neck, or the knees.

• Correct supine alignment •

Examples of Supine Corrections

Consider a forty-eight-year-old male stocker at a grocery store referred to therapy for left shoulder pain. His diagnosis seemed to be quite reasonable considering he used his arms and shoulders so much. When I asked him to lie down on the treatment table, his feet and legs were angled more toward the bottom left of the table. He also slightly bent to the right at his waist, so his torso and shoulders were leaning more toward the right side of the table. His head was side bent to the right, so his right ear was closer to his right shoulder. Finally, his head was also slightly rotated to the right and in mild cervical extension. He was crooked, but he felt very comfortable—and straight. He had no complaints of any abnormal tension anywhere in his body.

When I helped him reposition himself with his feet centered beneath his pelvis, his shoulders centered over his pelvis, and his head and neck centered over his body, he rated a sensation of "full body weirdness" at 4–5/10 (1/10 = minimum discomfort, 10/10 = maximum discomfort). Correcting his cervical extension with a mere four centimeters of support reduced the "weird feeling" to 0/10. (I will discuss correction of the head and neck after completing the body position explanation.)

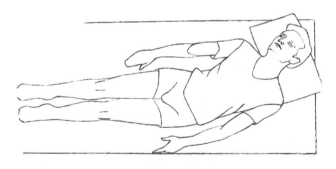

• Distorted supine alignment •

Next, consider another forty-six-year-old male patient with right shoulder pain. This patient looked surprisingly good regarding the posture of his torso, head, and neck when he first lay down in supine. He preferred to put both hands behind his head, in external rotation of the shoulders, but he was able to maintain a good cervical position even after his arms were put down by his sides. He had no complaints of pain or tension in his neck, shoulders, or lower back. The only thing abnormal about his posture was the extreme external rotation of both legs, which caused his feet and toes to fall out to each side.

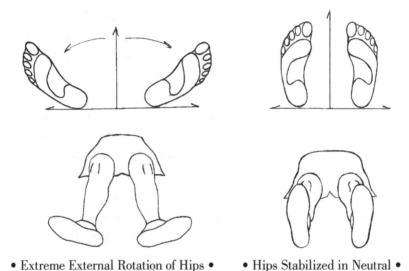

• Extreme External Rotation of Hips •   • Hips Stabilized in Neutral •

When his legs were repositioned and stabilized in neutral so his toes were pointing to the ceiling, **the arch in his lower back increased, his chest lifted toward the ceiling, and his head tilted back so his chin was, also, pointing up to the ceiling. He now sensed a tension in his lower back, torso, and neck of 4/10. When the abnormal position of his legs was corrected, the tension in his lower back, upper body and neck was exposed.** After repositioning his torso, neck, and head on a fifteen-degree wedge from his tailbone to the back of his head, he was relaxed in supine with 0/10 tension everywhere.

This patient was employed as a "floor mechanic" or a tile setter. He spent most of his time on his hands and knees installing tile or wood flooring. Considering his vocation, it made perfect sense that as a right-handed dominant person, he would have pain in his right shoulder secondary to overuse. He had also broken his right arm in a backward fall eighteen months ago while playing baseball, so he had even sustained a direct trauma to the shoulder. His response to supine positioning, however, revealed there was more to his problem. Specific injuries from his traumatic history included job-related lifting injuries to his lower back as well as two motor vehicle accidents in his twenties.

The effects lower body tension had on his shoulder motion were clearly evident by my measurements. When I initially measured his right shoulder internal rotation in supine with his legs incorrectly positioned, he was able to move the shoulder through only *forty degrees of motion*. After realigning his lower extremities and accommodating the tension in his lower back and torso on a fifteen-degree wedge, he was able to move the right shoulder through *eighty degrees of internal rotation*. When the tension below the shoulder in the torso was relaxed, he was able to internally rotate the shoulder through a full range of motion. As this patient systematically released the tension in his upper body, head, neck and eyes and *improved his lower body flexibility*, he was able to resolve the issues he was having with his shoulder.

This patient clearly illustrates how increased fascial tension affects posture and movement. By correcting his alignment, accommodating the tension, and then releasing the soft tissue restrictions through gentle lengthening movement, he returned to a full pain-free range of motion without any functional restrictions in his shoulder, or lower back for that matter.

Passive Hip Stabilization

As I mentioned in the last case study, I look at the position of the lower extremities when correcting full body alignment. The legs and feet should be directly underneath the pelvis. The knees and the feet should be pointing toward the ceiling. Most of the time, I see one of these abnormal postures instead:

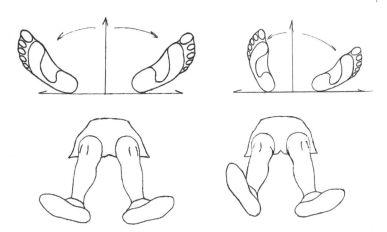

Tight hip rotator muscles pull on the leg so it falls to the outside, sometimes evenly and sometimes not. The primary function of the psoas muscle is to flex the hip, but it is an accessory muscle also for hip external rotation. When the legs fall out into external rotation while the patient is in supine, you can be sure an abnormality of the psoas, in addition to tight external hip rotators, is contributing to at least part of the misalignment.

I prefer to use passive stabilization as much as possible to alleviate tension and correct alignment. This enables my patients to relax in the correct position rather than work to maintain it. To correct abnormal rotation of the legs, I gently wrap a towel around my patients' knees to help them hold the correct position without effort as illustrated.

As the last patient example demonstrated, repositioning the legs in proper alignment can have a very interesting effect on the entire torso, shoulders, neck, and head. The influence the hips and lower back was having on the shoulders *would not have been recognized or addressed if the rotation of the hips and legs had not been corrected.* The contribution lower back tension was making to the total picture would have been overlooked as well if the unacceptable method of compensation for lower back pain and tension had been allowed.

I have worked with a couple of patients who found it necessary to slowly progress to the correct position for their lower extremities. One patient experienced cramping along the lateral aspect of both thighs after being in the fully corrected position for ten minutes. Another patient immediately began to cramp in the buttocks and the low back as her legs were repositioned from extreme external rotation of the hips to the neutral position. These side effects can be avoided by gradually working toward a full correction. Or delay implementing this correction until after you have done the exercises for several days.

Changing the Position of the Foot

The final area to notice in the lower body is the position for the ankle and the foot. When the exercises are begun, the foot may be in its normal resting position, which is slightly pointing down at the ankle. By pulling the "toes to the nose," a stretch is placed on the back of the calf. This position change has the potential to increase the difficulty of the eye, neck, and upper extremity exercises and engage otherwise unaddressed restrictions. I have noticed on several occasions that patients who demonstrate correct alignment of the head and neck in supine will not tilt their head back into extension until the back of the calf is stretched. (The correct position of the head and neck will be explained later in this chapter.)

• Correct supine alignment •

Modifications to the Upper Body in Supine - "Positions of Ease"

The use of an upper body wedge to alleviate uncomfortable fascial restrictions in supine was the final positioning strategy this method needed to facilitate the most gentle release of fascial restrictions. By using an upper body wedge of the appropriate size, the tension in the upper body, head, neck, and eyes, which is, more often than not, contributing to the lingering pain in the lower back and legs, can be relaxed. The body is "eased" into positions of more length on a smaller wedge as the tissue releases tension in response to gentle movement.

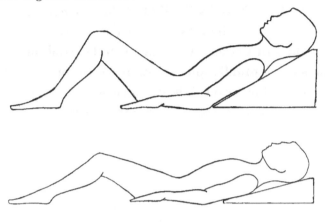

• Modified supine positions •

When you consider the water balloon illustration, it makes sense tension and pressure from above would provoke lower back pain. As I have educated my patients regarding the effects of the upper body, head, neck, and eyes on their lower back and how positioning can be used to manage and treat their symptoms, the response has been overwhelmingly positive.

Goodbye, Low Back Pain!

The most incredible revelation has come as I have witnessed the effect the eyes are having on the lower back, and almost everything else for that matter. Elevating the eyes, head, neck, and upper body alleviates the pressure seemingly translated into the lower back and legs from the elevated areas of tension. Even for my patients who are complaining of severe lower back pain, positioning the upper body on a wedge of variable sizes from as small as five degrees to as large as thirty degrees or more will finally provide them with relief from their symptoms. Sometimes one, two, or three pillows are also needed under the knees. It is not uncommon, however, for the lower back to be very comfortable, or even pain-free, without any support under the knees when the upper body is correctly positioned. This is surely one explanation for the popularity of recliners.

It is worth repeating that this modified supine position is not to be used *habitually* as a solution for lower back and leg symptoms. **This position serves as the BEGINNING POSITION for the exercise program when it is done in supine. As the movement from the exercises lengthens the soft tissues, the wedge is to be gradually reduced. The goal is to eventually tolerate supine positioning without any compensation whatsoever.** (The case examples on pages 225-288 will show you how positioning and the other exercises were used to alleviate lower back pain.)

• Correct supine alignment •

Modified supine positioning can be used for temporary pain relief when it is done several times a day for short periods. It can also be used to ease the pain at night so much-needed sleep can occur. Feel free to sleep in this position if it helps, but it is not expected that everyone should, or even could, do so. It is always recommended to follow up any prolonged time in this position with lengthening exercises to the anterior side of the body. These exercises are illustrated in chapter 3, p. 92-95, 97, "Lower Body Exercises Prone and Standing."

The easiest way to modify the supine position is in a recliner, adjustable bed, or hospital bed. Imagine the person in illustration A is long sitting in his or her recliner or bed. Lowering the back of the chair allows for a gradual progression from sitting up at a ninety-degree angle to lying flat at a zero-degree angle. The back of the chair can be lowered incrementally to a sixty-degree, forty-five degree, or thirty-degree angle and then finally to a more flat position as in illustration A. *The exercises are done in each position to release tension, which allows for progression to the next more lowered and more lengthened position.* The soft tissues are "eased" toward a more lengthened position. If you are forced to sleep with your upper body elevated secondary to breathing difficulties or digestive issues, these exercises should be done daily to offset the tension that develops in the front of the body while you sleep. Please refer to p. 133 for an explanation about *correct eye position* as the upper body is lowered to flat supine.

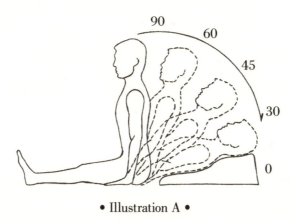

• Illustration A •

In the most extreme or unusual cases, it may be too difficult to perform the exercises for the upper body, head, neck, and eyes while the legs are extended. In this case, exercise the upper body with the knees bent and the feet on the floor. Then repeat the exercises again as you *gradually elevate the legs* from ninety degrees to forty-five degrees or to zero degrees. Continue this progression until you tolerate full knee extension. The position of the torso may now

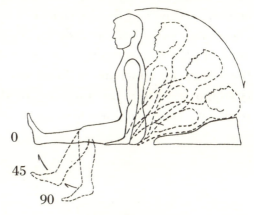

• Illustration B •

be lowered. The torso may also be gradually lowered as the knees are gradually straightened. The beginning position for this illustration is simply "sitting." Sitting in any type of stable chair will do. Most of my patients learn and do the exercises in sitting before ever completing them in modified supine.

If a recliner, an adjustable bed, or hospital bed is not available, the same thing can be accomplished by using a wedge behind the back as seen in illustration C.

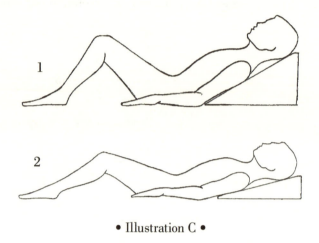

• Illustration C •

Be sure the trunk is supported so the entire spine is straight and the head is correctly positioned. (The correct position of the head will be discussed next in this chapter.) If a wedge is not readily available, a temporary wedge can be made out of pillows, folded blankets, and/or towels. Flatter pillows tend to work better than thicker pillows. **I prefer the wedge be constructed in such a way that the entire spine is supported from the tailbone to the back of the head.** The sequencing below shows how to stagger the pillows to construct the wedge.

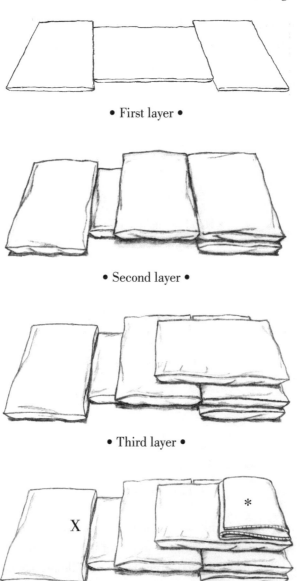

• First layer •

• Second layer •

• Third layer •

• Fourth layer •

The X indicates the approximate placement of the coccyx or tailbone. The * indicates the placement of the head.

Keep in mind there is no "correctly sized wedge" to be used to relax your body and begin the exercises. The size of the wedge will depend upon how much tension is in your body. Don't skimp on the compensation. The more tension you can alleviate through the positioning, the better your body will release the tension as you move through the lengthening exercises.

Sometimes a full wedge is not needed. Below are examples of other pillow configurations. Use whatever configuration best supports your back and neck to improve your tolerance for supine.

• Head to Shoulder Blades •

• Low Back to Head •

• Tailbone to Head •

If one, two, or three pillows are needed under the knees as illustrated on page 21, in combination with the wedge, it is worth noting the hips may only be bent at twenty to thirty degrees by using pillows as opposed to sixty to seventy degrees when a person rests his or her feet flat on surface. When my suggestion is followed, minimal deviation is made away from the desired position of flat supine. Good length is kept in the tissue while often reducing the pain as much as the unacceptable compensation position does.

I never suggest my patients purchase a pre-made wedge from a medical supply store or the like. **The purpose and use of the wedge is temporary. The repeated use of the wedge without improving the flexibility of the body with exercise will ultimately only make you worse.** Using the wedge without exercising to reduce and eliminate the wedge does the same thing bending at the hips and knees does to reinforce tension.

"Give a Little, Take a Little"

Finally, the body sometimes needs to be "worked like a teeter-totter" to comfortably release tension. In the elderly population I have worked with, they understand this principle best when it is phrased "Take from Peter to pay Paul". As I have previously stated, the ultimate goal of the exercises is to lengthen the fascial planes of connective tissue. The achievement of this flexibility is demonstrated when a person is able to stretch out on his or her back comfortably without requiring any support under the knees, torso, head, and/or neck. Sometimes this is a process that requires "shortening" one end, or putting the tissue on slack, so the other end can tolerate being "lengthened," or stretched out. "Lengthening" occurs when the body is positioned more closely to flat supine and/or the exercises are more easily tolerated through a greater range of motion. Eventually, all areas of the body should tolerate being in a lengthened state simultaneously. Refer to illustration C again for this explanation. I will walk you through this in steps.

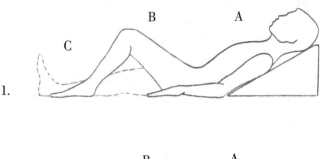

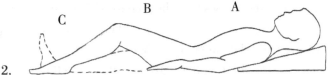

• Illustration C •

1. Figures 1A and 1B illustrate someone who requires much compensation for the fascial tension in his or her body. The upper body is significantly elevated, and there is also a significant bend at the hips and knees. The first goal for this person is to gradually release enough tension in his or her eyes, head, neck, and upper body to allow a gradual lengthening of the legs like in illustration 2B and finally fully straighten the legs like in illustration 1 or 2C (the dotted leg) while still being able to move his or her eyes, head, neck, and upper body. *The upper body is still shortened, while the lower body is lengthened.*

   Clinically, this illustrates what often happens with people who have significant upper body, neck, or eye/head tension. It can be very difficult for them to move their eyes, for example, when they stretch out their legs. When the legs are bent at the hips and knees, the exercises are more easily accomplished. *It is okay to elevate, or "shorten," one end of the body temporarily if it facilitates improved tolerance for movement at the other end* (patient example, p. 296-301, p. 373 - #2).

2. The next step is to lower the upper body toward a more flat position while the legs are fully lengthened as in illustrations 2A–C. When this is done, pretend it becomes more difficult to move the eyes, stick out the tongue, and/or move the neck when the upper body has been slightly lowered. To make the exercises easier while the upper body is in this more lengthened position, the hips and knees should be bent again, or shortened, like in illustration 1B. *The lengthened upper body will be able to move better when the legs are shortened.* The goal is to gradually extend the legs like in position 2B and finally 2C and still be able to move the eyes, tongue, neck, and arms.

3. Finally, the upper body is positioned flat on the surface (not pictured on this page). If it is difficult to move the eyes, tongue, and/or neck again in this new more lengthened position, the process of shortening the legs and working toward progressive lengthening of the legs should be repeated.

   This "give and take" works the other way as well. It is acceptable to increase the size of the upper body wedge, "shorten one end," like in illustration 1A to enable the legs to be "stretched out or lengthened" more comfortably.

4. If you are able to lie flat on your back comfortably while you are lying still but movement of the legs provokes too much pain in the hips,

lower back, shoulders, or neck, *shorten the upper body by elevating it so lengthening the lower body is better tolerated.* If the upper body must be elevated as much as is illustrated in position 1A, the goal will be to continue moving the lower body while the upper body is progressively lowered to position 2A and then finally flat.

5. If you do not have extra blankets, pillows, and/or towels to construct a wedge to accommodate painful or restricted upper body, neck, jaw, and eye movement, see if you are able to position the upper body flat on the surface and bend the hips and the knees to the extreme. This can be accomplished by lying down on the floor, scooting the buttocks up to the couch or a chair as closely as possible and bending the knees over the seat portion of the furniture. The hips and knees will be bent approximately ninety degrees in both areas. Continue to do the eye, jaw, neck, and arm exercises in this flat upper body position and then begin to slowly lengthen the lower body as tolerated.

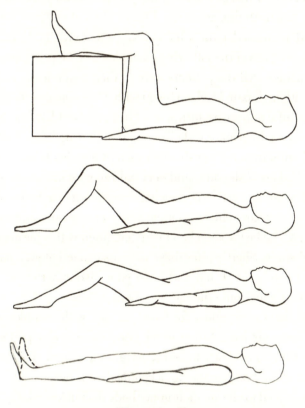

• Illustration D •

6. A word of caution: If you tolerate lying flat comfortably, regardless of where your pain is, *I would still recommend some elevation of the upper body, neck, and head when you first do the lower body exercises in supine.* This is being more conservative but will help prevent any potential aggravation of the head, neck, or shoulders, which could be potentially caused by lower body movement. Sometimes this elevation is much needed to improve the lower body's tolerance for movement, which pain would otherwise prevent.

Examples of How Modified Supine Positioning Can Be Used to Control Pain and Improve Tolerance for Movement

It was my original habit in the early years of using this method to begin most of my patients with the lower body exercises because of the positive effects they had on the lower body *as well as the neck*. After several years of success with this approach, I suddenly had multiple patients who experienced increased pain after starting the lower body exercises in supine. The purpose of the following examples is to help you avoid making the same mistake. All the patients were in their seventies or eighties and presented with high pain levels to begin with. One woman suffered from an extremely painful adhesive capsulitis or "frozen" shoulder. Another woman was experiencing intermittent shoulder pain following lower back surgery. She did not suffer from neck or shoulder pain prior to her lower back surgery but now lacked good shoulder and cervical range of motion in addition to pain. The next woman was experiencing debilitating headaches after being rear-ended in a motor vehicle accident one year after she underwent open heart surgery. The last woman had been diagnosed with a herniated disc in her cervical spine. Shortly after these patients exacerbated, a patient with sciatica and another with hip and knee pain also experienced the same increased pain after doing the lower body exercises.

The soft tissue restrictions for those patients with shoulder, neck, and head pain were obvious. When lower body motion was performed, the movement of the lower body forced a certain amount of pressure upward into an area of the body unable to accommodate it because of preexisting tension. Their need to elevate their upper body during lower body movement was understandable. If you have shoulder, neck, or head pain, a conservative way to begin the supine exercises is in the modified supine position to avoid an exacerbation of your symptoms by doing the lower body exercises.

The patients with sciatica, hip and leg pain, *were not clearly manifesting upper body tension* based upon their tolerance to lie flat comfortably in supine. When you consider the water balloon illustration to determine the cause of pain, you will conclude that tension in the upper body, head, and/or neck can create lower body or lower extremity symptoms like sciatica or hip, leg, and/or knee pain. This negative response to lower body movement was reduced or eliminated when the upper body was elevated as in illustration C #1 or 2 on page 33 during the movement of the lower body. As time went on, the patients gradually progressed toward a more flat supine position for exercise. It was this group of patients that helped me understand the need for the modified supine position as in illustration C.

I have also found it helps these patients to change the sequence of the exercises. Begin with the eye exercises and then add the neck and the arms. The lower body exercises would be initiated only after the upper body has been moving for a few days. This is the sequence I now use most commonly.

2. The Position of the Head and Neck

There are three continuous systems in the body. Each system has no beginning and no end. There is no location in the body not energized by the nervous system, fed by the circulatory system, or held together by the connective tissue or fascia. Each of these systems is at risk of impingement when the position of the head and neck, or cervical spine, is misaligned. For this reason, the position of the head and neck is a critical part of this exercise program.

• Cervical Neutral •

The illustration on the previous page represents *cervical neutral*, the correct head and neck position to be used throughout this exercise program. This is the "0" position for the head and neck on the exercise flow sheet on page 98. There are two important things to notice about this position. First, weight bearing of the head is on the lower part of the back of the skull, not on the top of the head. Second, the face and chin are parallel to the ceiling, or the chin may be gently tucked. **The chin is not pointing to the ceiling.** It is very important to be sure both of these areas are positioned correctly.

It is possible to tuck the chin to the throat, like a nod, and still keep the upper cervical spine in too much extension. To position the upper cervical spine correctly, the entire head should rock forward and down as the chin goes down. This will "open up" or "flatten out" the top part of the neck. This positions the neck in a posture more closely resembling the natural curve of the neck rather than an exaggeration of the normal curve.

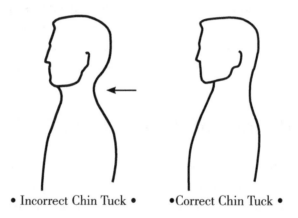

• Incorrect Chin Tuck •   •Correct Chin Tuck •

Correctly positioning this very specific location at the top of the neck and base of the head is key because of how it potentially affects the lining of the spine that proceeds up into the cranium. Correct alignment keeps restrictive pressure off critical anatomical structures located in this area, which will be discussed later. Imagine you wanted to hold a wooden spoon or the handle to a hammer at the top of your neck. You would have to tilt your head back enough to apply a certain amount of pressure on the object *outside the neck* so it would not fall. This is theoretically the same type of pressure the position of the neck exerts on the spinal cord and other structures *inside the neck* when the position of the head and neck is incorrectly tilted backward.

• No Cervical Impingement •   • Head Tilt with Cervical Impingement •

Another helpful word picture is to consider a garden hose. Bending, or kinking, any place in the hose, regardless of its distance away from the faucet, will restrict the amount of water that comes out of the hose. *Kinking the hose up close to the faucet will restrict the way the water flows through the entire distance of the hose.* Holding the head back into an abnormal amount of extension is similar to kinking a hose up next to the faucet.

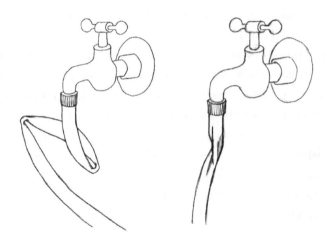

Most people will not correctly position the head and neck in cervical neutral when they lie down in supine; instead, they weight bear on their head somewhere between the crown and the back of their head. This incorrect positioning is often the result of incorrectly supporting the neck to alleviate neck pain in the same way low back pain is reduced with overcompensation. The overwhelming majority of my patients who suffer from neck pain habitually place a rolled towel or pillow under their neck while they sleep or relax.

• Acceptable •

• Unacceptable •

This position is acceptable only if the back of the head is supported also. If the back of the head is not supported, the head will passively extend to rest on the surface. This reinforces the tension that needs to be released at the base of the head and the top of the neck. Placing a rolled towel just under the neck with the head in extension may be done temporarily to reduce an exacerbation of lower back pain or neck pain but should always be followed up with stretching the chin to the chest as gently as tolerated. While the previous "unacceptable" illustration shows the head in extreme extension, chronic tension can develop even with the head habitually positioned in mild extension.

Cervical pillows designed to support the head and neck correctly can be purchased. A homemade version of a cervical pillow can be accomplished by inserting a rolled-up towel lengthwise inside the pillowcase of your normal pillow. Position the towel so it supports the natural curve of the neck, while the pillow supports the back of the head. This type of pillow offers assistance to correct posture and to support the neck, but it does not guarantee correct positioning. It is always possible to "cheat" even with the best of props, *so you must make a conscientious effort to position yourself correctly.*

I also recommend a folded towel be used in place of a pillow if the only pillows available are too thick or too thin. A folded towel can be personalized to accommodate a person's neck as in the previous "acceptable" illustration. Eliminating the use of a pillow is impossible, however, if there is a *kyphosis* of the upper back, which is an exaggerated curve between the shoulder blades, or "humpbacked." Reducing the amount of the kyphosis will be necessary to effectively correct the position of the head and neck. A certain amount of pillow support will also be needed to support the head in side lying.

In the following illustration, the position of the upper cervical spine is correct. The face is parallel with the ceiling. The chin is not pointing upward.

What is incorrect is how the thickness of the pillow forces the head to be in front of the shoulders. This is indicated by the position of the ear in relation to the shoulder. Using a pillow that is too thick or sleeping on two or three pillows will push the head forward in relationship to the shoulders, creating a different postural distortion. *The ear should always line up with the shoulder whether you are sitting, standing, supine, or side lying.* When choosing a pillow, the most important consideration is the effect it will have on the posture of the head and neck.

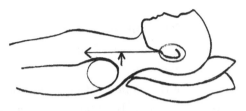

As I previously mentioned, most people lie down in supine with the head in a certain amount of extension with the chin pointing to the ceiling. The "incorrect" illustration below shows an exaggeration of this posture. When the position of the head is corrected, *the head will often be elevated off the surface. Support underneath the head and neck is required to achieve and stabilize the head in cervical neutral.* These positions are referred to in negative numbers on the exercise flow sheet.

As greater flexibility is achieved in the back of the neck, less support will be required to maintain cervical neutral. The goal is to comfortably achieve and maintain cervical neutral without support.

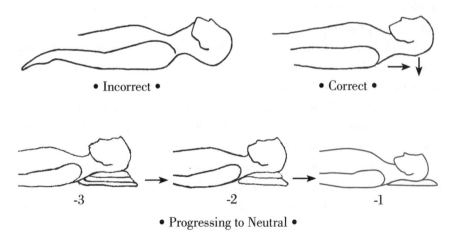

• Incorrect •   • Correct •

-3   -2   -1

• Progressing to Neutral •

3. The Type and Quality of the Motion

Rapid Release involves *active range of motion only*. It is good to move at a moderate speed and unnecessary to hold the movements to achieve a stretching effect. One very important aspect of this program is the *quality* of the motion. At no time should any discomfort greater than 3–4/10 on a scale of 1–10 be experienced anywhere in the body (0/10 = no pain, 10/10 = excruciating pain). Discomfort may be perceived as pain, tightness, pulling, pressure, achiness, dizziness, or nausea. Movement should always be *gentle* and *comfortable*. This subjective standard for assessing discomfort applies throughout this exercise program regarding how your body feels in each position to do the exercises and/or the symptoms possibly provoked by the exercises. If a full range of motion for a particular exercise is achievable but symptoms exceed 3–4/10 at a certain point in the range, the motion should be completed only through the comfortable range of motion. *Negative reactions to the exercises should be minimized by limiting the range of motion.* If four to five repetitions are comfortably completed within a shortened range of motion, an increase in the range will usually result with less discomfort during the sixth or seventh repetition. **Motion should not be forced.** Forcing the motion creates a resistance within the soft tissues, which will hinder increases in sustained flexibility. "No pain, no gain" is wrong thinking if your goal is to release fascial tension. *This mentality will hinder your progress through this exercise program.*

It will be helpful for you to refer to an exercise handout as you read this paragraph. Remember the body is divided into four different sections, or quadrants, to do the exercises. The entire body is addressed with movement when all four quadrants are done in one session of exercise. These quadrants are for the eyes, the neck, the upper body, and the lower body. Now please refer to pages 84-85, the upper body exercises. Notice how the exercises are *grouped in pairs on the page*. The first pair is the "1A. Angels" and "1B. Pullovers." The second pair is "2A. Elbow Winging" and "2B. Reaching Up and Shrugging Down." The third pair is "3A. Overhead Lift" and "3B. Reaching Down and Shrugging Up." Three pairs of exercises are done in each quadrant, except for the eyes, which include four pairs.

Each individual exercise is done three times. Each pair is repeated for two to seven sets before progressing to the next pair. For example, three repetitions of the "angel" is done, and then three repetitions of the "pullover" is done. This is equivalent to one set of three repetitions for the first pair of exercises for the upper body quadrant. Another three repetitions of the "angel" exercise is done, and another three repetitions of the "pullover" is done to complete the second set of the first pair of exercises in the upper body quadrant. A third set of the first pair, 1A and 1B, should be completed before progressing to the next pair, 2A and 2B. "Alternating movements and repeating them" seems to be how the connective tissues are gently warmed up and lengthened to address the "plastic" quality of the fascia. It is important to do the exercises as they are laid out on each page to *release fascial tension by alternating the movements*.

To summarize, connective tissue tension is released in the first two motions, 1A and 1B, before proceeding to the next pair. Exercises 2A and 2B are then completed three repetitions for two to seven sets. The final pair, 3A and 3B, are finally completed three repetitions for two to seven sets. This completes the exercises for the upper body quadrant. *The purpose of the six exercises in each quadrant is to release tension in an area of the body, not necessarily individual muscles.* The effect is different from stretching, which is sometimes unproductive and temporary.

When my patients desire to do more repetitions of the exercises, I *will always recommend they do more sets* as they reach the total number of repetitions they desire to do. For example, it is better to do "six sets of five repetitions" than "three sets of ten repetitions." Each pair of exercises consists of opposite movements. The more these opposites are "alternated and repeated," the more they tend to release tension in one another.

I have also noticed it is best not to cross midline with the motion. Initially, I stopped the movement at midline because I discovered it loosened me up more quickly. Over the course of time, I have recognized an additional benefit to this feature. Our muscles, tendons, and ligaments contain *proprioceptors*, which are components of the sensory nervous system that provide information to our brain concerning movement and body position. When your proprioception is intact, you will correctly know how your body is positioned in space, even if you close your eyes to eliminate visual confirmation. Whenever the soft tissue has been out of balance for an extended period, the proprioceptors lose their ability to interpret information correctly.

This is most clearly demonstrated during any type of postural evaluation. It is not uncommon for a person to believe he or she is standing straight, but his or her head and/or torso is, in fact, slightly rotated to the right or the left of the center. When this deviation is corrected, the person *then* complains of feeling "crooked" or "twisted." His or her body has received the "wrong" information for so long that what is "wrong" now feels "right," and what is "right" now feels "wrong." Positioning the body in correct alignment and utilizing midline as a reference point for movement helps retrain the body regarding its center and correctly reprograms positional information. In the long run, this has critical implications for balance and fall prevention.

Nearly everyone notices balance improvement overall by doing this program, even though the process of restoring balance and symmetry can be disorienting at times. Dizziness can be randomly provoked throughout the program. I personally experienced mild dizziness after doing the head and neck exercises for the first time *each time* I progressed my positioning in that area. (Progressive positioning will be discussed later.) I do not usually suffer from dizziness, so for anyone who already has these problems, **extra caution must be exercised to prevent a fall**.

The final point to remember regarding actual movement during the exercises involves *isolation of motion.* It is very important to *stabilize*, or keep still, all other parts of the body not directly involved in the specific exercise being done. When all undesired motion is eliminated, it is as if the fascia is being gently "ironed out" as the body is forced to move correctly. This is one of the ways a release of tension can be initiated in another area of the body even before that area is directly exercised. For example, I have noticed it is very common for people to pull their head back and forth doing the heel slide or single knee-to-chest exercise. Other times the head may roll to one side and back to the center in unison with the lower body during the lower trunk rotation exercise. This type of motion is dysfunctional and should not be allowed. This observation clearly demonstrates whenever the soft tissue is restricted, the body will make whatever compensations are necessary to achieve the desired movement. In other words, we cheat. This can happen deliberately, but most of the time, it is done unconsciously.

The range of motion will often decrease during the desired exercise when the undesired motion is restricted. *This brings me to the point of making an exception to this guideline.* If the amount of movement for an exercise significantly increases by allowing a compensatory movement to occur simultaneously, then it is okay to allow the compensatory motion to occur for the sake of moving the desired part through a greater range of motion. Eventually, the desired motion should be accomplished fully while the compensatory area is stabilized in correct alignment. As the exercises continue to be performed correctly, increased flexibility will be achieved in both areas.

I have noticed this result frequently as I have watched my patients do the eye, tongue, and jaw exercises. It is not uncommon for my patients to position their eyes "anywhere but in midline" as they do the exercises but especially as they do the tongue exercises. When they are asked to keep their eyes centered in midline, their ability to stick out their tongue will be noticeably less. Sideward movement of the jaw often occurs during lateral, or side to side, movement of the eyes. When the patient is asked to keep the jaw still during the eye exercises, the amount of eye motion decreases. In the lower body, this extra movement is noticed as a difficulty stabilizing the opposite hip during the seated and supine hip rotation exercise, the "windshield wiper." In supine, the head may rock back and forth during the heel slide exercise or roll side to side during the lower trunk rotation exercise.

And finally, if the range of motion in the shoulders is sufficiently limited, it is frequently easier to first move the arms one at a time. After each arm has improved on its own, then both arms should be moved together to assure maximum flexibility. The best example of this is the "angel" exercise. The shoulder shrugging exercises should always be done unilaterally.

Our bodies are designed for isolated movement. That is why we have joints and the ability to rotate as well as flex and extend. We should be able to turn our head without turning our body, reach overhead without extending our trunk, or look down without bending at the waist. The loss of the ability to isolate motion precipitates injury and falls. By releasing tension that hinders isolated movement, current pain is reduced, and the risk of future loss of balance and injury is also reduced.

4. The Manner of Exercise Progression

Once a person comfortably tolerates being flat on his or her back, the exercise program is then progressed by elevating the entire body on top of three pillows longitudinally aligned. Support is provided completely under the body from the head to the heels.

The arms, however, remain unsupported and drop down below the surface of the pillows. *This is a more difficult position for the body than it is to lie flat supine.* Because the arms are unsupported, a gentle stretch is applied throughout the body. This position will identify the areas of greatest fascial restriction immediately or within one minute or so. Postural discrepancies will be magnified with this positioning. Most people will be able to identify a localized area where they perceive more stretch or tension. Others may notice a feeling of being "crooked," "twisted," "off-balance," or "dizzy" when they first lie down on top of the pillows. These symptoms are evidence the soft tissue is being challenged. As the exercises are done in combination with the positioning, these symptoms will subside.

If the original discomfort in the lower back, for example, had reduced to 0/10 in flat supine after exercising, the pain will usually increase again with this positioning. This is acceptable as long as the discomfort does not exceed 3–4/10. The exercises are now done in this new position. *A release of fascial tension is achieved by combining a very gentle stretch with gentle active motion.* The exercises are then progressed even further by slowly moving the body down off the pillows so the legs gradually become unsupported as well.

The *basic exercise program* is now done in this slightly different supine position. The nice thing about this program is the exercises never change. Improved flexibility is achieved through *progressive positioning*. *A release of fascial tension is achieved by combining a very gentle stretch with gentle active motion.*

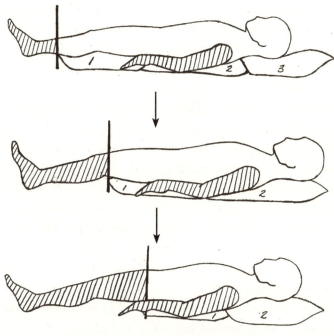

• Examples of Lower Body Progression •

There are a few lower body exercises done in the prone position or on your stomach. Continue to use the same pillow positioning in prone that you use in supine. Begin with the body fully supported (level #1) and progress through each level until you are using only one or two pillows under the pelvis (level #7).

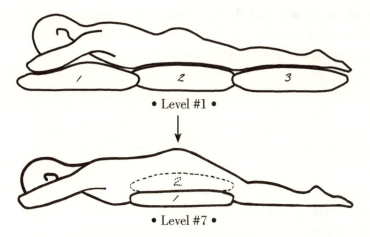

• Level #1 •

• Level #7 •

The levels of progression can easily be followed on the flow sheet on page 98. Each level of progression represents an approximate six-inch change in position and is suggested as a general guideline. *Most of my patients progress in three-inch increments.* Others with extreme tension may literally progress their lower extremities off the pillows one inch at a time. Individualize this aspect of the program to suit your body. The exercises should be done at each level of progression so there are no areas of adverse fascial tension left unaddressed. It is suggested that progression from one level to the next be made every two to three days. This is also a general guideline. Some people may progress daily, while others take five to seven days to progress from one level to the next. Individualize this aspect of the program also to accommodate your body.

This manner of exercise progression makes the program a *progressive flexibility* one as opposed to a *progressive strengthening* program like those most often used in physical rehabilitation. This is the way *to further promote myofascial release.*

This step has been innocently neglected in most exercise programs simply because such a method has not been available. I am convinced, however, that every problem cannot initially be corrected with conventional stretching and strengthening. Flexibility must be restored first to the soft tissue so tension does not hinder the strengthening process. By working the body through the levels of progression on the flow sheet, it is well prepared to tolerate and succeed with progressive strengthening. This process would begin at the completion of this program or as sufficient flexibility allows.

If increased discomfort is felt at the head and neck as the body moves down on the pillows and the lower extremities become less supported provoking an increased cervical extension, provide the amount of support required to comfortably correct the posture of the cervical spine.

In those cases where the discomfort exceeds 3–4/10, an additional wedge under the upper body may be necessary to reduce the strain on the upper body created by the positioning.

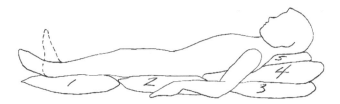

Or place a pillow under the knees to allow for some hip and knee flexion as in the illustration below.

These compensatory pillows allow a person to begin this form of progression he or she might not tolerate otherwise. After progressing down the flow sheet to reach the level where the legs are unsupported below or above the knee, for example, the person's tolerance on full pillows without any compensation should be reassessed. If the compensation can be reduced, it should be reduced. Or if the compensation is no longer needed, it should be eliminated. The exercises continue to be done in the fully supported position and progressed down the flow sheet as originally designed.

The thickness of the pillow you will tolerate best depends on where your greatest fascial restrictions are. Thinner pillows provide a more superficial stretch; thicker pillows reach a deeper level. One patient of mine only tolerated the depth of a braided rug because she had so much restriction in her superficial fascia. Beginning on thinner pillows and progressing to thicker pillows typically works the best if you so desire to do so. Most of my patients have not progressed beyond the thinner pillow stage. Experiment with different depths to see what works best for you.

It may be necessary to gain additional flexibility in the lower abdomen first by doing the standing modifications of the prone lower body exercises before you will tolerate this first position of progression. Doing the prone exercises at level #1 (p. 98) can also improve the tolerance for the supine exercises at level #1 if they are not well tolerated initially.

Consider the Confusing!

At first, I was confused by the various initial responses to this positioning. I eventually gleaned insights from these responses I now believe hold the key to effectively treating many different types of pain and dysfunction. As I stated before, this positioning exposes the body's greatest area of myofascial restriction. One of the most interesting things to notice about this is that the greatest area of myofascial restriction is frequently not in the same place as the patient's current primary complaint. This resonates with what has been known about myofascial pain for many years. The exciting part about this revelation is that *the positioning exposes the probable origin of the pain* that could have otherwise been neglected during the course of treatment.

Sometimes the exposed area is symptomatic, but many times, it is not. In other cases, *new symptoms* that have not been previously experienced will be provoked by this positioning. It is exciting for me to think this technique enables us to identify problems or problem areas before they actually manifest themselves through pain or dysfunction. In this way, the exercises become preventive as well as corrective therapy. Consider the following examples:

#1 — A fifty-six-year-old woman was referred to physical therapy for hip pain. When her full body is positioned on top of the pillows for the first time, she noticed a tension in the back of her neck as well as a "thickness" in her throat. When the pillow was removed out from under her calves and feet to increase the challenge to her body even more, the symptoms in her throat were magnified, and she could barely speak or swallow.

#2 — A thirty-eight-year-old female was referred to physical therapy for neck pain. She faithfully did her home exercise program on a flat surface and tolerated it very well. As her condition improved, her positioning was progressed so that her full body was elevated on top of the pillows. She immediately felt "off-balance" to the point that she could not maintain her position and *literally* rolled off the pillows.

#3 — A sixty-two-year-old man was referred to physical therapy for low back pain. When he was positioned on top of the pillows, the first thing he noticed was not the pain in his back; instead, he immediately complained of a very disturbing dizziness.

#4 — A nineteen-year-old female college student was referred to physical therapy for persistent knee pain following arthroscopic knee surgery. No specific rehab was ordered immediately post-op because the patient did a lot of cycling, walking, and running on her own. Full recovery was anticipated to occur as the result of her lifestyle; instead, the knee pain worsened over the next three months, which, in turn, hindered her tolerance for any form of exercise. When this patient was positioned on top of the pillows, the only discomfort she experienced was in the back of her head at 7/10.

Sometimes the exercises themselves can be very telling in regard to the origin of the pain. For example,

#5 — A seventy-four-year-old female was referred to physical therapy for vertigo. The neck was extremely tense posteriorly, so I assumed releasing the tension in the back of the neck would help resolve the vertigo. The patient tolerated the eye, head, and neck exercises without any difficulty but without any improvement either. It is not until the patient was instructed in the **lower body exercises** that the vertigo was initially provoked but then gradually began to subside.

#6 — A fifty-year-old man was complaining of right scapular (shoulder blade) pain that had been constant at 6–8/10 for about two weeks. Both hands were also cold and swelling with a noticeable loss of grip strength. After performing the **lower body exercises** for four to five minutes, the pain at the right shoulder blade decreased by 50 to 60 percent. The blood flow to both arms and hands increased so much that they pinked up, became warm to the touch, and both hands actually began to perspire. (These are all very positive responses that indicate increased blood flow and felt very good to this man). The pain reduced again by another 50 percent after the **eye, head, and neck exercises** were completed.

#7 — A forty-four-year-old female was referred to physical therapy for sciatica, which is a radiating nerve-type pain in the leg commonly believed to originate from problems in the lower back. I initially instructed the patient in the lower body exercises, which she tolerated without any difficulty, restrictions, *or improvement*. As I completed the exercise instruction for the remainder of the exercise program, it was very apparent **the eye exercises** were, by far, the most challenging. As her tolerance for the eye exercises increased, her leg pain decreased.

> This concludes the most important information to understand about positioning to succeed with this method.

Expanding the Basic Program

Before I close this chapter, I would like to explain the two different ways to expand upon this program. The first way is by suggesting **supplemental exercises** in different positions. The Seated Worker exercises, in particular, are an *easier* form of the basic program. I use this group of exercises for every patient. The second way is by making **variations** to the progressive positioning plan. These variations place the body on more of a stretch than the basic program. They are *more challenging* than the basic program. They may never be used by some people.

Supplemental Exercises and Positioning

There are several sets of exercises to complement the basic supine program. The **Seated Worker** series is a simplified version of the original series. These are the exercises I use to introduce whole-body movement before the exercises are done in supine. They have become foundational to this approach. The second set is the **supine isometrics**. These exercises gently contract the muscles while they are lengthened in the modified supine or supine position.

The **simplifications or variations** offer alternatives to some of the supine exercises for the upper and lower body (pp. 78-79, pp. 86-87, pp. 94-97). Some people will never need these simplifications, but for others, they will be a necessary step to comfortably tolerate the basic program.

The variations offer a way to achieve even greater flexibility around a joint by changing the angle or position of the joint during active motion.

There are additional lower body exercises that can be done in the **side-lying** or **long-sitting** position. I have found the side-lying exercises (page 102-103) to be particularly helpful in releasing tension throughout the torso. The long-sitting exercises (pp. 107-111) have been especially helpful in releasing tension over my sacrum. Restrictions in this area will often make standing straight very difficult. They also help decrease tightness in the hamstrings or the back of the thigh.

The final group of exercises for the lower body is the **"90 Degrees & Beyond"** exercises (p. 104-106). These exercises are for those individuals who can lie on their backs and bend at the hips enough to point their legs and feet straight to the ceiling while keeping the knees straight. Some people may never do these exercises. For others, they will be quite helpful. This progression encourages flexibility through a greater range of motion at the hips.

1. The Seated Worker Series

The Seated Worker series is an adaptation of the complete supine series. It deserves special attention because it has become such an important part of this approach. These exercises were originally organized for my patients whose jobs required mostly sitting. I have since found them to be a good place to start for most of my patients. They are especially good for patients who are extremely uncomfortable in supine and require excessive amounts of compensation to tolerate supine.

For many people, returning to work after an injury demands prolonged sitting for up to eight hours each day. It is a well-documented fact that sitting *always* increases the pressure in the lumbar discs or cushions. For anyone attempting to heal from an injury or break the cycle of chronic pain, prolonged sitting each day will definitely impede their recovery and/or hinder their progress. And what does the person do *who has not been recently injured* but the demands of prolonged sitting alone are causing pain and disability do? The advice most commonly given to seated workers is to interrupt periods of sitting every sixty minutes by standing or walking around. While this can be somewhat helpful, often, it isn't enough to curtail the negative effects of prolonged sitting.

The more I worked with people who had no choice but to sit all day, the more I recognized the need to help them counteract the negative effects of this requirement. In an attempt to meet this need, I modified the supine program so it can be done in the seated position. I suggest it be done midmorning, early afternoon, and mid to late afternoon. The active motion interrupts the progressive tension and increased pressure from accumulating in the body secondary to prolonged sitting. Even if the complete series cannot be done, doing the lower body exercises alone but frequently can reduce the amount of tension that develops in the lower back. This, in turn, will reduce the amount of tension that develops further up into the middle back, shoulders, neck, head, and eyes.

Interrupting a steady gaze at the computer or from reading or stitchery is especially important. Every hour or two, make two to three large circles in one direction and then in the opposite direction with your eyes. Look as far as you can across the room and then pull your gaze back in close. Do this at various angles. In short, do calisthenics with your eyes several times a day to negate the effects of prolonged time on the computer, reading, or crafts.

Patients of mine who have implemented this program during their workday have noted decreased tension throughout their body as well as reduced headaches and more energy to complete their evening tasks at home after work. One patient of mine was literally going to bed immediately after work each day because her pain was so great and exhausting. After doing her seated exercises three times a day and her supine program one time a day for three consecutive days, she was able to stand at home after work long enough to prepare a complete meal plus run her vacuum cleaner. Another patient of mine started her complete office of sixteen employees on the program after they had noticed her improvement. As people began to feel better, there was a noticeable improvement in the morale throughout the office as well as a general increase in the level of productivity.

In addition to helping people who work all day behind a desk or at a computer, I have personally used these exercises very successfully to decrease my upper body pain while *driving*. I had planned a trip to see my mom, which required a three-hour drive in my car. My left shoulder was already aching from working at my computer for the past three days. I was dreading the drive ahead of me as I suspected it would make my shoulder pain worse. I frequently alternated the trunk rotation, trunk side bend, knee winging, and forward reaching over the course of my complete trip. Even though I did not follow the entire seated series, by the time I reached my mom's house, *my shoulder pain was gone.*

2. Supine Isometrics

Once you are comfortably positioned in the supine position that best suits you, a gentle way to begin the myofascial lengthening process is by completing a series of isometric exercises. **Isometric** muscle contractions are static contractions that tighten the muscle without moving the joint the muscle attaches to. If the upper body is significantly elevated on a wedge, it may be necessary to support the arms on pillows to avoid straining the chest. It is better to elevate the arms with the elbows straight than it is to bend at the elbows and rest the hands and forearms on the chest or abdomen if this is tolerable.

Begin at your feet and work your way up your entire body, completing five to seven isometric contractions or small active movements in each area of the body as listed below. Hold each contraction for two to five seconds. Move at a slow, relaxing pace. The following is a suggested sequence. Extremities can either be worked separately or simultaneously.

1. Curl your toes.
2. Pump your ankles.
3. Press the back of the heel into the surface. Feel the back of the thigh contract.
4. Press the back of the knee into the surface. Feel the front of the thigh contract.
5. Squeeze your inner thighs together.
6. Squeeze your butt cheeks together.
7. Pull your lower abdomen down toward your spine. "Navel to the table."
8. Pull your lower ribs down and in toward midline.
9. Push your straightened arm into the surface, palm facing down.
10. Turn your palm in toward your body. Squeeze the sides of your body.
11. Push the backs of your shoulders into the surface as you squeeze your shoulder blades together.
12. Keep your chin down. Push the back of the head into the surface, leading with the base of the skull.

13. Open and close your mouth.
14. Open and close your eyes.

Completion of these exercises should only take five to ten minutes. If your body only tolerates ten minutes of this positioning, then that is a fine length of time to begin with. If you tolerate less time in this position, consider repeating the positioning and the exercises two or three times a day. Increase your time to fifteen or twenty minutes as you tolerate. Repeat the series of isometrics two or three times in each session if you like.

A few of my patients started their experience with supine positioning for one to two hours. Even though they were comfortable at the time, they experienced adverse symptoms the next day. *Surprisingly, the positioning and these exercises can make you very sore and even provoke flu-like symptoms.* I recommend you *begin slowly and then progress as tolerated.*

Be sure your body is positioned in correct alignment as much as possible. Keep your eyes centered in the orbit of the eye as much as possible. In some cases, it may initially be necessary to allow a slight amount of cervical extension to improve your comfort level in this position. This is permissible if it improves your overall tolerance for the position. After a few days, reassess your tolerance for a more neutral position with your head and neck.

Or you may find it to be initially helpful to alternate the correct position of the neck and/or lower extremities in a more relaxed position. For example, use the corrected position for the neck while the hips and knees are bent for the first five minutes of your session and then relax the neck into slight extension while the hips and knees are straightened for the next five minutes. "Give a Little" at one end so you can "Take a Little" at the other end. Repeat this cycle for the next ten minutes. *Soon you will tolerate the correct fully lengthened position at both ends simultaneously for the full twenty minutes.* Sometimes the neck must be allowed to extend slightly to allow for movement of the lower body. Or the neck and the upper body may both need to be shortened on a wedge. Other times, the hips and knees may need to be bent to improve the tolerance for movement of the upper body, neck, jaw, or eyes.

Variations to Progressive Positioning

There are two final ways to modify the progressive positioning to achieve a different effect. *Positioning plus* and *isolating the position of the neck* may be used to enhance the stretch created by the positioning.

1. Positioning Plus

The following are two suggested variations that provide an additional or alternative stretch to the progressive positioning. While these positions can virtually be used at any time, they can specifically be used if you are having difficulty progressing from one level to the next.

A. Moving the Arms Away from the Body

The lower body, head, neck, and eye exercises can all be made more difficult by repositioning the arms further away from the body to whatever extent is comfortable instead of keeping them down along the sides. If you are no longer challenged by any given level of the program but do not tolerate the next level of progression, reposition the arms and continue to do the exercises at the level you do tolerate for one to two days. Then reassess your tolerance for the next progression. If the soft tissue continues to be restricted, discuss this with your therapist, who can assist your progress with some additional modalities or manual techniques.

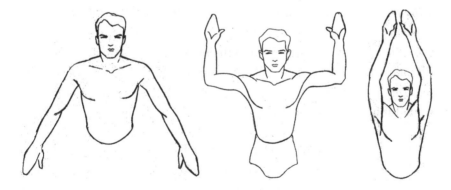

• VARIATIONS FOR GREATER DIFFICULTY •
(still lying on the back)

Examples of when to use:

1. The exercises for the lower body are no longer challenging at level 4, for example, when the arms are positioned straight down by the sides of the body, but the level 5 position places too much of a strain on the lower back. Continue to do the exercises at level 4 but move the arms away from the body or even position them overhead if possible. This additional stretch can help facilitate the release the body needs to progress to the next level.
2. You have progressed to level 7 for the lower body, but the stretch you perceive is only about 2/10 when the arms are straight down by your sides. Move the arms away from the body or place them overhead to increase the stretch to 4/10.
3. The exercises for the head and neck or the eyes are no longer challenging in position 3, for example, while the arms are positioned straight down alongside the body, but cervical neutral cannot be maintained in position 4. Continue to do the exercises at level 3 but move the arms away from the body to create a slightly greater stretch to the neck. This additional stretch can help facilitate the release the body needs to progress to the next level.

To summarize, if an additional stretch is needed, *modify the position of the arms. Continue to do the exercises at the level you tolerate for one to two days. Reassess your tolerance for progression.* Raising the arms can also relieve tension in the eyes and the neck at times. If you are having a difficult time with the eyes or the head and neck exercises, repositioning the arms away from the body may give you the advantage you need to comfortably complete the exercises.

B. Increasing the Support under the Lower Back and Buttocks

The second suggestion is specifically for the lower body. Increasing the depth of support used under the low back and buttocks by laying over two pillows instead of just one can promote a different or more challenging stretch.

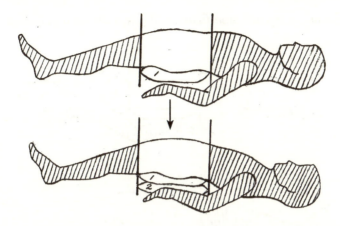

To increase from one pillow to two pillows all at once may be too difficult but can be achieved by adding a folded towel to one pillow and then two folded towels, etc., until two pillows are comfortably tolerated. Another suggestion is to maintain support under the upper body while two pillows are used under the buttocks.

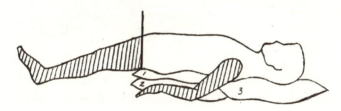

(The above position is particularly helpful if progression from position #6 to #7 on the flow chart is not comfortable for the lower body.)

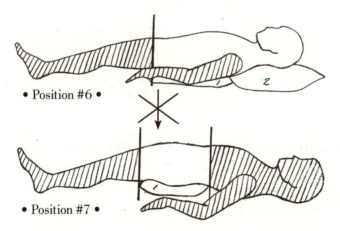

In summary, try this modification to help with the progression:

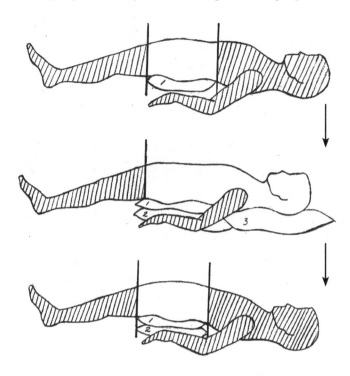

For a more direct stretch specifically to the spine, roll a towel up in the shape of a cylinder. Place this on top of the pillow directly under your spine from your shoulder blades to the back of your head or from your tailbone to the back of your head.

2. Isolating the Position of the Head and Neck

Once you can maintain cervical neutral without support, you can isolate the positioning of the head and neck to achieve even greater flexibility in that area. Tuck the chin slightly more and use a towel or a pillow underneath your head to *stretch* the back of the head and neck rather than just *stabilize* them.

The stretch will be increased as you move the pillow further down underneath the shoulders and the shoulder blades as demonstrated in the previous illustration. This type of positioning can either be more or less difficult for your neck than when the body is elevated on top of the pillows. It may be more difficult because the back of the neck is already being stretched by virtue of the position. Or this positioning may be easier because the body is on slack while only the neck is being stretched. You may find that positioning the head and neck in neutral or in flexion will each have a different effect on your neck. Your response is not predictable because we are all unique.

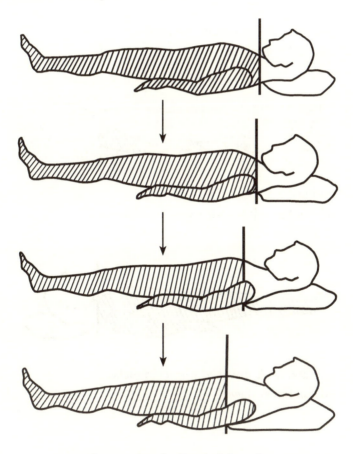

• Progressing the Cervical Stretch •

In an effort to be thorough, it should be noted there are a total of four different ways to position the head and the neck to achieve a different result. Of course, the B and D positions can be further progressed through all the lower body positions on the flow sheet. Theoretically, A should be the least difficult and D the most difficult. Again, each position must not necessarily be mastered but is mentioned to provide awareness of these options.

A.

- Head and neck *stabilized* in neutral.
- Body on flat surface.

B.

- Head and neck *stabilized* in neutral.
- Body on full pillows with arms unsupported.

C.

- Head and neck *stretched* with chin tucked.
- Body on flat surface.

D.

- Head and neck *stretched* with chin tucked.
- Body on full pillows with arms unsupported.

5. The Theory of the Program's Effectiveness

The final way **Rapid Release** is different from other exercise programs in the way it is affecting people. The results you can expect by doing these exercises are different from the results you might achieve by doing other exercises. I will present several ideas, or theories, in chapter 6 to potentially explain the results I am seeing.

Chapter 3

Rapid Release

Better Than Stretching!

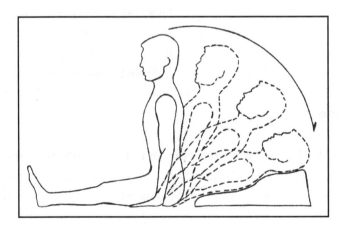

Beginning the Program

The following pages contain the exercises and the handouts I use to teach this method. They are sequenced in the order that seems to work best for most people: the Seated Worker series; the supine eyes, neck, and upper body; and the supine and prone lower body exercises. Or the upper body exercises may be taught last after the tension has been released above and below the shoulder joint. More about the reasoning behind the sequencing is answered by the second question in chapter 4. The instructions on each page of exercises are to do three repetitions of two to seven sets of each pair of exercises. This is a more conservative approach I adopted when I started working with more acutely ill patients. **Feel free to begin with 7 sets of 3 repetitions if you tolerate more activity.** *The original program design suggested the exercises be done in 3 sets of 7 repetitions.*

If you choose to do any of the supplemental exercises, they can be done in addition to the basic program in whatever way they work for you. The side-lying exercises can be done either after the supine and prone lower body exercises *or* after all the supine exercises are done. If I do the long-sitting exercises, I usually add them at the end of the program as a matter of convenience. Other times, I have used only the long-sitting exercises to quickly stretch out my lower body. If you have managed to maintain good flexibility, the "90 Degrees & Beyond" exercises could be used for the second and/or third set of the supine lower body exercises. If you are less flexible, they may never be included as part of your exercises.

Remember, the exercises in each area help release tension in one another. Plus, the different areas help release tension in one another. This is why the completion of these exercises in their entirety is ***"Better Than Stretching."***

WARNING: Doing this exercise program may provoke brief spells of dizziness, particularly with position changes. Take the time you need to allow this feeling to subside before you stand or begin to walk. Be careful with your first few steps. *Be sure you have your balance so that you do not fall.*

Focusing on the Eyes

Before you start these exercises, there is more to consider about the eye exercises. This small group of movements is the epitome of the statement "simple but profound." Even though the actual movements are very simple, for many people, these exercises are not easy. Sometimes the range of motion for the eyes is extremely limited. Other times, the motion is very uncoordinated or tiring. The effect(s) they can have on the body initially can be tremendous whether it be "for better or worse." *The vast majority of the time, the eye exercises are tolerated very well with no adverse side effects.* Even though it is often this group of exercises that ultimately makes the biggest difference in a person's improvement, there are certain times when extra care is needed, or you should proceed with caution.

It has been my observation that the eye exercises in particular can provoke a flare-up of lower back pain. Sometimes when this happens, a herniated lumbar disc has been previously diagnosed but not always. If chronic or acute low back pain is already present, it has usually been moderate to severe. You should be aware of three situations to alert you to be cautious with these exercises.

1. *The eye exercises do not provoke low back pain at the time, but as they are being done, the exercises themselves are very difficult to do.* Moving the eyes through full range of motion can be very difficult for some people. For others, movement of the eyes may immediately provoke a headache or nausea, etc. In these cases, lower back pain or soreness may be noticed shortly after the exercises are done or even the next day or two. Sometimes this painful period is very brief. Other times, the pain can last for days and be quite severe. Being careful not to provoke any symptoms greater than 3–4/10 by limiting the range of motion can reduce this negative response in the lower back as well as prevent a headache or more nausea. Assuming a more slouched position in sitting can help decrease tension in the body that hinders eye movement; bending at the hips and knees can reduce the tension provoked on the eyes from the body while in supine. If you choose to bend at the hips and knees, the legs should gradually be lengthened, or stretched out, a little bit every other day or so while the eye exercises are done.

2. *The supine eye exercises immediately provoke a pulling, pressure, or pain in the lower back.* The way to manage this symptom is the same as in no. 1: limit the range of motion for the eyes or bend at the hips and knees during the eye exercises. **In extreme cases, it may be necessary to discontinue the eye exercises altogether until some of the tension in the lower back has been released with the other exercises.**

On a few occasions, I have applied light, direct compression over the pelvis by wrapping a bath towel over the pelvis and tucking it in under each hip (see illustration on pages 135-139). This artificially provides stabilization to the pelvis, which always increases the body's tolerance for any type of motion. If you are able, the preferred method is to brace the pelvis with an isometric contraction of the abdominal muscles. Try both ways to see what works best for you. When the abdominal strength is so poor or if there is extreme pain, tightness, and/or pressure in the lower back or around the eyes, the artificial method provides better support than none until the muscle strength improves.

3. *The eye exercises are effectively reducing the pain in the leg, so they are done too frequently.* Several patients have done the eye exercises five to ten times a day once they realized this group of exercises was helping reduce their leg pain. They continued to do the remainder of the program only one time each day or less. Within a day or two, each of these patients was complaining of a "new" pain in the lower back or over the sacrum. Their response varied from moderate to quite severe. For some, it was present only with position change, but for others, it made all position changes and walking very difficult. To avoid this situation, some lower body movement should be done each time the eye exercises are done. At least alternate a few standing forward bends with standing trunk extension. Another option is to be sure the ratio of eye exercises to the rest of the body is more balanced.

It is worth repeating that it is acceptable to delay the start of the eye exercises if they are too difficult to do. Sometimes the eyes may lag behind the rest of the body a little. It is uncommon, but I have had a number of patients who continued to do the eye exercises in sitting for several weeks after the rest of their body was progressing from a modified supine position to a more flat supine position. As I previously mentioned, it is much better to temporarily *omit* the eye exercises if it means preventing a potential exacerbation of lower back pain. Acute pain, extreme pain, and a herniated disc are not necessarily a *contraindication* for the eye exercises, but they are situations where *caution* should be exercised or necessary compensations should be made to avoid unnecessary episodes of increased lower back pain. Sometimes it helps to complete rows 2-5 of the Seated Worker series for three to four days before including the eye exercises in the seated series.

On the other hand, I have worked with some patients who became very nauseated, even to the point of vomiting, when they did the eye exercises through partial range of motion in sitting for the first time. They used cool compresses or ice to their neck, jaw, or over their eyes that evening. The following day, they tolerated all the eye exercises through the full range of motion without any side effects. *Most of the time, people adapt to doing the eye exercises very quickly.* The benefits from doing the eye exercises will also be experienced very quickly.

Contraindications and Precautions

There are no contraindications for a program that focuses on correcting posture with pain-free, range-of-motion exercises. If there are times when this program is used simultaneously with post-surgical protocols that include restrictions, then of course, those restrictions should be observed. The most obvious type of injury would be to the neck directly when 24/7 bracing is required. The time when active motion may begin following a serious neck or spinal injury should always be cleared with the physician or the surgeon. Even though there may be times when portions of the program cannot be done because of a recent surgery or injury to a specific joint that requires immobilization, other portions of the program may be done to maintain good flexibility in the rest of the body.

There are times to exercise caution, however. Any patient who is medically frail, especially those in their seventies, eighties, and nineties and, even more particularly, with a cardiac and/or pulmonary diagnosis, should be treated cautiously. It may be necessary for these individuals, and/or those who are experiencing high levels of pain, to cut their neck a little slack each time the exercises are progressed, or the body is more lengthened. Be gentle with the eye, tongue, and neck exercises by decreasing the range of motion of the exercises as needed. Or do the eye and tongue exercises after the rest of the body has been exercised. *To counteract a negative response to the exercises, assume a modified supine position, tilt your head back and bend the hips and knees. Apply something cool, or even ice if you tolerate it, to the back of the neck.* Please refer to "Flare-Up Positioning" in chapter 4.

There are three occasions to be particularly conservative as you begin the exercises:

1. *Do not combine eye stabilization with head movement on the first day the eye exercises are done.* Be sure the eye and tongue exercises are well tolerated before you make them more difficult. "Well tolerated" can be defined as no adverse effects have occurred, such as excessive increases in heart rate or blood pressure. If you have a pulse oximeter and/or blood pressure cuff available, it would be useful to monitor your vital signs before and after the exercises are completed.
2. *Elevate the head of the bed as much as sixty degrees or more when you begin the lower body exercises in supine* if you are recovering from an acute cardiac, pulmonary, or CVA incident. This also applies when the neck has been directly injured. Tilting the head back slightly while the leg exercises are completed will further reduce the strain on the head and neck the first time the leg exercises are done.
3. *If you have experienced multiple face or head traumas, or demonstrate significant pressure in your head while lying down in supine, begin the exercises in sitting from the feet up the body instead of from the eyes down.* Excessive pressure in the head is revealed (a) whenever the head and face turn exceedingly red while lying flat, (b) whenever you are unable to lie flat because of uncomfortable head pressure or difficulty breathing, or (c) if you feel like your body is tilted "head down" when you are lying flat. "Head down" can be defined as feeling like your head is lower than your body when the body is actually in a flat supine

position, or you do not feel flat until the head of the bed is elevated. (The most extreme case I have seen of this was a woman who needed to elevate the head of the bed at thirty degrees before she felt like she was lying flat on her back. She had a long history of domestic abuse. The worst incident she remembered involved being kicked in the face and head by a person wearing steel-toed boots). The same supine advice as #2 applies here as well. Be sure to elevate the head of the bed at least sixty degrees when you begin the lower body exercises in supine.

Using the modified supine position may potentially increase the pain of an acute herniated disc. People with an acute irritation of a lumbar disc typically prefer to be in the position of "arching their back." This is the position of the prone prop up or prone press-up on page 92. This is the direct opposite of the modified supine position. Refer to the case examples on page 280-288 for complete instructions if you are suffering from the symptoms of a possible acute herniated disc. If the disc is not acute, modified supine may not only be tolerated but can also be very helpful.

And finally, beginning the eye exercises can potentially provoke lower back pain or soreness. Sticking out the tongue can provoke a sore throat and, if continued, provoke symptoms similar to bronchitis. This has been rare in my practice, but because the potential is there, it is worth mentioning. In both of these cases, discontinue the eye and tongue exercises until the symptoms subside. Begin again through a limited range of motion after your negative symptoms have subsided. Extend the range of motion to full range as you are able.

The following page (page 72-73) gives my recommendation on how to begin and progress through this exercise program.

Determine your beginning supine position.
- Correct the alignment of the cervical spine as needed. Use a negative (-) position on the progressive positioning flow sheet as needed for the neck.
- Use a position of ease (preferably) as needed to relieve lower back or upper body pain and/or tension.
- Complete the supine isometrics to familiarize your muscles with contracting while in the lengthened position.
- Do not begin the supine exercises in positions 1–7 on the progressive positioning flow sheet. It is best to complete the exercises in the zero ("0") supine position for a few days even if you tolerate one of the more difficult positions.

1. Begin the complete exercise program with the Seated Worker series. ***Familiarize yourself with the guidelines for the exercises.***
2. Do the eye exercises in the supine position.
    - If the eye exercises provoke low back or head pain in sitting, limit your range of motion and/or repetitions or slouch your posture in sitting; in supine or modified supine, bend at the hips and knees as needed to improve your tolerance for eye movement.
    - In extreme cases, if lower back or head pain is provoked even when taking these precautions, **discontinue** the eye exercises until there is less tension and pressure in the lower back or around the eyes.
3. Do the head and neck exercises in the supine position.
    - Sticking out your tongue can provoke a sore throat. Limit the range of motion of the tongue or discontinue the exercise temporarily to relieve the symptoms and prevent a bronchitis.
4. Do the upper body exercises in the supine position.
    - Refer to the upper body simplifications/variations as needed for those exercises that are *initially* too difficult for you.
    - **Progress** from the simplified exercises to the regular exercises as soon as you tolerate them.

5. Do the lower body exercises in the supine and prone positions.
   - Refer to the lower body simplifications/variations as needed for those exercises that are *initially* too difficult or if you do not yet tolerate lying on your stomach.
   - **Progress** from the simplified exercises to the regular exercises as soon as you can tolerate them.
   - Optional: Do the side-lying and/or long-sitting exercises.
        Do the "90 Degrees & Beyond" lower body exercises for greater flexibility.
6. Modify, or reduce, your position of ease as you progress toward tolerating flat supine.
7. After you tolerate the exercises in flat supine, further improve your flexibility, if you so desire, by progressing your position for exercise according to the progressive positioning flow sheet.

REMEMBER:

- Work your way down the page of the progressive pillow positioning flow sheet.
- Record the dates of your progress on the exercise log. Check off the exercises you did for accountability. This is the key to achieving myofascial release for greater flexibility, decreased pain, and increased function.

Rapid Release for the Seated Worker

1A. LOOKING UP AND DOWN	1B. LOOKING TO BOTH SIDES	1C. DIAGONALS	1D. DIAGONALS
• Look up and return to the center three times. • Look down and return to the center three times. • **Repeat two to seven sets.**	• Look to the right and return to the center three times. • Look to the left and return to the center three times. • **Repeat two to seven sets.**	• Look to an upper right corner and return to the center three times. • Look to a down and left corner and return to the center three times. • **Repeat two to seven sets.**	• Look to an upper left corner and return to the center three times. • Look to a down and right corner and return to the center three times. • **Repeat two to seven sets.**
2A. "NOD" AND TILT HEAD BACK	2B. STICK OUT THE TONGUE	2C. "CHICKEN" RETRACTION	2D. CONTROLLED OPENING
• Face forward. • "Nod" the chin to the throat. Return to the center. • Repeat three times. • Face forward. • Tilt the head back to look at the ceiling. • Return to the center. • Repeat three times. *Initially move the eyes with the head and then stabilize the eyes forward during head movement.*	• Sit up straight with the chin slightly tucked. • Stick your tongue out toward the bottom of the chin. • Repeat three times. • Stick tongue out straight and to the top lip three times each. *Remember, sticking out your tongue can give you a sore throat.*	• Sit up straight with ears directly in line with the shoulders. • Glide the head directly back. Keep the chin tucked. • Do not allow face to tilt toward the ceiling. • If the range of motion is very limited, first, reach forward with face and then pull back. • Repeat three times. ***Repeat this row two to seven times.***	• Place the tip of the tongue on the roof of the mouth just behind the top teeth. • Drop the jaw comfortably. Return to start. • Maintain tongue position throughout the exercise. • Repeat three times. *Make a clicking noise with the tongue if you are unable to maintain the tongue position.*

3A. SCISSOR AND PINCH	3B. HEAD ROTATION	3C. REACH AND ROW or PUSH AND PULL	3D. HEAD SIDE BEND
• Begin with the forearms crossed in front of your body at shoulder height. • Pull the elbows back behind you while squeezing the shoulder blades together. *(motion as seen from above)* • Return to start with the forearms in front of your body. Alternate which arm is on top. • Repeat three to seven times. *Complete exercise one arm at a time as needed.* *Lower the arms below shoulder height initially as needed. Return to shoulder height and above as tolerated.*	• Sit up straight with chin slightly tucked. • Look over the right shoulder and return to the center. • Repeat three times. • Look over the left shoulder and return to the center. • Repeat three times. *The eyes follow the head or look straight forward.*	• Begin by pulling the elbows together behind back. • Now point fingers to the ceiling. Push both arms forward as far as possible. Lead with the heel of the hand. • Pull back and push forward three times. *Complete exercise one arm at a time as needed.* *Push forward and pull back at various angles.* **Repeat this row two to seven times.**	• Sit up straight with chin slightly tucked. • Continue to look forward while the ear drops toward the shoulder. • Repeat three times. • Repeat three times to the other side.

4A. KNEE WINGING	4B. TRUNK ROTATION	4C. KNEE WINGING	4D. TRUNK SIDE BEND
• The trunk faces forward. • Drop the knees apart from each other and then pull the knees back to the center. • Repeat three times. • Go to 4B.	• Tuck the elbows into sides and cross the arms on the chest. • Twist **at the waist.** One shoulder should come forward; the other shoulder goes back. • Return to the center. • Repeat three times. • Repeat three times to the other side. • Go to 4C.	• Same as 4A. • Repeat three times. • Go to 4D.	• Place one hand on seat of chair for support, place the other hand at front of the shoulder. • Lean sideways while pushing the hand in front of the shoulder up and over your head. • Return to start in the center. • Repeat three times. • Repeat three times to the other side.
Position feet slightly apart.	*The head and face turn with the trunk,* **or** *the face stays forward as the trunk turns.*	*Position feet slightly apart.*	

Repeat this row two to seven times.

Releasing Pain | 77

5A. HEEL SLIDE or KNEE to CHEST	5B. KNEE PUMP	5C. HIP ROTATION	5D. ANKLE PUMP
• Move forward to the edge of the seat. • Lift the knee to the chest as tolerated. • Lower the foot back to the floor. • Repeat three times. *It is okay to lift the knee through partial range of motion.*	• Stay on the edge of the seat. • Straighten the knee. • Return the foot to the floor. • Repeat three times. *Begin by sliding the foot back and forth on the floor if necessary*	• Stay on the edge of the seat. • Move one foot to the outside two to three inches away from the midline. • Drop the knee to the center and then return the knee to the outside. • Repeat three times.	• Stay on the edge of the seat. • Pump the foot up and down at the ankle. • Lift the heel higher off the floor as tolerated. • Repeat three times. *It may be necessary to slightly lift the foot from the floor to keep the knee straight during the ankle pump.*

⟵ *Repeat this row two to seven times and then switch to the other leg.* ⟶

	SIMPLIFICATION OF 4D
*The exercises on this sheet are **options** to the standard program* **Simplification:** *These exercises are for those individuals who simply do not yet have the strength or the range of motion to perform the standard exercise.* **Variations:** *These exercises are changes to the standard exercises that will provide a slightly different stretch to promote an even further increased range of motion.*	• **TRUNK SIDE BEND** 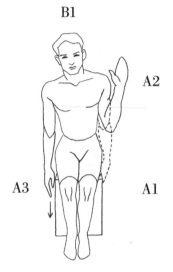 • *Modify the position of the arm as the trunk bends to the opposite side.* • Keep the hand down (A1) or at shoulder height (A2) as the opposite hand reaches toward the floor (A3). – OR – • Reach to the top of the head (B1) as the trunk tilts. Return the hand to shoulder height as the trunk straightens. • Repeat three to seven times.

Releasing Pain | 79

Seated Worker Modifications

VARIATION OF 3A	VARIATION OF 3C
• **FLIES**	• **FORWARD REACH**
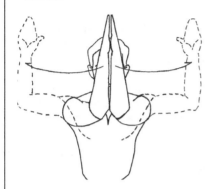	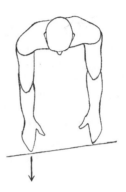
• Begin with the elbows touching in front of the chest, hands together, fingers pointing up. • Roll the arm and hands back so they are even with the body. • Return to the beginning position with the arms in front of the chest. • Repeat three times. *Alternate the height of the elbows as tolerated.*	• Stretch your arm(s) out in front of you at shoulder height. • Reach with one arm as if to make it longer. • *Keep the elbow locked* and pull the arm back from the shoulder. • Repeat three to seven times with each arm. *Move one arm at a time for 3A and 3C as needed.*

Modify the height of the arm or support the arm on the desk, etc., as needed

Guidelines for Eyes, Head, Neck, and Upper Body Exercises

Do three repetitions of each exercise.
Do two to seven sets of each pair.

- Lie on your back on a firm surface. **Keep your chin gently tucked.**
- Keep the lower half of the back of your head in contact with the surface.
- Keep the head still during the eye exercises, particularly the jaw.
- Keep the head and neck still during the upper body exercises.
- Keep your legs as straight as possible. Stabilize the ankle so the heel of the foot, the bottom of the foot, and the toes are as flat up against the wall as tolerated. If you must bend your knees, do so as little as possible to compensate for any discomfort.

All movements should be done GENTLY and COMFORTABLY.
– Do not strain or force motion –

- Limit your range of motion if necessary to minimize your symptoms.
- Keep any tension, nausea, dizziness, or "thickness" in the throat to 3–4/10 or less on a scale of 1–10.
- Move at a moderate pace—not too fast or too slow.
- Do not cross the midline with your motion.
- Do two to seven sets of each pair before you progress to the next pair.
- *It is possible* to experience a scratchy sore throat or a swollen/thick feeling in your throat in response to the tongue exercises as you progress through the head and neck exercises. Gargling with ice water and/or applying ice packs to your throat can reduce these symptoms. *Do not force your way through the progression if you experience this symptom.*
- The sore throat sensation can progress to a "burning" sensation in your chest, similar to a bronchitis. Discontinue the tongue exercises temporarily if necessary to avoid this symptom.

WARNING: **You may experience brief dizziness with position change as you progress through this program. Be careful during position changes to prevent a fall.**

REMINDER:
- Lying flat on the floor or another firm surface is the "0" (zero) position.
- Initially, you may need support under your head to help you *stabilize* your neck in the correct chin-tuck position.
- As you gain flexibility in the back of your neck, you will require less support under the head to maintain your chin comfortably tucked.
- As an option, when you are able to tuck your chin comfortably without any kind of support, you can put a folded towel or pillow under your head to *stretch* the back of the neck and make the exercises **more difficult**.
- The exercises become even **more difficult** as you move the pillow further down your upper back while maintaining the correct chin-tuck position.

Releasing Pain | 81

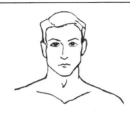

FACE FORWARD

EYES IN THE MIDLINE

- Lie flat on your back with the chin gently tucked.
- Position yourself directly under a light fixture, etc., to establish a midline reference point.
- Keep your jaw, head, and neck still while you move your eyes.
- Minimize any symptoms of nausea, dizziness, or pain by limiting your range of motion as needed.
- Achiness in the small of the lower back indicates that you are pushing the eye exercises too hard.
- Minimize lower back pain by limiting your range of motion, elevating the upper body, or bending at the hips and knees.
- If necessary, continue the eye exercises in the seated position until improved flexibility is noticeable in the rest of the body but especially in the lower back.

1A

- Look up.
- Return to the midline.
- Repeat three times.

1B

- Look down.
- Return to the midline.
- Repeat three times.

> Repeat this row two to seven times.
> Progress to the next pair.

2A

- Look to the right.
- Return to the midline.
- Repeat three times.

2B

- Look to the left.
- Return to the midline.
- Repeat three times.

> Repeat this row two to seven times.
> Progress to the next pair.

3A

- Look up to the right corner.
- Return to the midline.
- Repeat three times.

3B

- Look down to the left corner.
- Return to the midline.
- Repeat three times.

> Repeat this row two to seven times.
> Progress to the next pair.

4A

- Look up to the left corner.
- Return to the midline.
- Repeat three times.

4B

- Look down to the right corner.
- Return to the midline.
- Repeat three times.

> Repeat this row two to seven times.

Rapid Release - Head and Neck

1A. CERVICAL ROTATION

- Begin with the chin gently tucked.
- Turn the head to the right as if to look over your shoulder. *Direct chin down toward the shoulder.*
  - ☐ Eyes follow the head.
  - ☐ Eyes stabilized forward.
- Return to the midline. Repeat three times.
- Repeat to the left and back to the midline three times.

1B. CERVICAL "NOD" and CERVICAL EXTENSION

Incorrect chin tuck ⟶

- Lower the chin to the throat without lifting the back of the head from the surface.
  - ☐ Eyes follow the head.
  - ☐ Eyes stay forward.
- Return to start.
- Repeat three times.

- Tilt the head back, pointing the chin to the ceiling.
  - ☐ Eyes follow the head.
  - ☐ Eyes stay forward.
- Return to start.
- Repeat three times.

Repeat two to seven sets. Progress to the next pair.

2A. RETRACTION - "CHICKEN"

- It is critical to keep the chin gently tucked throughout this exercise. *Do not push with the top of your head.*
- Push the back of your head into the surface **with the lower part of your skull**.
- Relax to neutral. Repeat three times.
- *Clasp fingers together at the base of the head to help direct motion as needed.*

2B. TONGUE PROTRACTION - "Stick Out Your Tongue"

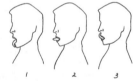

1   2   3

- Begin with the chin gently tucked.
- Open your mouth comfortably.
- Stick your tongue out gently to reach down for your chin. Gently exhale during motion.
- Pull your tongue back into the mouth. Repeat three times.
- Next, stick your tongue straight to the ceiling. Gently exhale during motion. Repeat three times.
- Finally, stick your tongue out to reach your top lip or nose. Gently exhale during motion. Repeat three times.

Repeat two to seven sets. Progress to the next pair.

3A. SIDE BENDING

- Begin with the chin gently tucked.
- *Keep the back of the head in contact with the surface. The nose should always point to the ceiling.*
- The crown of the head is at "12:00" position. Tilt the head to "10:00" and back to the center. Repeat three to seven times.
- Begin at "12:00" position. Tilt the head to "2:00" and back to the center. Repeat three times.
- *Place the hands at the base of the head to help direct motion as needed.*

3B. CONTROLLED OPENING

- Begin with the chin gently tucked.
- Relax the bottom jaw.
- Place the tip of the tongue on the roof of the mouth just behind the top teeth.
- Drop the jaw comfortably.
- Return the jaw to the starting position maintaining the tongue in contact with the roof of the mouth. *Be sure you are not just moving your lips.*
- Repeat three times.

Do not allow the head to tilt back.

Rapid Release - Upper Body

1A. ANGELS/JUMPING JACKS

- Begin with the arms down by the sides, palms up.
- Slide your arms up and out while maintaining contact with the surface, keeping the elbows straight.
- At the top of your motion, or slightly lower, turn the palms down and slide the arms back down to the sides.
- Repeat three times.

1B. PULLOVERS

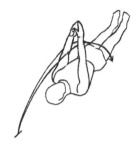

- Raise the hands from the sides of the hips to meet in the center of the body. Continue to lift the hands overhead.
- Keep the elbows as straight as possible.
- Lower the arms and hands back down to the sides of the hips.
- Repeat three times.

**Repeat two to seven sets.
Progress to the next pair.**

2A. ELBOW WINGING

- Touch fingertips behind the base of your head.
- Let the elbows drop down to the surface.
- Pull the elbows together in front of the face at the level of the mouth and chin without forcing the motion.
- Return the elbows to the starting position.
- Repeat three times.
- Optional: Demonstrate in varied positions.

2B. REACH UP AND SHRUG DOWN

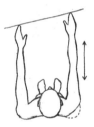

- Raise the arm to shoulder height so the hands are pointing to the ceiling.
- Keep the elbow straight as you reach for the ceiling with one arm and then pull the same shoulder back down to the surface.
- Stabilize the elbow with the opposite hand.
- Repeat three times with that arm.
- Repeat three times on the opposite side.
- Optional: Demonstrate in varied positions.

**Repeat two to seven sets.
Progress to the next pair.**

3A. OVERHEAD LIFT	3B. REACH DOWN AND SHRUG UP
	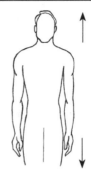
• Begin with the elbows bent at your sides and the backs of the hands on the surface. The hands and elbows maintain contact with the surface throughout the motion. • Slide the hands straight up to make a steeple overhead. Keep the elbows as straight as possible. • Slide back down to the starting position. • Repeat three times.	• Keep the elbows straight. • Reach the hand down toward the feet and then shrug the same shoulder up toward the ear. • Repeat three times on one side. • Repeat three times on the opposite side. • Demonstrate at different angles away from the body.

WINGING VARIATION OF 2A	**REACHING VARIATION OF 2B**
• **WINGING AT VARIED ANGLES** 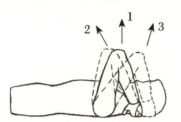 • Begin with the finger tips just behind the ear lobes - #2. • Pull the elbows together across the chest and then return the elbows to the surface. *– or –* • Begin with the hands at the upper back of the head - #3 • Pull the elbows together across the face at the level of the nose and eyes and then return the elbows to the surface. *Alternate winging **above** the midline with reaching **below** the midline.*	• **REACHING AT VARIED ANGLES** 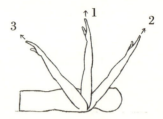 • Reach the arm and hand toward the ceiling. • Raise the arm above shoulder height to reach and shrug. - #2. *– or –* • Lower the arm below shoulder height to reach and shrug (reach and shrug) - #3. • In addition to modifying the angle of the arm, change the rotation of the arm so that the palm is facing in toward the body. *Alternate winging **below** the midline with reaching **above** the midline.*
HOLD-UP VARIATION OF 3A	**REACHING VARIATION OF 3B**
• **WINDSHIELD WIPER**  • *This exercise is helpful if you are unable to keep your forearm in contact with the surface for the hold-up exercise.* • Move the elbow away from the body as much as you can toward shoulder height. • Bend the elbow so the hand is pointing to the ceiling. • Drop the back of the hand to the surface and then return to the starting position. Repeat three times. • Drop the palm to the surface **directing the hand toward the hip** and then return to the starting position. Repeat three times. Alternate movements.	• **REACHING AT VARIED ANGLES** 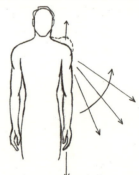 • Keep the arm resting on the surface but move the arm away from the body at thirty degrees to reach and shrug. • In addition to modifying the angle of the arm, change the rotation of the arm so that the palm is positioned up or down as well as facing the body. • Repeat the reach and shrug exercise with the arm moved away from the body at forty-five degrees and sixty degrees.

Releasing Pain | 87

Upper Body Modifications

*The exercises on this sheet are **options** to the standard program.*

Simplifications: *These exercises are for those individuals who simply do not yet have the strength or the range of motion to perform the standard exercise.*

Variations: *These exercises are subtle additions to the standard exercises that will provide a slightly different stretch to promote an even further increased range of motion.*

SIMPLIFICATION OF 1B

- **REACHING TO THE TOP OF THE HEAD**

- Clasp the hands together at the midline in front of the chest.
- Keep the elbows bent as you lift overhead.
- Lift the hands and arms overhead as far as tolerable as you reach for the nose, forehead, or top of the head.
- Pull the elbows in toward the center as much as possible.

SIMPLIFICATION OF 2A

- **REACHING TO THE OPPOSITE SHOULDER**

- If you are unable to put your hands behind your head or neck, try to simply reach across the body to the opposite shoulder and then return the elbow to the surface.
- This can be done at various angles, such as reaching for the forehead or the ribs.

SIMPLIFICATION OF 3A

- **REACHING TO THE TOP OF THE HEAD**

- Begin with the backs of the hands resting on the surface at shoulder height as much as possible.
- Reach for overhead so that the hands meet just above the head.
- Keep the arms and hands on the surface as much as possible.
- *If this is even too difficult*, reach for the nose or the forehead.

Guidelines for Lower Body Exercises

Do three repetitions of each exercise.
Do three to seven sets of each pair.

- Exercises are to be done lying on your back on a firm surface.
- Keep your eyes forward, looking straight up at the ceiling.
- Keep chin gently tucked. Keep your head and shoulders still.
- Keep the lower half of the back of your head in contact with the surface.
- Keep your legs straight. If you must bend your knees, do so as little as possible. It is more preferred to modify supine by using an upper body wedge.

All movements should be done GENTLY and COMFORTABLY.
– Do not strain or force motion –

- Keep any negative response to 3–4/10 or less on a scale of 1–10.
- Limit your range of motion if necessary to minimize the symptoms.
- Do not cross the midline with your motion.
- Move at a moderate pace—not too fast, not too slow.
- Do two to seven sets of each pair before you progress to the next pair.

Bridge three times between each supine pair.
– Do not force the prone exercises –
– Do not force the hip shrugs or extension –

WARNING: You may experience brief dizziness with position changes as you progress through this program. Be careful during position changes to prevent a fall.

REMINDER:

- Lying flat on the floor or another firm surface is the "0" (zero) position.
- Initially, you may need to use one to two pillows under your knees or a wedge under your upper body (preferred) to relax your lower back or alleviate other symptoms.
- As you gain flexibility and symptoms reduce, gradually remove this support until you are lying flat.
- Lying with your body on top of the pillows from head to heels with *arms unsupported* is **more difficult** than lying flat.
- The exercises become even **more difficult** as your legs gradually become **less supported** also.

Supine and Prone Transitional Exercises

Bridge in Supine: Do three repetitions between each pair of supine exercises.

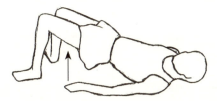

- Bridging allows the pelvis to unweight and balance as the soft tissue releases.
- Begin by bending your hips and knees comfortably with the feet flat on the floor.
- Gently squeeze the buttocks together.
- Lift the buttocks off the floor or surface as high as you comfortably can.
- Lower the buttocks to return to the surface.
- Repeat three times. Straighten the legs one at a time and relax.

A–B: Prone   **C: Prone Prop Up**   **D: Prone Press-Up**

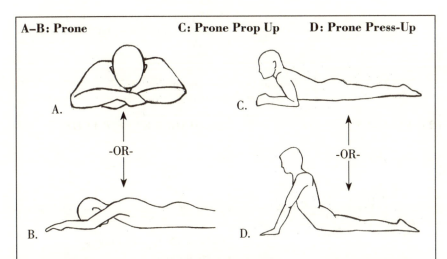

A. Lie as flat as possible with the chin tucked. Rest the forehead on the backs of the hands or on the surface.

-OR-

B. Straighten the arms overhead as tolerated.

C. Gently prop up the trunk so you are comfortably on your elbows.

-OR-

D. As you gain greater flexibility in your back and/or abdomen, you may progress to straight the elbows.

- Prop up anywhere within your comfortable range of motion.
- Keep stretch in the stomach and/or low back to 4/10 or less.
- Your goal is *not necessarily* to achieve position D.

Rapid Release - Lower Body - Supine

1A. HEEL SLIDES

- Begin with both legs as straight as possible.
- Bend one knee sliding heel along the surface toward the buttocks.
- Slide the heel along the surface to return to the starting position.
- Repeat three times on one side.
- Repeat three times on the opposite side.

1B. LOWER TRUNK ROTATION

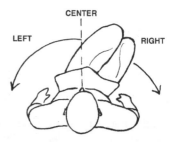

- Comfortably bend at the hips and knees one leg at a time.
- Lean the knees from the center to one side and then return the knees to the center.
- Repeat three times on one side.
- Repeat three times on the opposite side.

**Repeat two to seven sets.
Bridge three times.**

2A. FALLOUTS

- Slightly bend at the hips and knees one at a time, keeping the feet together.
- Lower your knees as they fall apart.
- Bring the knees back together in the center.
- Repeat three times.

2B. SINGLE KNEE TO CHEST

- Bend the hips and knees comfortably.
- Bring one knee toward the chest and then lower the heel down to the surface.
- Repeat three times on one side.
- Repeat three times on the opposite side.

**Repeat two to seven sets.
Bridge three times.**

3A. WINDSHIELD WIPER

- Hips and knees are comfortably bent.
- Place the ankle of one leg just above the knee on the opposite leg.
- Drop the knee out and away from your body and then pull the knee across the body towards the opposite shoulder. Repeat three times.
- Now go to exercise 3B using the same leg.

3B. STRAIGHT LEG RAISE WITH AN ANKLE PUMP

- Straighten the knee of the top leg so the foot is directed to the ceiling.
- Pull your foot/toes toward your head and then point your foot away from your head (bending at the ankle).
- Repeat the ankle pump three times.
- Complete two to seven sets of exercises 3A and 3B with one leg before repeating this pair of exercises with the opposite leg.

Repeat two to seven sets.
Bridge three times.
Roll onto the stomach.

Rapid Release - Lower Body - Prone

• **Begin with a prone prop up to your comfort level three times** •

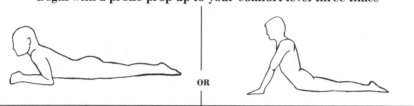

4. HIP SHRUG 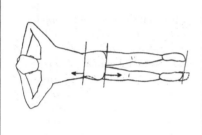	• Keep the forehead on the hands and the body flat. • Reach with one foot as if to make your leg longer. • Now pull the top of the pelvis up on the same side toward the ear. • Do not bend at the hip or knee. Do not rock side to side. • Repeat three times on one side. • Repeat three times on the opposite side.
5. HIP EXTENSION 	• Keep the forehead on the hands and the body flat. • Lift the leg straight from the hip. • Lower the leg back down to the surface. • Repeat three times on one side. • Repeat three times on the opposite side. *It is unnecessary to lift the leg very high; ten degrees to fifteen degrees is sufficient.*
6. HAMSTRING CURLS 	• Keep the forehead on the hands and the body flat. • Keep the front of the hip down flat on the surface. • Bring the foot toward the buttocks by bending the knee. • Return to the starting position. Fully straighten the knee each time. • Repeat three times on one leg. • Repeat three times on the opposite leg.

Prop up or press-up three to seven times.

- **Repeat prone series two to seven times** •
Log roll onto your back – Bridge three times – Lie out flat

- Position yourself flat or on top of the pillows at the appropriate level to correspond with supine positioning.

PRONE EXERCISE VARIATIONS IN STANDING

STANDING EXERCISES	PRONE PROP UP	VARIATION #4
• If you do not tolerate lying on your stomach, begin the prone exercises in standing. • Keep the chin tucked and eyes forward in all the exercises. *Modifications - Perform:* 1. Isolated back bend three times. 2. Isolated head tilt back three times - &/or - isolated chin tuck three times. 3. Isolated eye elevation three times. 4. Combine 1&2, 2&3 &/or 1,2,& 3.	**STANDING BACKBEND** • Stand with the feet slightly apart for balance. • Place your hands below the waist in the small of the back for support. • Lean back to stretch the lower abdomen and front of the pelvis and possibly the lower back. *Note: It will be helpful to back up to a counter for support.*	**STANDING HIP SHRUG** • Shift all your weight onto the leg next to support. • Lock the knee of the unweighted leg. • Shrug the hip of the unweighted leg up toward the shoulder. • Reach to the floor with the same leg as if to make the leg longer or drop the foot off the edge of a step. • A greater range of motion may be achieved if you hold the leg slightly in front of you.

VARIATION #5	VARIATION #6	ADDITIONAL EXERCISE
STANDING HIP EXTENSION	**STANDING KNEE BEND**	**STANDING HIP ABDUCTION**

• Stand straight with the front of the pelvis as close to counter as possible. • Lift the leg behind you from the hip. Keep the knee straight. • Keep the upper body and the pelvis still. **Do not allow the trunk to lean forward.**	• Stand straight with the front of the pelvis as close to counter as possible. • Bend the knee as if to kick the buttocks. • **Do not allow the trunk to lean forward or the knee to come forward.** *Note: It will be helpful to face a counter for support.*	• Stand straight. • Lift the leg to the side from the hip. • Keep the leg in the same plane as the body.

SIMPLIFICATION OF #3A LOWER BODY EXERCISES

SIMPLEST WINDSHIELD WIPER	SIMPLER WINDSHIELD WIPER

• Lie on your back with the chin gently tucked. • Keep the knee as straight as possible. • Roll the entire leg out and in **from the hip**.	• Lie on your back with hips and knees bent or straighten the non-exercised leg. • Move the foot of the exercised leg away from the midline as much as is comfortable. • Drop the knee to the inside and then to the outside as much as possible.* ***After total hip replacement, DO NOT cross the midline with the knee.**

SIMPLIFICATION OF #3B LOWER BODY EXERCISE

SIMPLEST STRAIGHT LEG WITH THE ANKLE PUMP	SIMPLER STRAIGHT LEG RAISE WITH THE ANKLE PUMP

• Lie on your back with the chin gently tucked. • Keep the knee as straight as possible while the leg rests on the surface. • Do the ankle pump three to seven times.	• Support the leg under the knee and thigh. • Lift the lower leg to straighten the knee. • Do the ankle pump three to seven times. • *Support can be provided by bending the opposite leg. Rest the exercising leg on the opposite bent knee.*

Releasing Pain | 97

ANGELS OR JUMPING JACKS	PULLOVERS	OVERHEAD REACH
Refer to Upper Body exercise instructions	*Refer to Upper Body exercise instructions*	*Refer to Upper Body exercise instructions*

 Unsupported Areas

Progressive Pillow Positioning Flow Sheet

HEAD, NECK, AND UPPER BODY PROGRESS EVERY TWO TO THREE DAYS AS TOLERATED			LOWER BODY PROGRESS EVERY TWO TO THREE DAYS AS TOLERATED		
LEVEL	POSITION	DATE/ COMMENTS	LEVEL	POSITION	DATE/ COMMENTS
-3	8–12 CM SUPPORT		-3	THREE PILLOW SUPPORT	
-2	4–8 CM SUPPORT		-2	TWO PILLOW SUPPORT	
-1	0–4 CM SUPPORT		-1	ONE PILLOW SUPPORT	
0	FLAT SUPINE		0	FLAT SUPINE	
1	0–4 CM		1	HEEL TO HEAD	
2	4–8 CM		2	MID-CALF TO HEAD	
3	BASE OF NECK TO HEAD		3	BELOW KNEE TO HEAD	
4	TOPS OF SHOULDERS TO HEAD		4	ABOVE KNEE TO HEAD	
5	MID-SHOULDER BLADE TO HEAD		5	MID-THIGH TO HEAD	
6	SHOULDER BLADE TO HEAD		6	BUTTOCKS TO HEAD	
7	WAIST TO ARMPIT		7	BUTTOCKS ONLY	

Progressive Positioning Reminders

1. The exercises become **more difficult** when they are done on top of the pillows.
2. Do not skip levels in the progression.
3. Your goal is to progress to the bottom of the flow sheet.
4. Each level of progression is a **suggestion** to keep you moving down the page. It may be necessary for you to progress in **three-inch increments rather than six inches**. Modify your progression as needed to accommodate your tolerance.
5. **Thinner** pillows will provide a superficial stretch. **Deeper** pillows will provide **a deeper** stretch. It is recommended to begin on thinner pillows.
6. In cases of extreme tightness, it may be necessary to position yourself on top of a folded afghan or blanket. After you work through all the levels of progression on the thinner support, repeat the complete progression on top of the pillows.
7. If you experience too much body tension on top of the pillows, construct a small upper body wedge *on top of the pillows* initially. This includes tension or pressure in the lower back, chest and head, thickness in the throat, and/or tension in the neck.

Positions of Ease

Choose from these position modifications to gently lengthen the body IF:
- you do not tolerate the flat supine position after successfully completing the seated series.
- your pain is significantly exacerbated when the exercises are done in supine.
- you have recently (within the last year) had any type of abdominal or thoracic surgery.
- you suffer from severe and/or chronic pain or frequent respiratory infections.
- you are seventy-plus years in age and *especially* if you are eighty-plus years.

1. **If you have a recliner,** an adjustable bed, or hospital bed, begin with the upper body elevated and the legs straight out in front to address the symptoms referred to the low back, hips, knees, ankles, and feet from above.

   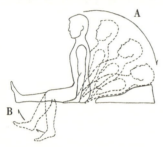

   - Slowly lower the position of the torso while the legs are fully extended (A).
   - In extreme cases, it may be necessary to gradually raise the legs to straight forward (B).
   - Shorten one end of your body to help the other end lengthen as in box 2. and 3. in the next column.

2. **Begin with the head elevated.** This best applies when the symptoms are referred to the lower back, hips, knees, and feet from tension in the upper body, neck, and head.

   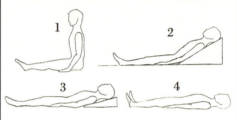

3. **Shortening the lower body** best applies when the lower body tension refers the pain to or limits motion at the head, neck, and shoulders.

   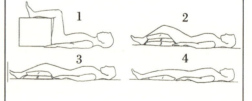

Progressive Pillow Positioning

The **Rapid Release** exercise program is progressed by doing the same exercises while you lie on top of the pillows. *The exercises never change.*

REMEMBER: for the lower body
- Lying on top of the pillows with the **arms unsupported** is **MORE DIFFICULT** than lying flat.

Less difficult   More difficult

- As the body moves down off the pillows and the **legs gradually become unsupported also,** the exercises become **EVEN MORE DIFFICULT.**

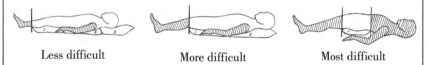

Less difficult   More difficult   Most difficult

- - -

REMEMBER: for the upper body, head, neck, and eyes
- Lying on a pillow to **stretch** the back of the head and neck while the rest of the body is **unsupported** is **MORE DIFFICULT** than lying flat.
- As the pillow is moved down the body to **stretch** the shoulders, shoulder blades, and ribs, the exercises become **EVEN MORE DIFFICULT.**

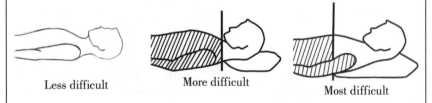

Less difficult   More difficult   Most difficult

- The thickness of your pillows will affect your tolerance for the positioning. If the pillows are *too thick*, the positioning will be *too difficult*. If the pillows are *too thin*, the exercises will be *too easy*.

Note: The size of the pillows should provide a slight stretch to your body so that the exercises are comfortably challenging initially.

- **The suggested levels of progression may be modified in smaller increments as needed.**

Rapid Release - Side lying

1A. HIP SHRUGS	• Lie on your side. Position the bottom arm under your head with the elbow straight or bent. The top hand rests on the surface for balance. Both legs are straight. The top foot drops behind the bottom foot. • **Keep your trunk still** from the waist up. • Reach with the top leg as if to make the leg longer. • Repeat three times. • Progress to exercises #2A and #2B.
2A. ISOLATED HIP ROTATION **2B.**	• Lie on your side. Position the bottom arm under your head with the elbow straight or bent. The top hand rests on the surface for balance. Both legs are straight. The top foot drops behind the bottom foot. • **Keep your trunk still** from the waist up while the pelvis rolls back and then pulls forward to return to the starting position. • Repeat three times and then progress to exercises #3A and #3B.
3A. ISOLATED TRUNK ROTATION **3B.**	• Lie on your side. Position the bottom arm under your head with the elbow straight or bent. The top hand rests on the surface. Bend at the hips and knees for balance. • **Keep the pelvis still** while the trunk and shoulder roll backward and the top arm drops back toward the surface. Extend the elbow if possible and then reach across your body to return the arm and trunk to the starting position. • Repeat three times.

4A. SIDE-LYING FLEXION "Shorten" **4B.** 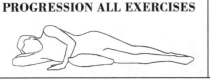 "Lengthen"	• Lie on your side with your hand under your head so the neck stays as straight as possible. Bend the bottom leg slightly at the hip and knee for balance. • Begin with the top arm pulled back behind the trunk and the top leg bent at the hip with the knee pulled up to the chest. • Reach forward and up with the top arm in a semicircular motion, while the top leg straightens down and back. Return to the starting position. • Repeat three times. Repeat the side-lying series two to seven times while on one side. • Flip to the other side. Repeat the side-lying series two to seven times.
PROGRESSION ALL EXERCISES	• Position the pillow underneath the hips and waist. • Add additional pillows to increase the stretch.

Rapid Release – 90 Degrees & Beyond

For those who tolerate it, even greater flexibility may be achieved by progressing the exercises past a ninety-degree straight leg raise. Some people may never reach this level. For others, these exercises will be very helpful.

• **STARTING POSITION:**	**1A. KNEE TO CHEST**
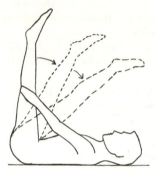	
• Begin with both legs pointing straight to the ceiling with the hips bent at ninety degrees. • As you become more flexible, begin with the hips bent at angles even greater than ninety degrees, progressing toward a "pike" position.	• Begin with both legs pointing straight to the ceiling or closer to the chest as tolerated. • Support the back of the thighs/knees with your hands. • Pull one knee toward your chest and then return to the starting position. • Repeat three times. • Repeat with the opposite leg. • Go to exercise #1B.

1B. TRUNK ROTATION

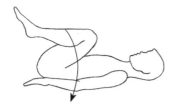

Assist the knees with the hands as needed to return to the center.

- Begin with both hips bent at ninety degrees or more. Bend the knees comfortably. The feet will not touch the floor.
- Place the hands on the knees or outer thighs for support.
- Drop both knees to one side and then return the knees to the center.
- Repeat three times.
- Repeat three times to the opposite side.
- Go to 1C.

1C. ABDUCTION/ADDUCTION

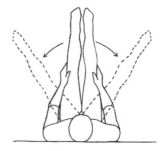

- Begin with both legs pointing straight to the ceiling.
- Place both hands outside the thighs for support.
- Keep the knees straight and let the legs fall out to the side and then return to the center.
- Repeat three times.

Repeat two to seven sets. Progress to the next pair.

2A. ANKLE PUMPS

- Begin with both legs pointing straight to the ceiling.
- Support the legs at the back of the thighs or knees with your hands.
- Gently pump the ankle on one leg three times.
- Alternate with exercise 2B.
- Repeat 2A and 2B two to seven sets.

2B. HIP ROTATION

- Begin with both legs pointing straight to the ceiling.
- Support the legs at the back of the thighs or knees with your hands.
- Bring the knee toward the outside of the chest. Lower the knee to the floor if possible, just beneath the armpit, and then return to the starting position.
- Repeat three times.

- Following these exercises, it also feels good to use your hands to gently distract the legs upward to gain an additional stretch to the back of the legs. Or ask for the assistance of another person.

Always finish with two to three prone prop ups or press-ups.

Guidelines for Long-Sitting Low Back Release Exercises

- Begin in the long-sitting position with the back as straight as possible.

- Initially, it may be necessary to lean back on your hands to minimize the strain on the lower back or to the backs of the thighs. If you are sitting on the floor, back up to a couch, chair, or the wall for support.

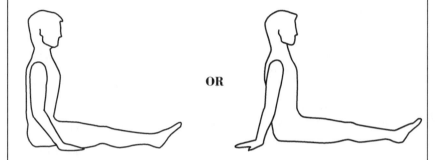

OR

- Keep all motions gentle and comfortable.

- Decrease your range of motion as needed to minimize any initial discomfort or tightness.

- Continue to stabilize the head and neck in the correct position.

- Whenever the trunk leans forward, the return motion should always begin by straightening the spine from the bottom to the top. For example,

   Forward Reach: To recover from the trunk and arms reaching forward, begin to straighten the back at the spinal level even with the bottoms of the shoulder blades and continue to straighten up to shoulders and neck.

   Long-Sitting Ankle Pump: To recover from being bent forward at the waist, start to straighten the back at the spinal level below the waist. Continue to straighten up to the waist and to the bottoms of the ribs, arching the back as you sit up straight.

Rapid Release Long-Sitting Low Back Exercises

1A. HEEL SLIDE

- Slide the heel of one foot toward the buttocks.
- Return to the starting position.
- Repeat three times.
- Repeat the exercise on the opposite side.

Use the hands to assist through a full range of motion as needed.

1B. QUAD SET

- Sit with the legs as straight as possible and toes pointing to the ceiling. (You may need to begin by leaning back on your hands slightly as in illustration 1A.)
- Lock the knee straight by pushing the back of the knee into the floor.
- Repeat three times.
- Repeat on the opposite side.

Additional stretch may be achieved by leaning the trunk forward.

**Repeat two to seven times.
Progress to the next pair.**

2A. HIP SHRUG

- Reach forward with one leg as if to "make it longer."
- Pull hip and leg back to the starting position.
- Repeat three times.
- Repeat the exercise on the opposite side.

2B. FORWARD REACH

- Raise the arms in front of you to shoulder height with the hands together.
- Reach forward with the arms as the trunk leans forward.
- Pull the shoulders and arms back to the starting position as you squeeze the shoulder blades together and sit up straight.
- Repeat three times.

Additional stretch can be achieved by reaching across the body at different angles.

**Repeat two to seven times.
Progress to the next pair.**

Releasing Pain | 109

3A. TRUNK ROTATION	3B. STRADDLE	3C. TRUNK SIDE BEND

• Sit with the legs apart to *whatever extent is comfortable for you*. • Position the arms as shown or fold across your chest. • Rotate the trunk and return to the center. • Repeat three times. • Repeat on the opposite side. • Go to 3B.	• Sit with the legs apart to *whatever extent is comfortable for you*. • Place the hands down on the floor in front of you to support the lower back. • Lower the chest toward the floor, keeping the lower back as straight as possible. • Return to the start. • Repeat three times. • Go to 3C.	• Sit with the legs apart to *whatever extent is comfortable for you*. • Begin with one hand at shoulder height and the other hand supporting you on the floor. • As the trunk leans to one side *from the waist*, the hand pushes toward the ceiling and across to the opposite side. • Repeat three times. • Repeat on the opposite side. • Repeat 3A, 3B, and 3C two to seven times.
Be sure that motion occurs at the waist, not just at the shoulders and arms.	*Additional stretch can be achieved by leaning to each side three times.*	*Additional stretch can be achieved by reaching across the body at different angles.*

4A. WINDSHIELD WIPER

- Sit with the hands by your sides on the floor.
- Slide one foot out to the side away from the midline and then bend the leg at the hip and the knee.
- Drop the knee in toward the midline and then return to the starting position.
- Repeat three times. Go to 4B.

4B. LONG-SITTING ANKLE PUMP

- Begin in long-sitting starting position.
- Keeping the knee as straight as possible, pump the ankle up and down three times.
- For an additional stretch, lean the trunk forward at the waist and then do the ankle pump.
- Alternate the ankle pumps and windshield wipers for two to seven sets.
- Repeat on the opposite side.

Below: It feels good to complete this series with a few gentle static stretches.

5A. DOUBLE KNEE TO CHEST

- Lie flat on your back with the hips and knees bent. Keep the chin tucked.
- Pull the knees to the chest. Hold for twenty to thirty seconds.
- Release the stretch.
- Repeat two to three times.

5B. SEATED FORWARD BEND

- Sit on the edge of a chair.
- Drop the trunk forward to rest the chest on thighs.
- Reach the arms underneath the chair as much as possible.
- Hold the stretch for twenty to thirty seconds.
- Repeat two to three times.

To return to the upright position, place the hands on the knees. Use the hands to help push the trunk upright as needed to avoid low back strain.

6A. PRAYER STRETCH	6B. TUCKED SITTING
 • Sit upright facing a table. Drop the chest forward and reach across the table as far as you comfortably can. -OR-  • Sit on your feet with the knees tucked into your chest as closely as possible. • Reach forward with your hands to stretch the lower and mid-back. Hold for twenty to thirty seconds. • Repeat two to three times. • **Increase** the stretch by reaching to either side and/or going up on your toes. -OR- Sit on the tops of the feet with the toes back (not shown).	 • Sit back on the heels. Drop the chest to the knees. • Hold for twenty to thirty seconds. • Repeat two to three times.

7. Always finish with two to three prop ups or press-ups.

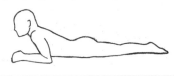
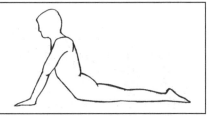

Rapid Release Exercise & Home Care Instruction Record

INSTRUCTION DATE							
1. LOWER BODY - Supine: heel slides, lower trunk rotation, single knee to chest, abd/add, hip IR/ER, straight leg raise w/ankle pump, bridging.							
• Prone: hip shrugs, hip extension, hamspring curls, prop-ups or press-ups; <u>standing modification</u>.							
• Modified: hip IR/ER, straight leg raise, hip extension, hamstring curls.							
2. UPPER BODY: angels, pullovers, winging, reaching up, hold-ups, shrugging down.							
• Modifications: angels, pullovers, winging, hold-ups.							
3. CERVICAL: rotation, flex/ext., retraction, tongue protraction, lateral bend, controlled opening.							
4. EYES: all planes of motion.							
5. SIDELYING: hip shrugs, isolated pelvic rotation, isolated trunk rotation, flex/ext.							
6. LONGSITTING: heel slides, hip shrug, forward reach; straddle, trunk rotation, trunk lateral bend; hip IR/ER, forward bend w/ankle pump.							
• Stretches: double knee to chest, seated forward bend, prayer stretch, tucked sitting.							
7. SEATED WORKER: 1) hip flex, hip rotation, knee extension A/P; **2)** hip abd/add, trunk rotation, trunk lateral bend; **3)** shoulder abd/add, reaching cervical rotation, cervical lateral bend; **4)** cervical flex/ext, tongue protraction, cervical pro/retraction; **5)** eyes.							
8. 90° & BEYOND: straight leg raise w/ankle pump, hip abd/add, single knee to chesr, hip IR/ER.							
9. SUPINE POSITION (SP), **CERVICAL POSITION (CP)**							
10. PROGRESSIVE POSITIONING (PP) **POSITIONING (P+)**							
11. LIGHT COMPRESSION							
12. CRANIAL FASCIA TRACTION							
13. POSITIONAL TRACT/PASSIVE HIP STAB.							
14. FLARE-UP POSITIONING							
15. COLD PACK TREATMENT							

Chapter 4

Answering Your Questions . . . Helping Yourself

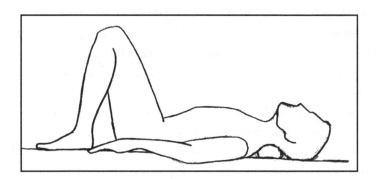

Q: Which position should I begin the exercises in?

A: This is an important question, so it is best for you to keep in mind some principles to help you make the best decision for yourself.

1. **The most conservative way to begin the exercises is in the seated position.** You will never go wrong by beginning at the very beginning. If your body is moving well in the seated position and your symptoms have not increased by doing the exercises, you can move on to a slightly more difficult supine position even the next day, but beginning global movement from the seated position is the most gentle way to do so. Progress to a modified supine or semi-reclined position on whatever size wedge is appropriate for you. As the exercises are done and your flexibility improves, gradually reduce the size of the wedge or upper body elevation. Eventually, you will be doing the exercises in the flat supine position.

If you do not feel like you need to be this easy on yourself, at least begin in some form of modified supine. The head and neck should be in good alignment. The upper body should be slightly elevated to reduce the risk of increasing symptoms in the head, neck, and shoulders in response to lower body movement; or lower back, hip, knee, or ankle pain will not be aggravated by increased pressure from above in the head, neck, and shoulders. If you find you have started in a position too difficult for your body, simply digress to an easier position.

Some of the hospitalized patients I have seen are initially unable to transfer to a chair to assume the seated position. There are some hospital beds that can be converted to the "chair mode" position. This type of bed can be extremely helpful for repositioning highly immobile patients. If such a bed is not available, elevate the head of the bed as much as is comfortably tolerated and use the bed controls and/or pillows under the knees to bend the hips and knees as much as is needed prior to beginning the seated exercises.

2. **Keep in mind there is no universally correct modified supine position to begin in once you progress from the seated position to supine.** When the strain on your body has

been minimized by using a modified supine position, you have met the objective of the modified positioning. Your body is more free to release tension through movement when you first reduce the strain on the connective tissue through your positioning. Don't be discouraged if you must begin on a fairly large wedge. You are simply doing what you need to do for your body to enhance your chances to improve.

Q: Which section of my body should I begin the exercises with?

A: Indirect movement, or movement not involving the painful body part, will always be tolerated the best. Remember, most of the time, *the source of the pain is at the opposite end of the body from the site of the pain.* Since most of our body is located below the eyes, I start most of my patients with the eye exercises in the seated position. Once they progress to supine, I begin again with the eye or neck exercises. If the greatest tension is in the eyes and neck, I attempt to at least move them through a partial range of motion. Tolerance for eye and neck movement can also be enhanced by bending the hips and knees. If limited motion of the eyes and neck is still too difficult or provokes uncomfortable symptoms, I shift my attention to the lower body with the upper body elevated. Moving the lower body will often provide enough relaxation of the neck and head to then allow for improved movement tolerance in those areas.

If the problem happens to be headaches, neck pain, or shoulder pain, begin with the lower body exercises in the seated position rows 5-4. Progress up the body to the shoulders, neck, and eyes. It may be necessary to reduce the range of motion of the arms and the neck once you reach rows 3-2. It may be necessary to skip row 3 for the arms altogether or move one arm at a time, actively or active assistively, through a limited range of motion. After completing the neck exercises (row 2) and the eye exercises (row 1), try rows 3-2 again to see if there is any improvement. When the position is progressed to modified supine, begin again with the lower body. Then move to the top with the eyes and work down the body to the neck and the shoulders.

If the problem is strictly with the shoulder, begin movement at whichever end of the body tolerates movement the best. If flat supine is tolerated, try to begin with the eyes and work down the body, skipping the arms and moving from the neck to the lower body. Finish the exercise sequence with the arms. Attempting to work straight down the body from the eyes, to the neck, to the arms, and then to the lower body is not *wrong*. I have just found it typically helps the shoulders to move better if tension is first released above and below the shoulders. If the lower body tolerates movement the best in supine, be sure to begin in *modified supine with the upper body elevated* as a precaution to avoid an exacerbation of shoulder pain, even if flat supine is tolerated well without increased shoulder pain.

If eye motion in sitting, modified supine, or supine is not tolerated well, complete the rest of the exercises and then recheck the tolerance for eye movement. Releasing tension in the abdominals will facilitate release in the eye muscles, so complete *the standing prone, or standing trunk*, exercises to relax the eye muscles. It will also help to do the prone exercises *in prone, or on the stomach*, to lengthen the front side of the trunk. If tolerance for lying on the stomach is poorly tolerated, even after doing the standing exercises, place one or two pillows under the abdomen to make lying prone more comfortable. Remove the pillows as tolerated.

One thing about eye movement should be noted. After a concussion or head trauma with a positive loss of consciousness, several of my hospitalized patients have had extreme difficulty with the eye exercises. Eye movement may be very uncoordinated and/or limited. Moving the eyes may provoke nausea or dizziness. Most of the time, these symptoms reduce when the hips and knees are bent. I usually restrict this first exposure of attempted eye movement to two sets of two or three repetitions. In spite of the difficulty, the change in the mental status of these patients the next day has been remarkable.

I have also witnessed this same scenario among several hospitalized patients who have suffered a concussion or some form of head trauma years ago and then travel to a significantly higher elevation. They may be admitted to the hospital for a variety of reasons, but "altered mental status" is also among their problem list. Completion of the eye exercises is always a challenge, but the change in their ability to mobilize is apparent immediately. Their mental status may clear some immediately, as well, but if not immediately, changes will be apparent by the following day.

Q: Is *Rapid Release* better for me than my current exercises (whatever they may be)?

A: I do not believe ***Rapid Release*** is **better** than other forms of exercise. I do believe, however, it is the "missing link" for many people to accomplish one of three things:

1. The exercises provide a new *starting point* for those people who have not yet tolerated any other form of exercise. If you know your body needs exercise but you have been unable to find any exercises that don't actually make you feel *worse*, these exercises may be *part* of your solution. I emphasize the word "part." Sometimes our physical conditions are so complicated they cannot be corrected by using only one treatment modality. Such is usually the case with chronic pain or full body pain.

It is my hope for anyone who benefits from these exercises to eventually tolerate a more difficult form of exercise. For instance, if your problem is balance, you must eventually master exercise done in the standing position to fully restore or correct your balance issues. Ultimately, some form of strengthening will be required to improve strength. ***Rapid Release*** is helpful for those patients who cannot begin at these levels.

2. These exercises can also provide an *option* for those people who have tried various types of exercise but are not completely achieving their goals or tolerating their complete workout. For example, I have had several patients who practice yoga regularly. While their overall tolerance for yoga may be good, there are certain poses they do not tolerate, or their pain is persistent in spite of regular exercise. By temporarily changing their form of exercise to the ***Rapid Release*** program, they are usually able to overcome their particular hindrance and return to their previous form of exercise. At times, they have required the assistance of my manual skills in combination with the

exercises to promote this progress, but for some, the exercises alone have provided the necessary relief.

3. The longer I use this program, the more convinced I am that *posture should be corrected as much as possible* before specific areas are rehabilitated. There may be some components of the rehab process that can overlap, but addressing postural deviations should not be omitted, which it usually is. For some reason, we all seem to have developed the belief that nothing can be done about poor posture. Posture can improve. Addressing postural deficits should be a mandatory part of the recovery process regardless of the problem. By helping to do this, **Rapid Release** is not better than other forms of exercise, but it will bring out the best in other forms of exercise.

Q: What is the best way to approach these exercises if I suffer from multiple pain sites?

A: Movement under these circumstances will always begin in sitting. Apply the principle to move your body at the opposite end from the most severe pain first. Initiating movement for some people may require a bit of picking and choosing. If you do not tolerate all the exercises in each row of the seated series, do the ones you can tolerate. Reassess your tolerance each day for movements you previously found to be difficult. Once the exercises are progressed to the supine position, be sure to elevate the upper body, head, and neck even if you do not appear to need it.

The key is to start moving. Gentle movement is always the objective. When the movement is too forceful, the soft tissue will respond by tightening up worse than it was before the movement was attempted. If movement is poorly tolerated all over the body, start where movement is tolerated the best, even if it is through a limited range of motion. If motion must be initiated passively, begin passively. I have been surprised to watch patients progress rather quickly in their tolerance for arm and leg movement, from passive to active assistive to active movement, when eye and neck movement is included in their exercises from a position of correct alignment.

Q: Do I have to do the complete program? How often should I do *Rapid Release*?

A: Because the four different sections of our bodies affect one another, it is best if the complete program be done at least one time per day. Depending on the amount of tension present, or the level of pain, initially, a person may need to do the full program more than once a day. *Remind yourself this phase is only temporary but may be required to initiate the process of change.* Reduce your frequency when you are feeling better to every other day, and then twice a week, and finally, once per week. By the time you are lying flat, you should be able to begin light strengthening and/or gentle low-impact aerobics. Walking *as tolerated* is always appropriate.

If it is impossible to do the full program all at the same time, or your body does not tolerate that much movement yet, try to do as much as you can before you even get out of bed. If your activities throughout the day reinforce or encourage tension, such as sitting at a computer or driving for extended periods, take a break from sitting every hour or so to do the standing exercises. Choose a couple of exercises from each row of the seated series to do frequently throughout the day. Keep moving as much as possible while you are sitting.

Q: Will *Rapid Release* work for me if I am a "naturally tense person" or if I have always had bad posture?

A: Yes, it will. As a matter of fact, this exercise program might help you change this perception of yourself. Many of my patients tell me they "just don't know how to relax." Their spouses, friends, or families always tell them to "loosen up" or "don't be so uptight." The truth may be this is not something they can voluntarily change just by making up their mind to do so. We all live under various amounts of pressure and stress, so *some* of this tension is probably influenced by our circumstances, attitudes, and coping skills. I do not believe, however, that *most* of the tension I see in my patients can be voluntarily reduced with an attitude adjustment and strenuous exercise. Many of my "uptight patients" are already avid exercisers spending significant amounts of time each week stretching and exercising but never gaining much flexibility. Almost without exception, there has been a motor vehicle accident, fall, or some type of trauma in their past. When the fascia is addressed with this gentle program, people begin to experience a new level of relaxation unfamiliar to them in the past. Their tension was not entirely a personality trait or the result of poor coping skills; instead, it was a very real anatomical response to previous trauma.

Along those same lines, poor posture is not necessarily the result of laziness or repetitious poor body mechanics. I am more inclined to believe poor posture "eventually happens to us" when the abnormal stresses and strains from a previous trauma are left to run their course. Abnormal posture is very difficult to consistently correct and maintain if there is enough tension within the body to visibly distort its external appearance. By releasing tension throughout the entire body, improved posture is more easily maintained.

Do not assume bad posture is uncorrectable because of your age. You do not have to look "like an old person" just because you are getting older. I have been pleasantly surprised by the improvements in the posture of my elderly patients once they started the standing exercises, particularly the eye exercises.

On a more personal note, if you are one of those "uptight" people, or you feel sloppy or lazy because of your posture, I encourage you "to cut yourself some slack." *Stop criticizing yourself.* **Do your exercises**, and you may find you are not the uptight, lazy slob you thought you were.

Q: What if I do not feel a stretch when I first lie down on top of the pillows? What if my body stretches too much when I lie down on top of the pillows?

A: If you do not initially perceive a stretch in the #1 progressive position, you may feel more of a stretch as you progress further down the flow sheet. The depth of the pillows has a definite effect on which level of the soft tissue it stretches. Very flat pillows tend to stretch the fascia just under the skin or very superficially. Deeper or thicker pillows tend to stretch more into the muscle and the viscera of the abdomen. The pillows I use in the clinic have always been more flat than thick. These pillows always provide an adequate stretch for my patients to begin with. I discuss the option with my patients to work from level #1 to #7 a second time through on deeper pillows after progressing from level #1 to #7 on more shallow pillows if they are inclined to do so. Be sure to clear the more superficial layer first before going deeper.

If you do not immediately feel a stretch when you position yourself on top of the pillows, lie still for one to two minutes. This is usually enough time for the area(s) of greatest restriction to identify themselves through feelings of tension, achiness, pressure, etc. Once the active motion is begun, these symptoms should begin to subside again. If you still do not perceive a mild stretch anywhere, try lying down on the top of thinner or deeper pillows or move your arms away from your body. Just remember to keep the stretch mild or gentle.

I do not usually encourage my patients to lie still on the pillows until they experience discomfort. This method should only be used to determine if the challenge from the pillows to your body is sufficient enough to provide a stretch. The following case example demonstrates the effect the depth of the support *under the body* can have on the amount of stretch being translated *through the body*.

I worked with a fifty-year-old female who had full body pain she rated at 6/10 constantly, but the pain in her lower back was even worse at 8/10 constantly. After exercise tolerance was confirmed in sitting and flat supine, the time finally came for her to progress her positioning on top of the pillows. This immediately increased her low back pain that had reduced to 2–3/10 in flat supine back up to 8/10 again. After much trial and error, she found the most elevation her body could tolerate was on top of a *braided rug*. I saw this patient years before I started providing *supine compensation on top of the progressive positioning pillows*. She would have been a perfect candidate for this modification.

This patient was in an accident with a wheat thrasher at three years of age. Her right arm was pulled into the machine and was later amputated below the elbow. Her whole body was surely traumatized by the excessive force at the time of the accident. Over the years, the dysfunction became more solidified in the soft tissues to the point that full body pain was now her constant companion. By gently confronting the tissues at a level they could tolerate, she regained her hope of overcoming her constant pain.

It is best for everyone to begin their progression on the pillows at level 1, from head to heels. I have tried to start the progressive positioning at whatever level provoked a stretch anywhere in the body at 4/10. While this worked for some people, others experienced a significant exacerbation of their symptoms within two to three days. Sometimes the flare-up lasted for seven to ten days. This is much too long to experience increased pain if it can be avoided. Starting at level 1 of the progressive positioning and gradually working through each level of progression almost always prevents these types of flare-ups.

The exception to this is for some patients suffering from knee or hip pain. About halfway through the progression, the knee might swell, or the hip pain may intensify again. Regress to sitting for the eye, neck, and upper extremity exercises to let the symptoms subside. When you resume the exercises at the level of progression where the exacerbation was experienced, try adding an upper body wedge for the first couple of days. Maybe even continue to use the wedge for several more steps in the progression and then return to the level of concern without the wedge.

Q: Should I continue to do my regular stretching and strengthening exercises?

A: The answer to this question really depends on what kind of *results* you are experiencing. While strengthening is a very good thing, it can be a hindrance to your overall progress with this program if it is begun too soon. *You want to avoid strengthening a dysfunctional pattern.* It may be necessary for you to take a temporary break from your strengthening or significantly decrease the amount of weight you are lifting until your flexibility improves. **Remember, this is only a temporary phase.** Chances are your strengthening will be enhanced in the end if you develop your flexibility first. More of the muscle will be freed up to participate in the strengthening process.

Stretching is also an excellent practice. Continue to do the stretches you enjoy without bouncing or forcing them but do them after you have completed the **Rapid Release** program. Your body will be more responsive to static stretching following dynamic lengthening or gentle active movement.

It is also worth mentioning that the *amount* you exercise can be contributing to your problem(s). Some individuals insist on pushing their bodies at the same level of exercise they did prior to the onset of their pain. To suggest to some people they decrease their running, for example, from thirty miles per week to twenty miles per week or less is like asking them to sacrifice their firstborn child to a pagan god. Don't forget your pain is present for a reason. It will not go away by ignoring it or bulldozing over it. *Temporary modifications* in your current program may be necessary for the best long-term results. Or if I may dare say so, it is possible some changes may need to be made permanently as we age. A seventy-year-old does not necessarily need to work out at the same level as a twenty-year-old for the workout to be productive.

Also, consider your body mechanics while you exercise. Being sure to correctly stabilize your low back and neck during exercise will not only protect you from injury, but it will also help you experience a more satisfying workout. If you do not know how to stabilize your low back and neck properly, seek out the advice of a health-care professional or an athletic trainer.

Q: Which other types of therapy complement *Rapid Release*?

A: There are many different types of valuable therapies and treatment modalities that can be enhanced by **Rapid Release,** including massage, chiropractic or spinal adjustment, acupuncture or acupressure, and various forms of gentle bodywork, such as craniosacral or visceral manipulation therapy. Nutrition plays a big part in how we feel and tolerate activity. Walking, as much as is comfortably tolerated, is a great adjunct to any treatment. I personally instruct my patients to do this exercise program once per day, and then I use my manual skills of neuromuscular therapy, manual trigger point therapy, myofascial release, muscle energy, craniosacral therapy and/or taping during their appointment times to further release soft tissue restrictions. The type of manual therapy techniques used by clinicians will vary widely depending on their individual training. Many of my patients combine their physical therapy treatments with acupuncture and/or chiropractic and/or massage.

I should mention all massage is not the same. I have seen the most improvement in my personal symptoms when I have received a basic Swedish massage. This massage consists of long superficial strokes to the skin. The therapist does not intend to direct their force deeper into the muscle. I have received bodywork to deeper levels of tissue that were relaxing or felt good at the time, but they also did not produce any lasting change in my body. On another occasion, I received bodywork that was especially deep, resulting in unnecessary injury. Many people respond well to deep bodywork, but if you have been injured recently, undergone surgery recently, or your soft tissues have been unhealthy for an extended length of time, my advice is to start very light and superficial and progress toward deeper treatment if you so desire.

I have found most therapies *enhance* one another when they are used simultaneously and sequenced wisely. If people do not improve with chiropractic adjustments or physical therapy or *whatever*, it could be the *timing* was not right for that modality, or a combination of therapies was needed. If the soft tissue is too tight, it can hinder or negate the effectiveness of a spinal adjustment. On the other hand, I have experienced soft tissue tension in my own elbow and forearm release immediately with a chiropractic adjustment after not responding to months of stretching and gentle strengthening. I have had patients who could not respond to any type of soft tissue modality or exercise until they received trigger point injections, etc. Be encouraged to know your situation is not necessarily hopeless. Maybe you just need to rethink it and explore some new options.

Q: What is the tape you refer to in some of the case examples in chapter 5?

A: The tape I use is called *kinesiotape*. It was developed by a Japanese chiropractor who has lived in Albuquerque for many years. It is stretchy and different from the tape most people are familiar with commonly used by athletic trainers and therapists to provide joint stabilization. I use this tape to promote myofascial release in the soft tissues. Kinesiotape is a familiar modality to therapists, trainers, chiropractors, and other health-care professionals. You may have seen it on several Olympians.

Q: Is it possible for this program to make me feel more pain or soreness?

A: Initiating any form of exercise can provoke pain or soreness. Also, remember you may demonstrate different types of side effects with these exercises. Increased urine output, increased sleep, and/or increased anxiety, nausea, or dizziness are a few of the potential responses you may experience in the beginning. The program can also be helpful in alleviating these types of symptoms. If your reactions are severe, give yourself a couple of days for the symptoms to resolve, simplify your positioning, decrease your repetitions, or decrease your range of motion when you resume the exercises.

Exacerbations, or flare-ups, in your condition can be the result of several different things as you make your way through the progressive positioning. On rare occasions, I have seen aggravating symptoms return from a *completely different old problem*. This does not mean you are doing the wrong thing. It does mean you are experiencing changes in your body. Being "right" in your body will not necessarily feel good initially if you have been "wrong" long enough.

Most importantly, do not force your way through the progressive positioning. It may even be necessary to regress your positioning and/or decrease the frequency of the exercises or discontinue the exercises temporarily if your symptoms are severe. Use other therapies as needed to help you get through an exacerbation. Discuss these flare-ups with your therapist so he or she can help you work through and overcome this phase in your recovery. Follow up with your doctor if you feel like an official reassessment is needed or would give you some peace of mind. You can best decide how to help yourself by considering some of the following reasons **why** you are feeling worse:

1. *You experience "normal soreness" as the result of beginning any new form of exercise.* Even a strong, healthy, uninjured body will become sore initially with a new exercise. You may experience this *plus some* if you are not working with healthy soft tissue. Sometimes a new, more localized pain or discomfort will develop as the body becomes more balanced. This usually presents as tension, or a cramp, in a muscle that will not relax. One or several massages to the area will usually resolve this, or your therapist may try to relieve the tension with an electrical stimulation modality. For *localized* symptoms of pain, try ice or cold packs. A hot tub can promote *general* relaxation of the tissues.
2. *You have reached a level in the progressive positioning challenging the soft tissue at the origin of the pain.* For example, the symptoms you are experiencing are mostly in your outer thigh, but the *source* of the pain is in the lower back or the neck. When the soft tissues are engaged and challenged in the lower back or neck by a new position, the pain in the leg may actually *increase* somewhat or quite a bit.
3. * *The exercises are being done in a position that is too difficult for you.* You will know a position is too difficult if you experience any symptom or discomfort greater than 4/10 on a scale of 1–10, or you are unable to maintain your head and neck in the correct neutral position.
4. * *Your effort is too aggressive.* Motion should always be gentle and comfortable.
5. *You increase your activity level too quickly as you begin to feel better.* It is very common to overdo it once you start to feel better. It's interesting how quickly we forget about our pain once it begins to subside. While this is a good thing, it can leave you sore and in more pain again. Even though your body is moving better and feeling better, muscle endurance has not yet developed. Walking is a great exercise but will create pain and soreness if a person decides to walk twenty miles in one day to make up for the last twenty years of not walking at all.

---

* While nos. 3 and #4 may or may not necessarily provoke a flare-up, **they will almost always hinder your progress.**

Pace yourself as you return to more normal activities. Always use good body mechanics.

6. *If you experience extreme nausea to the point of vomiting, your body may be purging.* Refer to the case example on page 217-221. I have spoken with several massage therapist who have told me this response is not necessarily an adverse response to the treatment. When the body is overloaded with toxins, the exercises can facilitate a "ridding of" these unwanted toxins. This response is typically provoked by the eye, tongue, and/or neck exercises. Do not do those exercises for several days if you experience this reaction. When you decide to try them again, be sure to begin the exercises from your feet up. Get your whole body moving before engaging those sensitive areas. When you do the exercises, only move through a partial and/or limited range of motion. I also suspect this could happen in response to the massage directly to the muscles of the jaw. As a precaution, apply a cool compress or ice pack to the back of your neck after these exercises or after massaging your jaw.

7. *You may be doing nothing wrong, but the barometric pressure in your area changes.* People with arthritic-type conditions say they can tell when the weather is going to change based on how they feel. I have noticed a decline in many of my patients, coworkers, and family members during those times when the colder, more windy weather hits Albuquerque the hardest. Even patients who have been making consistent progress will experience an unexplainable setback. In my opinion, a body suffering from the effects of increased fascial tension is less resilient to external pressure changes. Most of my patients require more "hands-on" treatment during this time and must regress slightly in their home exercise program.

Along these same lines, I have noticed a commonality among my patients in regard to altitude and/or elevation. Albuquerque is approximately one-mile high in elevation. For individuals who moved to Albuquerque from a lower elevation, the symptoms they experienced in regard to their current complaint were *milder or nonexistant* at the lower elevation. There is always a history of some trauma that occurred at the lower elevation. I speculate the change in elevation put their body at a disadvantage, which then manifests in the person's current complaint.

The reverse of this phenomenon is also true. When people who have always lived in Albuquerque travel to a lower elevation, their symptoms either partially or completely resolve while they are away from home at a lower elevation. This is always very puzzling to the patient who is inclined to believe the improvement is the result of being less stressed while on vacation, etc. While this may be partially true, I believe the main reason for the improvement is the change in altitude. I have had only one patient who reported feeling much worse at a lower elevation, but the location was extremely humid, which produces a different type of atmospheric change. I have had one patient whose pain completely resolved, and her function was unrestricted when she traveled to a higher and colder elevation. I have no explanation for the change in her condition.

Q: Is it better to apply heat or cold to sore muscles?

A: Many of us have been taught to apply ice packs to muscle sprains or strains the first forty-eight hours after an injury and then switch to heat. By the time I meet most of my patients, they are using heat frequently and regularly but realizing only partial and temporary pain relief. Even though it is *much longer than two days* after their injury, I still recommend they use cold packs to any area(s) of tenderness we discover during their initial evaluation. While both modalities are ultimately helpful because they increase blood flow to the area, the cold seems to be more effective in promoting a *change* in the tissue, even though the heat is more soothing at the time. Cold packs are usually the most uncomfortable at the initial application and then five to ten minutes after the application. These two episodes of discomfort can be better tolerated by following these suggestions:

1. Wet a thin kitchen towel or paper towel with hot water. Wring out the excess water. Or warm the damp towel in the microwave.
2. Place the warm towel over the skin in the area of the soft tissue tenderness.
3. Apply the cold pack on top of the warm towel. This makes the *initial application of the cold pack less shocking.*
4. Leave the cold packs in place for fifteen to twenty minutes.
5. It is normal for the cold to burn and/or sting before the area actually becomes numb. If the cold pack becomes too uncomfortable, lift it

away from the body for ten to fifteen seconds and then reapply. *This side effect can be minimized* by breaking contact with the cold even if it is only for these few seconds.

Or in cases of extreme tenderness, apply a bag of ice to the area for five seconds on and then five seconds off. Continue with this "on again, off again" process for five to ten minutes and then leave the cold pack continuously in place for another ten minutes or so.

The frequent use of heat or cold is acceptable for as many as six to eight times per day if there is no adverse reaction from the skin. Either modality can burn the skin if the temperature is too intense or if it is left on too long so be sure to check your skin for tolerance. The skin will turn red during the application, but then the color should dissipate and return to normal. The more frequent applications are indicated in those situations where the pain is most intense or most recent. Surgery should even be considered as an "acute injury."

Some people with different types of arthritis may not be as tolerant of the cold applications, but since most of the locations I suggest for placement are not directly over the bony surfaces of the joint, they should at least be attempted. Decreasing the treatment time or the intensity of the cold may be helpful initially if your tolerance for cold is low.

There are specific areas of the body where the cold will best be utilized. These areas fall along the *unilateral pathway of pain* found in most people. Topical treatments can be applied directly to the location of the pain, but the best results will be achieved by treating the following recommended areas. These are locations in the body where either the circulation or the innervation can be impinged by adverse tension in the soft tissues.

1. The base of the head where it connects to the neck plus the front and side of the neck. Because it is easy to do, *use cold packs all the way around the neck whenever possible.* Alternate the full front side with the full back side if this is more comfortable or alternate the right side and then the left side, etc.

2. Directly over your closed eyes. I have been told it is contraindicated to apply ice directly to the eyes, so I usually recommend a cold wet cloth over the eyes.
3. Directly on the ribs from the inferior angle of the shoulder blade to as high up into the armpit as possible.
4. From the lateral end, or outside end, of the collarbone in front to just above nipple line and slightly under the arm. *Numbers 3–4 are particularly helpful following any type of shoulder surgery.*
5. From the belly button to the top of the upper inner thigh.
6. About six inches above the waist in the low back to the top of the pelvis.
7. The side of the buttocks from the top of the hip at the waist to the top/side of the thigh.
8. In the center of the buttocks.
9. The top of the inner thigh as high up into the groin as possible. Extend down the inner thigh as far as the inner knee if necessary.
10. Behind the knee from above the joint line to the mid-calf. *This is particularly helpful following any type of knee surgery.*

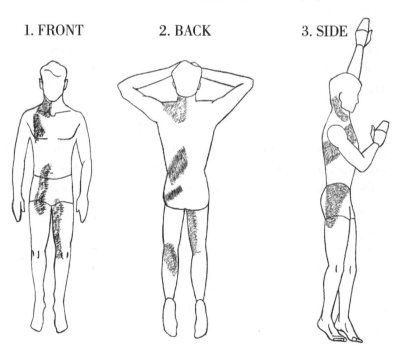

1. FRONT   2. BACK   3. SIDE

There are hot or cold packs available for purchase at most drugstores. Large bags of frozen peas are often suggested to use as a cold pack. Ice packs can also be homemade in one of two different ways:

1. Ice cubes in a ziplock bag.
2. Combine one part rubbing alcohol with two to three parts of water in a ziplock bag and then place in the freezer. This mixture will freeze to a "slushy" consistency and conform well to the body. It is best to use a doubled bag in case of leakage. I put mine on a cookie sheet in the freezer.

Contrasting the use of heat and cold can also be very effective. Apply the cold packs to the area for ten to fifteen minutes and then replace the cold pack(s) with hot pack(s) for the last ten to fifteen minutes. If it is possible to immerse the part in water, use hot and cold water instead of hot and cold packs.

For my patients who have suffered a recent fall or motor vehicle accident, I usually suggest they take a lukewarm bath or cold shower as tolerated. Begin the shower with hot or warm water. Gradually reduce the temperature for the effects of the contrast in the temperature. Finally, complete the shower with warm or hot water. The water should cover the entire body as much as possible, including the head and the face. Soaking as much of the head in a tub of water also helps. Wrapping the head in a cool to cold towel is another idea. *Gargling with ice water* can help the sore throat or the "thickness" in your throat that might develop after sticking out your tongue.

Q: How can I be sure my eyes are moving correctly if I do not have anyone to help me with tracking?

A: Following a target or a diagram works the best for most people. Begin by standing or sitting in front of a mirror. The mirror is sure to reveal whatever postural asymmetries there may be. Be sure your body and face are straight in respect to the mirror. Next, use a dry erase marker or put a strip of masking tape horizontally on the mirror at the level of your eyes. Also, put a vertical strip of tape on the mirror to divide your body in half. The intersection of the two strips of tape represents "the middle." Smaller lines can be drawn on the main lines if a full range of motion is not initially tolerated. It may be necessary to sit or stand two feet or so back from the mirror to make this work. Be sure to either sit or stand in the same place each time you do the exercises.

Do Eye Exercises in Sitting. Put masking tape on the mirror to follow with your eyes.
Mark off smaller increments as needed.

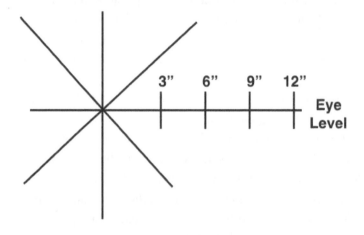

Begin by moving through a short distance. Increase distance as tolerated.

This is a little more difficult when lying on your back. It is helpful if someone can assist you. Try to position yourself on the floor or the bed underneath a light fixture or ceiling fan. If those items are not in a good place for you to lay underneath them, find a spot on the ceiling you can remember. You may consider marking the spot with a piece of tape. Once you have established where your center spot will be, stand back up to determine where the spot will be for you to look up to, down to, to the right of, to the left of, etc. It may help to also mark these spots with tape.

Q: Where do I position my eyes while I am lowering my upper body towards flat supine, but still in a modified supine position?

A: The answer to this question can be easily explained with an illustration.

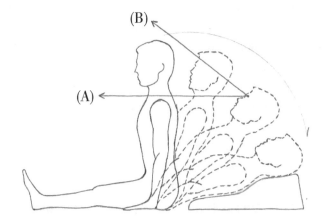

When the body is lowered to a forty-five-degree angle, for example, the eyes will be positioned in the bottom of the orbit when the person looks straight forward (A). *Movement of the eyes should always begin, however, from a position of being centered in the orbit.* When a person is leaning back at forty-five degrees, the eyes should be focused higher up on the wall in front of the person or possibly even on the ceiling. Lifting the line of sight upward is required to stabilize the eye in the center of the orbit (B). This is an important distinction to note as you progress through the modified supine positions toward flat supine.

Q: Is there anything else I can do at home to manage my symptoms besides the use of heat and cold?

A: There are several simple techniques I teach my patients for relaxation and to promote myofascial release between their treatment sessions. They can be helpful options if they work for you. One technique is widely used by massage therapists. The other techniques are my best attempt to duplicate light touch in a home program. All these techniques can be self-administered. As usual, the key to their effectiveness is *gentleness*.

- Tractioning the Cranial Fascia

This technique is incredibly simple but can be very helpful in promoting general relaxation of the head and neck. Begin by running your fingers through your hair. Rest your palm and the palmar surface of your fingers directly onto your head. Next, curl your fingers to make a fist. This will *traction the scalp*, which is different from pulling your hair. Always be very gentle with the traction to avoid provoking a headache. Squeeze your fist together tightly enough to *meet* the resistance of the scalp but do not force your way *through* the tension.

Start with the hand just to the right or the left of the center of the head where the hairline meets the forehead. Gently squeeze to make a fist. Hold the stretch for eight to twelve seconds or longer if you wish. Release briefly and then repeat as needed. Now move your hand to the side of your head over your ear at the hairline and stretch again. Next, stretch the crown of the head. Continue to move your hand to different locations down the back of the head to the hairline until you have covered one complete side of your head. Repeat on the opposite side. Use your right hand to stretch the right side of your head and your left hand to stretch the left side of your head.

When this type of stretch is no longer challenging to the tissue, progress the stretch by tractioning the scalp and then gently lifting it off your skull. This is more like pulling the hair, but you are actually lifting the skin. You can also add a clockwise or counterclockwise twist to this stretch. Or pull in a straight downward, upward, or sideways direction.

Another way to treat the cranial fascia is by gently pulling the ears. Grip the ear at the base where it attaches to the head by placing your thumb behind the ear and folding your index finger inside your ear. Gently pull the ear *away* from your head. The ear may also be stretched toward the face or the back of the head as well as up or down. It too can be twisted clockwise or counterclockwise.

- Manual Cranial Compression

Headaches or pressure in the head can often be eased by applying light direct pressure to the skull to decrease the intensity of a headache or to provide some temporary relief. There are three different ways to do this. Each compression should be sustained for approximately eight to twelve seconds and then repeat two to three times or as needed.

1. Place the palms of the hands on the back of the skull. Stretch your fingers up to the crown of the head; place the thumbs directly under the base of the skull. *Gently* squeeze the fingers and thumbs toward each other like a vise-grip on the head. Hold for eight to twelve seconds. Relax and repeat two to three times or as needed. Move the thumbs to a different spot at the base of the skull. Repeat the technique two to three times. Continue to relocate the thumbs until the complete base of the skull is treated.
2. Place one hand horizontally across your forehead so that your middle finger is at the level of your hairline. Place your other hand horizontally across the base of your skull so that your pointer finger is at the level of the prominent bones that form the base of the skull. *Gently* squeeze your hands toward each other. Hold for eight to twelve seconds. Relax and repeat two to three times or as needed.
3. Place the heels of your hands on the temples of your head. Rest your palms on your head as the fingers lie across the top of the head. *Gently* lift your palms and then gently squeeze together. Hold for eight to twelve seconds. Relax and repeat two to three times or as needed.

- Passive Cranial-Chest-Pelvic Compression

In an effort to duplicate my hands for my patients, I created a very simple method to promote relaxation and myofascial release. This technique can usually be done without the assistance of another person.

Begin by lying down comfortably in flat supine or whatever form of supine you tolerate. Create a blindfold by folding a pillowcase in half lengthwise and then again in thirds lengthwise. Place the blindfold over your eyes, using it to apply a very light but firm compression across the eyes, the bridge of the nose, and on the sides of the head. Overlap the ends of the blindfold behind the head. **Do not tie the ends together. Do not apply a hard, tight compression through the blindfold.** This technique can reduce pressure in the head and decrease tension in the neck. Some people even report a general sense of relaxation throughout their entire body.

You may want to use a scarf on your head that is either tied under the chin or on the top of the head to release tension at the crown of the head or in the jaw. It's okay to tie the ends together if the compression remains light but firm.

Another variation of this compression can be accomplished by wrapping the head from the base of the head to the front over the forehead like a turban. Place the center of the blindfold at the base of the head in the back. The blindfold may need to be lowered slightly to include the top of the neck. Position it as needed for your comfort in whichever way is most effective for you. Next, give a slight upward pull to one side of the blindfold as you bring it across the *side of the head and eye* to finally pull it across to the opposite side of the forehead. Repeat on the opposite side.

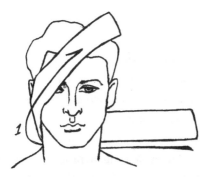 

It will be necessary to secure the ends on the forehead by applying a separate wrap just across the forehead or across the forehead and the eyes. Do this by placing the center of this second wrap at the center of the forehead. Hold the center in place with your right hand as you roll your head to the right. Use your left hand to tuck the left end in behind your head and then roll the head back to the center. Secure the right end by rolling the head to the left, etc.

As odd as it may seem, this technique should be used cautiously. Your body will make adjustments in response to the light compression, so you must be careful not to rush things, especially with more intense or acute conditions. Because the response to this technique is so *individual*, I will share some of the more diverse reactions I have seen so you will not be alarmed by your potential response. One patient who had been in a recent motor vehicle accident only tolerated the blindfold lying across *the top of her eyes* for about three minutes. The pressure in her head then became so intense that she had to immediately remove it. Another woman felt *completely relaxed* for six to seven minutes and then suddenly became claustrophobic. Yet another woman started very comfortably with the blindfold for ten minutes twice in the first day but was so stiff and sore in her lower back for the next three days that most of her usual daily tasks were too difficult to perform.

At the other end of the spectrum, one patient fell asleep with the blindfold in place for forty-five minutes the first time she ever tried it at home. She was pleasantly surprised to be more relaxed and much more energized when she woke up. She suffered no adverse reaction whatsoever. Another patient jumped from ten minutes to forty-five to ninety minutes in just a matter of days. He continued to use the compression on a daily basis during his afternoon nap of one to two hours. The compression relaxed him and produced more restful sleep.

Most people are able to start with five minutes one, two, or three times per day and then gradually increase their time up to twenty to thirty minutes one to two times per day without any problem. Beginning with five minutes may be too conservative in many cases, but I would rather err on the side of caution to avoid an exacerbation even though these problems are only temporary. Progression from this starting point may or may not be quick. Design your progression to your tolerance.

If your tolerance for this technique is poor, do not feel compelled to use it. Discontinue it until you have loosened up your body and/or head through other methods and then try it again. *Any of these suggestions should only be used if they are helpful.*

Interestingly, I have had two of my older patients tell me they remember their grandmothers doing something very similar to manage their headaches. Another patient thought she remembered seeing this technique in an old book of her grandmother's.

I should also clarify that the eye guards used to block out light *do not* serve the same purpose as the cranial blindfold. The effects produced by the blindfold are responses to the *width* of the blindfold and to the compression on the *sides of the head* as well as to the compression across the eyes and nose.

In the same manner, a folded towel can be used to apply a light compression over the top and sides of the pelvis and/or across the chest and/or lower ribs as in the following illustration. Again, do not tie the ends together.

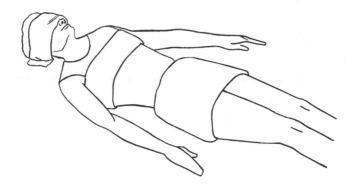

Do not *squeeze* your body with a hard compression. The idea is to *meet* the restrictions in the body with just enough pressure to facilitate a release. Because the body does not seem to be as sensitive to the time factor as the head, most people easily begin with a pelvic compression of twenty to thirty minutes without any type of adverse reaction. This time can be increased according to your tolerance. My only caution would be for patients suffering from fibromyalgia or even more particularly chronic fatigue syndrome. Begin briefly and progress in the same way I suggested for the head.

These compressions can be used individually or in combination. Some people respond best to the cranial blindfold alone, while other people prefer the pelvic and cranial compressions together. Design your treatment to your body and your schedule. You may treat one area in the morning and another area at night. If you only have enough time to treat one area per day, you may want to alternate the treatment areas, etc. It has helped my patients to keep a pillowcase and/or a towel by their bed to use just before getting up or just before going to sleep.

Most recently, I have wrapped my patients with one continuous pressure from under their arms to the level of their hip sockets. I have not yet applied the cranial compression simultaneously because I am usually treating the patients' head while their body is wrapped. I have noticed the gentle body compression often will make the head more responsive to my touch. Along those same lines, if you do not tolerate the light compression to your head initially, treat the lower body for several days or more and then reattempt the cranial compression. The sensitivity of your head may decrease in response to your body being more relaxed. This corresponds to the principles behind the water balloon theory.

- Passive Positional Low Back and/or Neck Traction

Sometimes a very light, sustained traction to the lower back or neck can be very relaxing. There are traction units available for purchase that can generate more force, but light traction can be created in the lower back by simply elevating the legs on a pillow from the knees down to the heels. Two pillows can be tried, but most people surprisingly respond *better* when their legs are elevated on only one pillow. Cervical traction can be created by tucking the chin and elevating the head or the head and shoulders on a pillow.

If you have previously tried mechanical traction unsuccessfully, it may have been too much for your body *at that time*. You may respond better to this more gentle approach.

These two areas can be tractioned together or separately. If the tension in your spine is severe, it may be necessary to bend at the hips and knees some while you stretch your neck or extend the head and neck some to stretch the lower back as in the illustrations below and on the next page:

To directly stretch the lower back, try lying facedown, or prone, over one or two pillows.

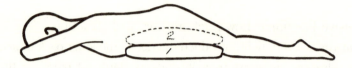

I usually suggest that my patients begin with only ten minutes of this positioning since the traction is static and then increase to twenty to thirty minutes as tolerated once or twice each day. If ten minutes is too long to begin with, do not force yourself to maintain the traction for that amount of time. It may be necessary to interject some active motion too during the traction to better tolerate more time.

- Headache-Migraine or Flare-Up Relief

While the goal of **Rapid Release** is to achieve maximum flexibility in the fascia, it can be very helpful during times of exacerbation to do *just the opposite*. During these times, it is okay to cut the body some slack by *bending* at the hips and knees and by *extending* the head and neck. I have been surprised at how quickly this positioning can reduce symptoms that have been extreme or have persisted for several days. Those suffering from tension headaches and severe migraines have found relief with this positioning.

This position comes quite easily for most people. The examples below illustrate two variations of this positioning. Feel free to bend at the hips and knees as much as needed to feel comfortable through the low back and legs. Allow the head to fall back into extension *to whatever degree is comfortable* so that the chin *is* pointing to the ceiling. Place a rolled towel of whatever size is needed under the back of the neck if it helps to further decrease the strain on the neck.

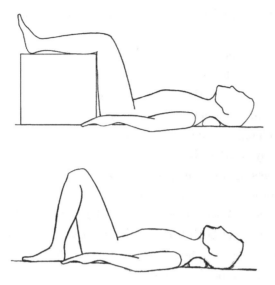

Maintain this position as long as necessary for your symptoms to subside. Most people will begin to notice a change in their symptoms within ten to twenty minutes. As the pain subsides, a slow, gradual effort should be made to return to as flat a position as possible.

NOTE: If you are using a wedge to help you tolerate the supine position better, be sure to include your wedge in combination with this suggestion. You will not, of course, attempt to stretch out flat at the end of your treatment time.

Two patients are especially memorable. One woman had a migraine so severe she had been to the emergency room three times over the past eight days for injections, which were ineffective in reducing her pain. When she came to therapy, she rated her headache at 8–9/10, which was a slight improvement over the 10+ she had been struggling with for the past week. We positioned her as I have suggested while I passively assisted the soft tissue of her lower abdomen to release. In only twenty minutes, the symptoms of her headache decreased to 2/10.

Another patient diagnosed with fibromyalgia for the past six to seven years was dreading a long flight she would be taking the next week. Flying always exacerbated her pain. This, in turn, would interfere with her ability to enjoy her vacation. The day after her flight, she did the basic program upon waking and relaxed for about twenty minutes in this position. She not only tolerated several full days of busy activity but also actually enjoyed herself with very minimal distraction from pain. She did notice a mild increase in her lower back pain after she flew home but rated the pain 2–3/10, which did not interfere with any of her normal daily activities. Her previous response to flying twice in one week was increased pain and decreased tolerance for activity at least two to three weeks.

When a change in the weather has provoked the exacerbation, this positioning may need to be repeated several times each day until the weather changes again. If progressing to a specific level of the exercise program has provoked the pain, regress one or two levels in the progression temporarily until you are feeling better. Patients who have previously suffered from a direct head trauma or currently experience more cranial tension sometimes are not helped by this positioning. For this population, lying prone seems to be more helpful.

- Intra-Oral Massage

I have saved the most helpful tip for last. By "intra-oral," I mean a massage to the inside of your mouth. We tend to forget we could not chew or yawn if we did not have muscles functioning correctly in our mouths. The muscles I will discuss with you directly affect the jaw or the TMJ, temporomandibular joint. While this is "one more thing I do not have an absolute explanation for," I have been *amazed repeatedly* by how much this technique helps all my patients, regardless of their diagnosis. My observation has been that these muscles must be affecting the status of the cranium in addition to the jaw. It has become a standard part of my treatment for everyone. Even though the environment of these muscles is different from other muscles, the muscles themselves are no different from your bicep, quadricep, or any other striated muscle.

Before I begin this treatment, I give my patients a full warning that these muscles can be very sensitive. It is not uncommon for my patients to rate the tenderness in their mouths at 7–8/10 or more. But there are just as many who rate their discomfort at 4–5/10. The sensation felt during treatment is usually sharp and/or pinprickly. The first treatment is always the worst so don't give up if your first experience with this technique is uncomfortable. It will get better. If you do not tolerate stroking over the muscle, hold light to moderate direct pressure into the sensitive area for ten to twenty seconds. Focus on your breath as you gently inhale and exhale to ease the muscle toward relaxation. If you tolerate both stroking the muscle and applying pressure, feel free to use both techniques. The improvement you will experience in your problem area after implementing this suggestion will motivate you to work through the discomfort. Applying ice to the outside of your jaw and face prior to treatment can also be helpful.

There are four muscles you should assess and treat. The first one, the *masseter*, is in your cheek.

Use the middle finger of the hand on the same side as the cheek you will massage to reach your cheek between the top teeth and your nose. Your fingernail should be resting against your top teeth and gum. Lightly pinch your cheek between your middle finger on the inside of your cheek and your thumb on the outside of the cheek. Stroke down the inside of the cheek toward the bottom jaw. Continue to stroke down the cheek, but each time begin your stroke a little further back on the cheekbone. Continue to move back on the cheek bone as far as you possibly can.

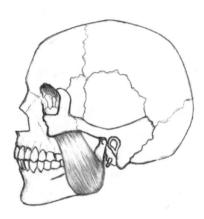

• The masseter •

One specific area in the cheek that is usually most problematic is in the very back of the cheek. When you clench your back teeth together, you will be able to feel an area that becomes very prominent. This deep section of the masseter is typically in need of treatment. The masseter is a muscle complement to other "adducting" muscles like the adductors of the inner thigh and the muscles in between the shoulder blades.

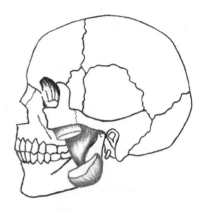

• The deep section of masseter •

The second area you will treat is where the *temporalis* tendon attaches onto the jawbone in front of your ear. Reach into your mouth and run the nail side of your middle finger along the outside of the top teeth to the very back of the teeth. When you reach the back, notice that you can feel your jawbone with the pad of your finger. Now rub your finger up this bone. When you reach the top of the jawbone, you are in the area where the temporalis muscle attaches to the jaw. As you drop your jaw, or slightly open your mouth a little more, you will be able to address more of the tendon.

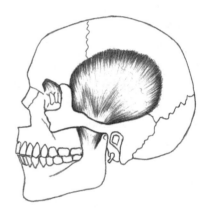

• The temporalis •

The next area you will treat is in this same area and usually the most tight and tender. The *lateral pterygoid* runs horizontally, or side to side, between the top of the jawbone (where you just treated) and the top teeth.

Run the pad of your middle finger all the way to the back of your top teeth. You will know you are in the right spot when you feel the tenderness. You may be the exception, but for most people, this area is quite tender. It is not uncommon for the muscle to be so tight that it cannot be treated unless the person shifts his or her bottom jaw sideways. (If the right side of the jaw is being treated, you may need to shift the bottom jaw to the right). *Be sure to go as far back and up into this area as you can.*

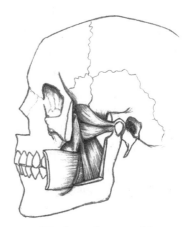

• The lateral pterygoid •

The final area is best treated when it is divided into two separate areas. The top portion of the *medial pterygoid* can be felt on the roof of the mouth. This time run the nail side of your middle finger all the way to the back of the top teeth. Now bring the finger inside the top teeth and reach slightly further back onto the roof of your mouth. You will feel a little bony "knob." As you come slightly down from the knob, you will be on the muscle. Continue to stroke down the muscle toward the inside of the bottom gum. If you begin to gag when you feel this muscle, that is all the more reason why you should treat it. Do not neglect to treat this area, but be very gentle with yourself. You may even want to first massage this muscle on the outside underneath your bottom jaw bone towards the back. As the muscle becomes less tense, your gag reflex will not be so sensitive. If you have difficulty with dental exams, releasing tension in these jaw muscles will be very helpful.

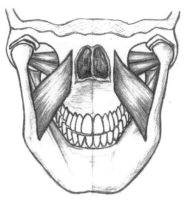

• The medial pterygoid •

The inferior portion of the medial pterygoid can be palpated as you continue to rub downward to the floor of the mouth past the jaw and the bottom teeth. Rub **side to side** on the floor of the mouth underneath the tongue. Also, rub **front to back** on the floor of the mouth underneath the tongue. You can actually compress this area between your fingers if you would like to push up with the thumb of your opposite hand under your chin to match the downward pressure from the finger inside on the floor of your mouth.

The best time to implement this massage is **immediately after an MVA (motor vehicle accident) or a fall**. If you find the muscles do not tolerate the direct massage, spend the first few days or even first week applying ice to your face, under your chin, and to the back of the neck. Don't forget to consider the soft tissue damage created by airbags and seat belts. Any place that is bruised or sustains a significant impact especially deserves the help that ice and massage can provide. Don't be discouraged if your accident or injury was not recent. This massage technique and the application of cold to the soft tissues of the jaw and the face can still be very effective whenever you are able to begin.

Chapter 5

Examples of Effectiveness

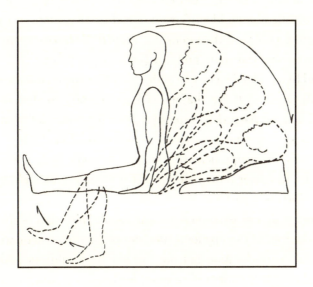

Examples of *Releasing Pain*

The following pages contain highlights from actual patients I have treated sometime in the past eighteen years. The diagnoses I have chosen represent some of the more common problems people deal with on a regular basis, ranging from knee pain to the after effects of stroke. I have included several different scenarios for each body part to provide you an opportunity to identify with a particular case example. While I will not necessarily take you from the start of treatment to completion each time, I will explain specific findings from each patient's evaluation or their responses to the exercise program to demonstrate the usefulness of this program in their particular case. Because **Rapid Release** is not the result of a meticulously strategized plan, many of the outcomes you will read about surprised me as much when they happened as they will surprise you now. Because these concepts are new, I've included many personal testimonies. This way, you don't have to only take my word for the effectiveness of this approach. I hope you will be able to identify with one of these examples if you suffer from lingering pain and then consider **Rapid Release** as an option to help you overcome your pain and functional restrictions.

I would like to clarify a couple of things before you review the examples. First of all, each of these diagnoses is frequently treated in physical therapy. When the **Rapid Release** program is utilized for treatment, the approach is more comprehensive than conventional methods or protocols used in rehab. By comprehensive, I mean the whole body is treated. I do not mean I administer an exhaustive list of various treatment modalities to one specific body part.

The following are examples to demonstrate how this is unique. If a patient is referred to therapy for a shoulder problem, the neck will usually be taken into consideration but not the low back and certainly not the hip or the knee. If a patient is referred for low back pain, the amount of treatment directed to the neck will vary from "minimal" to "some." If the hip, the knee, or the ankle is the primary complaint, the influence of the neck is rarely, if ever, factored into the treatment plan. The same dynamics apply for headaches, vertigo, or most shoulder problems. The low back is rarely, if ever, considered to help with these diagnoses. Treating jaw pain is often an area many therapist do not feel particularly comfortable with. To consider its influence on any area of the body aside from the neck is never considered. And finally, unless the diagnosis is vertigo, balance dysfunction, or an upper cervical spine disorder, the eyes are never factored in to the treatment protocol.

Treating the entire spine is needed because of the effect one end of the spine has on the other end. The jaw and the eyes should be included in every case as well. Anything less is incomplete.

Another thing to notice about these case reports is a common thread running through each history. Every person, except one, listed in these examples has previously been in a motor vehicle accident (MVA) or taken some sort of fall. To the best of my knowledge, there are no standardized follow-up care recommendations for traumatic musculoskeletal injury. If a person sustains injuries significant enough for hospitalization, the patient's condition is stabilized, and the major problems are addressed. Once the patient is able to care for himself or herself or other caregivers have been arranged, the person will be discharged from the hospital. Sometimes inpatient, outpatient, or home physical therapy is recommended but not always.

Another group of patients definitely know they have been injured by a traumatic accident, but they do not require hospitalization. The pain is noticed among this group of patients either immediately or shortly after their incident even in the absence of obvious external injuries or fractures. If the patient is seen in the emergency room (ER) or by his or her primary care physician (PCP), X-rays may be taken to be sure there are no fractures. If the X-rays are negative, the person is usually discharged with a prescription for muscle relaxers, anti-inflammatories, and/or pain medication. Sometimes therapy is recommended by an ER physician; other times, it is not. A follow-up visit with their PCP is often recommended if the patient was seen first in the ER.

A variety of things can happen once the person is seen by their PCP. One approach commonly taken is to continue the medication initiated by the emergency room physician and "give things time to heal." One patient of mine was even told to "just wait it out for two years, and whatever condition he or she was in at that time would be a good indicator of how he or she would feel from that point forward." If the PCP refers the patient to therapy, the orders usually specify treatment for the most functionally restricted or physically painful site at the time. If the injuries sustained from the accident seem to be mild to none, the ER doctor or PCP may not make any follow-up recommendations.

Many people will seek out chiropractic care. Some chiropractic offices now work together with a massage therapist. This is a good combination that worked well for me, but many people who see a chiropractor do not see a massage therapist or vice versa. Some patients take the initiative to begin acupuncture treatments. The final scenario is when the patient does not seek any form of medical attention, regardless of the severity of the injuries, unless there are obvious fractures.

Based on my clinical experience, I am convinced a shift in our thinking is necessary. The first shift in our thinking is we must acknowledge that an *absence of immediate symptoms* following trauma can be very misleading. As I have taken my patients' histories, I have been told dozens of times, "Yes, I was in a car accident, but I/everyone walked away from it just fine." Even when the impact involved was quite hard or if the patients were thrown around in the car, or even out of the car, etc., as long as they were able to "walk away" from the incident or were not bleeding profusely, they considered themselves to be uninjured. The thought of experiencing long-term effects never crosses their mind. One of the most interesting things I have observed is the patients involved in what seemed to be a minor accident will eventually exhibit *the same pattern of dysfunction* as someone involved in a "more serious" accident, but their symptoms may be less intense. Being involved in several "minor" accidents can eventually have the same effect as one more "serious" accident.

The second shift in our thinking involves educating ourselves about *comprehensive treatment of the soft tissues* following trauma. I have seen enough injured soft tissue to confidently say soft tissue does not heal *well or satisfactorily* when it is left to heal on its own. This area is certainly one place where improvements can easily be made in how we take care of ourselves and others. I hope you will have a good understanding of what this means by the time you finish this book. Please refer to pages 128-131, where I discuss where/how to apply cold packs or ice.

The following letters contain the comments from friends of mine who experienced firsthand what I have described. They contrast their outcomes after addressing their full body and directly treating their injured soft tissues with their responses to conventional care. The first letter is from a couple who was rear-ended in a car accident.

> *Dear Nancy,*
>
> *I am writing to thank you again for sharing your exercise program with us. We have been faithful to do them and have begun to see impressive results. After a few weeks, we were still sore and adjusting to the changes that were taking place. However, after six weeks now, we look forward to doing them because they make us feel so much better.*
>
> *As you know, I was in a car accident six months ago and suffered from a severe whiplash injury. I sought out chiropractic help in hope of finding some relief from my neck pain. The electrode treatments and the exercises prescribed did help, but they only gave me temporary relief. My neck and upper back pain made riding in a car or a plane longer than one hour very difficult. So when I saw you after a ten-hour ride in our car from California to New Mexico, my pain was even worse than usual. I was also beginning to feel pain in my right knee. I was beginning to dread the plane trip I would soon be making to Africa!*
>
> *Your exercise program has taken me beyond anything I gained from my chiropractic treatments or the pain medication I was given. I have recently been doing a lot of strenuous work around our house as we are preparing to move. In spite of all the painting, packing, bending, and lifting, I am not tired or sore. In fact, I'm actually feeling stronger! I don't think I would have been this strong even without my injury.*
>
> *Thank you again for sharing your tremendous gift and life's work with us. We are anxious to share it with others and give you the stories of their change and relief.*
>
> *God bless you for your work in helping others in this way. May He be glorified in all He has done and will continue to do in your life.*
>
> *Lovingly,*

This second letter is from a man who took a very serious fall off his motorcycle during a motocross race.

Dear Nancy,

This past June during a motocross race, I flipped over the handlebars of my bike while in midair and landed flat on my back. I was able to walk away from the accident, but by the next day, I went to the emergency room because my whole back was completely bruised, and the pain was severe. X-rays were taken that showed I had no broken bones, so I was sent home with pain medication and instructions to use heat and cold to my back as needed. I was told to avoid heavy lifting for two weeks and then go see my regular doctor if I was still in pain.

I took the first three or four days off from my regular job that requires repetitive bending, lifting, and carrying as well as climbing ladders and pouring concrete. During this time, I was using ice packs and my heating pad frequently to my back. I was on light duty for my first week back to work but returned to my regular duties by the second week. By this time, my pain was more localized to my low back, but it was becoming disablingly painful! I wasn't able to do anything at home after work—even changing positions on the couch was difficult and extremely painful. I was only sleeping a couple of hours total every night, which made going to work the next day even harder. Because I have a background as a weight lifter and personal trainer, I was able to start doing some stretching on my own. I also tried using pillows the best way I knew how to help position myself in ways to reduce the pain. In spite of everything I tried, the pain only got worse.

*Then I arranged a time to meet with you. After only two hours, the simple movements you showed me and some of your other new ideas started to help me right away. I immediately felt more flexible and started sleeping better. I started using the ice packs **on my stomach instead of my lower back** and was soon able to complete a day at work without being completely wasted by the time I got home.*

I can only wonder how much pain I could have been spared if I had started this program right after my accident. Your ideas gave me some very practical ways that really did help me to help myself. I would recommend this therapy for anyone with ongoing pain.

Thanks again,

I have worked alongside all different types of health-care professionals for the last thirty years. I know firsthand each one is doing the best they know how to do for their patients. The point I would rather make is *it would be helpful to have a protocol established to initiate early intervention to specifically treat and restore the soft tissue damaged in a traumatic accident. I believe* **Rapid Release** *is such a protocol.*

Physical abuse and amputation, or any type of traumatic injury that precedes an amputation, are additional areas where the damaged soft tissue is neglected. Surgery can be traumatic. I think primarily of abdominal procedures where the damaged soft tissue is rarely, *if ever*, considered until adhesions have already developed. Mastectomies can also affect a much larger area than just the surgical site.

As caregivers and individuals, we should acknowledge the many different ways soft tissue injuries can manifest themselves. There have been several occasions when I evaluated patients in the emergency room who appeared to be suffering from some sort of extreme internal disorder because of the severity of their symptoms. After numerous expensive tests had been run and much time had passed, physical therapy was consulted because all the diagnostic tests returned normal. In each case, the source of the problem was a chronic muscle strain.

We should not underestimate the use of conservative treatment modalities for soft tissue injuries. In our world of sophisticated technology and advanced pharmaceuticals, it is easy to minimize the value of simplistic and practical options like heat, cold, massage, and exercise. In reality, these are precisely the interventions most needed much of the time. More often than not, patients I meet report they are not experiencing the relief they are looking for in medications; instead, they are experiencing the side effects. More emphasis should be placed on the necessity of these conservative interventions immediately post injury. Educating ourselves regarding the placement of the heat, cold, or manual therapy based on the anatomy rather than on the symptoms alone will maximize the benefit of these modalities. And we should continue the treatment until the symptoms have resolved. Ice, for example, is a very effective modality long after the first forty-eight hours post injury.

The final concept to consider is most important. As I previously mentioned, when I evaluate my patients, I find the same *pattern of soft tissue dysfunction* in their bodies, regardless of the person's diagnosis or how the problem occurred. A previous trauma from a MVA or a fall appears to weaken the soft tissue along a particular neuromuscular pathway. When the person is subjected to an additional strain or trauma, repeated poor body mechanics, or poor posture, the result is pain, loss of function, and decreased quality of life. Identifying and treating this entire pattern of soft tissue dysfunction improves the outcome in the present and helps prevent future problems. *I am convinced that early intervention and thorough treatment of soft tissue damage following a traumatic accident could be as preventative to functional restrictions and chronic pain as hand washing is to infection.*

Keep this question in mind as you read the following case examples: how much pain, function, and quality of life could have been spared if each patient had been comprehensively rehabilitated and instructed to care for their damaged soft tissue immediately after their accident or fall?

Releasing Knee Pain

Every time I think a response I witness to this program is "the most amazing thing I have ever seen," something else will happen unexpectedly to amaze me again. This has certainly been the case as I consider the knee. The objective findings from the following patients enabled me to discern at their initial evaluation how the condition of their necks was clearly affecting the condition of their knees. Each one represents a different type of onset for their knee pain. These include the following:

- Pain that resulted suddenly and could not be associated with any specific injury.
- Pain that was *apparently* the direct result of a specific injury.
- Pain that did not respond well to conventional physical therapy.

These categories of onset apply to other body parts as well, but I will use the knee to illustrate how *insufficient* it is to only consider current information to treat a presenting problem. The key to successfully treating these patients was found by acknowledging the impact past traumatic injury was having on their current condition.

Spontaneous Onset without Injury

This seventy-three-year-old female was referred to therapy following arthroscopic knee surgery to repair a medial meniscus tear. She was unable to recall any previous or recent injury specifically to her knee; instead, she reported her right knee pain of 7/10 started "out of the blue" during weight bearing. Shortly thereafter, she noticed an achiness in her knee each night while she was lying in bed. She was virtually pain-free for the first four days after her surgery, but then her pain during weight bearing returned at a reduced intensity of 4/10. In addition, the knee now felt "weak" during ambulation and was noticeably "stiff" after ten to fifteen minutes of sitting. She was feeling "off-balance" but not to the point of falling.

Initial supine knee ROM (range of motion) with the head in moderate extension

- -10-degree extension (patient was not able to fully straighten the knee) and 110-degree flexion.
- Pain 4/10 during movement of the right knee.

Knee ROM after neck posture corrected and stabilized with three centimeters of support

- -5-degree extension and 121-degree flexion.
- Pain experienced during motion decreased to 2/10.

Traumatic history

- Thirty years ago, this patient was in a motor vehicle accident, resulting in "bad whiplash." There had been no treatment for the neck, which has been "very stiff ever since the accident."
- Three to four years ago, she experienced a very sudden onset of right sciatica without any specific low back injury.
- Two to three years ago, she was involved in another MVA, resulting in whiplash.

This example is a good illustration of a patient who was *unable to identify any specific injury directly to the knee*. What she had specifically injured in two separate MVAs was her neck. The posture of the neck was obviously a contributing factor to her pain based on her improved range of motion and subjective pain ratings after the alignment of the cervical spine was corrected.

Pain after Specific Injury

This fifty-one-year-old male fell onto a tile floor with his right knee approximately five to six weeks prior to our meeting. He had no knee pain until five nights after the fall when he was awakened by a sharp stabbing knee pain. The knee was constantly achy from that time at 5/10. Weight bearing on the right leg became painful at 5–8/10, which noticeably decreased his gait velocity. The knee also became extremely stiff after fifteen to twenty minutes of sitting, making full extension very difficult. The patient wore a knee immobilizer for three weeks, which made his daily tasks more tolerable but did not resolve or even reduce his overall pain.

Initial ROM with head in extreme extension

- -5–10-degree extension ➡ 75-degree flexion
- Pain at 5–6/10 during movement.

Cervical spine corrected to neutral and stabilized with eight centimeters of support

- Knee flexion increased to 130 degrees.
- Pain decreased to 2/10 during movement.

Traumatic history

- The patient sustained a whiplash injury from a MVA eight years ago. He considered his response to chiropractic care to be good.
- He had been thrown from horses several times in his life.
- His lower back has been "stiff" most of his life.

Again, this patient's extreme cervical tension greatly affected his knee pain. His fall onto the tile floor *provoked* his symptoms. While direct trauma to any given part may very well cause localized damage, direct treatment may not be enough to solve the patient's problems.

Negative Response to Conventional Therapy

Once again, I evaluated a patient who was unable to identify any specific injury directly to his right knee. This forty-four-year-old male worked at a job requiring frequent lifting, bending, and squatting. He attributed the sudden onset of soreness in his knee to "overuse." After playing frisbee with his dog one weekend in the park, he noticed he was walking with a limp most of the time in spite of the fact that he was unable to recall anything strenuous happening to his knee.

An arthroscopic medial meniscectomy was done five months after the onset of his pain. No physical therapy was scheduled as a "gradual recovery and return to normal function" was expected; instead, the patient continued to experience constant localized pain medial to the kneecap at 3/10. This pain would increase to 9/10 with forty-five minutes of driving. In addition, he was unable to recover from bending or squatting without the assistance of his upper extremities.

Traumatic history

- In 1982, the patient was in a MVA. He was treated by a chiropractor for lower back pain for eighteen months. He continued to experience lower back pain at 4/10 constantly that would increase to 7–8/10 with prolonged forward bending.
- The patient denied any noticeable neck pain. He acknowledged his neck would become stiff in response to stress.
- ROM measurements

	Right	Left	
Hip flexion	100°	105°	
Hip internal rotation	25° →	33°	*Notice that significant discrepancies lie at the hips as well as at the knee.*
Hip external rotation	35° →	25°	
Straight leg raise	46° →	70°	
Knee flexion	142°	150°	
Knee extension	0°	0°	

Following his initial evaluation, this patient was seen in physical therapy by a physical therapy assistant two times. He was instructed in standard leg lifts and light antigravity strengthening. He also did light strengthening on a total gym, stepper, and stationary bicycle.

When I reevaluated the patient, his constant pain had increased from 3/10 to 8/10. His limp was now so bad he had taken the previous day off from work. When I assessed his posture in supine, he was able to position his head and neck correctly with only a slight amount of difficulty. *His range of motion was easily within normal limits for looking over each shoulder.* When I positioned his full body on top of the pillows (progressive positioning, position #1), he immediately noticed the pain on the left side of his neck. When he tried to rotate his head to the left, he had *minimal range of motion.* Positioning this patient's full body on top of the pillows exposed his greatest area of myofascial restriction, which was *his neck.*

When I ran this patient through the lower body exercises of seven repetitions for two sets on a flat surface, his knee pain decreased from 8/10 to 4/10. After doing the eye, head, and neck exercises, his pain further reduced to 2/10. He demonstrated only a very mild trace of a limp as he left his appointment.

This is another good illustration of a patient who was unable to identify any specific injury directly to the knee. He was frustrated and confused because surgery and physical therapy had not helped. In fact, they were proving to be counterproductive. *Based on our treatment session, dysfunction in his neck was grossly affecting his response to treatment.*

I have been able to verify with objective findings how cervical involvement was contributing to each one of these different knee problems. Over time, I have been able to recognize lingering TMJ and eye dysfunction as contributors to most knee conditions. For example, if the right knee is the source of pain or limitation, the right eye and the left jaw *usually* will be a part of the problem. Sometimes the patient is aware of some trouble with either one or both places. Other times, they have not noticed anything specifically bothersome about one or either place until the soft tissue is assessed. My palpation exam will always uncover some amount of neuromuscular dysfunction in each place. Or difficulties demonstrating the exercises for the eyes or the jaw will occur. The ipsilateral, or same side, involvement of the knee and the eye is the point along the unilateral pathway of pain. I am assuming the involvement of the jaw on the contralateral, or the opposite side, is somehow compensatory.

Dr. Janet Travell and Dr. David G. Simons documented the relationship between the knee and the temporomandibular joint in volume two of their book *Myofascial Pain and Dysfunction - The Trigger Point Manual - The Lower Extremities* (p. 429). On two separate occasions, they observed ipsilateral jaw pain that was referred from an active trigger point in the soleus muscle of the calf. Their patient had noticed jaw pain with malocclusion in the ipsilateral jaw when the soleus muscle was either actively or passively stretched. When the soleus trigger point was injected, the pain and spasm in the jaw were immediately relieved. I have not kept a record of my findings considering this relationship, but I am sure the relationship is present more often than not. I have noticed in my observations, however, that *either side* of the jaw can be involved, but more commonly, I find the contralateral, or opposite, jaw and the ipsilateral eye are neuromuscularly dysfunctional whenever the knee is stiff, painful, unstable, swollen, or not rehabilitating well after injury or surgery. Consider how the following case study clearly illustrates this relationship.

Spontaneous Knee Pain Associated with TMJ Dysfunction

A forty-year-old male professor I treated was an avid cyclist. After taking a six-month break from his bike, he resumed his riding schedule and was increasing his distance once again. He was riding about thirty to thirty-five miles per day when he began to notice a "popping" or instability in his left knee during kneeling or squatting or when he would pivot on the left leg while the foot was planted. He had no recollection of any specific injury to the left knee. He had no pain in the knee unless the knee literally popped out of place. Fortunately, he was able to independently reposition the knee when a subluxation occurred.

His history quickly explained the spontaneous onset of his knee instability. Approximately eight to ten years prior, he had landed on both of his knees while in a shallow pool. He poorly tolerated running after this accident. In addition, he was in a rollover MVA in 1977. The airbag deployed, hitting him in the face and chest. He reported weekly cervical tension of 7/10. He also experienced chronic lower back pain he managed with medication and frequent chiropractic adjustments.

I instructed him in the supine exercises for his lower body, eyes, head, and neck at his first visit. At his second visit, he reported he had done his exercises daily. Squatting no longer provoked any noticeable instability in the left knee. Pivoting on the left leg with the foot planted continued to provoke a mild sensation of instability. Instructions for the upper body exercises were given at his second visit.

When he returned for his third visit, he confessed that his busy schedule had kept him from doing his exercises. His knee was "doing good overall," but he was complaining more of neck and upper body tension. This was when I asked him about some small scars around his right eye and jaw. This detail of his history was the most interesting of all.

He informed me the scars were the result of being bitten by his newly adopted dog a few months prior to the onset of his knee pain. He also reported some difficulty chewing for the past two to three months. The difficulty chewing occurred about the same time his knee instability started. My treatment that day focused on massage and myofascial release techniques to his head and neck.

At his fourth visit, the instability he experienced in the knee with squatting or during a planted pivot was only noticeable fifty percent of the time. I instructed him in self-massage to the muscles of his jaws and eyes during our visit. When he returned for his fifth visit, the instability in his knee was "rare." He continued to do his exercises three times a week and was now able to lie with correct cervical posture in supine without any compensation. At the time of his initial evaluation, he required four centimeters. Additional objective measurements verified improved symmetry at his hips. Measurements at the time of his initial evaluation were the following:

	Right	Left
Hip flexion	122	115
Internal rotation	26	30
External rotation	37	30

Measurements at the time of discharge were the following:

	Right	Left
Hip flexion	118	120
Internal rotation	40	40
External rotation	45	48

Improved symmetry and balance at the hips provided a more stable foundation for the knee. The soft tissue release of the neck and the jaw also helped facilitate this overall improvement. When I spoke with this patient three months after his discharge, he was still doing very well. He had gone skiing several times during Christmas break. His left knee did not give him even a hint of trouble.

This patient is a good example of a provocative dilemma for therapists and doctors. If exercising the knee was the solution to resolving knee pain and instability, cycling thirty-five miles a day should have helped; instead, exercise was the aggravating factor. This patient serves as a great example of knee pain and/or instability resulting from cervical and/or temporomandibular dysfunction, or dysfunction at the opposite end of the body from the symptoms.

Persistent Knee Pain after Arthroscopic Surgery

It's always rewarding to help someone overcome a long-standing problem. Such was the case with one of my close, personal friends. During a recent phone conversation, my friend told me about some of the physical problems she was having with her knees. She accepted my invitation to come to Albuquerque for a visit. She later wrote me to share her response to these exercises.

> *Dear Nancy,*
>
> *It has been my joy to have you as a personal friend for 30 years. I now have a deeper appreciation for you as a Physical Therapist. I know your own experiences of physical pain and disability have caused you to forge ahead to find some answers for relief. Your focus and perseverance in discovering solutions for those who have been restricted by their own pain will be literally life changing for so many. It already has been for me!*
>
> *Thank you for taking the time recently to share your insight with me about the* **Rapid Release** *exercises . . . they are a phenomenon!! Let me start by saying I have always enjoyed being physically active. I come from a family of athletes, so keeping in condition and good shape is very important to me. In 2001, however, I tore the meniscus in my left knee and had arthroscopic surgery. In 2004 I injured my right knee with the same diagnosis. Neither knee could be repaired so the torn cartilage was removed. I was told by my doctors to take care of the small amount of cartilage I still had intact. Ironically, I could not recall any specific injury to either one of my knees.*
>
> *In the last few years, the pain and stiffness in my knees has not responded to prescription anti-inflammatory drugs. I have come to dread standing to leave a movie theater. I have pushed many of my favorite shoes to the back of the closet! Walking in any type of heel has only been tolerable for about 10–15 minutes . . . UNTIL I began using the* **Rapid Release** *exercises. The difference is really amazing . . . in just a few weeks the pain is gone and I have very little stiffness! I recently walked up and down concrete sidewalks for several hours with very minimal discomfort. On another occasion, I wore a pair of 2" heels for two to three hours without any problem.*
>
> *A warning though is needed. Things may get worse before they get better! My right knee was more painful at first. The neck and eye exercises initially made me a little nauseous. It was more beneficial for me to do the neck and eye exercises first in the sequence with my knees bent to avoid the stomach*

uneasiness. Another alternative would be to perform them in a sitting position until you have built up a better tolerance for lying down. It takes perseverance and consistency in spite of what you feel in the beginning.

Again, Nancy, my gratitude for showing me I don't have to be a gym rat . . . exerting myself with high intensive cardio and strength training. Daily walking and implementing your formula for Releasing Pain has literally given me a new lease on my knees!

Sincerely grateful,

Pain after Total Knee Replacement and Hip Fracture

Several years ago, I worked in a home healthcare setting. The patients I saw were unable to leave their homes secondary to physical limitations. For some patients, this was a long-term arrangement. For others, it was only temporary until they were more fully recovered from surgery. Many of the patients I saw had undergone surgery to repair a hip fracture or replace a hip joint. I began to notice a large percentage of my patients with some type of hip diagnosis were not complaining of hip pain after surgery; instead, they were complaining of knee pain.

Most of these patients had not experienced knee pain until their hip was repaired. The next letter I will share, however, was written by a woman who did have a history of knee pain. In her particular case, she had bilateral total knee replacements performed four years prior to our meeting in September of 2006. In July of 2006, she had fractured her right hip. She had no hip pain after her surgery but was forced to spend two months in a skilled nursing facility because of restrictions created by her right knee. A chronic burning in the right knee of 6/10 limited her walking tolerance to approximately forty feet. Much to her dismay, this same burning pain had been with her for the last four years since her knee replacement was done. She also experienced a "pins and needles" sensation in her right foot at 9/10. The range of motion in her left knee had progressed to be functionally acceptable after joint replacement. Her right knee, however, did not achieve a good, functional motion. When we met, she only had ten degrees of active knee flexion in her right knee.

Over the course of the next two months, her walking tolerance increased to 120 feet with her walker. Her right knee flexion increased to 120 degrees. It should be noted her best improvement throughout the course of her treatment came in response to completing the eye and neck exercises. I also manually addressed her head and neck three times a week for the better part of the two months. Because her myofascial restrictions were so extensive, I doubt if this patient would have improved as much with the exercises alone. Nevertheless, by the end of our two months together, she no longer experienced any painful symptoms in her right foot or knee. She would notice some flare-ups with cold, wet, or windy weather, but the constant chronic pain was gone. This is her statement about her response to treatment:

> *Dear Nancy,*
>
> *When I met you, I had broken my right hip after falling in a parking lot. I had two separate surgeries on my hip and three months of rehab. When I went home, however, my ability to walk was hindered by knee pain rather than hip pain. When you explained your treatment methods to me, I knew this was something new in physiotherapy. As a retired nurse, I had never heard of anything like your treatments before! But I was willing and just crazy enough to be your guinea pig!*
>
> *As time went on, I came to realize your guinea pig was really a lucky duck! As my treatments progressed, it became obvious to me that my head, neck, and eyes were affecting my whole body. The knee pain I had felt for four years following bilateral total knee replacements had finally disappeared! In addition, your treatments and exercises have helped improve the range of motion in my left shoulder and arm. I have had multiple surgeries on my chest that finally resulted in a bilateral mastectomy to correct problems that developed from broken silicone implants.*
>
> *Compared to when I first met you, I am now loose as a goose! My improvement has surpassed my doctor's expectations! I plan to keep up my exercises and be rid of my walker by Christmas!*
>
> *Thanks again for all your help,*

It is easy to understand why this woman's rehabilitation did not go well when her progress is considered in light of her past medical and traumatic histories. She had suffered trauma to her head at twenty-eight years of age in a head-on collision. The scar on her left forehead was still noticeable from the many sutures required to repair the deep laceration she sustained from the impact of her head with the dashboard. In the 1980s, she was in another MVA. This time her vehicle was hurled into the air several stories high after hitting some ice and a guardrail. Her pelvis was fractured in multiple places when the vehicle landed on all fours. In addition, she had almost lost count of how many surgeries she had on her chest. Her best estimate was fourteen to fifteen different procedures before bilateral mastectomies were finally done. Even if she was off by one or two, half of that number could easily create some serious scar tissue.

Her history serves as a good platform for me to discuss another theory I have pondered. As physical therapists, our job sometimes places us in the middle of the doctor and the patient. When surgical results are less than expected by either party, as was the case following this woman's total knee replacement, it's human nature to blame the other party for the outcome, especially if each one knows they have done their part responsibly. On occasion, I will hear complaints from the patient suggesting their surgeon must have severed nerves or been asleep on the job during their surgery. Physicians, on the other hand, may tend to question the effort of the patient during the course of his or her rehabilitation. I now understand, in most cases, no one is to blame.

In this particular case, I know the surgeon who did this patient's total knee replacements. For him to have made some careless mistake or act irresponsibly is almost inconceivable. On the other hand, I witnessed firsthand the diligence this patient applied to every detail and instruction regarding her therapy. Neither party was at fault regarding her lack of progress. Previous traumas and complicated, indirectly related adhesions were to blame for her very difficult response to surgery and rehab. I can't help but wonder how things might have been different for her if more flexibility had been restored to her soft tissue after her two motor vehicle accidents or fourteen-plus chest procedures. I believe there are hundreds of patients just like her who would respond just as well to a more thorough therapeutic approach.

I've seen numerous patients whose recovery from surgery seems to be complicated by preexisting tension and lack of range of motion. I have often thought these exercises would be helpful for anyone *preparing for elective surgery*. Most recently, I had the opportunity to confirm my hunch. This next case example illustrates how preexisting adverse myofascial tension was a hindrance to a man who was trying to prepare for his upcoming ACL repair.

Knee Pain Preoperatively for ACL Repair

A forty-three-year-old patient of mine had torn his anterior cruciate ligament when he fell while carrying a heavy load of fencing materials. He was referred to physical therapy to strengthen his right knee prior to surgery. He had no tolerance for strengthening, however, because his pain level of 10/10 interfered with a simple active range of motion. He complained of a constant burning pain on the lateral aspect of the right thigh and along the medial and lateral aspect of the knee. On many occasions, his pain would radiate into his lower back on the right side. He was unable to bear any weight on his right lower extremity, which forced him to walk with crutches. The pain would interrupt his sleep every two hours. Upon evaluation, this patient had a very poor tolerance for the supine position. He complained of lower back and neck pain of 8/10. He required a thirty-degree wedge under his upper body with an additional six centimeters of support under his head and neck to be comfortable in supine with good cervical posture.

The first exercises I gave him were the standard exercises given for the range of motion of the knee and isometric strengthening. After doing these exercises for one week plus using cold packs frequently to the medial and lateral knee, his pain level persisted at 10/10. Next, we tried moving his neck and his eyes. These exercises reduced his pain to 8/10. The prone lower body exercises further reduced his pain to 5/10. It was not until I gave him the upper body exercises that his pain reduced to 4/10. Once he started moving his arms, he started sleeping at night and was able to ambulate without his crutches. Within four visits, he tolerated supine with only three centimeters of support under his head and neck, and his pain level rarely exceeded 4/10. His final range of motion was -5 degrees of extension to 136 degrees of flexion in comparison to 0–140 degrees on his non-injured leg. Plus, he was tolerating a variety of strengthening activities for the right knee.

The significant component in his medical history included a gunshot wound to the right side of his chest and open-heart surgery seventeen years prior to his knee injury. His range of motion in the right shoulder was limited, approximately fifty percent, when he started his home exercise program. Once he started moving his arms while his neck was correctly positioned, his overall improvement was quite fast. He was then better prepared to undergo surgery.

Chronic Degenerative Arthritis of the Knee

When I met this fifty-nine-year-old female, she was desperate for a quick solution to resolve a long-standing problem. A total joint replacement had been recommended to resolve the pain she had experienced in her right knee for the past twenty years. Her problems all started when she fell off her bicycle as a young girl. Her right knee had always been a bit of a problem. Walking had always been nonrestricted but with pain of 2–3/10. Standing from sitting, squatting, and stair-climbing had been difficult but doable. Three months prior to our meeting, her walking tolerance suddenly dropped to two or three blocks. Standing was restricted to fifteen minutes. Both activities were limited by anterior and medial knee pain of 7/10.

The unique part of this woman's history included a congenital deformity. She was born with "AVM" or arteriovenous malformation of the brain. The result of this defect was a mild weakness on the right side of her body most of her life. She suffered three mild strokes after her second pregnancy that did not compound her weakness but left her with more noticeable cognitive and memory deficits. I was not sure if this patient would respond to this program as well as others had, but we were both very pleasantly surprised by her results.

This is her story in her own words:

Nancy Griggs PT

Dear Nancy,

It was May 2008 and my knees were a wreck! I had a long history of knee problems, but I was making a very concerted effort to improve my situation. My kids had promised to take me on a backpacking trip to Ireland for my 60th birthday in mid-September. I started walking two miles a day to prepare for my trip. Just as my stamina was improving, I suddenly was unable to walk without a cane! I hurried to see my doctor to discuss the surgery I had been putting off for the past five years. She told me I would never recover from the surgery in time to enjoy my trip, so she referred me to physical therapy.

P.T.!!??! I thought. I had been through therapy before. I didn't want any more exercises that I knew would not work! (sigh) I reluctantly went to therapy anyway out of desperation. As I watched various therapists pass through the waiting room, I wondered who I would be working with. There was a jock PT, a young waif PT, an old hippie PT, and a long-distance, runner-looking PT. Then I heard you calling my name. You were down to earth and middle-aged. You put me at ease immediately even though I was still very skeptical about being at therapy.

It was obvious from the very start that your approach to therapy was different. The first exercise you gave me was to lie down on my back with my arms down my sides. Well, I thought, I can do that! but how will this help me get to Europe?! I was running out of time, so I did the exercises you gave me each week. Much to my surprise, I first noticed my mind seemed more clear! Then I started to feel taller and I moved about more freely.

*To make a long story short, my trip was great! The scenery and the food were definitely worth writing home about. But what was so personally gratifying for me was to carry my own forty pound backpack while climbing aboard the train all by myself. I walked and I walked! I stayed in a fourth-floor apartment in Venice, Italy for a week. I climbed those stairs and **smiled**! I was walking and climbing without pain!*

' I could have been placed with any therapist. I'm so glad it was you!!

Patellofemoral Pain

Discomfort experienced between the kneecap, or patella, and the bottom of the long bone in the thigh, the femur, is referred to as patellofemoral pain. The cause of the pain can vary but is most often attributed to weakness of the medial, or inner, thigh muscles and increased tension in the lateral, or the outside, thigh muscles, creating a misalignment of the kneecap in relationship to the bones of the leg. Exercises are usually prescribed to help restore the proper strength relationship of the muscle groups around the knee. Taping techniques are often implemented to realign the patella correctly during exercise to reduce pain.

When my twenty-seven-year-old patient was referred to our clinic for this diagnosis, she had already been dealing with patellofemoral pain for ten or eleven months. She had been very active for the past ten years, whether she was hiking, biking, running an hour per day, or playing volleyball twice each week without any difficulty or injury. She first noticed her pain as a "mild straining sensation" just above her kneecap after exertion. A high-intensity activity eventually provoked her knee pain to become a constant problem. Within five or six months, she was forced to discontinue running, but she continued to play volleyball twice per week. Her pain would last for twenty-four hours after each match and was becoming more easily provoked. Any amount of hiking that required more exertion or ascending and descending stairs was the next activity to become extremely difficult. She consulted with her doctor, who, in turn, referred her to PT.

Her first therapist instructed her in the usual protocol of exercises for the next four weeks, including straight leg raises, quad sets, leg presses, and hip strengthening. Her pain had not improved by the end of her six weeks of therapy, but her therapist was confident she just needed more time to respond to the exercises. She was very disciplined to continue with her exercise routine for another four weeks, but her pain remained unchanged. She discontinued playing volleyball and rested from all strenuous activity for three to four weeks. Her pain reduced to almost 0/10, but she missed her regular activities and exercise. She received a cortisone injection in her left knee a week prior to our evaluation but continued to experience a straining sensation of 5/10 above both kneecaps when ascending or descending stairs, walking for an hour, or waking each morning.

Her physical exam revealed nothing particularly alarming, but there were some asymmetries in her motion. She was fit and flexible. The strength at her knees and ankles was easily within normal limits. She was able to fully extend both knees to 0 degrees, but her flexion was asymmetrical with 125 degrees on the right and 135 degrees on the left. Her left knee moved the best but was more painful than the right. Hip flexion was equal at 100 degrees, but her ROM for hip rotation was "flip-flopped" (see page 207 for explanation). Internal rotation on the right was 38 degrees and 45 degrees on the left. External rotation was 45 degrees on the right and 35 degrees on the left. The numbers should all be 45 degrees. These imbalances in her hip ROM surely could have been contributing to some of her discomfort.

The final discrepancy was exposed in supine. She required six centimeters of cervical stabilization and a ten-degree upper body wedge to tolerate supine comfortably. Her medical history was insignificant for any type of chronic illness. Her traumatic and surgical history included repair of a right fractured ankle sustained ten years ago when she fell down five stairs.

I instructed her in the supine isometrics and the seated upper body, head, neck, and eye exercises following her evaluation. Coordination for lateral eye motion as well as looking up and down were obviously her greatest challenge. She was unable to report any improvement in her knees at her first follow-up appointment in spite of correcting her supine posture daily and doing parts of the seated program. I ran her through the complete supine program at this visit. Fortunately, her right knee pain decreased from 4/10 to 1/10, and her left knee pain decreased from 4/10 to 2–3/10. Thankfully, she saw the potential in trying a different approach at this visit. If she had not already worked so hard at a more conventional approach and seen no improvement, she might not have hung in there with me.

The exercises helped improve her upper torso flexibility as she did them throughout the next week. When she returned for her second follow-up appointment, she was able to lie comfortably in supine with only four centimeters of cervical stabilization. Even though her body was showing signs of improvement, she continued to experience pain of 5/10 on stairs or with thirty minutes of biking. I instructed her in the pillow progression and the use of light cranial compression to add to her home program.

She was somewhat discouraged when I saw her for our third follow-up visit two weeks later. She underwent arthroscopic surgery to her left knee eight days prior. She continued to experience 5/10 pain along the medial aspect of her knees with any kind of movement. I massaged the muscles of her temporomandibular joint (TMJ) and her ocular muscles. Lateral motion at her jaws was significantly restricted. She repeated the massage to her jaws three to four times during the next week.

She was happy to report at her fourth follow-up visit her pain was now only experienced in the evenings at 2/10. I suggested she focus on cervical and upper body strengthening during the next week. As I instructed her in antigravity strengthening for her neck and moderate resistance exercises for her upper body, her strength deficits were apparent. By the time we were done, however, her knee pain was barely noticeable at .5–1/10.

At her final visit, she had been doing her upper body and cervical strengthening every other day. She had also tolerated sixty minutes on an upright bicycle, thirty minutes of walking, and thirty minutes of jogging twice pain-free. She said she was a little reluctant at first to pursue these activities that usually provoked pain during and after the activity, but each time she was pleasantly surprised when the pain never came. She was "amazed by her progress and how quickly she improved," especially after her last two treatments.

It was interesting to note at her reevaluation what had and had not changed. All her hip measurements were exactly the same, except right hip external rotation now measured 42 degrees instead of 45 degrees. Overall, the imbalance at her hips was intact. The ROM for knee flexion was now symmetrical with 130° bilaterally. Her biggest change was in her upper body and neck. At the time of her evaluation, she required a 10-degree upper body wedge and six centimeters of cervical stabilization in supine. At the time of discharge, she required four centimeters of cervical stabilization only.

Knee Pain after Tibial Plateau Fracture

I decided to add this interesting case study for a couple of reasons. The first is because I did not use this method of treatment for this patient at her first couple of visits or for her evaluation. The second is because of what made me wish I had. I remember thinking when we first met, *This seems like a straightforward problem. She should respond to conventional therapy as well as anyone could.* Instead, she will serve as another good example of why she did not respond well to conventional physical therapy.

This rather quiet thirty-four-year-old female came to her evaluation still using a front-wheeled walker to ambulate after fracturing her tibial plateau, the area at the top end of the calf bone that forms the bottom half of the knee joint. She had been pushed down to the ground two months prior to our meeting, which caused her leg to fracture. She had been using a brace to stabilize her knee and a walker during ambulation to maintain her non-weight-bearing status after surgery. She reported a constant dull ache and a heaviness in her left knee at 3/10. She was unable to walk even two blocks and could not navigate stairs. Her normal ROM for knee flexion and extension on the right was 0–125 degrees. The flexion and extension on the left measured at -5–110 degrees.

The time had now come in her recovery to begin to strengthen her leg and bear partial weight through her injured leg during standing and walking. Because she was *so afraid* to do this, I spent much of our first appointment reassuring her that her body was ready for this next step in her recovery. We also spent time working on her knee ROM while she was either sitting, supine, or prone. At her second appointment, we did more weight shifting, gait training, and ROM and strengthening in standing, sitting, supine, and prone. By this time, she had no complaints of any pain around her injured knee. She was also able to demonstrate active knee flexion on the left of 130 degrees during a supine heel slide.

At her third appointment, she began to tell me about some very unusual side effects she was experiencing after activity. Her knee would become very stiff and tired if she ever attempted to walk more than fifty yards at one time. Riding her bicycle for just ten minutes would fatigue her entire body and make her very nauseated. Prior to her injury, she rode her bike for three miles three times per week. Her left knee was also beginning to feel very stiff and painful each morning upon waking at 7/10. In addition to these problems, she was suffering from an earache and congested sinuses on the left side for the past week. She would become dizzy at 5/10 while sitting or during her sleep. Left knee pain or dizziness had interrupted her sleep and forced her to change positions several times each night during the last week.

At her initial evaluation, this patient failed to mention her hearing loss since birth and her experience with seizures for the past two to three years. She wore hearing aids and controlled her seizures with medications, so it was easy for her to overlook these conditions. She also did not see how her hearing loss or seizures could affect her knee so she did not include that information about her medical history. She told me her hearing loss was probably the result of having scarlet fever as an infant. The only trauma she was aware of was a fall she took from the back of a pickup truck at age two. The scar from this accident was obvious over her left eye.

When I assessed this patient in supine, she was practically standing on her head. She was profoundly dizzy and nauseated until we finally got her comfortably positioned on a twenty-degree upper body wedge with ten centimeters of cervical stabilization. When I instructed her in the supine head and neck AROM (active range of motion), she was barely able to reach her bottom or top lip with her tongue because her range of motion was so limited. After spending five to ten minutes in modified supine positioning and completing the head and neck exercises, the stiffness and heaviness in her knee was gone. Her walking "felt normal." She was instructed to continue to do the head and neck exercises each day in the modified supine position. She was also given rows 2–4 in the Seated Worker series.

She canceled and rescheduled two appointments and returned for her next follow-up one month later. She had been compliant with her exercises and positioning for fifteen minutes each day for the first ten days after her last appointment. When all her nausea and dizziness resolved, she discontinued the positioning and postural exercises. She started walking 250–300 yards and riding her bike for thirty minutes each day instead. She told me her knee still felt very fatigued after the activity but had no complaints of stiffness. Cramping around the left knee continued to interrupt her sleep each night, but dizziness was no longer a problem. Her knee was stiff and weak each morning upon waking, making it difficult to weight bear, and sore at 5/10 after exercise but no longer painful.

The reassessment of her supine posture confirmed her continued need for a twenty-degree upper body wedge and ten centimeters of cervical stabilization in supine. She was instructed in rows 1 and 5 of the seated series. Her tongue movement showed good improvement. I suggested she do the full seated series, spend some time each day relaxing in modified supine again, and reduce the size of her wedge as tolerated.

At her next appointment, she was able to report that she had done her seated exercises each morning. Even though she no longer experienced any pain, soreness, or heaviness in her left knee with walking or biking, she had been unable to reduce the size of her wedge during supine exercise. I completed her instruction in the remainder of the supine program and how to progress her positioning to lie flatter. I also started her on some cervical strengthening exercises for her neck and closed-chain strengthening for her legs.

When I saw her one month later, she had been doing her supine exercises daily. She was now tolerating all the supine exercises flat with only four centimeters of cervical stabilization without any nausea or dizziness. She was riding her bike up and down hills for thirty minutes each day. I gave her mini squats and standing heel raises for light lower extremity strengthening and cervical antigravity strengthening. She found cervical strengthening to be very challenging. I also treated the soft tissue of her TMJ bilaterally, which was tender at 6–8/10.

I saw this patient for the last time one month after her previous appointment. She told me she had continued with all her exercises but paid particular attention to strengthening her neck. She was performing squats and heel raises with 6# in each hand. She was doing standing four-way kicks while using a 3# ankle weight. She no longer had pain or heaviness in her left leg and knee after walking or riding her bike. She had no pain during the day or the night. Her active ROM was easily 0–130 degrees. She tolerated being flat on her back in supine with only six centimeters of cervical stabilization. She was happy to say "I am on my way back to walking and riding my bike like before."

This patient is a good example of a phenomenon I have witnessed on multiple occasions. When sufficient upper body, head, and neck tension is present and the patient begins lower body AROM or strengthening in supine, adverse symptoms occur. Once the patient is careful to release the upper body tension first, he or she is *then* able to return to lower body strengthening and activity with fewer symptoms, restrictions, or setbacks.

Shoulder Restriction Affecting Knee Pain

For the longest time, I saw how shoulder pain was affected by neck and lower back pain. It wasn't until the last couple of years I began to see how much the shoulders are also affecting other areas. This next patient demonstrates how some of our patients with degenerative arthritis may have more potential to improve and feel better than previously expected.

This sixty-nine-year-old female had no history of lower back or knee pain until she fell directly onto her left knee while getting out of a car eleven years ago. Arthroscopic surgery resolved all the pain issues she was having at that time. Two or three years later, she took a second fall onto both knees but did not experience any pain as a result. She was pain-free for the next eight years. Then for no reason she could identify, she began to experience bilateral knee pain. She responded very well to her first cortisone injection, but the second injection made very little to no difference for her. Both knees hurt constantly at 10/10 without ibuprofen; 400 mg of ibuprofen twice each day would lower her pain to 5/10. Her sleep was interrupted by pain three to four times each night. Sitting for one hour or walking thirty minutes increased her pain to 10/10. She found herself dragging her feet while walking and would experience spontaneous buckling of her left knee several times each week. She had difficulty dressing her lower body and transitioning from sit to stand. She avoided stairs at all cost. Her goals for therapy were to decrease her constant pain and improve her sleep.

Range of motion restrictions were most significant for cervical rotation at 45 degrees in both directions and external hip rotation at 25 degrees each. Right knee motion was from 0 to 117 degrees of flexion. Left knee motion was more restricted at -10–95 degrees of flexion. Her posture was great in standing except the left shoulder appeared to be slightly elevated.

In supine, she felt good and only required four centimeters of cervical stabilization.

Improving her sleep turned out to be an easy fix. When she told me she slept on her stomach, I advised her to correct that as soon as possible. Sleeping habits can be difficult to break, but sleeping on the stomach, in prone, is the worst position for sleep because of its effect on the neck. The head is forced to turn to one side or the other for prolonged periods. This is no better than being upright with the head turned to the right or the left for several hours at a time.

This woman made the change to sleeping on either side the very first week of therapy. She was happy to report she had slept through the night every night of the week. Additionally, her ROM in her left knee increased to 0–102 degrees before she was given any exercises. After completing the cervical exercises on her back, her flexion improved further to 112 degrees. After completing the lower body supine exercises, her flexion was equal to her right knee at 120 degrees.

She received cortisone injections in both knees again the day before her second follow-up visit. Her knee pain was now gone while standing and walking, which made her more aware of the tension in her lower back. I instructed her in the standing exercises for her lower back and the eye exercises in sitting to address the tension in her lower back, which was easily visible and palpable.

At her third follow-up visit, she reported, "The eye exercises are relaxing my lower back." Her walking tolerance had increased to one hour. Her sleep continued to be noninterrupted. It was at this visit the relationship between her right shoulder and left knee became obvious. I had not been aware of her shoulder restrictions until I instructed her in the angel exercise. Left shoulder abduction was restricted to 120 degrees by pain and stiffness with 180 degrees being normal. *The same motion on the right was restricted to 90 degrees by pain, stiffness, and a sharp pain in her left knee at 4–5/10. The exercise was modified, so right shoulder abduction was completed while the left hip and knee were bent.* The angel exercise was alternated with the pullover exercise for multiple sets until shoulder abduction was within full limits. The left leg was then lengthened. The arm motions were completed again through a full range of motion and without provoking left knee pain.

Her fourth follow-up visit was devoted to strengthening her neck and upper body as well as progressing her eye exercises to the supine position. Doing these strengthening exercises daily helped her increase her walking tolerance to four hours. Then at her fifth follow-up visit, more time was devoted to strengthening instruction for the lower body as well as instruction for TMJ massage. At her final visit, she had 0/10 pain in her left knee, low back, and right shoulder. She had no functional restrictions. She had not taken any ibuprofen for the last month.

Knee Pain and Obesity

The next case study I'll share with you is for all those people who have been told their knees will not stop hurting until they lose weight. This fifty-year-old female would now beg to differ. *Of course,* carrying excessive weight is not good for your knees or any other part of your body. Even this patient would agree. We all either know someone or have heard of someone who has lost weight and reports relief from knee pain. This patient, however, clearly demonstrates that in some cases, blame is being incorrectly assigned to a person's weight. She represents the option for addressing knee pain before the weight comes off. Bear with me as I take you through the struggle she has been on for the last twenty-five years with her weight. Then I'll share with you her testimony and the hope her story can give to you.

At age twenty-five, my patient was five feet two inches tall and weighed a hundred and fifty pounds. This had been her steady weight since about fifteen or sixteen years of age. This was the year she was in a car accident. As the passenger in the vehicle, she was thrown to the driver's side of the car. She sustained a concussion and fractured her left collarbone as she broke the steering wheel with her body. Both knees were horribly bruised. She was surprised that her knees never hurt, even though it was painful to look at them. It took a full year for the bruising to fade. She also did not experience any pain in her lower back or neck.

Ten years later at age thirty-five, she gained sixty pounds during her first pregnancy. She was very active after giving birth. She rode her bike five miles each morning before work and would push her son in his stroller for sixty to ninety minutes every day. Her weight "yo-yoed" a lot after her first baby. She would lose twenty pounds and gain back twenty-five or lose fifty and gain seventy.

When her son was two years old, she slipped on some milk in the grocery store and landed in a modified version of the splits. Even though she had never been able to do the splits before, she was only sore for one day and then went back to work. Six months later, her lower back started hurting "out of the blue." Sitting and standing were very difficult for her. Plus, her sleep was interrupted several times each night by pain. She was no longer able to take long walks or ride her bike. She was diagnosed with a herniated disc in her lower back and was forced to quit the job she loved. She had become unreliable at work because of her lower back pain. Within one year of falling, her weight had increased to 275 pounds. Her weight loss plateaued at 225 after three months of very strict dieting. Once she reached that plateau, her weight once again "yo-yoed" between 225 and 275 pounds for many years.

By age forty, lower back pain was less debilitating. She was feeling good, so she returned to the gym to ride the bike and lift light weights. She seemed to tolerate her workouts just fine but would often be bedridden with back pain for two to three days at a time. In between these episodes, she felt "more back to normal" than she had in many years.

At age 43, she became pregnant for the second time. During this pregnancy, her weight increased to an all-time high of 325 pounds. After her daughter was born, she immediately returned to the gym. She worked out on the stationary bike, treadmill, and stepper and took water aerobics classes. Her weight *decreased* to 275 pounds as her lower back pain *increased*. By age 46, her lower back pain was quite severe. Plus, her neck and head were hurting. For the first time, her body became very sensitive to changes in the weather, especially the wind. She started gaining more weight in spite of the fact that she tried to be conscientious about her diet. When her weight reached 350 pounds, she gave up dieting. She felt helpless as she reasoned that losing weight by dieting alone without exercise was hopeless.

Over the course of the next three years, she spent much of her time bedridden. Her general physical condition was declining. She suffered from pneumonia three times per year for the next three years. Even minimal, very light housework like straightening up her dresser or folding laundry would put her back to bed for two to three days. She was no longer able to cook for her family or take care of her children. Then in January 2010, she experienced her last bout with pneumonia. Her legs and feet swelled beyond anything she could have imagined. From January to September of 2010, she watched her weight climb an additional 90 pounds. At 440 pounds and still only 5'2" tall, she was diagnosed with congestive heart failure, sleep apnea, and depression. She was hospitalized for ten days in September of 2010 when her blood pressure skyrocketed to 210/115. Her sister moved in with her and her family after her discharge. She became a patient in her own home. Even her children became her caregivers as she was afraid to ever be left alone.

Within several months of being back home from the hospital, her weight dropped to 372 pounds, and she was breathing better. Her knees started giving her trouble when she started cardiac rehab. She had noticed some knee pain prior to her hospitalization, but when her blood pressure went to 210/115, she forgot about her knee pain. She tried to ride the stationary bike at the cardiac rehab, but this increased her knee pain so much she was bedridden once again for two weeks. This was her response to any form of exercise whether it was the recumbent bike or the treadmill. By the time it was determined she could tolerate *four minutes of exercise*, her doctor picked up the phone and scheduled her an appointment in physical therapy himself.

As he was on the phone, she recalled how she felt like therapy in the past for her lower back and shoulder had been a waste of her time. Because our access for scheduling her first appointment was so backed up, her evaluation was scheduled four months later. She admitted to me she had no intention of keeping the appointment. I will let her tell her story from here.

> *Dear Nancy,*
> *I had no faith in physical therapy to help my knee pain. I had been in the past for my back pain as well as for my shoulder. The treatments and exercises I was given did not help me. I was hoping **anything** would come up so I would not have to keep my appointment, but at the last minute, I decided to go. When you started telling me your theory about how past trauma can affect our current problems, I thought you were ridiculous! I*

was raised to be polite, so I smiled and nodded as I thought to myself, "You will never see me again!"

Then you positioned me on my back and corrected my alignment. I remember feeling "totally off." This got my attention! I became so comfortable and relaxed when you showed me how to position myself on a wedge. For the next week I used ice behind my knees and lay on my wedge for 20 minutes, three times each day. After only two days, I was able to get out of my chair without even thinking about it. I caught myself walking in my home without my cane. I could still only walk for about 10 minutes in my house, but my knee pain was only 4/10. Otherwise, my pain stayed at a 1/10. I could not wait to come back for my second appointment!!

You started me on the seated exercises at that appointment. I was **startled and shocked** when I experienced a very sharp cramp in my lower back as I moved my eyes! I was convinced then beyond a shadow of a doubt there really was something to what you were doing! I did the complete seated series of exercises three times a day for the next three days. I also continued to position myself on my wedge and use ice behind my knees for 20 minutes three times a day for the next two days. My pain further reduced to the point that it stayed at a 1/10 at all times.

I spent my third day after our second appointment shopping at the flea market for **four hours.** My pain never rose above a 1/10! I did my positioning, ice and exercises and was off again to the casino for another **four hours.** I followed this again with my exercises, more ice and positioning. The next morning, I woke up to knee pain of 1/10, so I was out again with my daughter for **another four hours** of shopping!!

I am now doing my exercises lying down. I am feeling better in other parts of my body too. I have been able to clasp my own necklaces for the first time in many years.

It's almost scary to believe that all it's taken for me to feel better is a few pillows, towels, ice and some very simple, natural movements. You are the "Hanna Montana of Physical Therapy"! If I had all the money in the world, I could not repay you for what you have done for me. You have given me back my life. My kids have a mom again! My husband has told me, "It's so good to have you back. I've missed you so much."

Releasing Hip Pain

Old Problems . . . New Solutions

Two of the first places I noticed something different happening with these exercises while treating patients were with headaches and hip pain. Curiously enough, a woman I will specifically discuss in this section finally resolved her hip pain by doing the eye exercises. Another time, I was treating a woman for sciatica when her headaches improved. It was while I was treating these two patients I began to suspect the answer to resolving many pain issues could be found at the opposite end of the spine from the patient's symptoms.

Sciatica is a general term often used to refer to leg pain believed to originate from problems in the lower back. According to *Dorland's Medical Dictionary*, sciatica is "a syndrome characterized by pain radiating from the back into the buttock and into the lower extremity along its posterior and lateral aspect, and most commonly caused by prolapse of the intervertebral disc; the term is also used to refer to pain anywhere along the course of the sciatic nerve." I remember treating a man years ago who had suffered with sciatica for more than forty years. I wish I had known then what I know now.

To offer a new treatment option to those who have "tried everything" or have been told "nothing can be done to help you" is so gratifying. Sciatica is often that type of problem.

Hip Pain or Sciatica

Hip pain is a common diagnosis treated in physical therapy. Sometimes the pain is very localized over the ball and socket of the hip. Other times, it is accompanied by pain that refers down the leg as well. This type of pain may be diagnosed as a *lumbar radiculopathy*, but other times, it will be called sciatica. The most common complaint for these patients is a poor tolerance for side lying on the affected side and for weight bearing on the involved extremity. Treatment for sciatica is often directed to the lower back as this is usually the area considered to be the source of the problem. The responses I have witnessed to my exercise program, however, and the results I am seeing have convinced me to think otherwise in most cases. I now predict the origin of sciatica to be "in the head." And I do not mean psychologically; I mean *literally*.

Regardless of how the hip pain or sciatica started or was noticed originally, there is always one common denominator found among these patients. They can all recall either falling directly onto their tailbone or their buttocks, or they have sustained a significant impact directly to the head. Almost without exception, the *eye exercises* are the most difficult for these patients to either demonstrate or tolerate. I believe this is because the impact sustained at the tailbone, buttocks, or low back traveled up the spine to settle in the head. If the impact was to the forehead, the force settles in the *back of* the head and vice versa; if the impact is to the right side of the head, the force settles on the left side of the head and vice versa. For one patient of mine who landed on her face when she fell forward down seven steps, the tension in her head was so severe she literally *could not budge her eyes* if she kept her head still. For others, the movement occurs, but it is as if the eyes are "moving through mud." Another common response is for the eye motion to be "ratchety" or "jerky" to one degree or another. For some patients, the eye movement may be somewhat strained and provoke the eye(s) to become bloodshot or watery. Lateral movement of the eyes to the opposite side of the pain is typically the most difficult. For example, if the leg pain is on the right, shifting the eyes to the left is usually more difficult than laterally shifting the eyes to the right. If you are currently suffering from hip pain or sciatica or have not responded well to previous treatment, be encouraged as you read how others have overcome this problem.

Sciatica Immediately Following Trauma

The first time I met this thirty-one-year-old female, she was sitting very crooked in her chair. The constant aching and tension she experienced in her left buttock at 5–6/10 forced her to sit on her right butt cheek only. She had not been able to sit normally, lie on her back, or lie on her left side for the past three months since she had been struck as a pedestrian by a careless driver in a parking lot.

Any of these activities or attempting a brisk walk would provoke left gluteus pain of 8–9/10. She did not tolerate even very light touch over her piriformis muscle, which can be palpated in the very center of the buttock. She was surprised to learn she was equally as tender in her suboccipital muscles on the left side as well. She had been using cold packs to the painful area in her buttock for months, which helped her mostly while the packs were in place, but the cold packs applied to her neck "felt fantastic." The first time the knot in her left buttock went away completely was after she completed the supine neck and eye exercises. Even though her initial response to manual release, or massage, of her eye muscles was an exacerbation of her buttock and leg pain to 9/10, her pain leveled off at a consistent 2–3/10 within a day or two. Like most of my hip and knee patients, she has been pleasantly surprised by the connection among her lower body pain, her neck, and her eyes as you will read.

> *Dear Nancy,*
>
> *This letter is not only to thank you for everything you have done for me, and everything you are still doing to help me, but to let people know how wonderful it is to get the right type of physical therapy. I was so skeptical about going to therapy because everybody told me it would not only be a waste of my time, but it would hurt me more! I was in so much pain I knew I had to give it a try anyway.*
>
> *I am so happy I decided to go and did not miss out on meeting you and experiencing your treatment. You explained to me how all of my muscles had been affected by the trauma to my body and they were all connected. I was so surprised when you not only treated my hip area with exercises, but you also treated areas like my neck, face, and eyes. I didn't think those exercises were going to help me, but my biggest surprise came when they were the exercises that actually released the pain in my hip! It was amazing! Some days I would come to my appointment and my hip would be hurting at a 6/10. You would take me through my eye and neck exercises and my pain would be gone! It was unbelievable. Even though my pain is not 100 percent gone, my pain level is now low enough that I can get through my workday which requires me to sit all day.*

> *I don't know how to thank you enough for being so professional and for finding a way to help people like me get back to life without pain. I would like to tell those who have no trust in therapy that therapy can help—if they follow through with the methods you suggest.*
>
> *Thank you for being in the right place at the right time for me!*

This patient also serves as a good example of someone who exacerbated and leveled off several times over the course of their treatment. When we finally initiated antigravity strengthening of her lower extremities, her pain once again peaked to 8–9/10. This was scary and discouraging for her, but once again, her symptoms leveled off within a few days. She was then able to slowly progress to more difficult forms of strengthening and aerobic reconditioning.

Sciatica Provoked by Cervical Flexion

As clearly as the last case report exemplified how the eyes affect lower back pain, this case report clearly demonstrates how cervical flexion can provoke leg pain or what was believed to be sciatica. A sixty-two-year-old female experienced a very dull localized ache over her right SI joint for two to three years. Suddenly, the pain began to shoot down the posterior aspect of her right thigh constantly. Any movement of the limb increased the pain to 7/10. Over the course of the last nine months, her pain progressed to 7/10 constantly and 10/10 with sudden movement. This woman who had previously walked a mile a day for exercise had been restricted to walking twenty to thirty yards with a front-wheeled walker. Sitting on her left butt cheek on a soft cushion reduced her pain to 3/10, but even under these circumstances, she only tolerated sitting for ten to fifteen minutes. Her sleep was interrupted two to three times each night, or every time she rolled off her left side onto her back or onto her right side.

She required only a ten-degree upper body wedge and four centimeters of cervical stabilization to correct her posture and improve her tolerance for supine. Using her wedge each day for forty-five minutes reduced her pain to 5/10, but her response to exercise at her first follow-up visit clearly revealed the source of her pain. During the seated exercises, she found it extremely difficult to hold her head in neutral as she pumped her ankle while her knee was extended. She naturally leaned her head back into extension during the ankle pump exercise. She was also able to report increased tension in her calf during the exercise if she looked down with her eyes instead of looked straight forward as she pumped her ankle. The most telling exercise of all was a cervical chin tuck in standing, which immediately referred the pain down the posterior aspect of her entire right leg to her ankle.

After doing the Seated Worker exercises for one week, her pain localized to a small area over her tailbone only. At her second follow-up visit, her exercises were progressed to supine. Her ability to move her neck while she maintained correct alignment was so restricted in supine she was directed to complete the supine and prone lower body exercises first. When she returned to the neck again to try the exercises, she reported a ninety percent reduction in tension. After completing the cervical exercises, her tailbone pain reduced from 4/10 to 0/10. She was then instructed in the remainder of the supine exercises for her arms and eyes.

She canceled her next two appointments. I called to invite her to return to PT so I could give her some strengthening exercises and manual techniques to complete her instruction for ongoing self-care.

I spoke with this patient one year following her discharge. She continued to keep her pain to 0/10 most of the time. For six to eight weeks during the colder winter months, the pain in her lower back and right leg might return to 6/10, but she stated she could always reduce it to 0/10 again by doing her exercises. She could still feel her lower back and posterior right leg relax while she did her eye exercises each morning before she got up. Her favorite exercise of all continued to be tucking her chin in standing prior to forward bending at the waist.

Not surprisingly, she had taken two falls in her lifetime directly onto her coccyx. At age eleven, she fell from the top of a camper onto her tailbone. Twenty-five years ago, she was standing behind a podium at the NM State Fair taking tickets when a large truck accidentally backed into the podium, knocking her back onto her tailbone with the podium on top of her.

Hip Pain Secondary to Suspected Overtraining

A forty-four-year-old female came to see me for right hip and knee pain that prevented her from running. The patient had previously run approximately thirty-five miles per week since she was a teenager but had not tolerated running at all for the past six months. She had very poor tolerance for right side lying and was waking up almost every night with right hip pain. This patient's pain immediately resolved after doing the lower body exercises, which were not the least bit challenging for her, except for some mild limitation of her external rotation at both hips. She continued to do the exercises for the next three days one to two times per day. Her pain did not return, and she slept through each night pain-free.

At her second appointment, I instructed her in the eye, head, and neck exercises. She was very challenged by the eye exercises, and her tongue was very hypomobile. When her full body was positioned on top of the pillows, the only tension she experienced was in the back of her neck. By the end of her appointment, her right hip was feeling slightly agitated. This resolved by doing the exercises again the next morning.

She continued to be pain-free with each level of progression until she reached level #4 for the lower body where the legs are left unsupported from above the knees. While she was doing the exercises in the #4 position, she noticed that *she could barely move her eyes*. She forced her way through the exercises and then forgot about it as she went about her responsibilities for the day. That night, however, she was once again awakened by severe hip pain when lying on her right side.

This is a good example of pain that initially increased when the area where the pain originated was addressed and/or challenged. This exacerbation lasted through part of the next day but then resolved after she took a very short run of about one mile and did her exercises in the #2 lower body position.

This patient is very fit and flexible but still had persistent pain that previously did not resolve with exercise; instead, it *prevented* exercise. When questioned, this patient recalled one significant lower back injury approximately twenty years prior when she was a waitress. She had also taken about five to six falls over the past ten years while she was running. She now continues to do very well with her exercise progression and is slowly starting to increase her running.

Hip Pain of Insidious Onset

My next patient ruptured a disc in her lumbar spine in 2001. Surgical repair of the affected disc had resolved all the pain she previously experienced in her left leg. When she noticed a gradual onset of pain in both of her legs, she wondered if something was going wrong in her lower back again. Her logical suspicion was soon replaced by an understanding she would have never suspected.

Her current pain reminded her of her previous experiences. The pain in her left inner thigh and groin made forward bending to put her shoes on impossible. Getting out of her car on the driver's side or crossing her legs provoked a sharp, burning pain at 8/10 in her lower back, hip, and leg. The hip and leg pain would interrupt her sleep when she rolled over in bed. Lower back pain limited her sitting and standing to ten minutes. Exercise for her was virtually nonexistent, except for infrequent short walks.

Her evaluation in supine revealed asymmetrical hip flexion of 95 degrees on the right and 112 degrees on the left. The internal rotation of her hips was very good with 45 degrees on the right and 40 degrees on the left. Her external rotation was equally *as bad* with only 15 degrees on the right and 12 on the left. The minimal cervical extension she demonstrated in supine required four centimeters of support to stabilize her posture correctly. In standing, however, she demonstrated a rotation in her trunk as her right shoulder was anterior seven centimeters, and her left was anterior three centimeters. Her cervical rotation was limited to 60 degrees bilaterally.

Her traumatic history only included the self-inflicted blows she sustained to her head as a child. Whenever she was unhappy at the dinner table, she would throw herself backward in her chair, hitting the back of her head into the kitchen window. She had multiple scars on her head as reminders of her behavior.

Because I suspected her symptoms were referred by her head, neck, and eyes, I instructed her to do rows 1–3 of the Seated Worker series and the supine isometrics after I completed her evaluation. Unfortunately, this patient returned to her first follow-up visit with hip and leg pain still of 8/10. There were even times it seemed to hurt more than it did prior to therapy. The isometric hamstring exercises aggravated her lower back, so she discontinued them. The eye exercises made her eyes so red, she stopped them. I took her through the supine lower body and neck exercises as well as the standing modifications of the prone exercises. Her leg and hip pain decreased from 8/10 to 0/10. Her response was encouraging, but it was short-lived.

She returned for her second follow-up visit to report that her energy was better as a result of doing her exercises, but she was still not seeing any improvement in her lower back, hip, or leg pain. I completed her exercise instruction for the upper body and prone lower body exercises.

Her situation appeared even more bleak when she came to her next appointment. She had taken oral steroids for the past four days, and her pain had not improved. I decided to massage her hip flexors and adductors as well as her jaw muscles. This helped her bend over better to reach for her foot. We repeated her treatment with more massage at her next visit. While this continued to help her bend over to reach her foot, it was still extremely difficult to pull her left foot up to rest it on her right knee to put on her shoes. She estimated a 50 percent improvement in her pain and function after the massage treatments.

This is when she started to figure some things out for herself. She was preparing for bed as usual that night after her treatment. She started to put her soft night jaw splint in her mouth when it occurred to her that maybe her splint was contributing to her problem. She left it out to see if it made any difference. To her amazement, she was able to easily cross her left leg over her right the next morning. At her next visit, I only massaged her jaw. After treatment, her hip flexion measured 115 degrees bilaterally (previously 95 degrees on the left and 112 degrees on the right); her external rotation on the right was 36 degrees and 30 degrees on the left (previously 15 and 12 degrees, respectively). She was able to easily pull her foot up to her knee while sitting to put on her shoes.

At her sixth follow-up visit, she was happy to report she had no pain in her left hip unless she crossed her left leg too far over the right leg. Her sleep was no longer interrupted by pain, her sitting tolerance had improved to ninety minutes, and she was able to stand for several hours without any pain. She was able to walk a hundred yards or more several times each day comfortably.

I have a better theoretical understanding of *exactly how* these exercises work, but I'm still not sure *how the jaw has such an effect on the hip and the knee.* This patient is a very gracious and enjoyable sister in the Catholic church. "Walking by faith" is a way of life for her. But in this instance, seeing was believing.

> *Dear Nancy,*
> *I want to thank you a thousand times for helping me! It was such a blessing that I was assigned to you when my doctor ordered physical therapy for me. I had such pain coming down from my back through my hip and down the inside of my left leg. I had lost so much mobility in both legs because of the pain. I was moving around less and had to lie down more which was not good for my diabetes. Having had back surgery in the past, I was afraid the only thing that would help me was another back surgery.*
> *I would never have imagined or believed my problem was actually in my head! If I had not experienced the improvement myself, I would never have believed it possible that the exercises, the massage and the icing of my head and neck could fix what I was experiencing in my leg!*
> *When I started noticing the improvement, I began to wonder if the night guard I was wearing in my mouth was contributing to the problem. I asked my dentist and he told me the over the counter night guards are made of a soft material that actually makes you work your jaw more during the night. When I stopped using my night guard and continued with what you taught me, I saw even bigger improvements in a short amount of time.*
> *Thanks so much. May God bless you abundantly in what you are doing to help so many.*

Hip Pain Associated with Long History of Sitting

A sixty-five-year-old male patient of mine had retired from truck driving approximately two years ago. During the last seven years of his career, he experienced intermittent sciatica frequently. Because sitting is the position that stresses the lower back the most, it was assumed his job was provoking the sciatica. In fact, he had not experienced any sciatica since his retirement until he made a pivoting turn on the right leg while the foot was planted. At the time of his evaluation, he complained that his sleep was interrupted two to three times each week secondary to right shoulder and right hip pain. In addition, leg pain of 6–8/10 limited his walking tolerance to twenty minutes and limited his driving tolerance to ten to thirty minutes.

The first series of exercises I instructed him in was the eye exercises. The exercises made his eyes "very tired" but did not seem to directly affect his leg pain at the time. At his next appointment, I gave him the lower body and the head and neck exercises. While doing the tongue motions the next day, he experienced a release of tension in the form of a "pop" at the base of his skull on the right side. He did not experience any sciatica after that incident.

He continued to progress his exercises through all the levels of progression. He then added light weight lifting at the gym and walking. He underwent arthroscopic surgery to trim the cartilage in the right knee shortly after he completed therapy. With everything he did, his recovery was very close to 100 percent.

I spoke with this patient about six to eight weeks after his discharge. He was very happy to inform me he had recently driven eight hours without any symptoms of sciatica.

The most obvious objective, or measurable, improvement this patient demonstrated was in the posture of the cervical spine. At the time of his evaluation, he held his head in twenty degrees of cervical extension. In other words, he held his head back with his nose pointing up in the air. At the time of his discharge, he held his head in only four degrees of extension. Again, the lower body exercises were never difficult for him. It was the eye exercises that were consistently the most difficult and tiring with each level of progression. Significant trauma for this patient included two falls off running horses at ages eight and fourteen, falling off a ladder onto his tailbone at age thirty, and finally, falling backward out of his truck onto his lower back and tailbone at age forty.

Hip Pain Secondary to Lower Back Pain

In the course of my career, I have met some patients whom I will never forget. Such is the case with a forty-nine-year-old female I met very early on in my experience with this approach. Her dramatic response to these exercises forced me to "pull out my books" in an effort to understand the bizarre things she was telling me. She had suffered from low back pain since her early twenties after being thrown headfirst through her car windshield during a head-on collision. Lower back pain made standing very difficult for her since the time of her accident. Sitting was uncomfortable after twenty to thirty minutes. She experienced recurrent episodes of sciatica involving her right buttock and foot pain, but for the past four months, the pain involved her entire right leg.

One month prior to our meeting, the pain became constant and so severe she was forced to go to the emergency room. She took her pain medications regularly and received regular massage therapy for the month previous to our meeting. At the time of her evaluation, constant leg pain of 5/10 made it very painful for her to stand from sitting. Her tolerance for sitting and driving was fifteen to twenty minutes, while her standing and walking tolerance was only about five minutes. The leg pain limited her sleeping tolerance to three hours. She was also experiencing excruciatingly painful and nauseating headaches at the bottom of her head on the right side that would interrupt her sleep each night at about three o'clock.

During her first three visits to therapy, she was given the series of lower body exercises as well as several lower body stretches commonly given for sciatica. She was also treated with manual techniques in an attempt to decrease the cramping in the posterior thigh and hip. By her fourth visit, she was seeing no change whatsoever.

It was at this time I instructed her in the eye exercises. They were incredibly difficult for her. She was only able to move her eyes through approximately 30 percent of full range of motion. Her response to this very minimal amount of motion was a feeling of *complete physical exhaustion all over her body* after completing only three to four repetitions. She repeated the eye exercises to her tolerance again that night before she went to sleep as well as the next night just before going to sleep. By the second night, she did all seven repetitions and had no leg pain throughout the night. Plus, she slept about four hours before her sleep was interrupted by a "nature call" instead of pain. She continued to be pain-free the next day until about 2:00 p.m. while she was sitting. That night she did all seven repetitions again just before going to sleep and slept roughly six hours. I saw her the next day during which time she had been pain-free until she had to drive for two hours. Driving provoked the leg pain again at 6/10.

She returned for her next treatment in two weeks. By the time she returned, she was convinced the eye exercises were the solution to her leg pain, even though she had to admit it was freaking her out a little bit. She was doing the exercises just before retiring and was sleeping from 9:00 p.m. to 6:00 a.m. without interruption. Not only was her leg pain improving, but she was no longer being awakened by the excruciating headaches she originally told me about as well. She also discovered she could reduce her pain immediately during the day as well by repeating the exercises throughout the day. *In fact, just prior to our visit, she sat through a weekend seminar without any restriction.* Each day while sitting, she noticed the beginnings of the leg pain at about 11:00 a.m., but the symptoms readily dissipated after doing the eye exercises while she remained seated. During this visit, I instructed her in the head and neck exercises. At the time of the instruction, she was unable to keep her eyes stabilized in the forward position while she turned her head.

She did not return for her final visit for another three weeks. During this time between visits, she faithfully continued to do all her exercises. She was elated to tell me the day before she saw me she had physically cleaned her whole house of 1,400 square feet by herself. She worked from 8:00 a.m. to 7:00 p.m., vacuuming, climbing up and down step stools, etc. She stopped to rest once in the morning for thirty minutes and once in the afternoon for twenty minutes. As a result of this prolonged activity, her low back pain was 3/10, right buttock pain was 6–7/10, and right calf pain was 1/10. Normally, this type of activity would have provoked pain of 10/10 in her lower back and leg. She planned to do her exercises at home that evening after our appointment. She was confident they would help resolve even the right buttock pain.

I contacted this patient several months after her discharge to see how she was doing. I was so pleased to learn she was still doing her exercises. She continues to enjoy the same benefits and results. She graciously agreed to share her experiences with this exercise program with you.

Dear Nancy,

I just wanted to thank you for the difference your therapy has made in my life.

When I first came to see you, I was in constant pain. My back, hip, and leg hurt all the time. I felt hopeless about ever being pain-free. I started doing the physical exercises you prescribed. I still didn't see or feel any difference. Then you prescribed the eye exercises. At first they were incredibly difficult to do and I was exhausted after doing them, but they worked! I soon was having less and less pain. I am now comfortable most of the time. I know when my body starts tightening up and feeling discomfort or pain, it is because I have not been true to my exercises. Often I can reduce the pain, and even eliminate it, if I do my exercises regularly. I find just doing the eye exercises on occasion can help reduce the pain temporarily. I am still working toward making the exercises a regular part of my life.

I so appreciate your help and the time and energy you have put into developing a program that actually works! I wish you the best in all you do. God bless you and your work!

Sincerely,

There are a couple of things about this patient I have not yet mentioned that I believe are worth noting. On two separate occasions, I applied a special type of tape to her low back and abdomen that I frequently use to facilitate a continuous myofascial stretch. Even though the tape stayed on her for only about twelve hours, it may have or it may not have made a significant contribution while it was on. The part it played in her overall progress cannot be measured, but I have seen many people make great progress in response to this tape, particularly when it is used in conjunction with these exercises. I say all this so as not to potentially mislead anyone regarding the effectiveness of the exercises alone. While this additional modality was implemented with this patient and may have contributed to her progress, the patient is convinced the eye exercises alone are responsible for her improvement. I have, on separate occasions, observed the same results when the tape was not used.

The good news is that the patients I have shared with you continue to enjoy life pain-free of hip pain or sciatica. When there is any hint the pain may be returning, it can be eliminated by doing the exercises. If you are suffering from hip pain or sciatica and choose to try these exercises to manage your pain, there are a few things to be aware of so you do not become discouraged.

First of all, patients who suffer with hip pain as part of a systemic arthritic condition take longer to achieve a consistent level of flexibility than someone who is not dealing with a chronic arthritic condition. I am assuming this is because the soft tissue involvement is more extensive in these patients. Some form of regular manual therapy *if tolerable* to complement the exercises may be helpful with this population. This does not mean a certain amount of pain reduction and increased tolerance for activity cannot be experienced along the way, but more patience is required to reach your final goal. And the goal to be *pain-free* may not be a reasonable goal.

Second, an exacerbation of your symptoms will probably occur at least once as you work through the levels of progression. Exacerbations can be managed by regressing the level of progression, decreasing the depth of the pillows at the current level of progression, decreasing the range of motion during the exercises, or decreasing the number of repetitions, particularly for the eyes. Do not let this discourage you. You are obviously addressing restrictions that need to be released. You will get back on track if you are careful to continue slowly and gently. Also, seek out the help of a massage therapist or a craniosacral therapist to reduce the effects of the exacerbation.

I have had a couple of patients with hip and leg pain who did not respond to these exercises or suggestions. Severe anatomical changes had been previously confirmed with an MRI in both of these cases. Surgery was finally able to provide them with the results they hoped for. It is interesting for me to note, however, that the most difficult movements for these patients were still the eye exercises, even though the defective anatomy was in the lower back.

Recovery after Total Hip Replacement

Total joint replacements are greatly appreciated by most patients who receive them. They are very effective in resolving the pain provoked by osteoarthritis and rheumatoid arthritis. Two women I treated after their total hip replacements seemed to be doing very well when I first stopped by their homes to do their initial evaluation. I quickly learned first impressions can be deceiving. They both validated the important contribution made by a supine postural evaluation.

The first woman was in her mid-seventies. She was so grateful to finally be rid of the hip pain that had made walking and sleeping very difficult. My initial evaluation of her did not reveal anything particularly alarming or even slightly troubling. I thought I would probably be discharging her very soon. It was not until I attempted to evaluate her in supine that a huge deficit surfaced. She had spent the last three years sleeping in an almost upright long-sitting position. This was the only way she could sleep through the night pain-free. So this was the position she demonstrated when I asked her to lie down on her back. When I explained to her the importance of maintaining good posture even while she slept, she was ready to break this bad habit. She initially needed a thirty-degree wedge under her upper body to tolerate a flatter supine position. She progressed from there very quickly. Within three weeks, she was able to lie perfectly flat and sleep through the night without any interruptions. She had almost forgotten what a really good night's sleep felt like.

Her excellent response to manual soft tissue release techniques permitted her to fully restore her supine posture to within normal limits without any assistance. Consistent compliance alone with her home exercise program was the key to her success. I remember her frequently telling me she could not believe how good it made her hip feel to stick out her tongue.

The next woman was in her early sixties. She too was thankful her surgery addressed her left hip pain 100 percent. Her sleep, however, was now being interrupted several times each night by lower back pain and left groin pain. But her primary complaint after surgery was not even this pain issue; instead, she felt as if her operated leg was now longer than her non-operated leg. She held her left leg out to the side about twelve inches as she walked just to keep it on the floor. Any attempt to weight bear straight down on the left leg produced left groin pain of 7–8/10.

When she lay down on her back, the position of her head and neck were good, but she was lacking a full twenty-five degrees of left knee extension. This was not apparent in standing because she was so forward bent at the waist! The flexion at her trunk allowed her knee to straighten.

Her attempted demonstration of a simple heel slide in supine created an uncomfortable pulling sensation in her left hip at a 7-8/10. This motion, also, made her feel very clammy and nauseated. We discovered the head, neck and eye exercises were challenging for her to complete in supine, so we progressed her incrementally from sitting to supine in her recliner to improve her tolerance for the exercises. This strategy combined with manual treatments directly to her eyes, head, and neck proved to be very successful. At the time of her discharge, she was ambulating with a cane for greater than one hundred yards without pain. She was sleeping through the night without lower back pain. And she had full extension in her left knee with only a trace sensation of the left leg being longer than the right.

After one of the first sessions we spent working on her head and neck through active exercise and manual release of soft tissue restrictions around her neck and jaw, her left knee extension improved from negative twenty-five degrees to only negative three degrees, and her left groin pain decreased from 6–7/10 to 2/10. Her immediate positive response to manual treatment encouraged her to be such a compliant patient. She, in turn, was confident to assure her husband she had not gone off the deep end whenever he happened to pass by while she was doing her therapy. This is what she remembers most about the exercises.

> *Dear Nancy,*
>
> *I will never forget my experiences after I had my hip replaced. You taught me that everything had to be in good working order for me to fully recover from my surgery and regain my balance. You made me aware of all the muscles that needed to be worked—many of them I never would have guessed! When my husband would see me exercising my neck or sticking out my tongue, he would curiously ask, "Why does Nancy have you doing that?" I didn't even try to explain. I simply told him, "I'm just working on my hip!" Thanks for helping me make so much improvement!!*

Hip Pain Provoked by Exercise

It is not uncommon for pain to develop when someone decides "it's finally time to get back in shape and lose weight." Poor body mechanics combined with "pushing too hard too fast" can derail the best of intentions for improving someone's health. As you will see from the next example, preexisting conditions also can complicate a person's best efforts.

A sixty-year-old female originally injured her right hip ten years ago when she fell off a ski lift. After the initial incident, she did not experience pain in her hip until five months prior to her PT evaluation. She was visiting her daughter in her home with a flight of stairs she climbed several times each day when she suffered from right hip pain at 7/10 by the end of each day. The pain reduced completely after taking ibuprofen daily for two weeks after she returned home.

Two months later, she started working out with a trainer at a local gym. Walking on the treadmill three miles per hour provoked right buttock and hip pain at 7–8/10 once again. Attempts to relieve the pain in the center of her buttock, in the piriformis muscle, with a foam roller were excruciating. Even though she could temporarily relieve her symptoms with ibuprofen, her trainer advised her to consult her physician about her symptoms, who then referred her to PT for evaluation.

The patient's primary complaint was her inability to tolerate the aerobic exercise she needed to do to help her reach her weight loss goals. It was difficult to ascend and descend stairs or stand greater than twenty or thirty minutes. She denied any lower back pain but experienced a stiff neck occasionally. The internal rotation of her right hip was very limited to eighteen degrees and slightly limited on the left at thirty-five degrees with forty-five degrees being normal. A few muscles around her right hip were tender at 4/10.

Doing the Seated Worker series every other day reduced her constant pain of 2/10 to 1/10. More significantly, the pain after stair climbing reduced from 7/10 to 3/10. While learning the supine eye exercises at her first follow-up visit, she experienced a stretch in her right piriformis while looking down and diagonally to the left; looking down and diagonally to the right provoked a stretch in her left piriformis. Another surprising discovery for her at her second follow-up visit was the 7–8/10 tenderness of the medial pterygoid muscle when palpated underneath her tongue on the right side. *This was the exact area calcium deposits had been removed from her salivary glands twenty-five years ago.* The remainder of the supine exercises and the prone lower body exercises was taught to her at this appointment. By her third follow-up visit, her right hip pain was 0/10 throughout the day with pain by the end of the day of 1/10. Antigravity cervical strengthening, light scapular strengthening, and closed-chain lower extremity exercises were started at this visit.

By her fourth follow-up visit, she was ready for discharge. She had been compliant with her home exercise program daily. She occasionally massaged inside her mouth. Right hip internal rotation increased from eighteen to thirty-five degrees. Her previous walking and standing tolerance of only thirty minutes had increased to five hours without pain. As she left her last appointment, she commented "I will never understand why the most difficult exercise you gave me was to tuck my chin while I looked straight forward with my eyes!"

Scapular Dysfunction Affecting Leg Pain after MVA

A twenty-three-year-old male patient clearly demonstrates how fascial tension can interfere with recovery from traumatic injury. His story also demonstrates how traumatic injury can begin a never-ending cycle of problems, symptoms, and dysfunctions.

This young man fractured his left femur when he lost control of his vehicle. He required surgical stabilization of the break with rods and screws the following day. Over the next two months, he used crutches to ambulate. During this time, he developed pain in his left knee. An MRI confirmed a tear in the posterior stabilizing ligament of his knee. This too required surgical repair.

When I met this patient, he was still walking with crutches and bearing only partial weight on his left leg. His brace could come off only while he was relaxing during the day. The pain he felt was localized to the left knee intermittently. At this point, he was not experiencing any pain in the area of his mid-thigh, where he had fractured his femur. Even though this patient's accident had been quite serious, he had no complaints of jaw, neck, or low back pain.

The rehab following the repair or reconstruction of a ligament always involves a specific protocol. Because I am convinced of the influence the flexibility and alignment of the neck plays in the quality of a person's recovery, I instructed this patient in the cervical exercises in sitting the day of his evaluation, even though there were no glaring restrictions in his cervical range of motion or posture. For the next eight visits, or until ten weeks post-op, I strictly followed the protocol suggested by his orthopedic surgeon.

The patient's range of motion had fully returned by seven weeks post-op. His strength was gradually returning as expected. He was no longer using his brace or crutches for walking. He chose to walk with a straight cane because of persistent pain at the femoral fracture site rather than knee pain. He experienced pain of 8–10/10 in the form of a sharp stab when he transitioned from sit to stand. The pain restricted fast walking and a smooth push off his toes while walking. He also demonstrated a Trendelenburg gait, or his right pelvis dropped slightly when he bore weight on his left leg.

Because his pain was provoked only when he was in a weight-bearing situation, the pain had not restricted his ability to regain his range of motion or progress his strengthening according to the protocol. When the pain delayed his return to a normal gait, however, I decided to look elsewhere for my answers. The first thing I found was muscle spasms along the full left side of the back of his neck. Relaxing this tension with massage partially helped improve his tolerance for weight bearing. The use of kinesiotape to the posterior muscles of his calf also improved his ability to push off more correctly. With this relaxation, his gait velocity picked up as well.

What was most noticeable when he lay down on his stomach was the position of his right shoulder blade. The right upper quadrant of his back did not relax as it should into the table; instead, the shoulder blade pulled more in toward his spine, lifting the right shoulder toward his ear and back off the table. This observation prompted him to remember he had fractured multiple ribs in his accident as well as his left leg. After completing the exercises to strengthen his neck and shoulder blade area, he stated "his whole body felt lighter and better, including his left leg." Doing the neck and scapular strengthening exercises the next week reduced his pain with weight bearing by fifty percent. The pain also did not occur every time he transitioned from sit to stand.

I continued to assess motion at his lower trunk and eyes. Diagonal eye movements to the right were uncoordinated and difficult. Lower trunk rotation of the torso was limited about fifty percent but increased dramatically when his eyes were allowed to look down and to the right in unison with the movement of his trunk. The tension of 4/10 in his lower back decreased to 0/10 after completing the prone prop-up exercise. It was at the end of this follow-up visit he was able to maintain a stable pelvis and demonstrate correct heel strike and push off with verbal cues only.

At his next follow-up, I examined the soft tissue around his jaw bilaterally. He mentioned to me for the first time he had been "unable to chew anything on his right side for two weeks after his accident." Not surprisingly, all the muscles around the TMJ on the right side were tender at 6–8/10. The same muscles on the left side were tender at 0/10. What was most noticeable too was the dramatic increased circulation in his neck and face during the massage as well as moderate perspiration. Once again, the release of tension in this "never treated before" area of his body promoted a sense of general relaxation, even in his left leg. The evidence of an abnormal Trendelenburg gait was no longer apparent after this visit.

His last two visits were spent on the strengthening equipment in our gym to verify he was ready to return to the gym he attended regularly before his accident. He was tolerating a slightly faster walk on the treadmill and planned to progress as tolerated to running. He continued to demonstrate some decreased stability around his right scapula during plank exercises but was ready to address that deficit at the gym as well. He experienced a sharp pain in the area of his mid-quadriceps two to three times a week, but the pain literally lasted a few seconds. The pain provoked a mild limp for those few seconds but resolved as soon as the pain passed. He was discharged from therapy doing much better than he had once expected.

Lingering Pain Post Hip Fracture

This next example of a patient who had recently fractured his femur is probably repeated by hundreds of patients each year. Approximately six months prior to our meeting, an eighty-five-year-old gentleman broke his left femur, or the long bone in the thigh. He was leaving a restaurant with a friend when he lost his balance and fell. The leg was surgically repaired and stabilized with pins and bolts. The incision for this type of repair is made along the outside of the thigh. The pain will frequently persist in the area of the incision as it did for this man. His chief complaint was the pain along his incision at 9/10 with weight bearing. This, in turn, forced him to ambulate with a walker. By the time we met, he was at the point of using a wheelchair to navigate any type of lengthy distances or for outings away from his assisted-living facility.

His evaluation clearly revealed a palpable tightness and tenderness all along the lateral side of his leg, which was undoubtedly contributing to the problem. My biggest concern, however, was the posture of his cervical spine. I would tease this patient about the complex he was giving me because he would rather look at the floor instead of me. His head was extremely forward, and his chin was nearly touching his chest. Unfortunately, this type of posture is fairly common in the elderly population but not usually to this extreme.

This patient was honest enough at his sixth visit to admit he was only "fairly" compliant with his complete home exercise program. His leg pain had only reduced by fifty percent, even though the original tightness in his leg was nearly completely resolved. I decided a clear demonstration was needed to convince him to be more disciplined regarding his head and neck posture while doing his home exercise program.

When he came to his next appointment, he rated his leg pain at 5/10. I asked him to lie down in supine and position his head and neck with six centimeters of support to correct the posture of the cervical spine. First, we went through two sets of seven repetitions of only the eye exercises. He then took a short walk with his walker down the hall. He had to admit that the pain had reduced to about 3/10. He then lay back down and correctly positioned his head and neck. We completed two sets of seven repetitions of the head and neck exercises while he kept his eyes stabilized forward. This time he was pain-free when he walked down the hall with his walker.

This example clearly demonstrates the most efficient and successful way to reduce hip and thigh pain, in this case and others similar to, is by directing treatment toward the head, neck, and eyes. This patient also serves as a good example of a patient who commonly would be discharged from therapy with his goals only "partially met" had I not used a more comprehensive approach.

Falls often occur when a person trips over an uneven surface. Once the person is off-balance, he or she is unable to make the necessary adjustments to compensate for the balance disturbance. In this man's case, he was unable to identify why he lost his balance. He could not recall tripping over anything. He said the incident "happened quickly for no good reason." Unfortunately, this is a common remark. This confusion as to why their fall occurred also breeds an insecurity regarding walking and future fall prevention.

Wouldn't it be wonderful if we could prevent the number of falls that occur by discovering and addressing underlying balance issues *before* they create a bigger problem? Some general observations I have made regarding balance might help us to do just that.

Releasing Balance Dysfunction

The ability to maintain one's balance is critical for safety purposes. Falling occurs when a person loses their ability to maintain his or her center of gravity over his or her base of support.

The maintenance of proper balance is dependent upon the successful integration of information from multiple systems.

1. The CNS, or central nervous system, must interpret and organize sensory information it receives from the eyes, the ears, and the proprioceptive receptors in the muscles and tendons. The proprioceptors inform the CNS of the body's position in space and how the body is moving in relationship to its support surface.
2. The musculoskeletal system must maintain postural stability.

3. The biomechanics of the body, or the way it moves, must be efficient in maintaining the body's center of gravity over its base of support, or feet, while the body is changing positions.

When inaccurate information is communicated or interpreted inaccurately to or by the CNS, or if deficiencies exist in our ability to maintain proper posture or move efficiently, the ability to maintain our balance is jeopardized. Traumatic injury to the body can affect any of these systems. There is a logical progression toward the loss of function when the effects of trauma are neglected. Good balance is one function particularly at risk.

At the time of impact, there are asymmetrical forces imposed upon the body, causing a variety of sprains and strains to the muscle and soft tissue. If left untreated, these soft tissues potentially become too tense. The system becomes asymmetrical in many different ways and places. Proper biomechanics of the joints are hindered by loss of motion and loss of strength. Next, compensatory postural and movement patterns develop as the body attempts to correct itself. At this point, the muscles are no longer pulling on the skeletal system as originally designed. The proprioceptors begin to send the wrong information to the CNS regarding body position.

At first, the CNS may recognize the information is incorrect. If the wrong information is communicated long enough, however, the body accommodates to it. Herein lies the danger because the body no longer recognizes its need for change. The "wrong" posture now feels like the "right" position.

When it is broken down into its most simple components, there are two basic players in the balance game. One is the surface, the other is the body. The *surface* is the constant component of the two. In other words, the surface will not change to accommodate deficiencies in the body. It is the body's job to make whatever changes are necessary to accommodate to the surface. When you ask a body that no longer knows where its center is to function on an unaccommodating surface, the body is inclined to become off-balance and potentially fall.

The lost awareness of the center is a very common phenomenon among most of my patients. As a matter of fact, the lack of body awareness demonstrated by most people is surprising. A postural evaluation quickly reveals the underlying cause for this. There are a few postural deviations I find in nearly everyone I evaluate.

One of the first things I notice when I ask patients to stand normally in front of me is that they do not stand with their feet evenly in the same plane as if their toes are on a line; instead, one foot is always behind the other. When they correct their stance, it becomes obvious that *one side of the body* is either in front of or behind the other side. This is most noticeable at the shoulder and the pelvis on the same side of the body, but sometimes the shoulder is *forward* on one side, and the pelvis is *backward* on the opposite side or vice versa. Either way, there is a twisting of the body in reference to the center of gravity. This is evidence of muscle imbalance and fascial strain.

Another common finding is in the position of the pelvis. Instead of being level when the hands are on the hips, one side is often higher than the other. Or, one or both sides may be tilted forward or backward. Any of these changes in the position of the pelvis will affect all the muscles attaching to it. This primarily includes the abdominals and the large muscles on the front and the back of the thighs. These muscles are considered to be the most important muscles involved in coordinating movement between the trunk and the lower extremities. Other muscles more indirectly affected are on the front and the back of the calf as well as in the arch of the back. This complete group of muscles is most responsible for our posture. Any deviation in the position of the pelvis alone has the potential to greatly affect our balance.

Finally, the position of the head is nearly always slightly turned to one side as well as tilted back. The head is also commonly held out in front of the chest instead of balancing evenly over the trunk.

Whenever any of these deviations are corrected, the person *then* begins to complain of "feeling weird." One of the most interesting and thought-provoking things I have noticed in these postural changes is that they are present to some degree in everyone I evaluate regardless of their diagnosis. They are surely evident in most of us.

Postural distortions are not limited to people who obviously have poor posture. Imbalanced bodies include many people who are not literally losing their balance; instead, people accommodate to the postural changes in their bodies so well they are not noticeable. Even the person doing the compensating has not yet noticed what he or she is doing.

The best illustration of this accommodation occurs when the rotation of the head is corrected. When the head is brought into the midline, the person reports feeling very awkward. A positional mistake made with the head and neck creates a positional mistake with the eyes and ears. All these areas provide critical sensory information to the CNS for interpretation and maintenance of balance. For the eyes to look straight forward when the head is turned, the eye muscles must pull on an angle rather than straight forward. When this position of the head is corrected and the eyes must now look straight forward, the person feels very uncomfortable. This discomfort is evidence of proprioceptive changes already present in the muscles of the eyes and the neck. The inner ear houses critical structures for balance. When the position of the ears is altered because the position of the head is altered, balance is further jeopardized.

Massage therapists suggest the soft tissues of our body have "memory" of previous trauma. I suggest these objective findings are the tangible manifestation of that memory. These discrepancies may seem minor at the time, especially if they are not creating any functional deficits. What kind of problems will they cause in the future if they are left untreated for the next five, ten, twenty, or thirty years? It's similar to the principle of a trajectory that is only five to ten degrees off course. Eventually, it is nowhere near its original course. If we could go back in time, would we have discovered these same problems in people who are now older and falling occasionally or frequently? I think we would.

If you are willing to consider this premise to be correct, this observation becomes very significant in a preventative way. When these asymmetries are detected in our posture and corrected *before they actually cause a balance disturbance*, we interrupt a dysfunctional pattern in our body that can eventually lead to more noticeable balance disturbances and potential falls. This is why it is critical to do these exercises from a position of correct posture. When the muscles are asked to move from a centered foundation, the proprioceptors are retrained to recognize the center of the body.

Check It out Yourself

There are a few ways you can check for asymmetries already existing in your own body.

1. **See if your hip rotation is equal on both sides.** The normal range of motion (ROM) is forty-five degrees in each direction. This can be easily assessed as in **illustration A**:

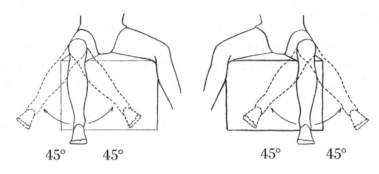

• Symmetrical hip rotation •

Illustration A

In reality, most patients present with an obvious imbalance. The measurements I shared about my knee patient on page 158 represent what I frequently see.

	Right	Left	
Hip flexion	100°	105°	
Hip internal rotation	25°	33°	*Notice that significant discrepancies lie at the hips as well as at the knee.*
Hip external rotation	35°	25°	
Straight leg raise	46°	70°	
Knee flexion	142°	150°	
Knee Extension	0°	0°	

His measurements look more like **illustration B**:

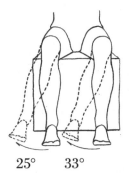 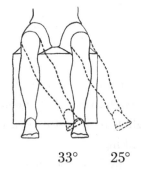

25°   33°   33°   25°

• Flip-flopped asymmetry •

Illustration B

Not only are the measurements unequal on each leg, but they are also reversed in their inequality when each leg is compared to the other. The external rotation is greater on the right leg, but internal rotation is greater on the left leg. The asymmetry is flip-flopped. Another very common imbalance is like **illustration C** (below), where the external rotation in both legs is significantly less than the internal rotation or vice versa. The legs are "symmetrically asymmetric." It's no wonder this type of imbalance can and will eventually lead to a loss of balance.

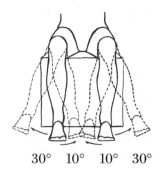

30°   10°   10°   30°

• Symmetrically asymmetric •

Illustration C

Imagine what it would feel like to ride in a car if the tire pressures varied to these extremes. I had a conversation about tire imbalance with a technician one day while I was having my tires rotated. I asked him what makes a car pull to one side or the other. Assuming the car is properly aligned, he said the car will pull to one side when there is a bad tire on that side. He went on to say the car would pull to the other side if the bad tire was moved to the other side. Each tire individually has the potential to create this effect.

People do the same thing. Even when a person is not losing their balance enough to fall, I frequently hear reports from those who cannot walk straight to their destination. They notice they "drift to one side" while they are walking.

This is why it is fundamental to this approach to exercise all the four quadrants of the body. Each quadrant is the equivalent of a tire on your car. When one area is "out of balance" within itself, it is capable of disturbing the balance of the entire system. That is what I mean when I say, "We are the sum of our parts."

UNbalanced x 1 + Balanced x 3 =
UNBALANCED
Balanced + balanced + balanced + balanced =
BALANCED

2. **Check for equality in your straight leg raise** (SLR). To check your ROM for this, position yourself like exercise 3B of the lower body exercises. Inequality in your SLR verifies that the large muscles of the thigh are not pulling evenly on the pelvis. Note the asymmetry in the previous ROM example. The SLR is forty-six degrees on the right and seventy degrees on the left. This type of deficiency can definitely disturb your balance.

3. **Check your endurance for completing a single heel raise.** This test will give you some quick information about your lower leg strength and endurance. Be sure your toes are even. Put your toes on a line if you need that kind of assistance. Now go up and down on your toes twenty times. Make a mental note of any difficulties. Now

try to do the same thing with one leg at a time. Try to do twenty heel raises on the right and then twenty on the left. If there is a difference in your tolerance from one leg to the other, there is the potential for this asymmetry to create a balance disturbance.

There are three things to watch for while doing this test:

1. Do not push yourself to twenty repetitions if you are having a hard time just doing ten, for example. This is just a test to assess your *tolerance*. Do what you *tolerate*.
2. Be sure your toes are lined up evenly. One patient had no difficulty completing this task through a full range of motion when I allowed her to keep one foot in front of the other. When we brought the left foot forward to be evenly aligned with the right, she had a very poor tolerance for the heel raise on the left. She also experienced a very sharp pain in her left calf during the exercise. This pain, in turn, limited her range of motion by fifty percent.
3. If pain, or a lack of strength, hinders your ability to go up on your toes at all, then try to stand on one leg at a time. Time yourself and see if your times are equal on both legs. Again, the differences in your outcomes are evidence of asymmetries already present.

Balance Disorder Secondary to Range-of-Motion Deficits

This next case history clearly illustrates how range-of-motion deficits eventually result in gait deviations. I met with a very gracious and vibrant eighty-six-year-old woman who felt unsure of herself on stairs or uneven surfaces while she was walking. A quick review of her medical history explains why.

At six years of age, she broke out the front windshield of the car she was in with her forehead during an accident. The scar over her left eye and top lip were still noticeable. The left eye had also deviated to the left since the time of the accident. She had not had any functional limitations because of her eye throughout her lifetime but required surgical removal of bilateral cataracts in 2004 and 2006. She was hospitalized numerous times in her twenties and thirties for severe bouts with asthma.

Her health was then very good until her late seventies when she developed hip and knee pain. Her left hip was replaced in 2003, and then both knees were replaced in 2006. She said she had always "hoped to feel a little better than she did" after surgery each time, but she thought her age was the obstacle hindering her improvement. Her joints were not painful, but they were stiff. The only pain she complained of was over her sacrum and in her lower back from 2/10 to 7/10 while standing or walking.

At the time of her evaluation, she required eight centimeters of support under her head to stabilize her head and neck in neutral. Her lower extremity range-of-motion measurements were as follows:

	Right	Left
Hip flexion	100°	60°
Hip internal rotation	32°	32°
Hip external rotation	16°	12°
Straight leg raise	—	—
Knee flexion	0°–120°	-15°–110°
Cervical stabilization required		8 cm

She was forward bent approximately thirty degrees at the waist. Her left shoulder dropped down lower than the right. Her tolerance for standing on one leg was eight seconds on the right and four seconds on the left while I held her hands for gentle support. Without support from her upper extremities, she was unable to stand on either leg alone.

The eye exercises were initially very fatiguing even when performed in the seated position, but she immediately noticed more relaxation in her left knee for straightening after she completed the eye exercises. She also stood much straighter at the waist but continued to be slightly tilted to the left. After completing the eye exercises in supine, she felt like she could move easily enough "to go dancing." Her standing posture improved even more as she was no longer tilted to the left. By the time she was able to complete seven repetitions of her eye, head, and neck exercises in supine, she no longer required her prescription medication for her morning lower back pain. If she needed any meds at all, Tylenol was sufficient. About one week after beginning the lower body exercises, she tolerated an outing with her family without any increased lower back pain. In addition, she felt very safe and steady with her cane for assistance. Prior to beginning her therapy, she did not attempt outings away from home without her walker.

The changes in her range of motion at the time of discharge were as follows:

	Right	Left
Hip flexion	70°	60°
Hip internal rotation*	32°	32°
Hip external rotation	22°	22°
Straight leg raise	—	—
Knee flexion	0°–93°	0°–85°
Cervical stabilization required		2 cm

It was interesting to note how much worse her measurements for hip and knee flexion were at the time of her discharge. As you will soon read, this change surprisingly did not have a negative effect on her function. This loss of motion was the direct result of progressing her exercises to the no. 1 lower body progression for full body on pillows four days prior to her discharge. She felt great the day she did the program on full pillows but noticed more stiffness the following day. This is a good example of what can happen in response to the pillow progression initially. I recommended she regress her positioning to flat supine or even seated again to regain improved flexibility. She could once again attempt the pillow progression if she felt like it was necessary. Some people are very happy with the extent of their improvement without ever including the pillow progression as part of their personal program. I am confident if we had more time to work together, the motion in her lower extremities would have been restored to her initial evaluation status.

Even more interesting to me was the continued improvement she showed in the range of motion of her neck. The amount of support she required for stabilization at the time of discharge was only two centimeters as compared to the eight centimeters she required at the time of her initial evaluation.

She will attest to noticeable improvements in her function and stamina in her letter. To what exactly can I attribute this improvement? Did she generally function better because the improvement in her neck overrode the decline in her lower extremities? Did she function better because her lower extremities range of motion were now more symmetrical in spite of the fact that they were somewhat less? Ultimately, the combination of these changes did provide her with an improved functional outcome.

There are already many good exercises and treatment strategies available to treat balance disturbances. I have treated a few patients who did not improve their balance by using the standard approach. On these occasions, **Rapid Release** has been a good program to begin with. In time, more standard balance activities are integrated into their rehab program. Eventually, their program may consist only of standard balance exercises and activities.

This patient had not previously experienced much change with standard exercises for balance and lower extremity strengthening. This is how she contrasts the different exercise approaches in her own words:

> *Dear Nancy,*
>
> *When my doctor suggested I see a physical therapist for my balance, I was expecting to go through the "same old thing" I had done when I had hip surgery and another time after I had fallen. Once I got started with you though, I realized I had never been given anything like what you were doing. Your exercises got me pleasantly excited as I felt my eyes having such a relaxing effect on my lower back, hips and knees. I knew I had never experienced anything like this in therapy before!*
>
> *Shortly after we completed our sessions, I went on vacation with some of my children. They were so surprised when I could walk up and down hills with them and keep up much of the time. I even surprised myself! My daughter who lives nearby says this is the best she has seen me do in quite a while. I look forward to getting out and do not even mind walking if a handicapped space is not available.*
>
> *One of the most amazing things that has come out of my sessions with you is I no longer have any lower back pain and I feel more energized. Before our therapy, I only had enough energy to sleep! And my doctor was sure pleased when she did*

not have to renew my prescription for my pain medicine. I have been able to maintain my "no pain" state by doing something as silly and as simple as correcting the position of my head while I sleep and by doing my eye exercises.

Experiencing your exercises firsthand has helped me understand how my whole body works together. The improvement I have seen has motivated me to keep up with my exercises. Your vision for change needs to be heard!

Thanks so much for all of your inspiration!

Poor Posture and Balance

It is not rocket science to presume that poor posture might contribute to poor balance. I am being reminded of this several times a day now that I am working entirely with the elderly. We are all familiar with the typical posture so many of our senior citizens demonstrate. The upper back is rounded out, the shoulders are forward to a certain degree, and the head is forward or out in front of the shoulders a certain amount. There is a trend in the supine posture of these patients that is easily corrected. Even though most of these people sleep on their sides, when I position them on their backs, they always position their pillow below their shoulders and across their upper backs. If they happen to sleep on their backs, they always pull the pillow down onto their upper back. This immediately rolls their shoulders forward. The amount of forward head they demonstrate varies, but sometimes they require a folded towel under their heads in addition to their pillow to stabilize their head. Looking up with their eyes is usually difficult for these patients, but as that particular exercise improves, standing more straight also improves.

In addition to developing a "forward head" posture, it is not uncommon to see an older person walking behind his or her walker a fair amount while bending forward at the waist. Interestingly enough, looking up with the eyes seems to have a strong connection to correcting this postural defect as well. This posture is illustrated by a current patient of mine who did not recall ever taking a significant fall in his lifetime or being in a MVA. The most traumatizing events he recalled to his body occurred while he was on the diving team in college. He remembered several painful "belly flops" and improper entrances into the water with his head. It makes sense to me that trauma to the abdomen in that way could result in fascial shortening on the torso because we so rarely stretch out the front side of our body doing backbends, etc.

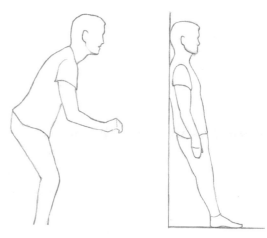

We used the standing extension exercises in therapy to correct this posture, but we modified the exercises a bit. When this patient was instructed to step away from the counter about a foot, he was able to stand with his torso upright. This provided the opportunity for the eyes, neck, jaw, tongue, and both arms to move from a position of correct alignment. The goal then was to gradually tolerate the exercises with the feet back underneath the body where they belong.

The most dramatic postural change I have witnessed involved a patient's sitting and standing posture. This particular seventy-seven-year-old female was admitted to our facility following a total hip replacement on the left. Six months prior, her right hip had been replaced. Her hips, however, were not hindering her rehabilitation as much as her eyes. *Her eyes appeared to be immovable from the bottom of her eye sockets.* It was so difficult for her to look up with her eyes while sitting that she literally slouched down as far as possible in her wheelchair with her head tilted back on the back of the seat so she could see the world from the very bottom of her orbits. This created a significant problem when it came to standing. When her head and neck were positioned in correct alignment while she stood so she could look straight forward with her eyes, she would immediately fall backward.

I began with her, as I do with everyone, by assessing and correcting her supine posture. She slept on her back but positioned her pillows in a way I had not seen before. She slept with two pillows, but they were not positioned on top of each other; instead, one pillow was under her upper back and the other pillow underneath her head. She then tilted her head back into an extreme amount of cervical extension, held her book on her abdomen, and read with her eyes positioned in the very bottom of her eye sockets every night for two to three hours. This was the position she fell asleep in every night. After removing the pillow from her upper back and repositioning her head in correct cervical alignment on one pillow, we discussed the option of holding her book parallel with the ceiling in front of her face to read. *Interestingly, she was unable to do this because she could not actively lift her eyes from the bottom of her eye sockets. When she attempted to lift her eyes, her head immediately pulled back into extension instead.* We raised the head of the bed ten degrees to help her maintain correct alignment of her neck. She was very compliant with the instructions I gave her to correct her sleeping position. She even discontinued reading at night to assure that she would keep her neck in the correct position. In addition to assuming this position for sleep, I suggested she rest in this position for an hour or so after lunch each day.

She required a moderate amount of assistance to stand from her wheelchair the next day and maximum assistance from myself to maintain her standing balance. Without help, she immediately lost her balance and fell back into her wheelchair. As we began the seated exercises, her eye motion was sluggish with poor endurance in all directions, but looking up was the most difficult. Her eyes did well to reach the center of the orbit. After completing 3x2 eye movements in each direction, I returned to the up and down movements for another 3x2. By the end of the eye series, she was easily lifting her eyes above the center of the orbit. We progressed our way down her body according to the handout. She was much like many others I have worked with who demonstrated a significant lack of coordination in their upper extremities and poor body awareness throughout their bodies. After the exercises were completed, she was able to stand from her wheelchair with only "contact guard assistance" or less than minimal assistance. She was also able to maintain her standing balance completely independently for more than thirty seconds.

It was also important for her to correct her sitting posture throughout the day, which took some concerted effort and attention on her part. She was so accustomed to being slouched down in her chair that she had great difficulty pulling her pelvis back in her chair. In fact, she could not do it completely. Her pelvis, or buttocks, lacked two inches or so of reaching the back when she tried as hard as she could to sit up straight. A pillow was needed in the back of her chair to help her sit up straight until this improved. After three or four days of doing the seated and modified supine exercises, she was able to correct her sitting posture and maintain her pelvis back in the seat comfortably.

She did not, of course, experience a steady uphill improvement with her sitting posture or her balance. She found herself slouching a bit and tilting her head back again out of habit. This would, in turn, have a negative impact on her standing balance. But overall, she was progressing in the right direction. On several occasions before the end of the week, she was able to stand independently for one minute at a time, even though it was very tiring for her.

The benefits of making sitting and supine postural corrections were most evident in her transfers and her balance. Within ten days of beginning the program, she was transferring "standby assist." This means she could stand herself from one surface using her front-wheeled walker or a grab bar and move herself to another surface while another person was close by "to spot" her activity but is not needed to provide any of the effort. She was also able to stand next to a counter for support for ten minutes to complete the standing exercises for her eyes, neck, and arms. During her last week at our facility, I instructed her family how to progress the exercises with her at home to further improve her flexibility and posture. She was in a good place at her time of discharge to begin more specific balance training with the therapists who would continue her therapy at home.

This patient also depicts an interesting observation I have made over the years. I have noticed that my elderly patients with knee pain often display a very swollen area in the upper medial corner of their eyelid. It will look like a pea has been slipped underneath their skin.

This patient also presented with excessive swelling, or "bags," under both eyes. This type of swelling around the eyes is not normal, even though it may be fairly common. It indicates that something out of the ordinary is going on around the eyes. It was clear this patient's eyes were involved in her dysfunction following surgery. If you have this type of chronic swelling around your eyes and pain elsewhere in your body, the swelling may be an indication that your eyes are part of your problem and may be part of your solution.

Poor Proprioception and Balance

This fifty-eight-year-old female's balance problems started after she twisted her right ankle and fell forward onto both hands eleven years ago. Later in the same year, she twisted her right knee during a slip-and-fall incident that required arthroscopic intervention. In spite of receiving PT for one year, she never fully regained her ability to weight bear on her right leg. Within one year, she injured her right knee again while completing a standing pivot transfer. After one more year, she underwent hemiarthroplasty on the right knee.

The surgery resolved her pain issues, and she regained a full range of motion. The only ongoing problem she struggled with was a loss of proprioception, especially when descending stairs. She became unaware of her foot placement on the last four steps. She was fearful of walking in any new area or on a different surface, such as grass in the park. She started requesting a wheelchair in airports as ramped surfaces made her "very dizzy and fuzzy in her head."

She continued to fall three more times, sustaining a sprained ankle on the left and broke each wrist. In addition to her balance and proprioception issues, it was not surprising she experienced chronic neck pain of 4–8/10 constantly with episodes of increased pain weekly of 8–10/10. Her X-rays were significant for C3-4-5 foraminal narrowing, which caused decreased room in the spine for the spinal cord. This explained the pain and numbness in her right arm after spending one hour on the computer without properly supporting her head and neck. She had also suffered from an ear infection in the 1990s, which provoked nine months of vertigo. She was diagnosed with sleep apnea and slept with a CPAP machine and three pillows under her head for three years prior to her PT evaluation.

Her traumatic history was not surprising. At age six, she was the passenger in a vehicle when it ran into a tree. She sustained a laceration to her right parietal lobe and a concussion. From that time forward and through college, she experienced frequent migraine headaches. For some unknown reason, she was free from migraines after college until she slipped and fell on ice in 1996, landing on the left side of her face. The left orbit was very bruised as was the left side of her brain. This accident provoked migraines on the left side of her head and face once each month.

Her cervical movement was, not surprisingly, restricted. Cervical rotation was forty-five degrees to the right and only twenty degrees to the left. Flexion was within full limits at fifty degrees, but extension was significantly restricted at thirty degrees. Unlike so many others with neck pain, this woman's range of motion in her lower body was excellent. In standing, the posture of her upper body looked good until she corrected her stance. When her left foot was brought forward and internally rotated to assume the correct position under her pelvis, her left shoulder immediately elevated and rolled forward five centimeters.

Correcting her posture in supine required a series of correcting many different compensatory strategies. Initially in supine, her head and neck felt as if they were pushing down into her shoulders at 6–7/10. Both ears ached at 5/10. Her lower back felt weak and unsupported at 5/10. When six centimeters of cervical correction was provided to alleviate her neck symptoms, her left lower extremity externally rotated excessively, and her pelvis rotated anteriorly on the right. When her pelvis and left leg were aligned correctly, her shoulders depressed and "felt weird 8/10," and both arms now rotated externally to the extreme. It was not until her upper body was elevated on a fifteen-degree upper body wedge with six centimeters under her head that she finally was able to lie down comfortably while her head and neck, pelvis, and lower extremities were all correctly aligned at the same time.

As I have previously stated, I begin the exercises with most of my patients in the seated position. Sometimes I wonder if I am being too conservative, so I will begin the exercises in the modified supine position.

Most of the time, the patient experiences some form of adverse reaction. For this patient, I instructed her to do the lower body supine exercises at her first follow-up visit while elevated on her wedge. She returned one week later to report that the bridge especially had aggravated her neck pain and decreased her time on the computer to five minutes secondary to increased right arm pain. After completing the full Seated Worker series, her neck pain decreased from 7/10 to 4/10, but her right shoulder pain persisted at 7/10.

At the following week's appointment, the patient was able to report that she had completed the seated exercises daily, and her neck and right arm pain did not exceed 4/10. She requested clarification about doing the eye and neck exercises, so that was the focus of our treatment session. She was provided with a diagram to serve as a chart she could make at home on her wall or mirror to assist her with correct eye movement.

She was unable to return to therapy for three weeks secondary to an episode of severe internal and external otitis with swelling. Otitis is an inflammation of the ear. She required two different antibiotics to relieve the condition. What was most interesting was "how much better balanced" she felt in her lower body after the infection cleared. She was steadier on her feet. The previous tenderness in her right medial pterygoid at 10/10 and left at 8/10 was now no more than 4/10. She resumed the seated lower body exercises daily after her infection cleared but decided to rest her upper body, head, neck, and eyes for an additional week. I chose to increase the size of her wedge to twenty-five degrees in an attempt to continue her lower body exercises in a more lengthened position. She was cautioned to minimize the range of motion for bridging. She was also instructed in the standing lower body exercises.

She was again unable to return to therapy for another three weeks, but this time it was because she had been out of town. She continued to use her wedge for positioning and exercise but found the eye exercises still the most difficult to do. Her eyes tended to wander even with a chart or when she attempted to follow another person's fingers for directions.

The good news, however, was the improvement she was noticing in her balance. The hotel where she was staying had a mock fire drill during her stay. As she was hurrying down seven flights of stairs, she realized she was slightly anxious but had no sense of falling or any dizziness. She also caught herself standing to put her pants on without holding on. At this fifth follow-up visit, she was instructed to begin the cervical exercises on a lower wedge of fifteen degrees.

At her sixth follow-up, she conveyed she felt the eye exercises were increasing the number of migraine headaches she had been having on the left side of her head. To improve her tolerance for eye motion, I instructed her to add the prone lower body exercises to her routine. In addition, I relaxed the tension around her TMJ and in her face with manual massage. She reduced the size of her wedge to only five degrees over the next week. The exercises and the massage both helped her report much fewer headaches the next week and "steadily" feeling more improvements in her balance.

I added kinesiotape to her calves bilaterally as part of her treatment plan over the next month to relieve the obvious tension in her legs that was probably contributing to her balance issues. She found the tape to be another asset to improving her walking tolerance and general sense of well-being. The tension in her neck could still become 5/10 at times but did not exceed 2–3/10 while the tape was in place. She was also started on light strengthening for her scapula, hips, and legs. During this time, her spouse was taught how to apply the kinesiotape. She was also given routine balance activities to further fine-tune her balance.

Before her discharge, she was able to completely remove her wedge for exercise. *She felt perfectly aligned in her body while her body was perfectly aligned* with only six centimeters of cervical stabilization. She also traveled to Canada for a week before her discharge. Even though she carried a straight cane and held onto her husband's arm "just in case," she walked for several hours each day without dizziness or loss of balance. She had achieved her goals to improve her tolerance for descending stairs and navigating with confidence on new or unfamiliar surfaces.

One of the most noteworthy occurrences in this patient's recovery was the otitis of her ear. Massage therapists will confirm it is not uncommon for the body to "purge" itself of toxins and negative energy during the course of healing. A response like this patient's has been rare for me to witness over the course of the last eighteen years, but I have seen responses of extreme nausea, vomiting, or diarrhea on a few occasions. It is far more common for people to experience what feels like a case of the flu, cold, or allergies. I cannot prove, of course, that the otitis occurred in response to her treatment, but I find it interesting that she began to significantly improve after that condition resolved.

Releasing Ankle Dysfunction

As I mentioned in the previous section, the proprioceptors in the muscles and tendons of the body help supply our CNS with necessary information to help maintain our balance. Some of the most important information comes, not surprisingly, from our feet and ankles. Three of my ankle patients will demonstrate why this program should also be applied to ankle rehab. Like all the other diagnoses, these patients illustrate the neck affects the ankle, and the ankle affects the neck. Trauma affects the whole body.

The first example is a twenty-six-year-old male who broke his ankle snowboarding. During his standing postural exam, it was obvious he was weight bearing more on the balls of his feet than over the entire surface of his foot. He also held his head three centimeters in front of his shoulders. When I gently helped him glide his head back so it would be correctly balanced over his neck and shoulders, his weight immediately shifted backward too. He was now weight bearing over the entire surface of the bottom of his foot. The way his weight is distributed down through the leg and then through the ankle to the foot will surely affect the way his ankle feels and functions for years to come.

The next example is a fifty-six-year-old male who fractured both ankles when he dropped seventeen feet straight down off a ladder. His head was in so much extension when he lay down in supine he was virtually standing on his head. He could not tolerate supine at all until he was provided with a fifteen-degree upper body wedge and ten centimeters of cervical support. If a three-centimeter shift in the position of the head and neck, as in the previous example, can affect how the patient distributes his weight in standing, imagine the problems this kind of discrepancy will cause.

And finally, this last patient demonstrates the latent manifestation of cervical tension following an injury to her ankle. She is one of the very few patients I have treated in the last decade whom I did not utilize this approach from the very beginning of her therapy. In spite of the fact that she fractured her ankle when she slipped and fell on ice, her postural evaluation in supine was excellent. She is one of the very few people I have met who demonstrated absolutely perfect cervical alignment in supine. I began her treatment by giving her active exercises for her ankle, knee, and hip. I then progressed her exercises, as most therapist would, to strengthening over the next several weeks.

She was doing fine until she started back to work four months after her injury. Even though she returned to work for only four hours at the retail store where she had previously worked eight hours shifts, she was now finding that ankle tension at the end of her shift was slowing down her walking speed. The ankle pain she previously experienced of 3/10 with exercise only was now fairly constant at 5/10 unless she took ibuprofen. She noticed a soreness in her lower back and tension in her neck and across the top of her upper back and shoulders at the end of her workday. Her supine postural exam now revealed cervical tension that required six centimeters of cervical support to correct her alignment.

Needless to say, I was sure to teach her what I should have taught her from the very beginning before she was discharged.

Ankle Pain after Fracture

Injuries resulting from physical violence should always be treated holistically. A fifty-three-year-old female fractured her right ankle when she was kicked down five stairs by her estranged boyfriend. She surprisingly had no complaints of neck pain and minimal complaints of lower back pain. The constant 3/10 pain on the anterior side of her ankle increased immediately to 7/10 with standing. She had a moderate limp on her right foot with each step, which restricted her walking tolerance to a quarter of a mile with a brief rest every fifty steps along the way. One of her goals for therapy was to return to walking one mile per day for exercise. She also needed to return to her job in the near future, which would initially require four hours of standing. Interestingly, aside from her primary complaint of pain through her right ankle while weight bearing, her next biggest concern was the fact that her eyes had been stinging constantly since her fall.

Her medical history was significant only for high blood pressure. Three months prior to her fall, she had experienced a very painful bout of shingles that affected her left eye, ear, and arm for two months. Sadly, her traumatic history included a forceful blow to the same area of her head and neck four years prior. She had also fractured both hands, her left ankle, and her right big toe secondary to some sort of fall as well as dislocating her left hip over the last five to ten years.

When her supine posture was evaluated, she required a ten-degree upper body wedge with ten centimeters of cervical stabilization to correct the alignment of her cervical spine. She reported at her first follow-up visit that resting for one hour on the wedge three times each day helped her generally feel much better. She was instructed at this appointment to begin the cervical and lower body exercises on her wedge once each day.

Secondary to scheduling conflicts and the holidays, she was not seen again in therapy for three weeks. Her pain had decreased to no more than 5/10, and her walking tolerance increased to a half a mile, but she had a very strange occurrence to report. For two of the three weeks since her last visit, she stated that she "looked like she had a mask on." Her upper and lower eyelids, left greater than right, were so swollen for two to three days she almost could not open her eyes. The whites of both eyes were blood red. As the swelling began to subside, her upper eyelids became very dry, flaky, and tight. The swelling was completely gone by the time she came to her appointment, and the eyes were no longer painful. The tension in her upper eyelid was her only remaining symptom.

I decided at this visit to assess her tolerance for eye motion in sitting. I knew either it would be too early for her to exercise her eyes, or it might be just what she needed. She did amazingly well even though both eyes fatigued quickly, left greater than right. We were both overjoyed when the 6/10 pain prior to the eye exercises that had covered her entire Achille's tendon became very localized to a small area on the medial aspect of the tendon at only 4/10.

I used kinesiotape on her calf for the next couple of visits to help increase her ankle motion and decrease her pain while walking. Even though the tape helped immensely, she continued to limp slightly. I then discovered she virtually had no flexibility in her soleus muscle, which is the calf muscle just beneath the superficial gastrocnemius. This is also when we discovered how much her soleus was affecting her tolerance for eye motion and vice versa.

Her tolerance for the eye exercises had improved over the last several weeks to the point where she only experienced 3/10 difficulty while looking up with her eyes in the seated position. Much to our surprise, the difficulty increased to 7/10 when she attempted to complete the same eye movement while her soleus was placed on a stretch. After completing 3x7 repetitions of the eye movements looking up and down through only partial range of motion while maintaining a stretch on her soleus, the anterior ankle pain and tension of 5/10 decreased to 2/10. Her mild limp was not completely gone but was negligible.

Kinesiotape was used over her anterior, posterior, and lateral calf over the next few visits. Her ankle pain did not exceed 2/10 while the tape was in place but could still increase with more walking to 5/10 without the tape. After instructing her in exercises to strengthen her right ankle, I gave her exercises to also strengthen around her scapula, or shoulder blade, and neck. It became evident her right side in general was weaker than her left side. After strengthening these three areas, she was able to walk on her right ankle pain-free and without a limp. Her final four visits were devoted to improving her core flexibility and strength. She expressed her impressions of therapy in the following letter:

> *Dear Nancy,*
>
> *The thing I will always remember most about my therapy is that even though we were not working on my ankle, my whole body started to feel better, including my ankle! When my family would ask me about my therapy, I would show them my tongue and eye exercises and tell them how much they were helping me! We got a good laugh out of that!*
>
> *Things started to change for the better for me when you taught me how to change my sleeping patterns. I have woken*

up with a stiff, tight, and painful neck 8/10 for the past ten years. Within one week of not sleeping on my stomach, I no longer needed to take the tramadol, ibuprofen, and naproxen I had taken for years to help manage my neck pain. The head and neck pain I had constantly experienced for years was much worse than my ankle pain. I did not believe I could be rid of those pains, but it is all gone.

I remember wondering what did all the different exercises you were giving me have to do with my foot. You explained to me about the fascia and how working out all of my kinks would help my whole body, including my ankle. You also explained how the tape you put on my foot, ankle, and leg would not only help my ankle, but other areas along the length of the fascia in my body. The tape to my ankle helped me get rid of my limp, but the tape to my lower back helped me feel better all over!

Looking back, I now realize it took this injury for me to finally realize I was the victim of domestic violence. Through the classes I took after this incident and by going through PT, I now understand how that relationship was affecting every area of my life. For all I know, I could be dead by now if something like this had not gotten my attention. Instead, I feel better than ever! I recently attended a basketball tournament and went up and down stairs three times a day for four days in a row with very little trouble from my ankle.

The only thing about this experience that makes me sad is how much I miss going to PT, but I don't have any reasons to go anymore! You have done such a wonderful job with me. I am amazed by how much better my whole body feels.

Thank you so much for your help!

Releasing Low Back Pain

A quick search on Google will boggle your mind when you look at the magnitude of the consequences in America alone by people who suffer with lower back pain. The impact low back pain has on our society has been extensively studied from many different angles. In a posting by the World Health Organization, low back pain was cited as "the leading cause of activity limitation and work absence throughout much of the world imposing a high economic burden on individuals, families, communities, industries, and governments. Their article estimates that in the United States alone, 149 million workdays are lost every year to low back pain with a total cost estimated to be between $100 and $200 billion, of which two-thirds is due to lost wages and lower productivity." An article by WebMD from February 12, 2008, cited a study conducted by researchers at the University of Washington in Seattle that appeared in the February 13 issue of the *Journal of the American Medical Association*. The paper stated that "more U.S. health care dollars are spent treating back and neck pain than almost any other medical condition, but much of that money may be wasted, a new study suggests. Researchers from the University of Washington, Seattle, found that the nation's dramatic rise in expenditures for the diagnosis and treatment of back and neck problems has not led to expected improvements in patient health. After adjustments were made for inflation, the total estimated cost associated with back and neck pain increased by sixty-five percent between 1997 and 2008 to $86 billion per year." After ten more years have passed, I would assume the number is even greater. They also commented, "Despite the nation's dramatic increase in spending, little improvement is seen in the patients." Another site, *Money Crashers*, recognized the differing information presented by various health-care providers recorded in an article by Laura Williams previously posted in *Health and Fitness*. The American Chiropractic Association estimates the financial burden of low back pain in America to be approximately $50 billion annually, but the American Association of Orthopedic Surgeons cost was calculated to be $200 billion annually. These totals include expenses for services and medications as well as short- and long-term lost wages and productivity to the employee and employer, respectively. Words like "staggering" and "epidemic" are routinely associated with lower back pain in discussions about the condition. Even with the lowest cost I observed to be quoted in association with low back pain to be $50 billion a year, it is evident the financial burden alone of lower back pain on America is enormous.

Low back pain and neck pain are two of the most common complaints treated by health-care professionals. It has been quoted frequently in medical literature that 80 percent of the American population will visit their doctor at least once in their lifetime for lower back pain. As I have already mentioned several times, 96 percent of my patients have previously experienced one or more falls, motor vehicle accidents, or any combination of both. Patients suffering from low back pain or neck pain constitute a large majority of this population. Unfortunately, most people not only follow up these traumas with limited forms of treatment, but they must also return to jobs that require prolonged sitting, standing, or frequent bending and lifting, which are all very stressful on the spine, particularly the lower back. Most workers who return to sitting also are on a computer for large portions of the day, which only further complicates the effects of sitting on the lower back.

Cumulative trauma, or the effects of accumulated "mini-traumas" in a person's body, has previously been one explanation given for most low back pain. The effects of cumulative trauma are best illustrated by the example of a person who bends over to pick up a pencil from the floor and experiences excruciating lower back pain even though there is nothing particularly difficult or strenuous about this task. As a result of this occurrence, recovering from the forward bent position is extremely difficult. In addition, standing up completely straight is usually not successfully accomplished. Most activities of daily living are restricted, such as sitting, standing, walking, and bending. Falling to sleep each night may be difficult, or sleep may be frequently interrupted by pain. Rolling over in bed or getting up from a chair now requires the assistance of the arms and hands for pushing up if the task is to be completed independently or with decreased pain.

It's hard to believe all this trouble is the result of picking up one silly little pencil from the floor. In fact, the back was not injured by picking the pencil; instead, the specific injury is the final result of incorrectly bending over repeatedly for the past several weeks, months, or years or *accumulative trauma*.

The tasks preceding this type of injury can range from strenuous to sedentary. For example, auto mechanics spend much of their day bending forward. The lifting they are required to do can range from lighter-weight parts to heavier engines. Sometimes this type of worker can identify a specific injury to the low back, but often, they complain of a pain that gradually developed over time or a very sudden intense pain they cannot relate to any particular injury. Prolonged sitting at a desk, computer, or sewing machine, etc., also provokes cumulative trauma to the lower back by virtue of the increased pressure it creates in the lower back, even though the task *is sedentary* rather than *strenuous*.

The solution for reducing the effects of cumulative trauma has been and is instruction in postural exercises and body mechanics training. While this type of education is very valuable, it is often given *after* an injury has occurred. Some employers have taken the initiative to train their employees and design work areas to promote accident and injury prevention, but these facilities may not constitute the majority.

Another common source of injury among the work force is *overuse*. This is another form of cumulative trauma but is usually related to more nonstrenuous tasks. For example, a plant in Albuquerque utilizes assembly lines of workers to organize computer parts or electronics. It is not uncommon for the workers to sit for several hours at a time while they pick up a bolt, for example, and then place it on a screw. Minimal exertion and strength is required, but this same task may be completed hundreds or even thousands of times each day. You would think this type of repetitive activity would develop strength and endurance, but instead, it results in all the symptoms of overuse. These symptoms include pain, swelling, and decreased range of motion and strength, which lead to a decreased tolerance for routine daily activities. Again, postural and body mechanics training and strengthening and flexibility exercises are given to address these problems but are often not prescribed or consistently adhered to prior to the injury; instead, patients are usually seen for strengthening and flexibility instruction after the problem has occurred.

The fact that cumulative trauma and overuse affect the body is understandable. But why can one person on an assembly line handle the same job so much better than the person sitting right next to them? Or, why can one mechanic work the same hours doing the same job as his coworker and never becomes injured, restricted, or disabled? The answer to this question is as diverse as there are people to ask it of. In general, however, the person who is conscientious of his or her sleep, diet, and exercise will fare better in any environment than the person who neglects these basic essential areas of self-care. I believe a previous trauma from motor vehicle accidents and falls also complicates our health far more than has been previously acknowledged. For some, the trauma may have occurred in the past several months or in the last two to three years, but for others, it occurred several decades ago.

One of the most interesting things to notice about people suffering from low back pain is the host of other problems they may have as well. TMJ, neck, and shoulder pain are common. Digestive problems and bloating are not uncommon. Some patients identify headaches ranging from mild to extreme as well as dizziness, shortness of breath, or difficulty swallowing to be problems they experience to one degree or another. When the lower back is addressed with a more holistic approach, the possibility is there to improve the patient's overall condition.

Because lower back pain is such a huge problem, I have included case studies from a wide variety of diagnoses. Let's look at what I believe to be the latent effects of trauma as they relate to a multitude of lower back of problems.

Acute Low Back Pain

I evaluated a thirty-eight-year-old male who presented with all the classic findings of a person suffering from cumulative trauma to the low back. He was unable to recall any specific injury to his lower back, even though his job requirements involved unloading inventory from delivery trucks all day. He estimated that he would forward bend at the waist three hundred to four hundred times each day, if not more. Additional responsibilities included stepping up and down two to three feet into a forklift several hundred times each day. His normal routine after work included sitting on the floor to watch the evening news.

On the evening of the onset of this patient's pain, he was unable to recall any signs of lower back pain earlier in his workday or when he arrived home. After sitting on the floor for thirty minutes, however, he was unable to get up. By using the furniture to help pull himself up, he was able to make it up from the floor but was not able to stand straight for the rest of the evening. The next morning he woke up with numbness in the right thigh and calf.

Attempting to fulfill his responsibilities at work decreased his ability to weight bear on his right leg. He was given light duty at work for two days, but prolonged sitting further complicated his posture to include side bending of his trunk and forward bending. Two chiropractic adjustments seemed to do the trick for him until all his symptoms returned the morning after the second adjustment.

I evaluated this patient at the end of the third day he had taken time off from work to rest. During these three days, he had faithfully taken his anti-inflammatory and pain medications plus used ice packs frequently to the low back. In spite of all his effort, he had seen no improvement.

At the time of the evaluation, his tolerance for sitting or standing was only ten to fifteen minutes. His posture continued to be very distorted by forward bending and side bending to the left. In addition, his head was tilted back significantly to the point that he required four centimeters of support to stabilize his head correctly in supine.

Interestingly, he did not ask for support under his knees to alleviate the low back pain in supine *until* the head and neck were correctly positioned. Positioning the head and neck in the neutral position created a pressure at the tailbone of 7/10. There was no pressure at all in the tailbone with only two centimeters of support under the head and neck, but his head and neck were not yet correctly positioned in neutral. I allowed this deviation in his positioning so he could comfortably perform the lower body exercises. The tethering effect positioning can have on the spine is very clearly demonstrated by this patient.

By the end of the evaluation session, I had instructed the patient in the lower body series of exercises. This alone gave him approximately 80 percent relief of his symptoms. Before he left, I suggested he apply his cold packs to his stomach instead of directly to his lower back. I also encouraged him to lie as flat as possible as much as possible.

The plan was for this patient to return to PT to receive the remainder of the exercise program; instead, he left me a voicemail to cancel his remaining appointments after two days of following my instructions plus doing his exercises two to three times a day. He happily told me all his symptoms were gone, and he would be returning to work. My attempts to contact him to encourage him to complete his therapy were unsuccessful.

On the surface, this looks like a success story that makes physical therapy look amazingly effective. For this employee to return to work after only one appointment of therapy would please any employer. Plus, the patient was eager to return to work. But from my perspective, his recovery was incomplete, and reinjury is just a matter of time.

Take a look at his traumatic history. Most recently, he was in a MVA two months prior to the onset of this incident where he T-boned another car. During this same month, he had fallen directly onto his tailbone, landing on the edge of a step. Four years prior, he ran into a telephone pole with his car, breaking his front windshield with the front of his head. Three or four other car accidents occurred while he was in college. Of these accidents, his car was totaled twice. One incident involved a head-on collision. The other time, the patient ran into a brick wall.

This patient was a very large man. When I met him, he was 6'7" tall and weighed 350 pounds. He attributed his original low back pain to *weight gain* since he had never experienced any low back pain until his weight then peaked to 270 pounds in 1995. From that time to the present, he was able to manage his infrequent episodes of low back pain with chiropractic adjustments but not this time. I believe this patient is now at the point where a multidisciplinary approach is needed to fully resolve his problems. The effects of the pain on his tailbone clearly indicate abnormal neural tension in his spine. By doing the lower body exercises alone, the patient was able to resolve his current complaints but probably only correcting the tip of the iceberg.

I would also like to address the idea of blaming pain on body weight. Of course, being overweight is nothing to aspire to and does not put our bodies at their greatest functional advantage. But on the other hand, I have evaluated people who are skin and bones whose back pain is more intense, more constant, and much more debilitating than this man's. I think blame placed on weight gain is quite often *inappropriately emphasized*. Excess weight can contribute to the problem, but I find lack of flexibility is more universally the cause of a person's pain, not their weight.

Chronic Low Back Pain

I evaluated a forty-seven-year-old woman for low back pain, which happened to be only one of her many problems. *Everything* about coming to her physical therapy appointment was painful for her. Getting out of bed, brushing her hair, getting dressed, riding in the car, and walking into the building all required painful, deliberate effort. *Everything* about my evaluation of her was painful from sitting long enough to answer my questions, standing still for a postural exam, to changing positions for range-of-motion measurements to be taken.

This woman had been plagued by chronic digestive disorders and difficult menstrual periods since adolescence. In her early twenties, she started to work as a telephone operator, which required eight hours of sitting each day. She kept the same job until her early forties when she was forced into an early retirement by disabling muscle spasms covering her entire back. After her retirement, she was diagnosed with fibromyalgia. Her tolerance for any type of activity continued to progressively deteriorate.

She required the assistance of another person to help get her out of bed each morning secondary to full body pain at 9/10. After rising, she ambulated very slowly with the assistance of another person to her kitchen. She kept a heating pad on her lower back while she ate her breakfast, which had been prepared for her by someone else. This helped decrease her lower back pain to 5/10, which enabled her to walk independently to the bathroom to get ready for the day. Her pain throughout the day without pain medication was 8–10/10. She could temporarily decrease her pain to 5–6/10 with her pain medication and/or using her heating pad. Sitting was always very uncomfortable for her with a maximum tolerance of twenty to thirty minutes. Her standing tolerance was ten minutes, and her walking tolerance was five minutes. She required the assistance of another person to stand from the seated position. Her sleep was interrupted each night two to three times by pain. Sleep had not been "restful" for her for at least the last five years. She was unable to even attempt the prone position during her evaluation. Attempting to lie flat supine during her evaluation provoked low back pain of 9/10. In addition to her low back pain, she was complaining of extreme tension and loss of motion in her neck with headaches each morning at 8–9/10.

One of the most interesting things about this woman's history was the absence of any direct low back injury or motor vehicle accidents *ever*. She could not recall any falls, *except* for the time she had fallen out of a tree at five years of age. She was reluctant to even mention it since it had happened so long ago.

In spite of this patient's disability and high level of pain, she responded very well to treatment. She was seen five times for treatment, which included instruction for the Seated Worker program, the lower body exercises, and manual therapy to her abdomen and lower back. By the end of the five visits, she reported the following improvements. She could lie flat supine without any difficulty. She was getting out of bed independently. She was comfortably sleeping through the night, except for one or two times each week instead of being awakened two to three times each night by pain. This had not occurred for at least the last five years. Her sitting tolerance had not increased beyond thirty minutes, but she was now sitting comfortably during that time. She was also able to stand without the assistance of another person. Her pain level now never exceeded 6/10. She no longer required prescription medication throughout the day but was managing her pain with ibuprofen as needed. This would further reduce her pain temporarily to 3–4/10.

The plan of care for the patient at this point was to continue with her therapy to address the remaining tension in her spine. She was in agreement with this plan but called to discontinue her therapy secondary to personal circumstances. There were two observations at the time of her last visit that told me there was still more work for this patient to do. Improving these areas would have helped her realize even greater pain relief and probably longer-lasting results.

First of all, she was still unable to bring her knee to her chest in supine. The full range of motion for this direction of movement is 115–125 degrees. Even though her range of motion had increased from 70 degrees to 90 degrees, there was more room for improvement. The amount of cervical correction she required improved from 9 centimeters to 5, but once again, there was room improvement.

Low Back Pain Secondary to Degenerative Disc Disease

We are all wearing out. Our bodies are largely a reflection of how they have been used, abused, and maintained. The wear and tear of life got off to a dramatic start at age sixteen for a sixty-two-year-old female patient of mine when she was ejected from a vehicle in an accident. In 2006, she was rear-ended. In 2007, she was broadsided. Additional trauma included a fall flat onto her back on concrete in January 2009. Surgical history included a total hip replacement on the right in 1999.

Not surprisingly, her experience with lower back pain started when she woke up one morning in 2004 with significant unprovoked lower back pain. She responded fairly well to eighteen months of chiropractic care. After her accident in 2007, her back did not respond so well to treatment. After several months of traditional physical therapy, she was discharged with many of the same symptoms she started with. It was explained to her that she would eventually improve if she remained committed to her exercises.

She continued to do her home program several times each week and reduced her work schedule at her desk job from full time to part time. Within one year of her accident, she was forced to quit work altogether because her tolerance for sitting decreased to twenty to thirty minutes. She required the assistance of another person to help her rise from the seated position. Once she was up, she found it extremely difficult to stand straight. Any form of walking, even behind a grocery cart, was limited to twenty to thirty minutes.

Her lower back pain never dropped below 3/10, but routine activities of daily living easily provoked her pain to 8/10. Her sleep was interrupted three to four times each night by pain. Reaching into her dryer or standing to cook provoked a burning sensation between her shoulder blades at 6/10 in addition to her lower back pain.

Her evaluation revealed her greatest restrictions were in her cervical spine. Lower back pain of 8/10 in supine reduced to 4/10 when the posture of her cervical spine was corrected with eight centimeters of support. Her pain further reduced to 2–3/10 when her upper body was elevated on a ten-degree wedge. After working through the seated worker series for one week and the full supine program for another week, she was much more flexible all over and in less pain.

By her third follow-up appointment, her lower back pain was isolated to one very specific site and only provoked by twisting. She appeared to be ready to progress her positioning to on top of the pillows, so she received instruction to do so at this visit. When she returned for her fourth follow-up visit, she reported she had done her exercises in the mid-calf position for two days when she experienced a sudden strain in her lower back. She could not recall anything she did to injure her low back, but the strained area restricted her from exercises for two days. I was able to help relieve the troublesome area with massage. She was instructed to regress her positioning to lying flat on the floor again to avoid restraining the painful site and then slowly progress to being on top of the pillows again. I also applied kinesiotape to her calves to gently assist with her soft tissue release.

When she returned for her sixth and final follow-up visit, she had ridden in a car twelve hours each way during the past week. She had no pain, just lower back soreness at 3/10. Her abdominal strength was poor, so I instructed her in a home exercise program to improve her core strength. She was ready for discharge. Here are a few of her thoughts about her therapy:

> *Dear Nancy,*
> *It was my lucky day when my doctor sent me to see you at rehab. I was suffering from a very bad lower back and a lot of pain. He told me of your nontraditional approach to therapy, but he highly recommended you. I'm so glad I gave therapy a try because your methods have been very good! My pain has gone from a 9–10/10 at times to a 2/10 most of the time. I could no longer stand up straight after sitting or roll over in bed without pulling on my night clothes to turn myself. I can now do those things without any effort.*
> *I had been through therapy before, but left there in no better shape than when I started. The "surprises" in your treatments seem to be what have made the difference. It was amazing for me to experience stretching and relaxation occur in my body while I was contracting another muscle elsewhere isometrically. Then I could not believe how difficult it was for me to hold my tongue behind my top teeth while I opened my mouth! I never*

would have thought to exercise my eyes, but I've felt how they have helped to straighten out my whole body! Then you applied tape to my legs and my abdomen that helped to relax my neck and across my shoulders. Another surprise!

I'm not 100 percent better, but I doubt if I ever will be with the injuries I've sustained and the amount of degeneration I have in my spine. But I do feel so much better. Thank you so much for all you have done for me!

Sincerely,

Sacroiliac or "SI Joint" Pain

One specific area in the lower back where pain is frequently reported is at the juncture where the bottom vertebra of the spine and the sacrum meet. This level is identified as L5-S1 for fifth lumbar and first sacral segments of the spine. Another area is at the joint(s) where the sacrum meets with the large bones of the pelvis that sit on either side of it, *the ilium*. These are the bones you rest your hands on whenever you put your hands on your hips. The juncture of the sacrum to the ilium is the *sacroiliac joint*. "SI" pain is felt in the small of the back below the waist. Many times, but not always, sacroiliac pain may also be experienced with unilateral or bilateral hip pain. My next patient, unfortunately, experienced pain at L5-S1, over her left SI joint, and into her left hip.

This fifty-five-year-old female's lower back pain started shortly after she took a fall onto her coccyx, or tailbone, in April 2004. The pain she experienced in her lower back and SI area was always present at 3/10 but could increase to 8/10 for no reason she could identify. Sharp pain in her lower back would refer a numbness and ache into her left lateral thigh as well. Occasionally, her pain extended into the left knee. She poorly tolerated forward bending to make up her bed and was unable to walk greater than fifteen to forty-five minutes. She could stand for only fifteen to twenty minutes. Sitting was restricted to sixty minutes if she could shift her weight from side to side multiple times while sitting. She was unable to lie on her left side, and her ability to fall asleep each night was delayed by hip pain. She had been diagnosed with mild osteoarthritis and osteopenia but otherwise was a very healthy woman. Aside from the fall she had taken in 2004, she had only experienced one other trauma in her life when she broke her nose as a teenager in a MVA.

This woman had received a steroid injection in her left hip two weeks prior to our meeting that had not reduced her pain. She was obviously discouraged by the time we met. My evaluation did not reveal anything drastically wrong, but there were a few minor discrepancies that proved to be significant. Her standing postural evaluation revealed her right shoulder was six centimeters *in front* of her ear, while her left shoulder was two centimeters *behind* her ear. In other words, her upper body was twisted in relationship to her head and neck. This was evidence of tension in her upper body. When she was positioned in supine, she required four centimeters of support to correct and stabilize the posture of her head and neck in neutral. This is actually very little considering most people I meet require six to ten centimeters of support to correct their cervical alignment. In addition, a sizable wedge under their upper body is often needed to comfortably tolerate supine.

I instructed her in the supine isometrics after her evaluation and the seated worker series at her next appointment. She is one of very few people who did not experience any improvement by doing these exercises. At her third visit, she continued to experience left hip pain of 5–6/10 constantly, but her lower back pain of 7/10 was now restricted to times of movement like forward bending.

I was fairly certain her pain was originating at her eyes based on her previously fractured nose. When there is extreme restriction in the area of the eyes and the nose, it often must be approached *indirectly* by beginning to move the lower body first. Unfortunately, the lower body exercises provoked lower back pain that prevented her from completing the supine lower body series. If she attempted to do the eye exercises in supine with four centimeters of stabilization, it strained her neck and provoked lower back pain of 6/10. I finally positioned her on a ten-degree upper body wedge with eight centimeters under her head and neck. In other words, I was now "cutting her more slack in her upper body" to improve her tolerance for movement. The eye exercises now only provoked lower back discomfort of 3/10. Even though we had to overcompensate in regard to her supine positioning, this new position allowed her to start moving.

Her next appointment confirmed it had been worth it to adjust her supine position. Her lower back pain while sitting on a softer type of chair was now 2/10, and she tolerated twenty minutes of left side lying. At her *next* appointment, she continued to report left lateral thigh and gluteal pain of 5/10, but her lower back pain stayed fairly consistently at 0–1/10. I instructed her in the progressive positioning, and of course, she had the most difficulty once again with the eye movement. After completing her supine exercises on the pillows, her leg and gluteal pain reduced from 5/10 to 3/10. It was during this time a friend of hers suggested she try wearing a sacral support to help address her leg pain. She did this for the next three to four weeks. I also treated her leg directly with massage and indirectly with craniosacral therapy.

By her seventh visit, she was doing her exercises in the #6 position on the progressive positioning flow sheet. Her pain was holding consistently at 1–2/10 with an occasional 3/10 after prolonged sitting or standing. She seemed to be ready for strengthening, so I gave her some entry level lumbar stabilization exercises. Unfortunately, she came to her *next* visit with reports of increased pain in her lower back, hip, and lateral thigh of 5/10 for *ten days*. I regressed her lower body exercises to active range of motion again and gave her some very gentle strengthening for her upper body. Fortunately, her lower back and hip pain reduced again to 1–3/10 by her next visit.

Whenever her pain increased, she could always reduce it with her exercises. We reviewed her lumbar stabilization for her to try again, instructed her in some gentle antigravity cervical strengthening, as well as instructed her in self-massage of her ocular muscles. At her final visit, she was able to walk for several hours without increasing her usual level of 1–2/10 pain. After her exercise, her pain would usually further reduce to 0/10.

If you felt a little bit like a yo-yo as you read this case study, then that makes two of us. It took thoughtful modification of the program to help this woman and much discipline and consistency on her part. She is to be commended for her efforts, especially when she initially had such reservations about my approach. By the end of ten visits together, however, she was very pleased with her final results as you will read.

Dear Nancy,

I cannot say enough about how helpful your therapy has been for me. I used to have days where the pain in my back and leg was so intense all day long that my accomplishments were limited to whatever I could do in a semi-reclining position. The pain I experienced significantly impacted my daily activities.

My husband accompanied me to my first several appointments with you. In the beginning, we were both very skeptical of your methods. The exercises seemed silly. How could moving my eyes, sticking out my tongue, and retracting my neck help my lower back and leg pain? But I went along with you and did the exercises. Almost immediately the intensity of my pain went down from a 6/10 to a 2/10 (on a scale of 1–10 with 10/10 being the worst pain ever). The exercises seemed so bizarre to me, but learning about the fascia helped me understand how tension in one area can affect a seemingly unrelated area in my body. Your exercises really helped me! These exercises work.

I still have mild pain almost constantly, but doing these exercises daily helps me manage and reduce my pain. I can now do the things I enjoy. It takes me about an hour to do the program, but the benefits far outweigh the inconvenience.

I consider these exercises to be an extremely valuable tool for maintaining good health. I will do them for the rest of my life!

Sincerely,

Acute Mechanical Low Back Pain

"Mechanical" low back pain refers to pain resulting from completing a particular task or a series of tasks with poor body mechanics that may or may not be associated with repetitive motion. A twenty-two-year-old male patient of mine originally injured his lower back four years prior to our first meeting when he caught a power wheelchair as it was falling out of the back of a truck. His symptoms resolved with physical therapy treatments consisting of stretching and strengthening the lower back. He advanced his exercise program at a local gym where he worked out daily to maintain his strength and flexibility.

He was pain-free for more than three years. He then started to notice "twinges" of pain in his lower back each evening after completing a day's work for a local medical equipment and supply business. His job entailed frequent bending, lifting, and carrying all different sizes, shapes, and weights of various items, such as wheelchairs or hospital beds. He also remodeled the insides of handicapped vehicles to accommodate his clients with all their necessary equipment. This aspect of his job involved contorting his body in unusual ways to remove parts and install whatever new parts were needed either inside or underneath the vehicle.

When his lower back pain returned, he assumed it was the result of using bad body mechanics every day at work while lifting, carrying, or twisting. His primary complaints included an inability to lift a standard wheelchair of thirty pounds into the back of his truck. This was a problem because many of the power chairs he needed to move could weigh as much as two hundred pounds. His sitting tolerance was fifteen minutes. He was able to forward bend at the waist for only fifteen minutes. Getting out of bed each morning was especially difficult secondary to extreme stiffness in his lower back. He experienced tension in the lower back with random sharp pains of 8/10 throughout the day.

Frequent bending, lifting, and carrying would be considered by most as the underlying cause of this patient's problems. Strengthening and stretching the lower body and body mechanics education would be the usual way to address this problem. These modalities are treatment strategies that will be necessary to *fully* rehabilitate this patient. Beginning his treatment with spinal flexibility *first*, in my opinion, was needed to assure him of better long-term results.

Significant traumatic history for this young man included two concussions sustained while playing high school football and a motor vehicle whiplash injury at age seventeen. These previous injuries explained why he was most comfortable in supine with his upper body elevated on a twenty-five-degree wedge and four centimeters of support to stabilize the posture of his cervical spine. His low back pain reduced from 6/10 to 2/10 while in this position at his first visit.

His response to the eye and tongue exercises was also very telling. He first experienced a "strain" in his lower back when he attempted to stabilize his eyes during seated cervical rotation and during tongue protraction. His ability to demonstrate the eye exercises in supine was also delayed by the cramping provoked in his lower back. Completing the lower body exercises in supine, however, facilitated a relaxation of his upper body evidenced by an improved tolerance for eye and tongue motion in sitting.

He soon tolerated supine on a smaller and smaller wedge. By his fifth visit, he was able to complete the supine program on full pillows, including the eye exercises. His comment when he finished was "I feel like a million bucks!" He elaborates more fully on his experience in the following letter:

> *Dear Nancy,*
>
> *When you first gave me stretches to help my lower back pain, I thought "Really, is she kidding?" I had played high school football and baseball and even gone on to play some minor league baseball. I felt like I needed to be in the weight room! Then it occurred to me on my way home from my appointment that my last physical therapist gave me strengthening exercises for my back when I originally hurt myself. The exercises helped at the time, but my problem had come back! So I decided trying something new would not hurt.*
>
> *The first thing about your treatment that surprised me was how relaxing it was for my lower back when I went through the simple isometrics while lying on my back. On the other hand, I must say I was **shocked** when I felt the tension **increase** in my lower back when I moved my eyes! Needless to say, the obvious response of my body to such simple things motivated me to better understand your approach.*
>
> *Not long after I started your exercises, the pain in my lower back was significantly better. And again to my surprise, I noticed other changes too. My daily posture was more relaxed. I felt more balanced. I thought I was only imagining that I felt taller until my friends and family asked me if I was still growing! The changes in my posture also helped my pitching. My left shoulder would not get as sore from throwing and would not stay sore as long. My leg kick became higher which improved my ability to drive my body into a harder pitch. I've also noticed that my running stride is longer.*
>
> *I've recommended your exercises to several of my baseball friends, but they are skeptical. Of course, I understand because I've been there! But you've opened my eyes to consider other*

> *kinds of exercise. When we're done, I may check out a yoga class!*
>
> *Thanks for your help, Nancy. I'd recommend your exercises to anyone!*

One of the things I have learned over the past few years of teaching these exercises to people of all ages is to not assume anything. On a couple of occasions, I assumed that because my patient was young and very active or exercised regularly, I could start him or her in the supine position rather than the seated position. I have been so surprised when he or she has returned with severely exacerbated symptoms that could have been avoided by starting things off more slowly.

What surprised me about this patient is that even though we *did* start his exercises in the seated position, the tension in his nervous system was such that eye motion even in the seated position provoked cramping in his lower back. Another patient of mine in his early sixties experienced the opposite effect. A noticeable *relaxation* immediately occurred in his lower back in response to the eye exercises. He had fractured the right side of his face in multiple places in an accident in his twenties. His head trauma sounded to be more significant, and he was almost forty years older than the patient I just discussed. If I had to predict who would have had more difficulty working their way through the program, I would have assumed it would have been the older gentleman. But I also would be wrong. My younger patient had additional difficulties as well.

I always caution my patients that the tongue exercises can provoke an extremely sore throat and even irritate the upper chest. When I first did these exercises, my sore throat progressed into symptoms that felt very much like bronchitis. This can usually be avoided by starting the exercises in the seated position, but this particular patient developed an extremely sore throat two or three days after starting the exercises even in the seated position. Then after progressing on the pillows to the no. 3 position, where the pillows are supporting the body from above the knee to the head, he developed severe chest pains in the left side of his chest. As he mentioned in his letter, the exercises initially helped his pitching shoulder. But as he progressed further, the positioning challenged the fascial restrictions in his left pectoralis major muscle, provoking chest pain.

It is documented in myofascial textbooks that active trigger points in the pectoral muscles are capable of provoking chest pain similar to the chest pain associated with a heart attack. My patient did the right thing to have his chest pain evaluated in the emergency room and was relieved to have all his tests come back normal. But his good test results left him wondering what *was* causing his pain. At his next appointment, I addressed the soft tissue restrictions in his left pectoralis major and minor. The muscles responded quickly to treatment. The result was improved internal rotation of the shoulder from fifty degrees to ninety-five degrees. His shoulder pain immediately improved but only lasted for three days. An MRI confirmed a torn labrum, or cartilage, in his shoulder. Surgery would ultimately be needed to resolve his pain issues, but he was on the right track to be fully prepared for that type of intervention.

Acute Low Back Pain Secondary to a Recent Motor Vehicle Accident

I have chosen the following example of lower back pain following a recent motor vehicle accident for two reasons. First, this patient responded to the exercises very quickly in a positive way. Second, the area that demonstrated the greatest *objective deficits* was not in the area of the patient's primary pain complaints or functional restrictions. As far as this patient was concerned, he had only injured his lower back in the accident he was involved in. He had not noticed any pain or tension in his neck, but his evaluation revealed cervical trouble that had not yet surfaced.

The patient was a twenty-two-year-old male who spent thirty hours a week at his job in retail sales. His ability to stand, lift, stock merchandise, etc., was nonrestricted prior to his accident. After hours, he went dancing frequently and lifted light weights regularly. He walked about two miles every day going from one class to another at the University of New Mexico.

At the time of his evaluation, he reported the following functional deficits. He had reduced his work hours to four to eight hours a week secondary to constant low back pain he rated at 6–8/10. His standing tolerance was limited to fifteen minutes by low back cramps at 8–9/10. He tolerated sitting for sixty minutes maximum. His lifting tolerance was limited to twenty pounds or less. Walking was always painful in the lower back with pain frequently referring into his left leg. He was sleeping through the night but only with the assistance of muscle relaxers. He had not noticed any balance discrepancies but did notice his "whole left side felt weaker whenever he did anything."

When he was evaluated in supine, he first noticed low back pain of 7/10, which readily subsided. *The tension in his neck, however, did not subside until he was correctly stabilized in neutral with five centimeters of support under his head and neck.* During his first follow-up visit, I instructed him in the Seated Worker series, the lower body supine and prone exercises, as well as the side-lying exercises. His lower back pain of 6/10 prior to the exercises decreased to 4/10 after the exercises.

He returned for his next visit eight days later. In between visits, he had done his home exercise program four times each day and was very pleased with the following improvements. He was sleeping through the night without medication. He sat comfortably through a two-hour movie. He was walking to all his classes pain-free. He was able to stand at work for four hours with lower back tension of 5/10 by the end of his shift.

He mentioned he had unsuccessfully attempted to run a little more than thirty yards. He only tolerated twisting his trunk for one hole of golf. During this second visit, I completed the exercise instruction for the remainder of the supine program.

At his third visit, he was only experiencing very brief episodes of low back pain provoked mostly by reaching. He was still sleeping through the night without medication. He felt his quality of sleep was enhanced by the eye exercises, which always made him very sleepy. Because he was now able to tolerate supine correctly and comfortably, I instructed him to progress his positioning to the lower body #1 position with his full body supported on the pillows. He immediately felt a stretch to his whole body of 6/10 that decreased to 3–4/10 after completing the lower body exercises. There was also a distinct elevation and posterior rotation of the right hip and shoulder in this position. This corrected to within normal limits after doing the exercises.

By his next visit nine days later, he had progressed the exercises to the lower body position #7. He had easily jogged one mile the day before his appointment. He had no standing restrictions at work. He had not tried to play golf again but was afraid he still would not tolerate the twisting motion required to swing his clubs. During this visit, I instructed him in core stabilization exercises for his lower body and light resistive strengthening for his upper body. There was an apparent weakness and lack of endurance throughout his complete left side.

At his next visit one week later, he reported continued improvement after doing the strengthening exercises for the first four days. On the fifth day, however, "his body seemed to tighten up in response to the strengthening." This, in turn, significantly reduced his standing tolerance again. We discussed complementing his exercises with a chiropractic evaluation and a full body massage. I also suggested he temporarily regress his home exercises to a level he could better tolerate.

This patient left the next day for a vacation in Mexico with his friends. Either he never returned home or he was able to successfully progress his strengthening program on his own because I never saw or spoke to him again. It is my hope the latter is true.

Many years have passed since I saw this patient. I have continued to learn more about the body's response to these exercises as time goes by. I now understand the tension he complained of on his last visit to be the result of premature strengthening.

Chronic Intermittent Low Back Pain Secondary to a Previous Fall

A fifty-five-year-old widowed female had suffered with unpredictable low back pain since 1988 after slipping on a slick kitchen floor. She landed on her tailbone and then hit the back of her head and neck. Some days for her were spent pain-free. On these "good days," she was unrestricted in any of her activities of daily living.

But it only took "sleeping wrong" to provoke a stiffness and muscle spasms in her lower back and neck of 4–8/10. It would be extremely difficult for her to turn her head on these days, and her walking was limited to "just getting around the house." These episodes occurred once or twice a month. She had no tolerance for sitting during these times; instead, she would spend anywhere from four days to two weeks flat on her back in bed.

Even though she clarified "this did not happen every month," I still thought how sad it was that an otherwise healthy adult had spent much of her thirties and forties incapacitated by pain. She treated her symptoms with chiropractic adjustments for the first year after her fall. For the past twenty years, she managed the stiffness and pain in her lower back and neck with over-the-counter medications, stretching, heat, and cold.

She rated the pain she felt in her neck and lower back at 8/10 when she arrived for her evaluation. In spite of her pain, she was able to demonstrate normal range of motion at the trunk, but her hip flexion bilaterally was restricted to ninety degrees. The internal rotation of her hips was limited bilaterally to twenty-five degrees. The external rotation of the left hip was also twenty-five degrees, while the right hip was a little better at thirty-seven degrees. Her back pain reduced to 3/10 in supine with two pillows under her knees. It reduced again to 0/10 when she was provided with six centimeters of stabilization for the cervical spine. I instructed her in the lower body series of exercises, suggested she apply her cold packs to her abdomen instead of her back, and scheduled her appointment for next week.

She returned to her first follow-up appointment to gladly report she could "make her back pain go away" by positioning herself in supine once or twice a day for ten to twenty minutes. She was already able to lie flat in supine and demonstrate correct posture without any cervical compensation by this visit. I instructed her in the seated worker series of exercises for her homework the next week. As would be expected, she had the most difficulty coordinating the eye exercises.

At her next visit, her lower back was "doing great." She told me, "I am moving around so much easier. I am less tense all over since I have started moving my neck and my eyes!" I completed her instruction for the rest of the program and sent her on her way. She called to cancel her next appointment because she had "strained her back." I did not know what to expect when she returned the following week, but I was glad to hear she recovered by doing her exercises and was "doing great again." I instructed her in the pillow progression and scheduled her to return in two weeks.

When next we met, she was "feeling so good." She had progressed her exercises to the #4 (above the knee) position. She noticed some low back pain if she skipped her exercises for two to three days but could always remedy her situation with her exercises. By her sixth visit, we started core strengthening exercises. With this addition, the occurrence of her lower back pain further reduced to once every two weeks or less. By her eighth visit, which was exactly three months after her initial evaluation, she rarely noticed any lower back pain. Plus, she had grown one and a half inches. Other objective improvements were increased hip flexion to 112 degrees and internal rotation to 36 degrees bilaterally and increased external rotation to 45 degrees on the right and 50 degrees on the left.

I should mention this patient experienced a bout with flu-like symptoms as she continued to progress her positioning on the pillows. During her illness, she experienced three to four days of vomiting and diarrhea as well as bleeding from her rectum for almost one full week. She appropriately consulted with her primary care physician during this time. He followed up on the bleeding but was unable to determine the cause. This was the first time any of my patients reported these types of extreme symptoms to me, but as I have mentioned, I have had several patients report flu-like symptoms occurring at some point in their exercise progression. Were these symptoms a coincidence, or were they provoked by changes in the myofascia? I cannot be positive of the answer to this question, so I am passing this information along "FYI." This patient correctly discontinued her exercises while she was ill, which is exactly what should be done if any type of illness occurs during the course of progressing the exercises.

Fortunately, she did not experience any lower back pain during her illness. Once her symptoms resolved, she resumed her exercises. When she was able to return for her sixth visit, she was ready to resume strengthening. From that time on, she has had nothing but good news to report. Here are some of her remarks:

> *Dear Nancy,*
>
> *I wanted to drop you a few lines to let you how I'm doing. The exercises you gave me have **drastically** changed my life! I have wanted to work outside the home as a volunteer for many years, but because of my unpredictable back pain, I felt it was impractical for me to do so. After discussing my back problems with my doctor, she made the arrangements for my therapy which worked out to be with you. And I consider it to be a miracle to have been placed under your care!*

> *For all the years I have had problems, I never would have thought that one series of exercises could straighten them all out. I never thought to try such simple positions to make myself feel better! If I feel a little something coming back on, I am quick to do my exercises and it all clears up. As a matter of fact, I took a severe fall on four steps in a dark hallway about six months ago. My knee swelled to twice its size. I was diagnosed with a severe strain to my right knee and ankle. I was told I'd be walking on crutches for at least three weeks. When I knew there were no fractures, I started using my ice. Three days later I started the lower body, head and neck exercises. In ten days, I was walking with a cane. In two weeks, I did not even need my cane. As of today, I still have no pain in my legs, knees or feet.*
>
> *I'm sorry it has taken us so long to get together to write this letter, but I've been working 24/7! I am on the go constantly and with no pain! Since I completed my therapy with you, I am now working for Vista, a government-sponsored organization that pays volunteers a stipend to help with needed community projects. I will soon be recruiting volunteers to tutor and mentor middle school students. I also volunteer for two different neighborhood associations. We are improving our streets in one association to provide safe routes for our students walking to and from school. In the other association, we are designing "safe places" for children and families to congregate and play comfortably. I've also rearranged all of my furniture in my house by myself without any back pain. That is a lot said in itself!*
>
> *I know this may sound strange to some people, but I praise and thank God every day I had the opportunity to meet you and to learn these simple exercises.*
>
> *Sincerely,*

I must say I was unprepared for my meeting with this patient once we were finally able to schedule some time together eight months after her discharge. My first clue things had changed for her was her new haircut and color and her French manicure. It has been rewarding to help people overcome their pain and return to life as they had known it before their pain, but I was not expecting to hear about the domino effect this patient's improved condition was having in her life. The combined income she now made from her social security checks plus her Vista stipend qualified her for Medicaid health insurance. Under Medicaid, she is eligible to receive dental insurance, which is something she has not had for most of her adult life. Her teeth are severely stained from tetracycline use as a child. She has multiple decayed old fillings and damaged gums. She is in need of multiple root canals and has an impacted wisdom tooth. Her dental needs are great, but she finally has the means to address these problems.

On yet another level, she is taking correspondence courses for computer training and interior design. She had not told me about the physical and sexual abuse she had suffered as a child that forced her to drop out of school in fourth grade. As you can imagine, several abusive relationships were to follow.

That is all behind her now. She is an overcomer and such an inspiration. She just needed to feel better so she could follow her dreams. As our meeting came to a close and we parted ways, she told me, "My life has changed in unbelievable ways."

Acute Low Back Pain Secondary to Recent Trauma

This forty-two-year-old male patient of mine had a history of "muscular" low back pain he associated with his work as a general contractor. His pain had never restricted his work, however, until he ran into a truck that pulled out in front of him while he was rollerblading. The six to eight weeks immediately following the accident required almost complete bedrest. Getting out of the house for even brief periods to run simple errands would provoke a burning and an ache of 10/10 in his lower back and neck and down both arms and legs. He began his quest for recovery from his injuries with massage therapy and chiropractic adjustments. This helped him get back to work, but 7/10 pain in his lower back and down the backs of both legs developed by noon each day, making it very difficult for him to complete a full day's work.

He went to see his PCP for a definitive diagnosis and advice. His doctor assured him "there was nothing wrong" with his lower back. In other words, his X-rays were unremarkable for any serious injury. On one hand, my patient was relieved to hear there was nothing seriously wrong with his back. On the other hand, he did not have any answers as to why he could not stand straight and why he was in considerable pain regardless of how he positioned himself. By the time we met, he was fearful he would not be able to continue working in the construction industry.

His evaluation revealed range-of-motion deficits in his trunk and hips. The posture of his cervical spine required four centimeters of support to alleviate cervical tension of 5–6/10. After we added the cervical and eye exercises to his home program, he started to notice some improvement in his lower back pain. By the time he had progressed his positioning on the pillows to the #4 above-the-knee position, his lower back pain was minimal at the end of a full day's work. On days his work required prolonged digging, his pain could increase to 7/10 but would decrease to 3/10 after completing his exercises.

His improved body awareness facilitated even further improvement after his discharge. He had sustained a severe whiplash injury ten years ago. When he started to massage his own neck, he was shocked to find it full of knots. He realized even more improvement as he continued to self-treat his own neck. When we met to record his progress, he was feeling great. He had this to say about his therapy:

> *Dear Nancy,*
>
> *The first thing that intrigued me about you was the fact that you had been in an accident yourself. You had experienced trauma to your body first hand, so in my mind, you were "in the know." When we met, I was confused and frustrated. My MD had assured me there was nothing wrong with my back. So why was I in so much pain? And why wasn't I able to do all the things I used to do? He gave me painkillers and a prescription for physical therapy as my only solution. I was not willing to accept constant pain or painkillers as a way of life, so I came to therapy as "a last ditch" effort. When I saw your ability to move around so easily, my "iffy" outlook on therapy began to change.*
>
> *I soon recognized your approach was more holistic and "almost mystical." I was so encouraged to finally met someone who understood my whole body had been traumatized in my accident, not just my back! And not only did you know that in theory, you knew what to do about it! I must admit a part of me was a little skeptical of your approach even though the other*

part of me was relieved and intrigued to hear of the option of a more nonconventional method. Western medicine had pretty much convinced me my options were limited. And moving my eyes was something I certainly never considered to be one of my options! When you suggested I move my eyes to help my back, I thought, "Yeah right," but I was so helpless and hopeless I was willing to do just about anything!

What I ultimately learned was the source of my lower back pain was coming from my neck! I had not recognized how much tension was in my neck until you pointed it out. When I started doing the eye exercises, I could really sense a transformation was taking place in my whole body. Then I started to massage my own neck. What I experienced was a release of muscular tension throughout my entire body! My legs, hips, and shoulders all spontaneously began to relax. Once the tension began to leave my body, I even felt better mentally. I was sensing I was becoming "OK" on many different levels.

Nancy, when I met you I was fearful I was on the verge of losing my life I loved as a builder and living my life out in misery and pain. I now understand life does not have to be that way! Thank you for the return to my well-being.

When I met with this patient several months after his discharge, he informed me he continued to start each day with his exercises and other light strengthening exercises. I was happy to hear he was tolerating anything his construction work required for up to twelve hours a day.

Chronic Low Back Pain Secondary to a Previous Trauma

At this point, I would like to share a letter with you written by a business associate who worked with the geriatric population in Albuquerque and their families. The first time we met, I explained to him the method of my practice. He wanted to experience the exercises firsthand to help him identify clients of his who could benefit from my work. Plus, he had a long-standing lower back problem of his own.

The main reason I included his letter is because I only spent one session with him. Depending on the complexity of a person's problem, there are times when these exercises alone would not be a person's complete solution. His testimony, however, demonstrates the potential of what can happen when these exercises are done consistently.

> *Dear Nancy,*
>
> *I wanted to thank you for helping me gain a handle on my lower back problems. Your expertise in your field and your exercise program has helped me alleviate all of my lower back pain for the past 24 months. Here is my story . . .*
>
> *I have suffered from lower back pain stemming from a helicopter accident I sustained in 1989 while serving in the United States Army from 1986–1989. I have seen many physicians and physical therapists since the time of my injury. Everything from prescription medications to a variety of modalities such as electrical stimulation, ultrasound, massage, and hot/cold packs has been tried. All of these things relieved the symptoms of the pain temporarily, but nothing ever got to the root cause of it.*
>
> *During one "episode" my back gave out and pain shot down my leg to my toes. My back muscles were in severe spasm. I knew then I had to see a specialist. My family physician recommended I see an orthopedic surgeon. The orthopedist discussed the options I had for either surgery or a cortisone injection. I opted for the cortisone shot in my back. The shot worked well. The muscles in my back started to relax and the swelling began to decrease. The cortisone treatment worked for a time, but the aching in my back returned. I knew the shot had been only a temporary fix. I resigned myself to the thought this back problem was something I was going to have to live with.*
>
> *In the years that followed, I developed a routine to help keep my back from giving out. It consisted of no heavy lifting, lift when necessary with my legs, and always keep some ibuprofen handy for pain and swelling. It was awful because I couldn't play with my children, hold them or run after them. I felt like a prisoner in my own body! I was living, but it was not a life of full quality.*

> *Nancy, since I met you and received your instruction on some very special exercises, I soon became aware my pain was not just stemming from my back. There were other causes that did not allow my body to heal itself correctly since the time of the accident. I followed your instructions and continued to perform the exercises and stretching. In ONE VISIT, you changed my life! I am pain-free from lower back aches. I have a quality of life I have not had in a long time. My children don't have to hear "be careful, my back!" from me anymore. For the first time I feel I can look to my future with a positive outlook. Life is tough when you can't sit for long, your legs fall asleep when you sit, or when your back spasms when your child wants a piggyback ride. Life is surely better since I met you. Thank you, Nancy, for all you do!*
>
> *Sincerely,*

This *patient* deserves a lot of credit for his progress. He faithfully did the complete program at least once a day for the first month. He then decreased his compliance to three to four times per week for the second month. Now he continues to a variety of different stretches each day. He is proof that all the good ideas and even the best advice in the world are meaningless unless a committed person applies them.

Back Pain Secondary to Scoliosis

Scoliosis is a deformity of the spine that typically creates two lateral, or sideways, curves in the spine, one on top of the other and in opposite directions. These two curves give the spine an "S" shape. Some scoliosis is mild and hardly noticeable to the average person. In more extreme cases, the curves are dramatic and very obvious because the shoulders and the pelvis become unleveled in response to the crooked spine. The rib cage protrudes and becomes very prominent on one side of the back. In these cases, surgery may be indicated because the imbalances created by the structural asymmetries begin to compromise organ function in the torso.

When I met this seventy-eight-year-old female, it was not because of her scoliosis; instead, she became a patient of mine at the skilled nursing facility where I worked after having a revision done of a previous total hip replacement. She was finally doing well in regard to the stability in her right hip. Her original hip replacement was done in June of 2012. The hip dislocated three times over the next couple of months, so the original surgery was revised in October of 2012. On four more occasions over the next four years, the hip dislocated again. She finally consulted with another orthopedic surgeon for a second opinion. He determined her preexisting scoliosis might be affecting the stability of her hip and agreed to revise her existing hip replacement.

What was interesting about her scoliosis was that it did not develop in her life until she was thirty-two years old. The onset of the scoliosis was a mystery to everyone she asked about it, but it is not so mysterious when you consider her traumatic history. At age twenty-six, she was in her first MVA. She was the passenger in a car that was broadsided directly into her door. She hit the right side of her forehead at her hairline on the dashboard. She explained, "I did not come to for three days." Interestingly, she was functioning during this time but did not remember a single thing she did during those three days. She was even interviewed with her husband for a job at a church. Her husband commented that she answered all the questions they asked her, but he got the impression she was not very interested in the position because of her lack of expression and engagement. She still does not remember anything about that time but distinctly remembers the moment "I came to." She went on to be involved in another six accidents in her lifetime. She was hit from the front, the back, and either side by the time it was all said and done.

Now that her hip was finally doing better, her biggest concern when we met was "the congested feeling in her head" that was affecting her concentration and memory. The chronic pain in her mid to lower back at 5/10 she had suffered with for the past seventy years was also still an issue. She explained to me she remembered crying at eight to ten years of age because her back pain was so severe. Her mother spent many nights rubbing her back with topical ointments. When I asked if there was anything unusual about her delivery at birth, her response was shocking. Her mother spent forty-two hours in labor with my patient. My patient was positioned breech, so the doctor at the time reached up into her mother's womb with forceps and dragged my patient into the correct birthing position while pulling on her head with the forceps. My patient was unable to lie on her back for the first month of her life secondary to the fact that the skin had been ripped off the back of her head and the upper half of her neck during the delivery. Her mother was bedridden for one month during which time she almost died. Upon closer inspection, I was able to see the scarring on the back of my patient's neck that had been there her entire life. Becoming more active in volleyball and basketball as an adolescent helped reduce her back pain during those years, but her back pain intensified once again during her first pregnancy at thirty-two. Thankfully, her pain was intermittent but increased in intensity to 5–10/10 when it did occur from age thirty-two to her present age of seventy-eight.

The way this patient responded to the exercises was remarkable. The first exercise session included rows 1–3 of the Seated Worker. She required frequent verbal cues to correct the left lateral bend and right rotation of her head and neck. The incoordination and rapid fatigue of the eye movements was obvious. She also had a difficult time coordinating the alternating movements with her arms. Because of time constraints, the exercises for her torso and both legs were not completed during her first session.

When we met the next day, she expressed her greatest appreciation lay in the fact that her "mind had cleared." The position of her head was now easily stabilized in correct alignment without any thought on the part of my patient. We repeated the entire seated exercise series, including the torso and the legs. This time when she stood, she was almost straight. She maintained a small curve to the left in her thoracolumbar spine, but this curve, after all, had been there for the last forty-six years. Of course, she easily collapsed back into her usual amount of deformity because strengthening over time would be needed to maintain her progress.

We continued to progress her exercises to the modified supine position and gradually lengthened her body as she tolerated. During her third visit, I attempted to progress her exercises to the standing position. This premature decision on my part became evident when movements with her arms provoked right piriformis pain at 7–8/10. The piriformis lies in the center of the buttock. She was not yet ready to lengthen her arms overhead while her hips were fully lengthened. Positioning her in the modified supine position with the head of the bed at thirty and her hips and knees slightly bent helped her reduce the piriformis pain to 0/10 again.

The next few days were spent making sure she understood her home exercise program. She also was instructed in the massage techniques for her TMJ. This treatment also proved to be very helpful in relaxing the curvature of her back. By the time I left for my vacation, she was fully prepared to progress to strengthening exercises for her back to maintain the new range of motion she had achieved with the flexibility exercises, or so I thought.

I was on vacation during her last week in the skilled nursing facility. We had made plans to reconnect when I returned to write a letter for this book, but I received a phone call from her earlier than I had expected. She explained to me that she had pulled a muscle on one of the pieces of exercise equipment the day before she was discharged from the rehab facility. A trip to the emergency room ruled out anything more serious and confirmed her constant pain of 7–9/10 was probably a strained muscle. It was a relief for her to know she was not suffering because of anything more serious, but she still did not know what to do about her pain. Neither heat nor cold nor topical creams made much of a difference. That was when she called me, and we set up a time for her to visit me at home.

The first thing we did was review the use of modified supine positioning. We then attempted to review the supine eye, neck, and jaw exercises. *We were not very far into the eye exercises when one of the motions provoked a sharp stab directly into the area of her pain.* (The muscle she had pulled was her psoas, where it attached onto her upper thigh bone). I transitioned her into the seated position and ran her through the seated exercises. By the time we completed the series, her groin pain had reduced to 3/10. I completed our time together by instructing her to back up to my kitchen counter. I asked her to move her feet forward so she would be able to stand straight with her torso (page 214). She tolerated the eye exercises well in standing without provoking any adverse pain. She felt good about leaving my house that day with suggestions of movement and positioning she could use if she got into trouble again. She was feeling good enough in one week to meet me to write up the following letter:

Dear Nancy,

I came to one of New Mexico's best rehab facilities on a Monday afternoon. Tuesday morning after a lovely breakfast, I met a dear lady by the name of Nancy. You told me, "I think what I do will help you relax so you can rest better while you sleep." I hoped you were right! After working for over an hour and doing some strange movements and exercises with my eyes and head, I was fascinated and eager for more rehab the following day. The Bible says the tongue is like the rudder of a ship. "Look at the ships. Though they are so large and are driven by strong winds, they are guided by a very small rudder wherever the will of the pilot directs" (James 3:4). Much good or bad can be accomplished socially by how we use our tongues when we speak, but I learned that first day how the small tongue can physically affect other parts of the body as well. When you left my room, I immediately went into the restroom and felt like I dropped 5 pounds! My bowels had never emptied so completely. I then went to bed thinking I would lie down to rest for just a bit. Someone came into my room 2 hours later to wake me up for lunch! For the first time since my hip surgery five days before, I was completely relaxed. My shoulders and neck felt like they had been "newborn." They were so free of tightness and cramping.

The osteoarthritis I have suffered with for the past fifteen years has caused me many aches and pains, muscle spasms and cramps over the years. I now know I can use your exercises that work me from the eyes down to relax and release all of the above.

I have been in several car wrecks leaving me with a great deal of damage to my neck and spine. I have a triple curvature of my spine. Conventional therapy has many times been too severe and added a great deal of pain to my damaged bone structure. Many therapists over the years have told me, "Stand up straight." You are the first one to show me how to do this. Your gentle and thorough approach built strength while relaxing and firming my muscles.

I plan to use "Nancy's techniques" for the rest of my life. The results I've gotten prove the body can respond in a very positive way when the correct approach is provided to rebuild damaged muscle and strength.

A Firm Believer,

Low Back Pain Secondary to Spinal Stenosis

My next patient was still driving and doing all her own shopping for up to two or three hours at a time prior to her current episode with spinal stenosis. Her activity level was remarkable for an elderly woman, and especially so considering she was ninety-three years old. She had most recently been homebound for several months secondary to very debilitating muscle spasms provoked by very minimal exertion. You would be correct to imagine she was wondering if this was how she would be spending her remaining time on this earth. For a woman who was still very independent, socially active, and mentally alert, the past couple of months had made her admittedly and understandably very depressed.

When we met, she was sleeping on the couch to restrict any side-to-side rolling, which provoked lower back cramps of 10+/10. She required pain medication each morning just to get out of bed. Even with medication, she needed her walker and the supervision of one other person to walk thirty feet to her bathroom. She had virtually no tolerance for sitting or standing, so she was completely dependent on others for any type of meal preparation.

During our first visit, I gave her and her two very helpful and dedicated sons instructions to correct her sleeping position. She was using three pillows under her upper back, shoulders, head, and neck to prop her up. These pillows not only forced her head into a very chin-tuck position but also pushed her head extremely forward. Instead, we arranged her pillows to form a thirty-degree wedge. This kept her upper body elevated but corrected the position of her head and neck. In addition, we put one small pillow under her knees to alleviate any potential strain to her neck the new positioning might provoke. Then I got her started on the Seated Worker series of exercises.

Her improvement was remarkable. It was very clear from our very first exercise session that cervical tension was contributing to her lower back problem. She tolerated all the exercises in the Seated Worker series very well until we tried to rotate her head to the left. This motion immediately provoked the cramp in her right lower back that had changed her life in recent months. She was disciplined to complete her exercises two to three times each day through the range of motion she tolerated. Within one week, she was able to complete her cervical exercises through a full range of motion without any cramping in her lower back. This allowed her to confidently ambulate alone 150 feet with her walker. Within ten days, she no longer required prescription medication to get out of bed each morning. By the end of the month, she was walking in her apartment without her walker, standing in her kitchen in ten-minute intervals, and walking in the community for ten to fifteen minutes at a time with her walker. By the end of the second month, she was driving again and independently running brief errands without her walker. Her spunk, tenacity, and willingness to work hard to restore her health are inspiring and praiseworthy. I hope you will enjoy knowing a small part of her through her letter.

> *Dear Nancy,*
>
> *For the past ten years, I have suffered from severe attacks of spinal stenosis. The pain is excruciating as it affects the spine and the nerves surrounding it. The treatment I would receive to remedy my situation would be "painkillers" and light physical therapy. Both of these would only give temporary relief. Most of the time the medical profession would admit the only help they could offer me was surgery. In some cases, that is not an acceptable option.*
>
> *Then shortly after one of the most intensive attacks I had ever experienced, I met you as my physical therapist. Your approach to treating me was in many ways quite different from any previous sessions I have had before. Twice a week, you would explain to me what you were trying to accomplish. At first, I'll admit, I was doubtful anyone could help me. I was very depressed and not a very receptive patient! However, your very professional manner and the confidence you displayed as you worked with me helped me to lose my negative attitude. Your enthusiasm began to motivate me as you thoroughly explained why you were certain these exercises would help me. I began to take my therapy more seriously and slowly noticed I was less depressed. An improved sense of "well-being" was returning. I began to work harder to be compliant with your program even though I did have to pace myself. I found I was developing a new interest, admiration, and belief in how one part of our body can*

affect another part. With the proper therapy, I was frequently surprised when I could feel my neck exercises relieving the intense pain in my lower back!

So, Nancy, I want you to know your dedication to your ideas and your thoroughness in your understanding of how one body part affects another brought me out of my depressing ordeal. I am no longer the "doubting Thomas" I used to be. While I have no illusions that the stenosis is "cured," I do feel this therapy can keep the severe and devastating pain in check. For that I am very grateful.

You are a "natural-born healer" who has helped put me back on track to live out my own philosophy—"As long as there is life, Life is for the Living!" Thank you, Nancy, Thank you!

Low Back Pain Secondary to Spondylolisthesis

Another common lower back diagnosis referred to therapy is *spondylolisthesis*. This is a condition where one of the vertebrae in the lower back has moved anteriorly in respect to the vertebral body below it. This misalignment typically occurs at L5 on S1. If the slippage is significant, nerve impingement may occur, provoking pain in the leg(s).

A very active forty-two-year-old patient of mine began to experience difficulty getting out of her car and poor tolerance for weight bearing on her left leg after taking a long road trip for the Christmas holiday in 2008. The trip consisted of two eight-hour days of driving to her destination and then two eight-hour days of driving back home. It was on the second day of her return trip her trouble started. Her entire left leg went "to sleep" after eight hours of sitting. During her normal work week, she would experience radiating pain in the posterior aspect of her left leg from the buttock to the knee that could reach 7/10 at times. By the time we met, she had been prescribed medication to help her sleep. She was also taking 600 mg of ibuprofen four times each day to improve her tolerance for walking thirty minutes each day. Sitting was not a problem for her, but her standing tolerance was limited to ten minutes even with medication. She commented her pain would have been much more debilitating throughout the day without the ibuprofen. She continued to exercise daily at her spin class for up to two hours without restriction.

She did not associate any particular injury with her current problem but recalled several traumatic events when she was questioned more specifically. She sustained a concussion in 2003 when a car door blew shut on her head, resulting in chronic stiffness in her neck. She had sustained a whiplash injury to her neck in 1993 and 1995. In May of 2007, she fell on her coccyx while hiking.

My findings during her evaluation were the usual but not anything extreme. Her hip flexion bilaterally was 110 degrees, which is quite good. Internal rotation of the right hip was thirty degrees and forty degrees on the left. External rotation was limited on the right at thirty-five degrees and on the left at twenty-five degrees. The range of motion for her trunk was within normal limits, but the torque in her torso was significant. Her right shoulder was anterior to her ear by eight centimeters, while her left shoulder was only anterior by three centimeters. Imagine the twist this created in her trunk. In supine, she only required four centimeters to stabilize her cervical spine. Five degrees of upper body elevation and one pillow under her knees took all the strain out of her lumbar spine. Her homework assignment at the end of my evaluation was to complete the supine isometrics in this position daily plus complete rows 1–4 of the Seated Worker series.

She was a very compliant patient and followed all her instructions. When she returned for her first follow-up appointment, she was happy to report she no longer required medication to help her sleep. She had not taken any ibuprofen for leg pain during the day for the past eight days. The leg pain would return with prolonged standing but was not significant enough to warrant medication.

Her only complaint was of a temporal and occipital headache that was provoked each time she completed the supine isometrics. I modified her supine position to fifteen degrees of elevation and six to eight centimeters of cervical stabilization. I instructed her in the seated eye exercises through all planes of motion, which caused significant nausea. I also instructed her to begin the cervical and upper extremity exercises while in supine.

She was doing very well when she returned for her second follow-up visit the next week. She had consistently done her exercises for the first four days after her last appointment but then had done nothing for the last four days. In spite of her noncompliance for four days, her pain had not exceeded 2–3/10. She was able to reduce those symptoms to 0/10 by doing the seated exercises. I completed her instruction for the lower body and eye exercises in supine. She now only required four centimeters of support under her cervical spine.

I instructed her in the pillow progression at her third follow-up appointment and manually released some of the tension along her spine and cranium. She was doing well at her fourth follow-up appointment in spite of straining her leg slightly while moving some boxes. A quick massage to the involved muscles of her leg got her ready for the trip she was taking to Scotland in three days.

She returned to her next appointment three weeks later after thoroughly enjoying her trip. She did not need any ibuprofen on her trip until her fifth day after spending most of the day walking up and down hills. Her leg became sore on her flight home, but she had not done her exercises for two full weeks. After completing her exercises, her leg pain again reduced to 2–3/10.

I followed up with this patient three months after her discharge to see how she was feeling. These were some of the things she had to tell me as she recalled her experiences in therapy.

> *Dear Nancy,*
>
> *I had started on a very focused exercise program regimen of Pilates, spin class, and weight training along with a specific diet in an effort to lose weight. Eighteen months into my program, I had not lost any weight and my leg started to hurt! When the tests I had run for a blood clot returned negative, I was referred to the Orthopedic Spine clinic. That's when I was diagnosed with a spondylolisthesis.*
>
> *When I met you, I knew one specific segment of my body was out of alignment in my spine, but I could not believe how uncomfortable I felt when you corrected the alignment of my whole body. I did not feel right at all! Then when you gave me the eye exercises, I felt nauseated and started to perspire. I wondered how feeling so rotten could help my back pain! But it did!*

Correcting my alignment and exercising my eyes were the two things that got me better. After doing your complete exercise program for 2–3 weeks, I was ready to go on my trip to Scotland. I had a great time!

I still experience leg pain of 1/10 most of the time. In spite of going to my spin class for sixty minutes four times a week and walking three to five miles once a week, I find I need to do your exercises every four to five days. This new awareness of my body has taught me how to keep my symptoms in check.

One thing I would like to add is that prior to starting your exercises, I did not perspire during exercise. I was exercising vigorously in spin class and weight training, but I did not sweat and I was still unable to lose any weight. I continue to do the same program, but I now perspire during my workout and have lost ten pounds in the last month. This may be a coincidence, but if not, thanks for that too!

Low Back Pain after Failed Back Surgery

I doubt if anything is more discouraging than suffering from pain significant enough to warrant surgery, agreeing to undergo the procedure and then waking up to the same pain you had prior to being cut open. Or maybe your original complaints are gone, but now you are feeling pain in a completely new area or in a different way. Modern medicine has made remarkable strides surgically to improve the quality of life for many people by replacing total joints, valves in the heart, or complete organs, if needed, to name just a few procedures that have only become available in the last several decades. While much good can be accomplished surgically, it is a mistake to ever assume that surgery will always solve all your problems.

This next patient is a perfect example of someone who had agreed to surgery because other avenues of treatment had been ineffective. Even though she could not recall a specific injury to her lower back, in April of 2007, she was very suddenly attacked by a piercing, stabbing sensation in her lower back that did not change for months. Her pain would not allow her to sit longer than five minutes. Her walking was immediately restricted to thirty yards. She soon was reliant upon a scooter for any ambulation outside her house. She "furniture walked" or held onto walls to get about inside her home. Her sleep was constantly interrupted by pain. She received a series of six different injections in her lower back over the course of 2007.

The most relief she experienced after her injections, and only on one occasion, was for two weeks. The other five injections were helpful for less than one hour. During this time, she continued to work at her job eight hours a day at the computer but only because her work station was modified for standing while she worked. By September of 2007, her pain forced her to quit her job and file for disability. She spent most of her days confined to her recliner.

She agreed to undergo a fusion at L4-5 and L5-S1 in January of 2008. She had successfully been through surgery before to correct the problems she was having with her neck, so she *welcomed* the idea of surgery to relieve her debilitating back pain. Unfortunately, her improvement was not what she had hoped for. The surgery successfully treated the *sharp* pain in her lower back, but she now felt a constant *pressure* sensation in her lower back on the left side at 6–7/10. Her walking was once again restricted to about thirty yards by spontaneous muscle spasms she rated at 9–10/10. Her sitting improved but was still limited to sixty minutes. It was extremely difficult for her to stand straight after sitting or upon waking each morning. Her sleep continued to be interrupted each night about six times by lower back pain.

She was tired, confused, and angry with her situation. Her family needed the income she helped to provide, so when her disability expired, she was forced to return to work "ready or not." And she was not ready. She spent her days alternating between an hour of standing and sitting. If this wasn't enough to deal with, a constant soreness of 5/10 in both of her knees was making it difficult to stand. Her persistent pain was a mystery to her surgeon because her X-rays and MRI confirmed her surgery had been *technically* completed successfully. So now what?

I was hopeful after listening to her history that therapy would provide her with the relief she was hoping for. Thirty years ago, she had fallen on a slick floor and fractured a vertebra in her thoracic spine. In the late 1980s, she sustained a severe whiplash injury. Frequent crepitus had been present with any movement of her neck for quite some time. In 2002, she began to experience a constant severe headache covering the entire crown of her head. Soon after the onset of her headache, her head began to bob up and down uncontrollably. She developed constant tremors in both hands. A shunt was surgically placed in her brain in December 2002 to alleviate pressure on her brain, but her symptoms continued. The shunt required corrective surgery for repositioning in January 2003, but her symptoms *still* did not change.

In March of 2003, her symptoms were finally successfully resolved with an *Arnold-Chiari decompression*. This surgical procedure enlarges the foramen magnum, the opening in the base of the skull where the spinal cord attaches to the brain. A portion of the top vertebrae of the spine, the atlas, is also cut away to relieve pressure on the cerebellum, which functions to coordinate movement.

After enduring all this, you can only imagine the frustration and depression she felt when her lower back started to hurt. When her surgical outcome was not good, she was understandably disappointed and confused. Eleven months after her failed back surgery, her doctor referred her to see me. She agreed to try physical therapy but was disillusioned and very doubtful anything could be done to help her with her severe pain.

She was glad she had kept her first appointment when she experienced her pain reduce from 8/10 to 2/10 after only a short time in a modified supine position. Her upper body restrictions were so severe she required a twenty-degree upper body wedge and six centimeters of support to stabilize her cervical spine in the correct neutral position. Placing two pillows under her knees made her even more comfortable. I instructed her in the supine isometrics to do once or twice a day as tolerated in hopes she would at least get some more rest.

She returned to her next appointment two weeks later in disbelief but so appreciative. She was doing "much better" and even had a couple of *pain-free* days for the first time in two years. She was doing her supine positioning at least once a day for fifteen minutes, even though it felt "really weird" at first. Some days she was even able to take fifteen minutes at work to go through her isometrics. Once she began to understand the effect her neck was having on her lower back, her husband started to massage her neck and shoulders each night. Her pain level at her second visit was only 4/10 after putting in ten hours at work. And we hadn't even started her exercises yet. I instructed her in the seated worker series for her homework, which she tolerated well until we got to her eyes. Not surprisingly, the most difficult part of the program for her was the eye exercises. She more specifically had a very difficult time stabilizing the position of her head while she moved her eyes.

At her third visit, she reported continued difficulty with the eye exercises, but she would move her eyes through only limited range of motion so as to keep her head and neck correctly positioned. Over the course of her next two visits, she learned the full supine program as well as the pillow progression. In addition, I instructed her in massage techniques to address the muscles of her face, jaw, and eyes. By the end of her fifth visit, her lower back pain consistently stayed at 1–2/10. She took a short break in her treatment to spend two weeks in Italy. Upon her return, I was especially pleased to hear her pain was still at 1–2/10 in spite of flying across the ocean and back, walking up to six miles one day, and helping her daughter move. These are her thoughts on her improvement:

> *Dear Nancy,*
>
> *Before my back surgery, I had gone through six different treatments through pain management. They stuck a total of twelve needles in my back at my last session. And all to no avail! By fourteen months after my fusion in my low back, my pain was only getting worse. After my doctor confirmed all my bones were in the proper place and healing better than was expected, he referred me to you. I really did not think any kind of treatment would help me because my pain felt like it was so deep in my bones.*
>
> *I was **amazed** at how rapidly my first few treatments caused a change for the better! My husband soon began to notice improvements in my walking. I even surprised myself when I could bend over or reach for things I previously had needed help with.*
>
> *I never would have imagined that stretching the muscles in my neck and upper back could relieve pain throughout my entire back! Or that something as simple as moving my eyes while keeping my head still could be so hard! I had not spent even one day without pain in over two years until I started therapy with you. Your methods work!*
>
> *I thank God my doctor referred me to you for therapy. I believe you and your methods are a "godsend." You have been such a blessing to me and my husband!*
>
> *Forever grateful,*

This patient was also happy to report improvement in her knees. She had lived with constant knee pain of 5/10 bilaterally since the 1980s. Arthroscopic surgery on two different occasions had not helped ease her symptoms. She had been advised to avoid stairs to limit the wear and tear on her knees that would only provoke more pain. But her knee pain also reduced to 1–2/10 in response to her exercises. While she was in Italy, she climbed 417 stairs in the Sistine Chapel without any increased pain.

Just as a little aside, this woman was the third patient of mine in a year who needed to feel better so she could enjoy a vacation in Europe. I joked with each of them about not inviting me to join them on their trip. You would think they would have wanted to have their therapist around just in case they needed a little personal attention. Thank goodness they were all able to thoroughly enjoy their vacations without any restrictions... and without me.

Low Back Pain Secondary to Recurrent Disc Herniation

It's a good thing to resolve the pain of a failed back surgery, but it just may be an even better thing *to avoid* what appears to be an inevitable surgery. That was the case with my next patient who just so happened to work on the orthopedic floor of the hospital. I was on my way to work on the orthopedic floor of another hospital when I was injured. You would think health-care professionals would be exempt from these types of injuries, but obviously, we are not.

This twenty-nine-year-old female was only twenty-three years old when she herniated a disc in her lower back as the result of a car accident. Her pain only got worse during the time she spent in physical therapy. It was decided a discectomy at L5-S1 was indicated. She did well for the next four years. Then for no reason she could identify, her pain slowly began to return. There had not been any new injuries to her back. Plus, she rode her bicycle six miles a day, five days a week to stay in shape.

She was initially referred to the pain clinic for three different epidural injections. The first one helped her for six months, but the next two were ineffective. Her physician ordered physical therapy. She scheduled her appointment, only to cancel it for fear of increasing her pain like she had during her prior treatments. The pain in her lower back continued to worsen over the course of a year from 3/10 to 7/10. The pain in the back of her right leg to her knee was also 7/10 whenever she sat, stood, tucked her chin, or sneezed. Her sleep was interrupted every night by pain. She rated the stiffness in her lower back at 9/10 each morning, which made lower body dressing especially difficult. Finally, one of her coworkers who had also been a patient of mine and the orthopedic spine specialist insisted she give my style of treatment a try. Her MRI confirmed she had herniated her disc at L5-S1 again. Her only option to therapy was a spinal fusion, so she reluctantly came to therapy.

In many ways, this patient looked like the picture of good health. Her initial evaluation revealed some minor discrepancies but nothing alarming. Her trunk motion was mildly limited for forward bending and rotation to the right. Her cervical range of motion was within normal limits, but tucking her chin immediately sent a shooting pain down the back of her right leg. The range of motion at her hips was very good, except for bilateral external rotation, which was limited to twenty-two degrees. In supine, she immediately complained of pain from her right lower back to her right knee at 4/10. This subsided with six centimeters of cervical stabilization and one pillow under her knees. Before she left her first appointment, I instructed her in the supine isometrics she was to do on a ten-degree wedge in addition to the six centimeters of support she required to stabilize her head and neck. I also ran her through the full seated worker series. She was quite surprised when she found it difficult to move her eyes. She was even more surprised when lateral eye motion reproduced her leg pain.

Her first follow-up appointment was not scheduled for two weeks later. I luckily ran into her about nine or ten days after her evaluation. She had been doing her supine isometrics twice a day for fifteen to thirty minutes and the seated worker series once a day. Her low back and leg pain had improved about 30 percent, but she had developed a very large swollen knot behind her right knee. I took a look at this knot for myself, which was easily the size of a golf ball. When I asked her if she was using the wedged position while in supine, she admitted she had forgotten that part of her positioning. I encouraged her to make that change while in supine and suggested she discontinue stabilizing her eyes while in supine and discontinue the eye exercises altogether while seated.

She had been able to implement these changes for about three days when she returned for her first follow-up visit. She was glad to say the swelling behind her knee had improved by 50 percent. I took her through the full supine program while she was positioned on a ten-degree wedge with six centimeters of cervical stabilization. The swelling behind her knee reduced by an additional 50 percent, her leg pain decreased to 0/10, and her lower back pain was only 2/10. We agreed for her to continue her full supine program on the wedge for two to three days. Then she could try the eye exercises again in sitting and reduce the wedge as tolerated.

She was not able to return for another appointment for twenty days. She had progressed her supine positioning, so she required only two centimeters of support under her head and neck. Her pain had reduced to 2/10 constantly in her lower back and leg. I instructed her in the pillow progression. The tension in her cervical spine and upper trapezius increased to 4/10 but reduced to 0/10 with four centimeters of cervical support. After completing the exercises, her cervical tension reduced to 2/10 even while she was elevated on top of the pillows. Her lower back and leg pain continued at 2/10.

She canceled her next follow-up appointment secondary to a death in her family, but I was able to catch up with her three months after her last appointment to see how she is doing. This is what she had to say:

> *Dear Nancy,*
>
> *As you know, I was deathly afraid to come to therapy because the exercises I had been given in therapy before only made me worse. I would recommend your style of therapy to anyone though! I could not believe that in two treatments, my pain was virtually gone! My coworkers were right when they told me you could help me with your different methods.*
>
> *I was so surprised when looking sideways with my eyes shot the same pain down my leg I had been feeling. I also could not believe how much of a difference it made when I did not do my exercises on such a small wedge. The knot I developed behind my knee when I did not use it went away as quickly as it came when I started positioning myself correctly.*

> *It is now three months later, and I have no pain in my leg and my lower back pain is only a 1/10. I'm riding my bicycle six miles, twice a week again, and hope to increase soon. I can be myself again and do the things I enjoy.*
> *Thank you, Nancy, for all of your help!*

I suspect the posture this patient assumed with her head and neck while riding her bike is partially responsible for the recurrence of her lower back pain. While discontinuing her bike riding was not an option, maintaining the flexibility of her upper body and neck as a precaution is. Her case example is a good illustration that some activities require additional exercise to help balance out the potentially negative effects the previous exercise may have had on our posture. This patient continues to do her head, neck, and eye exercises about twice a week.

Neural Tension Resulting in Low Back Pain

I evaluated a fifty-year-old man two months after he was broadsided while driving a company truck. His case example clearly demonstrates the principle of neural tension between the eyes and the lower back as well as the advantages of an early comprehensive intervention after traumatic injury.

This patient's constant pain of 7–8/10 was localized to the right side of his lower thoracic spine. Lightly touching this same area increased his pain to 10/10. His work as the maintenance supervisor for an apartment complex was hindered by his decreased tolerance for lifting, carrying, squatting, bending, standing, and walking.

After assessing his posture in supine, it was determined that he required a ten-degree upper body wedge with eight centimeters of cervical stabilization to comfortably tolerate the supine position. Because his pain was isolated to his right serratus posterior inferior muscle, he was first instructed to do the lower body exercises in supine. He was also instructed to daily apply cold packs directly to the painful area.

He returned the next week with pain of 0/10 as a result of icing and exercising daily. His walking tolerance increased from forty minutes to four hours. His sitting increased from fifteen to ninety minutes. He had slowly progressed his lifting tolerance to twenty pounds.

Regardless of his progress, I made the decision to assess his tolerance for the remainder of the exercises in supine. He now only required eight centimeters of cervical stabilization to tolerate supine while his legs were fully extended. Looking down with his eyes while in this position reproduced his lower back pain to 8/10. Lateral motion of the eyes was "ratchety." Moving the eyes diagonally to the right was very difficult. He demonstrated poor coordination of tongue movement. He was unable to lower his mandible when his tongue was stabilized behind his top teeth.

With his hips bent 55 degrees and knees 120 degrees, his pain was 0/10 while looking down. In 45 degrees of hip flexion with 95 degrees of knee flexion, his pain was 4/10. The eye and neck exercises were completed in this position. The upper and lower extremity exercises in supine and prone were completed with both legs fully extended. His tolerance for eye motion was reassessed upon exercise completion. He was now able to look down without provoking low back pain while his legs were fully extended. Additionally, he only required four centimeters of cervical support to maintain correct cervical alignment instead of eight.

By the end of this patient's last described treatment session, his LBP was 0/10. When he returned one week later, he had worked nonrestricted since his last visit. Bilateral hip flexion had increased from 80 degrees to 102 degrees on the right and 110 degrees on the left, right hip internal rotation increased from 12 degrees to 20 degrees, and hip external rotation increased from 25 degrees to 42 degrees on the right and 28 degrees to 44 degrees on the left. Bilateral cervical rotation increased from 45 degrees to 60 degrees. He stated it had been harder to stabilize his head position during eye movement the previous week than it was for him to dig a 3' x 4' hole.

Lifelong Lower Back Pain

There have been several times in my career I have caught myself wondering, *How many others are there somewhere just like this patient?* Such is the case with the next two case reports.

My twenty-nine-year-old extraordinary female patient could work circles around anyone I know. She worked eight to ten hours each day as a computer programmer, was a part-time English tutor and student, played guitar in a band with her friends, and spent five to six hours each week crafting. This may seem like anyone else you know who lives a full life, but this young woman did all this with constant pain in her lower back and down both legs of 8/10. In addition, she lived with constant left ankle and bilateral knee, hip, and shoulder pain.

It is no wonder she collapsed onto her left side from sheer exhaustion six months prior to our meeting. There was not a time in her life she could recall living free from low back pain or without an abnormal gait, but the fall she took increased the intensity of her pain from 5/10 to 8/10.

Pain also interfered with her function. It was extremely difficult for her to stand from sitting. Her walking tolerance was only ten minutes with a front-wheeled walker she steered with her right hand only because it was too difficult to keep her left elbow straight enough to reach the walker with her left hand. Her best effort to reach forward with her left arm was one and a half inches less than her forward reach on the right. She stepped forward with her right leg while her left leg dragged behind. Her sitting tolerance was ten minutes, her sleep was interrupted by pain two to three times each night, and she was unable to carry more than two or three pounds. Her current exercise consisted of walking as tolerated, even though she had been a very accomplished bodybuilder until just one year before her fall. The pictures she showed me of her bodybuilding days were incredible.

This young woman had never been in a motor vehicle accident but had fallen frequently over the years secondary to left ankle instability. Her medical history included heart arrhythmias, but more importantly, she was born three months prematurely and received a right occipital shunt at one month of age. Her shunt was surgically revised at age two and age eleven. She had corrective surgery at age twenty-nine to address abnormal tension in the muscles of her left eye that caused the eye to constantly pull up and out to the left. She could not remember life without the constant pain and tension she experienced on the right side of her neck.

I made some very interesting observations about her eyes on the day of her evaluation. The first thing I noticed was a poor tolerance for looking up with both eyes. Her left eye immediately pulled to the center. The right eye motion created intolerable tension in her right occipital lobe at the site of her shunt. It was only when she moved one eye at a time while the other eye was covered that the eyes moved correctly and comfortably. Rotating her head to the left with her eyes stabilized forward increased the occipital tension across the bottom of her head; rotating her head to the right was impossible to do with a stabilized forward gaze. Her left eye automatically pulled down and to the left when she plantar flexed her left ankle. It was also extremely difficult to maintain a forward gaze during active eversion of the left ankle.

This patient did not normally experience symptoms worth mentioning over her sacrum, but after eye movement, she stated she felt cold and numb at 7–8/10 in the area of her left SI joint. Prior to exercise, the sensation in the same area was only 2/10. I used the flare-up positioning page 140-142 for fifteen minutes to reduce her discomfort to 5–6/10. She was instructed not to attempt the eye exercises until I saw her back for her first follow-up but to use a twenty-degree upper body wedge with six centimeters of cervical stabilization and three pillows under her knees to alleviate her symptoms and to begin the myofascial lengthening process.

I started her exercise instruction at her first follow-up with her lower extremities in the seated position. We attempted to finish with the eye exercises, but her motion was too uncoordinated. Her endurance for repetitive motion was also incredibly impaired. The obvious fatigue and heaviness of her eyelids as she attempted to complete her third repetition was unlike anything I had ever seen before. The eye exercises were postponed for this patient until a later time.

By her second follow-up visit, this patient was already seeing improvements she was excited about. She found it was much easier to accomplish normal heel-toe gait mechanics with her left foot while walking. Because she was no longer dragging her left foot, the callous she had developed on her left little toe was already gone.

By her third follow-up visit, she was sleeping seven and a half hours each night on her wedge. Doing the seated exercises four times per day had reduced her lower back pain to 7/10 and occipital tension from 8/10 to 5/10. Walking was becoming "less of a struggle." She was also able to turn her head to the right 1/4" to 1/2" while stabilizing her gaze forward.

Because of this patient's extreme head and neck involvement, I decided to assess the soft tissue of her bilateral TMJ at her fourth follow-up appointment. Even though all the muscles addressed were tender, she was especially so on the right side of her face and jaw. Interestingly, massaging the right side of her face referred frequent very sharp pains into her right eye. She was also instructed to begin the lower body, upper body, and cervical exercises on her wedge.

After doing the supine exercises for her complete body for one week, she came to her fifth follow-up appointment able to lie flat on her back with four centimeters of cervical stabilization and lower back pain of only 4/10. Lower back pain while she was up had reduced to 5–6/10 most of the time. She was instructed to rock back and forth on her left foot and ankle to help further improve her gait. She was doubtful about how much this could change because she had tried many times over her life to stretch out her left calf without success. In fact, her ability to stretch "her toes to her nose" on the right measured at twenty degrees of active ankle motion and negative five degrees on the left. Her right ankle was more flexible than usual, and her left ankle was stiffer. I applied kinesiotape to her calves and feet in a relaxed amount of plantar flexion, with toes pointing down, to help relax the tension in both calves. With the tape in place, she immediately found it easier to stand with a more upright posture.

She returned to her next appointment with lower back pain of only 4/10. Almost more importantly to her was her new ability to walk on the treadmill at a one to four incline for seventeen minutes at two and a half miles per hour. She had never tolerated any amount of incline because of the extreme tension in her left calf. When her dorsiflexion, or toes to nose position, on the left was remeasured, she now had positive five degrees.

She also came without her walker to this appointment. Because she had developed some anterior shoulder tightness from leaning forward onto her walker, we decided to apply the kinesiotape to the anterior side of her right shoulder instead of on her calves this time. Her ability to stand upright with her upper body immediately improved.

Even though itching under the tape forced her to remove the tape after only three days, her upright posture was looking better than ever and required minimal effort to maintain. Her low back pain had reduced to 3–4/10. At her seventh follow-up visit, I applied the tape to her psoas muscle/hip flexor bilaterally to achieve greater flexibility in that area to further reduce her low back pain. Unfortunately, the tape to her psoas muscle increased her back pain to 5–6/10.

When she returned for her next appointment three days later, she was walking more forward bent than I had seen her for a while. Applying kinesiotape to her calves bilaterally and actively stretching and moving her psoas enabled her to stand straight again by the end of her session but did not reduce her back pain. At her next visit, she reported spasms in her lower back that were interrupting her sleep again. She wondered if this was not being provoked by a harder new chair she had been sitting on at work. She was instructed to continue with the flexibility exercises she was already doing and was given a few strengthening exercises but mostly for her upper back.

Her lower back pain had reduced to 3/10 by the time she came in the next week. Surprisingly, as I began to review her home exercises, I realized she was not yet doing the eye exercises in supine. Even though she was tolerating the rest of her exercises in flat supine with only four centimeters of cervical stabilization, we learned something very interesting about her eyes when we attempted to move them in this position. With her legs stabilized in neutral rotation, she required two more centimeters of cervical stabilization, or six centimeters. Looking up and down with her eyes decreased her lower back pain on the left to 0/10 but increased her lower back pain on the right to 6/10 and almost provoked muscle spasms. When she was finally positioned on a twenty-degree upper body wedge with six centimeters of cervical stabilization and her legs fully extended and stabilized in neutral rotation, she no longer felt any pulling in her low back with eye motion but felt tension in her left eye at 6–7/10 with movement. She was encouraged to either bend slightly at the hips and knees during her eye exercises or slightly increase her wedge to reduce the strain around the left eye. She was instructed to do the remainder of the exercises for her neck and upper and lower body with her body flat and four centimeters of cervical stabilization since the more lengthened position was very comfortable for the rest of her body during movement.

Two weeks later, she arrived in PT with lower back pain of 1–2/10 most of the time. She continued to have great difficulty tolerating the eye exercises with her legs out straight. In fact, doing the eye exercises with leg extension had provoked three days of occipital headaches. By positioning her on a thirty-degree wedge, bending her hips at forty degrees and her knees at twenty degrees, her lower back pain further reduced to 0/10 after completing the eye exercises.

At her final appointment, she had not experienced any lower back pain since her last appointment, but she was still unable to lower the size of the wedge she required to do the eye exercises. As a general rule, releasing tension in the body helps alleviate tension in the eyes, so she was instructed to use the progressive positioning with her entire body supported on top of thin pillows to provide a mild stretch to her body while she did her neck and upper and lower body exercises. She immediately perceived abdominal tension at 7/10 in this position and felt as if she were "going to roll off the pillows." This sensation was alleviated to 4/10 when she was provided with a five-degree upper body wedge from her scapula to her head to be used on top of the full body support.

At this point, the patient had reached all her goals to decrease her pain and improve her ability to walk and exercise. She was very independent with her home exercise program and motivated to continue to work through the flexibility process to release more tension around her eyes. I followed up with her one year after her discharge to see how she was doing.

> *Dear Nancy,*
>
> *I had been having a very difficult time for about 6 months prior to meeting with you. It all started when I began to experience very erratic heart palpitations. I was sent home without an explanation from the emergency room when all of the tests they ran were inconclusive.*
>
> *One week later I spontaneously collapsed and fell at my work as a computer programmer. I didn't know what was going on, but knew something wasn't right, so I took 2 days off work to rest. As I was walking in the door to return to work, I collapsed again, so I quit on the spot. I was admitted to the hospital's neurology unit where my condition still could not be diagnosed. I was issued a front- wheeled walker by my physical therapist during my short hospital stay. I was then discharged to go home with a walker I could barely use. Two weeks later my PCP gave me a referral to PT to address my lower back pain, but also gave me a psych referral to help me accept my disability.*

When I met you I was skeptical about reducing the back pain I had my entire life, but decided to give therapy a try. I was also convinced there was nothing I could do to improve my movement dysfunction.

Conversations I had previously with different providers about my function usually ended with comments like, "We'll monitor this," or "We'll keep an eye on you." Over the years I came to understand these phrases really meant "We can't help you." When you mentioned at my evaluation that you hoped my gait would improve as you attempted to reduce my lower back pain, I thought, "I'll believe this when I see it." I did not think improvement was a possibility for me.

The next response I remember having to your treatments was being so surprised at how difficult it was to do some of the very simple things you asked me to do. I realized my condition had deteriorated to a greater extent than I had realized. When you told me the tension in my body probably extended all the way to my eye, I wondered if that could really be true. Then when you touched the right side of my head and I flinched, I realized, "She just might be right."

As my eyes started to move better, I could feel my whole body releasing tension. At first I wondered if it was a fluke that I was enjoying so much time without lower back pain. As time went on, I thought, "This just really might be working." It is now one year later. I still do my exercises 3x/wk. Lower back pain is not an issue.

When I look back on my therapy experience, I am still so amazed at how much changed in literally 1 short season of my life! Not only was I able to reduce my constant lower back pain from 8–9/10 to 1–3/10, but I was able to progress from walking with a front-wheeled walker to ambulating without any type of assistive device.

Thank you for not dismissing my concerns. Thank you for believing you could help me and then spending the time it took to help me. I have proven people wrong about my abilities since one month of age when I was not expected to live. I never considered myself as disabled.

Now others have no reason to believe that of me either.

Low Back Pain and Blindness

Helping someone reduce their pain and improve the quality of their life never gets old. It is even more rewarding when I begin the patient's treatments wondering, *How much will I be able to help this patient?* Such was the case with a forty-five-year-old female suffering from extreme lower back pain. She was more tolerant of her pain for the first two years as it came on gradually and intermittently, but when it suddenly became constant and more disabling, she knew she needed help.

Bilateral lumbar pain was 5/10 each morning upon waking. After getting up and about throughout the day, her pain hovered at 1–2/10 for most of the morning but would reach 5–6/10 again by three o'clock in the afternoon. If she waited until six o'clock to go to bed, her pain would be 10/10. This made it extremely difficult to climb the thirteen stairs to her bedroom. Most of the time, she could complete the stairs in three to five minutes, but it had taken her as much as ninety minutes on one occasion. She had to be especially careful not to overeat, which was sure to increase her lower back pain regardless of the time of day.

She tolerated sitting, standing, and walking in fifteen increments with 800 mg of ibuprofen on board twice each day. She required the assistance of another person to transfer from sit to stand. If help was not available, she relied heavily on her upper extremities. She was unable to carry a ten pound laundry basket of clothes.

This patient had never been in a motor vehicle accident nor had she taken a fall. Her medical history was completely clear of any chronic illness or abnormalities, except for one thing. This patient had suffered from bilateral detached retinas during her third pregnancy. Within two years, she was totally blind in both eyes. By the time we met, she had been blind for sixteen years. She wore dark glasses at all times. She had no reason to move her eyes.

One of the things I found to be so interesting about this patient was the fact that her range of motion throughout her body was easily within full limits. Her supine posture was very good, but she complained of 5/10 pressure and heaviness in her head and throat. She required a twenty-five-degree upper body wedge and six centimeters of cervical stabilization to reduce these sensations to 1–2/10. It was truly remarkable how quickly this patient responded to this technique.

When she returned for her first follow-up visit, she stated she was sleeping on her wedge every night with pain of 0/10 while she was on the wedge and upon waking each morning. Her pain throughout the day did not exceed 4/10. The first set of exercises I attempted with her was the eye exercises in sitting. The tension around her eyes was evident and made attempts at movement very uncoordinated. After completing two sets of two repetitions looking up and down and side to side, she was experiencing a slight increased cervical tension. It was virtually impossible to stabilize her head in neutral during eye motion, so I moved on to the neck and upper extremity exercises. Upon completion of only these exercises, she stood from her chair independently without the assistance of her upper extremities. Her lower back pain had decreased from 4/10 to 0/10.

By her second follow-up visit, she continued to transfer independently with caution. Most of the time, she did not use her upper extremities for assistance. She had extended her bedtime to eight or nine o'clock with lower back pain of 5/10 by the time she retired. She was now able to stand long enough to wash dishes without having to go to bed immediately afterward. At this appointment, instruction was completed for the Seated Worker series, including the torso and the lower extremities.

At her third follow-up visit, she no longer referred to her back as painful; instead, she described the abnormal sensation in her lower back as a pressure that never exceeded 2/10. Even at eight or nine o'clock in the evening, her discomfort did not exceed 2/10. Her eye movement in sitting was reassessed and was now very coordinated. When she was instructed in the neck exercises on her wedge, she immediately felt a dull pulling sensation in her lumbar spine at 8–9/10.

At her fourth follow-up, she was able to report 0–1/10 lower back pain all week. On the day of her appointment, the pressure in her low back was 3/10, but it was a very windy day. Windy weather will almost always increase symptoms regardless of the problem. She had even been able to discontinue her wedge for sleeping. I reviewed the cervical exercises with her in flat supine with only six centimeters of cervical support. Cervical retraction in this more extended position provoked a very sharp pain at 10/10 in her lumbar spine. In hook lying, the same exercise provoked a dull pulling sensation again at 4/10. She was instructed to continue to use a fifteen-degree upper body wedge for exercise to minimize lower back pain, even though she no longer needed the wedge for sleeping.

She was instructed in the prone exercises while lying with one pillow under her abdomen at her fifth follow-up visit. Kinesiotape was applied to both calves to further promote myofascial release along posterior fascial lines. She immediately felt "looser all over" when she stood. At her sixth visit, she was able to report she was going up and down her stairs in thirty seconds. She even tolerated a four-hour road trip while the tape was in place.

She then experienced a slight setback when she started school. She spent four hours a day from Monday to Thursday sitting in very hard chairs. She reverted to waking up with lower back pain at 5/10 but was able to reduce her pain to 2/10 by doing her exercises. Her last four visits were devoted to educating her significant other in the application of the kinesiotape to her lower extremities and her torso. Supine exercise instruction and general light strengthening was also completed. Overeating continued to temporarily increase her back pain to as much as 9/10, but her pain stayed at 0–2/10 most of the time. She was much happier since she could stay up later and navigate her stairs more normally.

Acute Immobilizing Lower Back Pain

I will conclude this section on lower back pain with a case example that many people, unfortunately, will relate to. I hope it will be especially helpful because I will include specific instructions to walk you through this problem. I have treated patients who were transported by ambulance to the emergency room and then admitted to the hospital after suffering a situation similar to the one I will share with you now.

You will be encouraged to know, as I spoke with this person on the telephone, we were able to progress him from 10+/10 pain in side lying to standing with 2/10 pain in one hour and seven minutes. He woke up with lower back pain and right leg pain that prevented him from weight bearing on his right leg, frequently referred to as sciatica. He was not completely out of the woods by the end of our call, but he was able to avoid a visit to the emergency room and/or prolonged disabling lower back pain. Staying home from work the next three to four days was needed so he could spend more time lying down. It also gave him time to complete the exercises several times a day. Multiple visits to his chiropractor over the next two weeks proved to be additionally helpful. Within one week of the incident, he was back to work with very little discomfort.

His story went like this: My daughter called me one Sunday morning asking if I would speak with my son-in-law who was completely immobilized by lower back pain. He explained to me how he experienced some lower back stiffness 4–5/10 the day before while sitting in a slouched position on their deep leather sofa. During the night, severe lower back pain of 10+/10 developed. He slept very little as the pain forced him to roll from side to side all night with great difficulty. The next morning, he was unable to sit upright to get out of bed. He was able to "position himself like a backpack on my daughter's upper back" as she dragged him to the restroom. He was 100 percent unable to weight bear on his right leg.

My thirty-five-year-old son-in-law sits at a desk on a computer forty hours each week. When I asked him about his traumatic history, he recalled being in multiple motor cycle accidents as a teenager. I made an educated guess he was experiencing the symptoms of a "bulging" disc. I was hopeful the disc was not "herniated," which is a more serious version of a disc problem. In these situations, the disc, or the cushion in between the vertebral bodies, "squishes out of shape" in response to adverse pressure. When a disc is bulging, the interior contents of the disc press out on the external edge of the disc to distort the shape. The enlarged shape of the disc then applies pressure to nerve roots exiting the spine in the same area, provoking pain. When the disc herniates, the tough outside ring of the disc tears, which allows the interior gel-like contents of the disc to ooze out onto spinal nerves. This is a problem that may require surgical intervention.

The most comfortable position for this condition is prone, or on the stomach. This position alleviates the pressure on the disc and affords gravity the opportunity to assist the disc back into its rightful place. I will number the instructions I gave my son-in-law over the phone so you can follow these instructions step-by-step if you are ever so unfortunate enough to need this advice. Illustrations for most of these exercises are on page 92 "Lower Body Prone."

Protocol for Potential Acute Disc Protrusion or Herniation

1. From the side-lying position, roll over onto your stomach. Sometimes positioning a pillow lengthwise underneath the torso from the armpits to the front crease of your hips will make this position more comfortable or make it easier to do the exercises in the beginning. If you use a pillow, place it on the bed so you can roll over onto it. It will be more difficult to position the pillow if you are already on your stomach.
2. Next, bend your elbows so they were tucked into your side, hands at the level of your face, palms facing downward on the surface, and forehead resting on the surface.
3. Gently lift your chest off the surface by arching your back. Begin with a very small range of motion, if necessary. Remember to keep any symptom you may feel to 3–4/10. (My son-in-law tolerated a very small prop up, so he only completed three to four of them.)

If this direct motion involving the site of the discomfort is painful, you are not yet ready to move this area. Begin movement above and below the site of pain instead. The motion should at least be attempted to give you a baseline for your tolerance of the movement.

4. Now keep your torso flat. Stack your hands together under your forehead. Lift your forehead off your hands so you are looking straight forward three to four times.
5. With your forehead resting again on your hands, look up with your eyes three to four times and look down with your eyes three to four times. Always begin eye movement from the center.

(Steps 4–5 gently move the spine above the site of pain.)

6. Now keep your forehead resting on your hands or the surface. Shift your attention to the lower body. Shrug, or glide, one hip up toward the shoulder, then reach down with the foot and leg, as if to make the leg longer, while maintaining the leg in contact with the surface three to four times. You may choose to begin on the side opposite your pain if one side is hurting more than the other. Again, it is fine to begin with

a very small motion. Assess your tolerance for the exercise on the other side and complete three to four repetitions as tolerated.

If you do not tolerate this exercise at all on one or both sides, then omit the exercise in the beginning. You can reassess your tolerance for the movement during another set. This principle applies to any of the exercises.

7. Next, attempt to keep your leg straight at the knee and lift the leg from the hip, or your buttocks, three to four times. If this is uncomfortable, squeeze your butt cheeks together in an attempt to lift the leg but do not lift the leg. (This is an isometric contraction. This is an easy way to engage the muscles of the lower body. If you are able to lift the leg but can only do so slightly, this is an acceptable way to begin this exercise.) Now attempt the exercise on the other leg.
8. Finally, bend one knee as if to kick your bottom with your foot. Be easy with your movement. After completing three to four repetitions on one leg, repeat on the opposite side.

(Steps 7–8 gently move the spine below the site of pain. The muscle used for #6 attaches directly to the spine. If you do not initially tolerate this movement, come back to it after you have done multiple sets of the other exercises.)

9. Return to the prone prop-up exercise (#3). This time see of you are able to prop up a little further. If you can, then do so. If you cannot, do what you tolerate. In this patient's case, his tolerance for the prop up began to improve immediately, and he was able to extend his range of motion.

*If your tolerance for the prop up is not improving, you may need to do multiple sets of the exercises above and below the pain before attempting to do the prop up again.
In extreme cases, you may need to use cold packs to the abdomen and the lower back a time or two to improve your tolerance for movement and then attempt the exercises.*

10. Repeat #4–8 a time or two or as needed.
11. Repeat multiple gentle prop ups again after completing the series of exercises.

Remain in the prop-up position. Increase the amount of prop up as you tolerate.
12. Tuck the chin to the chest, return to neutral three to four times, and tilt the head back three to four times.
13. Keep the face forward. Look up with the eyes three to four times and look down three to four times.

Place the torso back down on the surface with the forehead on the hands.
14. Repeat #6–8 for the lower body.
15. Repeat multiple gentle prop ups.

Remain in the prop-up position to whatever extent you tolerate.
16. Repeat #12.
17. **Now keep the chin tucked.** Look up with the eyes three to four times and look down three to four times.

Place the torso back down on the surface with the forehead on the hands.
18. Repeat #6–8 for the lower body.

Return to the prop-up position.
19. **While the torso is propped up,** repeat #8.
20. Repeat several prop ups with or without the knees bent.

Stay in the prop-up position with the knees bent.
21. Repeat #12.
22. Repeat #13.

Stay in the prop-up position with the knees bent and the chin tucked to the chest.
23. Look up with the eyes three to four times and look down three to four times.

Stay in the prop-up position with the knees bent, chin tucked to the chest, and eyes up.
24. Repeat #8.

Return to lying flat on the surface, forehead on the hands.
25. Prop up and down three times. Return to lying down flat on your stomach.

In addition to the above exercises, we also discussed using the Seated Worker series to keep his body moving throughout his workdays, taking frequent breaks to look away from his computer to do some "calisthenics with his eyes" and completing the standing extension exercises a couple of times each day to prevent a reoccurrence of his symptoms. We also discussed that he had reached the point where specific strengthening to support his lumbosacral spine was needed to maximize the effects of the therapy.

His letter verifies the effectiveness of the exercises to help him out of an emergency and how they continue to keep him going.

> *Dear Nancy,*
>
> *I want to thank you for your help when my back went out a few weeks ago. I have never been that incapacitated in my life! It is remarkable that you were able to help me finally get out of bed on my own by* **simply talking me through eye and leg exercises over the phone.** *I don't know what I would've done without your help that day. I likely would have had to call an ambulance. If you had not gotten me moving, I also wouldn't have been able to get out of my house to get the additional help I needed from my chiropractor.*
>
> *Since returning to work, I will occasionally begin to experience stiffness in my low back again. I am shocked* **every time** *at how much your eye exercises help in those circumstances. After completing the exercises for only a few minutes, the stiffness in my back will improve dramatically. Taking regular breaks from looking at my screen as you suggested is helping prevent the pain from recurring.*
>
> *I look forward to receiving a printed copy of the exercises so I can share them with my colleagues at work. Thanks again.*
>
> *Sincerely,*

Seated workers are advised to take short walks away from their desk to protect themselves from the adverse effects of sitting. It is even *more advantageous to do the standing extension exercises* to lengthen the soft tissue that becomes so restricted during prolonged sitting.

Add these exercises to your short walk around the office to maximize the benefit of being out of your chair. Marching in place will actively contract and then lengthen these tissues as well.

Another Acute Disc Protrusion

A few weeks after the last incident, my cousin called for help. His wife had been experiencing sciatica for the past several months. Her condition was not as acutely debilitating as my son-in-law's, but painful nonetheless. Her symptoms were sharper, stabbing and followed no pattern of provocation. While my son-in-law had X-rays to verify a prolapsed disc, my cousin's wife had MRI results that confirmed mild bulging of her discs at four different levels in her lumbar spine. The most concerning was the bulge at L5-S1 which was consistent with the area where she was experiencing pain in her right leg.

I walked her through the same series of instructions you just read. All the exercises were reasonably easy for her. It was not until step #17 that she experienced a cramping in her right hamstring when she propped up, tucked her chin to her chest, and looked up with her eyes. Propping up and looking up with her eyes *while the neck was straight* did not provoke the same cramping. Step #23, propping up and looking up while the chin was tucked and knees were bent, provoked the same cramping but more intensely. I instructed her to bend and straighten her knee a few times and insert a few prop ups into the series between #23 and #25 to relieve the cramping. After three or four series of alternating these movements, she no longer experienced any cramping while doing any of the exercises. I spoke with her the following morning, and she felt much better than usual upon waking. When I followed up with her three months later, this was what she had to say:

Dear Nancy,

Just wanted to write and say THANK YOU! After dealing with sciatic nerve pain for months, I didn't think anything short of pain injections or surgery would provide relief. I couldn't sleep, could sit or stand for only short periods of time, and only walk short distances. The nerve compression was causing decreased muscle tone, foot tingling and numbness and eventually foot drop. I was a mess!

It was quite extraordinary to be pain-free from the 10/10 pain I had experienced for 3 months after my first treatment of following your program. I was especially impressed that the eye exercises were a key component of the plan. I had never exercised my eyes before but quickly realized the importance of including this muscle group in my overall treatment plan. After using your methods for three months in conjunction with regular physical therapy, I am thrilled to say I am completely back to normal.

Thanks to you, I have my life back again. You are a God-send and I'm so thankful for the healing power of your revolutionary program. Thank you for publishing this book and sharing your vision of hope and healing. I can't wait to get a copy and incorporate these methods into my regular exercise plan for long-term wellness.

The strategy I used for the above exercises is very simple. Initially, I asked her to stabilize one end, or keep it still, while the other end was moved. Then the opposite end was stabilized, and the other end was moved. Eventually, the stabilized end was also *put on a stretch while it stabilized*, and the other end was moved. This gently encouraged gradual lengthening in the soft tissue and along the nervous system. This is similar to the "give a little, take a little" principle. The body is worked back and forth like a teeter-totter, but instead of shortening one end to allow for greater length at the opposite end, *one end is stabilized in a gradually more lengthened position while the other end is moved.* This would be the final phase of progressing through the positions of exercise for anyone, but most people would not necessarily start at this level.

For my cousin's wife, it wasn't until she almost had her nervous system fully lengthened, and then stretched a little further, that she began to challenge her restrictions. It was very surprising to her when her hamstring cramped as she tucked her chin and looked up with her eyes. We had finally isolated the probable area provoking her pain. It would have been nice if we had been able to have an MRI done of her lower back immediately after the exercises were done to see if there was any change in the shape of the disc. Based upon her response to the exercise, it was clear the tension in her eyes and neck was contributing to her lower extremity pain. It is my conviction that the tension in her head and neck created a pressure that was pushing down into her spine. It was this pressure from above that made the disc protrude. Only time will tell if the disc will actually recede once the tension in her head and neck is alleviated for a longer period.

There is another interesting point to note about these two people. Both were experiencing high levels of pain. Both tolerated progression from the easiest position in prone to the most lengthened position in prone in one sixty-minute session. *I have grown so accustomed to being extra cautious and conservative with so many of my patients I tend to forget that everyone might not need to be so conservative as they begin the program and progress from one position to the next.* In these two instances, I progressed their position and continued to move them as long as they tolerated the next more difficult position. This worked for both of them without any adverse side effects the next day. The rate you choose to progress through the exercises is up to you. If you find you have progressed too quickly, allow your symptoms to calm down, then take things a little more slowly as you work through various positions of exercising.

Releasing Neck Pain

The immediate, sudden onset of neck pain is often the result of a motor vehicle accident. This type of injury is referred to as *whiplash*. Acute neck pain or strain can also occur secondary to any activity involving quick or forceful use of the upper extremities, such as throwing, reaching, pushing, pulling, or lifting. And of course, falling can provoke many types of problems, including neck pain. But for everyone who suffers from acute neck pain, there are probably a dozen other people who suffer from a chronic, nagging neck pain.

Poor posture and poor body mechanics are often cited as the causes of the problem as well as stress. For example, tilting the head sideways to hold a telephone between the head and the shoulder will create neck pain as will prolonged looking up to paint a ceiling. Correcting poor body mechanics and posture while we work is critical, but it is only part of the solution because it is only part of the problem. When body mechanics or postural training are taught, it is very important to create an awareness of the complete spine. Treating the neck locally may be successful initially, but long-term improvement can only be assured when the complete spine is addressed.

Regardless of the apparent reason for the neck pain, there is usually tension in the lower back or lower body. This produces the "squeezing effect" I have already described. This, in turn, increases the pressure in the spine above it, creating neck pain and tension. The postural response to this lower body tension and pressure is extension of the cervical spine. In other words, in an effort to alleviate the pressure in the lower body, the head tilts back to cut the system some slack. When the "squeeze" from below is eliminated, the posture of the neck is more easily corrected, and the neck responds to treatment more thoroughly. In the same way, the tension around and/or within the cranium can contribute to excessive extension of the cervical spine.

Any deviation in our posture away from the norm is an indication of trouble. Exaggerations of the normal curves in our spines are almost always *compensatory* in nature. In other words, the neck in these examples is not the source of the problem, even though it may be the site of the pain; instead, the posture of the neck has changed to compensate for tightness in an adjacent area. Releasing the adjacent tension will assure greater success in alleviating the neck pain.

The exception I have seen to this theory is found in patients who already have severe anatomical changes in the cervical spine that have been confirmed by an MRI or X-rays. The tension will still be present in the low back, but releasing the tension in this area will not be sufficient to satisfactorily reduce the patient's symptoms in his or her neck. In fact, I have seen symptoms exacerbate in the neck considerably in response to completing these simple lower body exercises if the anatomy is already altered enough in the neck. Utilizing the wedge positioning is certainly indicated in the case of progressed anatomical changes of the cervical spine.

If you have acute or chronic neck pain, review the following case examples. Each one confirms the necessity for treating the full body. If you have unsuccessfully tried to eliminate your neck pain, maybe one of these examples will give you hope for greater improvement.

Acute Neck Pain

A very fit and vivacious forty-six-year-old woman came to physical therapy about five weeks after straining her neck during her weight lifting class. She attributed the incident to insufficient time spent warming up or poor exercise technique, even though she thought she had been very conscientious about those things. She could not recall doing anything particularly strenuous during her workout. When I questioned her about previous falls or motor vehicle accidents, she quickly responded she had no previous history of other injuries. Her postural exam in supine was even within normal limits. It occurred to me maybe this was a rare case when a very specific injury had occurred solely for the reasons the patient had suspected.

We began her treatments directly to the muscle she had strained in her neck, the levator scapulae. This muscle runs from the superior and medial corner of the shoulder blade up to the neck. It is easily one of the most frequently problematic muscles in the neck. Conventional treatments of electrical stimulation and/or ultrasound were provided in addition to exercise instruction focusing on strengthening her neck and shoulder girdle. After three sessions, she reported some relief immediately following each treatment session, but the tightness in her neck would soon return.

It was during this session she told me about two previous incidents she had forgotten about. Approximately five years ago, she had taken a spill on her bicycle. She remembered skinning up her knees a little bit, but for the most part, she felt like the incident had not done anything to her neck. Then two years ago, she was rear-ended while she was stopped at a red light. Her neck was a little tense and sore for about a week, but she then completely forgot about it.

When I evaluated her posture while she was positioned on full pillows, an obliquity of her pelvis became very evident. In other words, her pelvis was no longer nice and symmetrical. The left side dropped deeper into the pillow and down some. When the bottom pillow was removed so her calves were no longer supported, she perceived a stretch directly in the neck muscle where her pain was located. It became very obvious through these positioning changes that the condition of her lower back was, in fact, contributing to the problem she was having in her neck.

Acute Neck Pain Secondary to Recent MVA

Every time I evaluate a patient who is now suffering from some type of pain I believe can be attributed to a MVA that occurred years ago, I wish this type of treatment had been available to them at the time of their accident. The next case study I will share is another good example of the potential results that would be nice to offer to any victim of a MVA.

I met this nineteen-year-old female three weeks after the vehicle she was riding in was broadsided from the right side. The morning after her accident, she noticed she could not look over her right shoulder. This would pose a problem for any driver, but it was a particular problem for her because she was now paranoid of being hit from the right side. She found herself looking over her right shoulder even when she didn't need to. She soon found it difficult to spend more than thirty minutes on her computer and had a limited tolerance for looking up at an overhead screen in one of her classrooms. She was waking up several mornings a week with a stiff, achy neck at 5/10. After spending her days either sitting in class or sitting at work, she suffered from neck pain and tension of 5/10 by the end of each day.

The results of her range-of-motion assessment were interesting as her motion was not measurably limited at her neck, waist, or hips. She was actually hypermobile in both shoulders. Her cervical posture was good in supine, but her neck felt tense and uncomfortable at 5/10. She was much more comfortable after she was positioned on top of a fifteen-degree wedge. She demonstrated mild strength deficits in her left serratus anterior and trapezius. She was tender to palpation in her suboccipitals, scalenes, and serratus anterior, but she was most tender over her psoas on the left.

At the end of her first appointment, I instructed her to correct her cervical posture each night before bedtime. When she returned for her first follow-up visit, she told me she had been lying in supine for twenty minutes before going to sleep each night. She was now waking up with stiffness in neck at 1–2/10 on some mornings. On the other mornings, her pain was still 5/10. I instructed her in the Seated Worker series at that first follow-up appointment, and her neck pain went from 5/10 to 1/10. Interestingly but not surprisingly, she demonstrated poor coordination of her eye movement, and her jaw tended to deviate to the left with opening.

At her second follow-up appointment, she was happy to report her neck pain and tension upon waking was now 3/10 consistently, and she no longer noticed any neck pain throughout the day. I instructed her in the full supine program at this visit. When she returned for her third follow-up visit, she was no longer experiencing any pain but would notice a mild "soreness" in her neck and upper traps at 3/10 each morning and at the end of the day.

When she returned for her fourth follow-up visit, she reported she had progressed her positioning for improved flexibility to below the knee. During the past week, she had noticed her eye motion was the most strained with each level of progression, even though it was only slight. She had not experienced any neck pain for the entire week until the day of her appointment. For reasons she was unable to identify, her neck was sore at 5/10. At this visit, I instructed her in a few core strengthening exercises. One of the prone exercises involved lifting her opposite arm and leg. Much to our surprise, she experienced a very sharp, stabbing sensation behind both of her knees during this exercise. Upon closer examination, it was clear the pain was localized to her *plantaris* muscle, which is typically activated by trauma as part of the unilateral pathway of pain.

At her sixth (fifth follow-up) and final visit, she was no longer having any trouble looking over her shoulder while driving, her neck was no longer stiff each morning, and she had no trouble looking up at her classroom screen. She could spend as much time on the computer as she needed to without provoking neck pain and stiffness. She reported improved balance during her quadruped exercise with very minimal strain now behind each knee. Before I discharged her, I decided to give her a few more core strengthening exercises to round out her home exercise program. She was slightly challenged by the new exercises but felt confident she could continue her exercises independently. She was happy to be feeling better, and I was pleased with how far she had come in only six visits.

I spoke with her five months after her discharge to see how she was feeling. She was still feeling good and had this to say about her time in therapy:

> *Dear Nancy,*
>
> *I started physical therapy because I was having trouble with my neck and upper back after being broadsided in a car accident one month prior. The day after the accident, I was unable to look over my right shoulder as I was driving to class. Later that day, I noticed how difficult it was for me to look up at one of the screens in my classroom. As time went on, my neck was noticeably painful each morning when I woke up.*
>
> *When I started therapy, I was expecting to get the same exercises for my neck and arm that my friend who was in the accident with me was getting. I was a little surprised when the first thing you had me do was lie down and correct the posture of my neck. I was even more surprised to feel how uncomfortable it was for me to do this! But the longer I did this throughout the next week, I noticed I was waking up with less neck pain.*
>
> *I honestly must say, I thought it was weird when you gave me the exercises for my lower back and my legs. Then I thought it was **bizarre** when you gave me the exercises for my jaw! But when I felt my neck relaxing almost immediately after opening my mouth and moving my eyes, I decided to go along with your suggestions even though I didn't understand them. The rest of the exercises you gave me for my arms and legs did not have the same immediate effect, but I could later feel how they were helping to loosen up the rest of my body.*
>
> *When you showed me how to lie down on top of the pillows, I really felt "out of my comfort zone." For the first time, I could really feel how much the accident had affected my whole body. I could feel how much everything was shifted!*
>
> *In spite of all this, I would complain to my mom about having to do things that did not seem to have anything to do with my neck! She helped me understand I would be better*

off if I worked on everything now. She was in a car accident twenty-five years ago and still has lower back pain. I was even more convinced everything is connected when you gave me the exercises for my lower back and I got a sharp pain behind my knee! Thank goodness, I soon got over that.

It's now been eight months since I last saw you. I will have some pain in my neck whenever I'm stressed, but this happened before my accident. It may be a little more intense now, but usually doesn't last long. Otherwise, I can sit at my computer for hours and waste so much time doing nothing! Or I can do whatever work I need to do. Your therapy was great . . . it really did work, even though I was surprised by most of the things you asked me to do!

Thanks a lot for your help!!

Acute Neck Pain Secondary to Recent MVA

Even though the last patient did not demonstrate range-of-motion deficits throughout her body, it became evident to her throughout her time in therapy how much her entire body had been affected by her accident. The next patient I will discuss also was not aware of lower body pain or restrictions, even though they were obvious in her evaluation. She is more like most of the patients I see who complain of neck pain, especially after a recent trauma.

This thirty-one-year-old female's primary complaint was also neck pain at 5/10 constantly after her vehicle was rear-ended and forced beneath a semi-truck in front of her. Her pain on the left side of her neck and across the top of her left shoulder usually increased to 8/10 by the end of her workday. Cervical motion was significantly reduced to only ten degrees of rotation to the right and twenty degrees to the left; cervical flexion was thirty degrees, and extension was twenty degrees. Her hip flexion on the right was ninety degrees, which is a slight limitation, but she was surprised by the fact that she could only flex her left hip at sixty degrees. In addition, internal hip rotation on the right of forty-two degrees was much less on the left at twenty-two degrees; external hip rotation on the right of thirty-two degrees was only fifteen degrees on the left. She had noticed how tender she was on the left side of her chest and neck but very caught off guard by the 6–8/10 tenderness in her psoas, gluteus medius, and adductor muscles of her left hip and thigh. She made the comment "Something has happened to the entire left side of my body!" Strength deficits on the left were also noted per manual muscle test. She required ten centimeters of cervical correction, a twenty-degree upper body wedge, and one pillow under her knees to tolerate good alignment comfortably.

I gave this patient the Seated Worker series on the day of her evaluation not only because it is a good way to begin complete body movement but also because she worked at a seated job on a computer eight hours each day. She was very caught off guard the next day when she only tolerated sitting at her desk for two hours because of left hip and lower back pain. Throughout the week, her pain was frequently only 2/10 during most of her day but still increased to 8/10 by the end of the day or even while she was sleeping.

Even though the lower body pain was new to her after starting therapy, she did not let it get her down; instead, she caught on very quickly to the "give a little, take a little" principle. We learned during her second follow-up visit that she needed to extend her neck initially to improve her tolerance for lower body movement. She also needed to bend her hips and knees a little more to tolerate neck and upper extremity movement better and to avoid a numbness on the right side of her face that was provoked by arm motion. Because eye motion in supine immediately increased tension in her neck and upper trapezius on the left side, she knew to continue her eye exercises in sitting. She understood to try the eye exercises again in supine after improving the general flexibility of the rest of her body.

She canceled her next two appointments because "she was feeling fine and had no pain." She was even able to wear high heels again without provoking neck pain, which, in her mind, was the whole point of her therapy. I convinced her to come in for at least one more visit for some strengthening instruction.

The next time I saw her, she had some difficulty exercising with a moderately resistive band for her upper body. Her endurance was also challenged by closed kinetic chain strengthening, which I chose for her because she could easily incorporate them into her workday. I also encouraged her to begin walking thirty minutes a day to speed up her recovery. She conveyed at her last two appointments she no longer experienced pain in her neck or upper back but did experience stiffness at 3/10 about three days a week. Our last two visits were spent on massage to her neck, TMJ, eyes, pectorals, serratus anterior, and psoas. All these areas were maximally tender in spite of her compliance with her home exercises three to four times each week. All these areas were also very responsive to treatment. I can only hope she got what she needed because she did not return for her last two scheduled appointments.

Cervical Pain with Upper Extremity Radiculopathy

I chose to include this patient's case example for a couple of reasons. He illustrates well how beneficial it can be to shorten the body at one end to help facilitate movement at the other end. He also represents another type of patient population who can benefit from this approach. The population I am referring to is rather difficult to define, but it is those individuals who may appear to have an obvious logical reason for their pain, but ultimately, the underlying reason for their pain is more about previous trauma. He also was referred to PT from an uncommon referral source.

This fifty-five-year-old male was referred to physical therapy by his infectious disease physician who suspected a reaction to his medications may be provoking his neck and upper extremity pain. He had previously taken *Zerit* to treat his positive HIV condition. One common side effect of this drug is the depositing of fat cells. This patient had developed a very large *lipoma* that covered the entire length of his cervical spine. In the same way a thoracic kyphosis causes the upper back to round out excessively, this type of lipoma gives the appearance of a "buffalo hump" on the back of the neck. He had experienced neck pain off and on for the past six or seven years, but the intensity of his pain started to interfere with his function during the last year.

It seemed logical to assume the abnormality in his cervical spine would be responsible for the constant cervical tension and "heaviness" in the right arm he had been experiencing for the past year at 3–7/10. Reaching in any direction with his right arm was most difficult for him and was sure to provoke a shooting pain of 7/10 down the arm. This very sudden pain had already caused him to drop several cups. After ten minutes of sitting or thirty to sixty minutes of driving, his pain would radiate down the posterior aspect of both arms. He was only able to sleep on his left side with his right arm carefully positioned on top of four pillows. When he moved out of this very specific position, his sleep was interrupted several times each night by a numbness in the right arm at 10/10.

The equally as significant information that came from taking his medical history was, of course, past traumatic injury. He was rear-ended in several MVAs from age eighteen to twenty-five. On one occasion, he was ejected from his vehicle and spent the next several days unconscious in the hospital. My hope was that these traumas were more responsible for provoking his pain than the lipoma. If the cause of his pain truly was the mass, how could I help him since I could not eliminate the mass? Since there was no way for me to do that, I initiated treatment to address the effects of a previous trauma in hopes the mass would not interfere with his ability to respond to the exercises.

Thankfully, he did so well. He is a clear example of how those with patience and persistent can work through the program as they "give a little, take a little" to achieve very satisfying results.

His cervical flexion and extension were within functional limits at the time of his evaluation but felt "stiff" at the end of his range of motion. Looking over each shoulder was limited to fifty percent both ways. His shoulder flexion on the right was 153 degrees and 157 degrees on the left. Abduction on the right was limited to 140 degrees but was only 155 degrees on the left. In other words, neither shoulder demonstrated a full range of motion of 180 degrees, but only the right shoulder and arm were painful with reaching. Interestingly enough, his internal rotation and external rotation for both shoulders was easily within normal limits with 85 and 90 degrees, respectively. His measurements for his lower body were exactly the opposite. The internal and external rotations *of his hips* were restricted to 23 degrees bilaterally, but his flexion was normal with 110 degrees bilaterally. He required eight centimeters of support to stabilize the posture of his cervical spine in supine and one pillow under his knees to ease his lower back pain.

I instructed him in the Seated Worker exercises for his lower body at the time of his evaluation with the hopes of improving his lower body flexibility. In spite of excellent compliance with his exercises and correcting his cervical posture whenever he lay down, he had not seen any appreciable change by the time he returned for his first follow-up visit. We worked on the seated head, neck, and eye exercises at that visit. The restrictions around his eyes became obvious when *he was unable to move his eyes without moving his head.* As I moved my fingers in simple straight lines either up or down or side to side, he could not follow my fingers with his eyes unless he moved his head also. Even though he initially had very little success with the eye exercises, just attempting them helped him to sense a subtle reduction in his neck pain from 5/10 to 4/10.

During the next week, he was very committed to doing his full seated program two to three times per day. At his third visit, he was able to report an improvement during reaching with his right upper extremity with pain now at 4–5/10. During this visit, he completed the head and neck exercises without difficulty while in supine with eight centimeters of cervical stabilization. *His eye motion was noticeably more strained while in supine, but the strain was obviously reduced when just one pillow was put under his knees.* When he sat up to assess his reaching tolerance after completing the head, neck, and eye exercises, his pain had reduced to 3–4/10. It was during his third and fourth visits that we realized we would need *to modify his supine positioning to improve his tolerance for moving his upper and lower extremities and eyes while in supine.*

At his fourth visit, I began instruction for the lower body exercises while in supine with eight centimeters of cervical stabilization. Much to both of our surprise, movement of the lower body provoked the sharp, shooting pain in the right upper extremity. Because he was already on so much cervical support, I decided to place him on a twenty-degree upper body wedge. *With this modification, he was able to move the lower body without provoking arm pain.* His homework for the next week was to slowly reduce the amount of his upper body wedge as tolerated during lower body movement.

The next challenge was posed when we attempted to finally move the arms while he was positioned in supine. He was taken off the wedge so the arms could move while in contact with the mat surface. When movement of the arms provoked arm pain of 5–6/10, he was allowed to bend at the hips and knees. This reduced his pain to 3–4/10. I then noticed his eyes were looking down toward his feet. When he was asked to stabilize his gaze so his eyes were centered in the orbit, movement of his arms provoked pain of 8/10 even with his knees bent. I placed him back on top of the wedge, stabilized his eyes in center, and bent his hips and knees. While in this position, he tolerated moving his arms with minimal discomfort. His homework for the next week regarding upper extremity movement was to begin with the upper body elevated on a wedge, his hips and knees bent, and his eyes stabilized in the center of the orbit. He was then to slowly lengthen the lower body and reduce the upper body wedge while keeping the gaze stabilized as he performed the upper body exercises. *His goal was to better tolerate arm motion with a more lengthened body while his eyes were stabilized in the center of the orbit.* Even after moving his arms in these varied positions only enough to decide how he should proceed with his exercises, he was able to sit up and reach with the right upper extremity *without pain*!

At his fifth visit, he was happy to report he had been doing his exercises with his legs out flat but still on a bit of an upper body wedge. Then he took a fall in his garden, giving himself a black eye on the right. I determined he should revert to positioning himself on a thirty-degree upper body wedge with six centimeters of cervical support and two pillows under his knees while he exercised. I then completed his exercise instruction with the prone lower body exercises. His 4/10 pain with reaching was reduced to 2/10 by the end of our session.

By his next visit, he was able to lie flat on his back with six centimeters under his head and neck and one small pillow under his knees during his exercises. He no longer experienced any arm pain during the day but would sometimes have pain at 4–5/10 in the evening when he would lie down to go to sleep. The pain was interrupting his sleep occasionally but no longer several times each night. I instructed him in the pillow progression and scheduled his last follow-up visit.

When he came in for his seventh and final visit, he was no longer experiencing any shoulder pain with activity or reaching overhead. He would experience a mild ache of 3/10 down the right arm while he was more sedentary each evening, but his sleep was no longer interrupted by pain. His shoulder flexion and abduction were now 180 degrees bilaterally, even though he continued to require six centimeters of support to stabilize the posture of his head and neck. His hip's internal and external rotations *on the left* had improved by 10 degrees, but there was no improvement noted on the right.

The lipoma over his cervical spine was unchanged. In spite of what had not changed, when we met five months after his discharge to discuss his impression about his therapy, he was no longer having any shoulder pain *ever*. These are his thoughts about his experience in therapy:

> *Dear Nancy,*
>
> *My initial reaction to my doctor's suggestion to try physical therapy for my neck, upper back, and arm pain was "Oh no." We had just discussed that my pain may be the result of a medication side effect. How could physical therapy help that? Being desperate for some pain relief, I decided to go with an open mind.*
>
> *When I first met you, I was suffering from limited movement of my head side to side, tilting my head back and forth, and pain shooting down to the tips of my fingers. At one of my first sessions, I was asked to follow your finger with my eyes, but without moving my head. That's when it hit me where my trouble really was! Why was I having so much trouble with such an easy movement?*
>
> *Next came the head, neck and upper body release. These were simple movements, but difficult and complicated to isolate because of my limited range of motion. I began to notice, however, that as my ability to isolate my eye motion improved, the pain in my arm also began to subside. Over the course of our sessions, I noticed a change in my flexibility for the better. The shooting pain in my arm had quit, so I took myself off the pain medication I was prescribed. Today, I am able to tilt my head back and forth, side to side, and I can rotate my head in a 360° circle without any pain!*
>
> *Five months later, I still use your handouts as a blueprint to address the proper way to keep my body in alignment. I appreciate the gentleness this approach offers to help me maintain my flexibility.*

> *I value what I have learned from you as an important part of my health care. I have never exercised regularly before, but these exercises have become a part of my daily routine . . . and they will be for the rest of my life!*
> *THANK YOU, NANCY! and Keep up the good work!*

Neck Pain Secondary to Previous MVA

At the time I evaluated this particular fifty-three-year-old woman, her neck pain was so bad by the end of each workday she went home to bed immediately after work. Dinner each night either was prepared by her husband or was something prepackaged or frozen. Her problems all started twenty-three years ago after she accidentally ran into a parked car while sliding on an icy road. Even though she had experienced nagging low back and neck pain ever since, she had never sought any type of treatment for either problem as her pain was not yet functionally restrictive. In other words, there was nothing her pain prevented her from doing, even though she was aware of some level of pain or tension in her body during most everything she did.

Three years prior to our meeting, she underwent surgery in both hands to relieve the symptoms of carpal tunnel syndrome. Carpel tunnel is a problem where pressure is put on a particular nerve to the hand as it passes through the wrist. The effects of this are pain, numbness, and/or burning in the hand and/or the fingers. When the effects of the anesthesia wore off, she immediately noticed a throbbing pain throughout her complete right upper extremity extending up into the right side of her neck as well.

Over the next three years, the intensity of the pain became progressively more constant and more intense. Before the surgery, she tolerated her job sitting at a computer for eight hours with only a moderate amount of discomfort by the end of the day. Her status at the time of her therapy evaluation was a different matter. She had a poor tolerance for her job with neck pain and tension of 8/10 at the end of each workday. Her neck was stiff at 8/10 upon waking each morning. Her tolerance for handwriting early in the day was thirty minutes maximum. By the end of the day, her handwriting was illegible within ten minutes, and she could no longer hold a pen. She was unable to hold a cup or a can without the assistance of her left hand. Her head, neck, and arm felt extremely "heavy," and her energy was depleted. Household chores were difficult to complete after work. She no longer enjoyed her free time on weekends. Instead of playing softball with her friends or fishing with her family, she spent much of her time resting on weekends to gear up for another week at work.

Sadly, I am sure there are *hundreds*, if not *thousands*, of people who can easily identify with her story.

By the end of her evaluation and first session, I had instructed her in the neck exercises as well as the relaxation techniques for light compression and traction. These combined techniques helped her somewhat but only temporarily. At her second session, I instructed her in the Seated Worker series of exercises to help her make it through her workday better. After doing these exercises three times each day for three days and doing her supine exercises each night before bed, she not only stood one night after work for one hour to prepare dinner, but she ran her vacuum cleaner as well. By the time her exercise instruction was complete and she progressed to doing the exercises on full pillows, she noticed some significant improvements. She was no longer experiencing any heaviness or numbness in her right arm. Her writing tolerance had increased to three hours. The stiffness in her neck upon waking and at the end of her workday now never exceeded 3–4/10.

Over the next five weeks, she continued to progress her exercises at home plus see me two times each week. My treatment consisted of manual techniques to her abdomen and low back followed by kinesiotaping to the same areas. By the time of her discharge approximately two months after her initial evaluation, she tolerated very busy weekends consisting of several hours of shopping and walking with only mild soreness the next day but no pain. On one particular day after work, she cooked supper, vacuumed her whole house, cleaned one bathroom, and did four loads of laundry. Her stamina after work had greatly improved. One other evening after work, she not only was able to help out with her hyperactive grandson, but she also actually enjoyed it.

Even though she felt like all the exercises were helpful to her, her most noticeable improvement occurred in response to the Seated Worker series. By keeping her lower back loose throughout the day, she was able to prevent the tension from traveling up into her neck. The additional progress we made to release the tension in her lower back and abdomen through my manual treatments and taping helped relieve her dependence on maintaining such a rigid exercise commitment. The final result of the combined treatment strategies was less tension in her neck and an absence of symptoms in her arms and hands.

I would now like to share a letter written by another patient of mine who had suffered from neck pain for twenty-seven years as the result of being involved in a motor vehicle accident. There was no mistaking this woman had trouble with her neck. She literally turned her whole body when she needed to turn her head. Needless to say, one of her primary complaints was she was having difficulty looking over her shoulders while she was driving. During her evaluation, I also noticed she was unable to lie down or sit back up without holding her head in her hands.

This woman was a great patient. She was very disciplined with her exercises. She started to notice significant improvement once she progressed her positioning to being on top of the pillows. Initially, doing the exercises on the pillows significantly challenged her ability to do the eye exercises and provoked some lower back pain. She reverted to doing the exercises on a flat surface for a few days to alleviate these symptoms. When she tried doing the exercises again on top of the pillows, she felt like her neck loosened up by fifty percent. She also noticed she had more energy. She was even able to cautiously lift her head off the pillow without the assistance of her hands. After performing the exercises in the no. 2 lower body position, she was able to complete a supine to sit position change without any support to her head. After completing her exercises in the no. 4 position, she was finally able to turn her head while she kept her torso still. It is now eighteen months since her discharge. She and I are both pleased to say she is still doing just as well. Here are a few of her comments regarding these exercises:

> *Dear Nancy,*
> *I can still remember the morning we had breakfast together when I told you about all of the problems I have had with my neck. I had sustained a very severe whiplash injury twenty-seven years ago tearing all of the ligaments on the left side of my neck. My neck had been uncomfortable most of the time since that injury, but it became constantly painful during the*

last ten years. Being from Kentucky, the best way I can explain my attitude toward my pain was that I just had to endure it. We call it having "grit in your craw." Nothing I had ever tried had helped to reduce my neck pain. I had reconciled myself to the fact this was something I was just going to have to live with. When you said you thought you could help me, I wanted to believe you!

Your exercises were the first thing I had ever done to improve my motion. And they got rid of all my pain . . . short term and long term! The only thing that hurts me now at a 3–4/10 is turning my head to the left. That is nothing compared to the constant pain of an 8–10+/10 I used to feel in that same area even when I was being completely still. The increased flexibility I now have in my neck has allowed me to better enjoy my nonimpact aerobics and Nei Gong classes. The increased energy I gained as I was freed from the pain has allowed me to live a more enriched life.

It is my desire to motivate and encourage others through the writing of this letter. There is hope and help available!

Thank you, Nancy!

Chronic Neck Pain after Cervical Fusion

Even though this patient was referred to PT for neck pain, his neck was only one of his very debilitating problems. The drive and tenacity he demonstrated throughout his therapy, however, helped him improve beyond my most hopeful expectations. This patient had undergone a cervical fusion from C4 to C7 four years prior to our meeting to relieve the constant numbness on the left side of his body. The surgery was successful in some ways, but he continued to experience 9–10/10 numbness on the right side of his neck constantly.

This patient's neck injury occurred fifteen years prior to his surgery when he was hit in the head by a 4x4 that dropped from sixty-five-foot overhead. After taking three to four days off work, the patient returned to work and had no follow-up therapy or any form of treatment. Surprisingly, he experienced no pain in his neck, but eleven years later, he started falling spontaneously. Within three years, he was forced to quit his job at the airport transporting wheelchair-bound travelers among other responsibilities requiring excessive walking.

Following his unemployment, he became less active. He soon developed neck and knee pain. The buckling persisted, forcing him to wear braces on both knees whenever he was up. Within two more years, he required a cervical fusion to stabilize his neck. Because he lost his insurance coverage shortly after his surgery, he received almost no therapy to assist with his recovery. Within one year after his surgery, he was unable to hold his head up without supporting it on his hands. He spent much of his time leaning his head back on the back of his couch after being up each day for one to three hours. This was also the position he used to drink most liquids since he was unable to lean his head back past neutral. He also suffered with very sharp spontaneous pains in the back of his head and eyes dozens of times each day.

When I met this patient, he wore knee braces continually to prevent buckling. His walking tolerance was sixty feet if he was wearing his braces. He was greatly in need of an assistive device for walking but was too embarrassed to use a walker or a cane; instead, he struggled through each step, dragging his left leg behind, leaning forward with his trunk rotated to the left as he seemed to pull himself forward with his head. His arms were devoid of any swing to help propel him forward. His right arm hung down by his side, while his left arm was bent at the elbow and tucked into his side.

This patient spent six months in therapy. His recovery was so tedious I decided to share only highlights from his recovery. I have never seen anyone in the last eighteen years who demonstrated such severe neural tension deficits. I've also had only a handful of patients who were as determined to recover as he was. He is the only patient I can recall who literally set his alarm to wake him up to do his exercises and walk before pain woke him up at 2:00 a.m. If he exercised at 12:00 a.m. or 1:00 a.m., he could fall back to sleep and sleep eight hours straight. Hopefully, the examples from his treatment will provide a better understanding of how neural tension can present, be treated and defeated.

I found it interesting as he explained to me at his evaluation that he forced himself to lie flat for an hour or so each day because he "felt like it was good for him to stretch out," but he had not been correcting the alignment of his head and neck. When his supine posture was evaluated, he required ten centimeters to stabilize his head in neutral. With two pillows additionally under his knees, he was fairly comfortable by his definition of "comfortable." By my definition of comfortable, which relaxed the tension in his body, he required a twenty-degree upper body wedge, four centimeters of cervical support, and two pillows under his knees.

He was very encouraged at his first follow-up visit that the sharp pains in his head and eyes had stopped almost immediately after he started lying down on a wedge each day. The excessive tension he was suffering from became very apparent at this visit also when simply moving a foot away from the midline in sitting provoked very sharp, jabbing pains in his neck and back of the head. He only tolerated hip rotation if he was allowed to position his foot away from the midline *but up on his toes.* Attempting a seated heel slide, knee fallouts, or ankle pump as well as opening his mouth also provoked the same jabbing pain in the back of his head and neck.

We were both surprised at his response to opening and closing his eyes five times in a row. It took about five seconds for him to lift his eyelid after looking down. Even though he had never noticed this when he blinked, he did not have the strength or endurance to open his eyes several times in a row. Eye motion also provoked severe head pain, but he tolerated a limited range of motion when he was *initially allowed to slouch and lean his head back* while performing the eye exercises.

Throughout this patient's treatment, he made good progress followed by a setback, but he refused to give up. He meticulously followed my suggestions and would always get back on track. Such was the case after doing the complete Seated Worker series for only one week. His knees were feeling better, so he walked fifty feet without his knee braces. Unfortunately, the next day, his knees were more painful, and the hard, stabbing pains in his eyes and occiput returned. He then relied on his knee supports more than ever for walking for the next several days. On the bright side, however, the ringing that had been "so loud" in his ears continually for the past ten years had reduced to 2–3/10, allowing him to "finally hear again." Even though his left leg remained stiff while he walked, he no longer was dragging the leg behind him, his torso was facing more forward, and his head was now lined up better over his body.

After being in treatment for six weeks, I attempted to lightly massage his head and neck. Even my light touch provoked severe head pain. I attempted to massage the other end of fascial lines on his feet, but even light touch to his right Achilles tendon provoked severe right suboccipital and right head pain. I postponed any form of manual therapy until later. After seven weeks of therapy, he was able to hold his head upright for three to eight hours a day. He even walked for two and a half hours one day. Then of course, he suffered for two very bad days.

Over the next several weeks, it became clear there was not any area of his body that did not affect his neck pain. Attempting to align his leg correctly to improve his heel strike and push off from the foot and ankle provoked sharp neck pains. Reaching across his body provoked a frontal headache. Even diaphragmatic breathing provoked a frontal headache. It was after he started to work through these restrictions that he experienced brief periods without any neck pain. Sometimes his pain would still be 9–10/10, but his pain mostly hovered around 6/10.

After ten weeks of therapy, he left his house to go downtown for the first time in one year. He walked, stood, and sat for a total of six hours without increased neck pain. His legs were swollen for two days, but his neck pain did not increase. It was during this time he was finally able to tolerate an ankle pump in sitting without neck pain.

After eleven weeks, he was able to mow his grass and trim his hedges. Twenty minutes' worth of work took him four hours, but he did it. He was "sore all over," but it only lasted one day. Interestingly, attempting the eye exercises with his head and neck properly aligned still provoked very sharp, jabbing eye pains.

I'm not sure why I did what I did at his twelfth-week appointment, but I decided to see how well he could move his eyes while he was standing. Surprisingly, lateral deviation to the right or the left referred pain into both knees. The left knee even buckled when the eyes were shifted to the right. Because the prone exercises generally improve a person's tolerance for the eye exercises, we worked on the prone exercises while he was positioned over two pillows.

After doing the prone exercises for several days, he started squeezing his eyes shut plus made large and small circles in both directions several times each day. His movement throughout his body became more fluid and less guarded without causing sharp head pains. He rarely experienced feelings of falling backward, which had been a fairly common occurrence.

After fifteen weeks of therapy, he was finally able to tilt his head back to drink from a glass. He was able to walk half a mile slowly. He was "okay with slow" considering how difficult it had been to walk from room to room before therapy. He also had progressed from being mostly homebound to leaving home three times a week for four to eight hours at a time.

Once he started doing his eye exercises on a forty-five-degree wedge, his legs started feeling stronger. Within two weeks, he did not have an inkling of a feeling that he might fall backward. He was even able to lift a fifty-foot roll of wire without any soreness or pain the next day. He was able to complete what was previously three to four days' worth of yard work done in three to four hours.

At six months from the time of his evaluation, this patient's constant 9–10/10 neck pain was 0/10 most of the time. His pain could escalate back to 8–9/10 on days he did an excessive amount of yard work or walking but would decrease again by the next morning. His biggest concern at this point was left knee pain for which a total joint replacement had been recommended.

After spending so much time with this patient, I was sad when circumstances changed with his insurance. He discontinued therapy very suddenly, and I never saw him again. I can only hope he is still doing well. Based upon my experience with him, I'm sure he will continue to do whatever he can to maintain his improvement.

Acute Neck Pain after Cervical Fusion

This very athletic thirty-year-old male patient was taking his usual fifteen-mile bike ride like he had done each day for the past ten years. When his front tire hit a dip in the road, he was thrown forward, landing on the right side of his face. He immediately felt pain and numbness throughout his entire body. The next day, his cervical spine was fused together from C3 to C6. Four of the seven vertebrae of his neck were surgically fused together with stainless steel rods and screws.

By the time we met eight months later, he was riding a stationary bike thirty to sixty minutes a day plus doing fifteen to forty-five minutes of yoga or tai chi. He continued to work two days a week for eight hours as a waiter plus helped care for his two- and four-year-old boys every day. The only residual symptom from his injury he continued to complain of was an achy tension of 2/10 in his neck and in between his shoulder blades after two hours of standing or forty-five to sixty minutes sitting at the computer.

What is most significant about this very muscular and active individual was what he found to be the most difficult and painful thing to do. When I first assessed his posture in supine, he demonstrated abduction of his right arm and his left leg. In other words, he held his right arm and left leg away from the midline of his body. He was also unable to pull his right knee straight up to his chest; instead, his knee fell out considerably to the right side of his body as he attempted to pull his knee to his chest. He initially only required four centimeters of cervical stabilization until I moved his right arm and left leg into proper alignment. Now all of the sudden, he needed eight centimeters of support under his head and neck as well *as* five degrees of elevation under his upper back.

This patient was able to demonstrate good supine posture with only four centimeters of cervical support by the time he completed his treatment in four visits. He was also able to pull his right knee to the center of his chest without difficulty. His only remaining complaints were of fatigue and some tension in his neck each night by six o'clock or seven o'clock after a busy day.

For someone who was an avid exerciser and felt like he knew his body very well, this patient was surprised at what part of his treatments seemed to challenge and help him the most. For the first three days, he spent lying in supine with corrected alignment for ten minutes, he experienced increased upper back and neck pain. His neck tension finally released in response to the positioning and became more relaxed in supine. He never knew lying still could be such a difficult thing to do. Then after being shown the lower body exercises, his upper back became tense once again at 5–6/10 and "locked up" for the next five to six days. In the end, however, he was more comfortable in his upper body and neck after releasing fascial restrictions in his lower body. He had a better understanding of how tension from below was contributing to his neck pain and tension.

Neck Pain after Previous Fall

A twenty-seven-year-old female thought her back and neck pain stemmed from sleeping three nights on a bad mattress because she first noticed lower back pain a few days after returning home from vacation. Neck pain and stiffness were not far behind. Within a month or so, she started back to school. Migraine headaches frequently interfered with her studying, which required one to two hours each day reading and two to three hours on the computer. This noticeably affected her concentration since her neck pain increased quickly from 2/10 to 8/10 after only thirty minutes of either activity. Helping to stock shelves and clean floors at her part-time job could provoke her lower back pain to also increase from 2/10 to 8–9/10. Her sleep was delayed each night for as much as two to three hours by headaches or neck or lower back pain. Her sleep was additionally interrupted each night two to three times by pain. Walking was restricted to sixty to ninety minutes by lower back pain. Her jaws also popped regularly, left greater than right. Both eyes had been unusually dry for the past couple of years.

After discussing her traumatic history, she agreed the bad mattress might not solely be responsible for her current struggle. At age sixteen, she sustained a whiplash injury in a motor vehicle accident. At fourteen, she was hit in the back by a closing elevator door that pushed her into a hospital meal cart. Her worst injury occurred at age seven when she jumped off a tree stump, landing in a sprinkler head with her lower back. She remembered being "paralyzed" for a couple of hours after the incident.

Even though her neck felt very stiff and tense to her, her ability to move through a full range of motion was deceiving. Her greatest restriction was in her hip flexion of only seventy-eight degrees bilaterally. In supine, she required eight centimeters of cervical stabilization and a twenty-degree upper body wedge to reduce a thickness in her throat from 7–8/10 to 1–2/10.

Because she did not have the supplies to construct a wedge at home, I instructed her in the Seated Worker series and the standing exercises for her lower body at her first follow-up appointment. Cervical pro and retraction were obviously the most difficult exercises to complete. Tongue protraction was the most noticeably restricted. While the seated exercises did not begin the process of improvement for her, the supine cervical and upper extremity exercises at her next visit reduced her neck and lower back symptoms by fifty percent.

At her third follow-up appointment, she reported to having done her supine exercises three times the previous week. Her lower back pain was now 0/10, cervical stiffness 1/10, and mid-thoracic tension 3/10. Light resistive scapular exercises only reduced her mid-back symptoms to 2.5/10, but after completing the eye exercises in supine, her mid-back symptoms reduced to 0/10.

Her next appointment came at the end of finals week. She learned that resting her eyes more frequently helped keep her cervical discomfort at 1–2/10, but her lower back pain had been more consistently at 4/10 during the week. Massaging her TMJ bilaterally at this appointment quickly reduced her lower back pain to 1/10. She was also instructed to alternate marching in place and forward bending with a couple of routine hip flexor stretches.

She experienced increased lower back pain the next week in response to heavy custodial work at her job. Her exercises helped reduce her pain from 9/10 to 6/10 and then 4/10, but it was the TMJ massage she depended upon to lower her pain to 1–2/10. She stated, "The jaw massage helps me more than anything else I've been shown."

Her final three appointments were devoted to core and cervical strengthening. At her last appointment, she stated she could still experience pain of 1–3/10 in her lower back, neck, or forehead, but she no longer experienced spikes in her pain up to 8–9/10. Her most significant change in flexibility occurred in her hip flexion, which increased from 78 to 100 degrees on the right and 108 degrees on the left. These are the comments she had to make about her therapy:

> *Dear Nancy,*
>
> *When I agreed to come to physical therapy for my neck and lower back pain, I was expecting to get a lot of stretches for my neck and upper traps. I was somewhat reluctant to come as I had been to PT in the past for lower back pain. The exercises I was given at that time were painful and did not reduce my pain, so I quite going before my sessions were completed. I was expecting you to find things wrong with my back and neck, but I could feel*

how screwed up everything was when you laid me down on your table! Your explanation about how past trauma to my body was affecting me today made perfect sense to me. By the end of my first visit, I more fully understood just how connected my body is. As a student of archeology, I am learning to appreciate the diversity of different cultures. This helped me to be more open to discovering new avenues in health care as well. I even called my parents to ask them why we had never sought out this particular kind of therapy in the past!

Even though your concepts made sense to me, I must say when you asked me to stick out my tongue, I remember thinking, "No way is this going to help anything!" Then I was so surprised to find out I really could not stick out my tongue very far! I was extremely surprised when the eye exercises took away all the pain from in between my shoulder blades. I was equally surprised when moving my eyes up and down helped the most to relax my neck and massaging in my jaw gave me the quickest relief from my lower back pain.

One year ago I was terrified I would never be able to do field work in archeology, but would be restricted to lab work or academia. I was afraid my limited options would make me less employable. This past weekend, however, I walked two and a half to three hours without any increased neck or lower back pain. I am looking forward to beginning my first field school in one month.

Thank you so much for helping me feel better about my future and participating in field school without any limitations!

Insidious Onset Neck and Shoulder Pain

A forty-three-year-old male could not recall ever injuring his neck or right shoulder. His traumatic history, however, included a whiplash injury ten years ago; a fractured right elbow sustained while wrestling fifteen years ago, which required surgical repair; and a fall on concrete at age four, lacerating the left side of his forehead. His first symptoms of numbness in his right upper trapezius and the back of his neck interrupted his sleep one morning at four o'clock. Within five days, the dorsal aspect of his right forearm was numb consistently at 7/10, and the tension in the right side of his neck and upper trapezius was also constant at 6–7/10. By this time, he was sent home from Afghanistan for therapy. His sleep was interrupted three times every night by right shoulder pain, he was unable to lift his twenty-two pound one-year-old son from the floor, and he found it very difficult to use his right arm to help carry a twenty-four pack of bottled water. The range of motion in his neck was minimally restricted, but hip flexion on the right was only 105 degrees compared to 120 degrees on the left. Bilateral hip internal rotation was restricted to 35 degrees. Right shoulder motion was easily within full limits, but the strength for all the scapular stabilizers, including the mid and lower trapezius, rhomboids, and serratus anterior, was only 4/5+.

Within two months, this patient was seen twelve times and ready to return to work. What was so interesting about his recovery was how much tension from above and below his neck and shoulder clearly affected his symptoms in several different ways. Sleeping on a five-degree wedge with six centimeters of cervical stabilization helped reduce his pain from 6–7/10 to 4–5/10. Extension of his right hip provoked burning in his right upper and mid-trapezius, so trigger point release to the right posterior adductors relieved the symptoms. Eye coordination was poor when looking up or to either side, and his ability to stick out his tongue and open his mouth was limited, but completing the eye and neck exercises through his available range of motion reduced his upper trap pain from 4–5/10 to 0/10. Unfortunately, hiking or extending his right hip in standing could shoot the pain right back up to 6/10, but massaging his jaw and eyes could reduce his symptoms right back down to 1/10. Kinesiotape was used over his abdominals, calves, hamstrings, and right forearm in addition to the exercises to help this patient relieve the myofascial tension throughout the right side of his body. Once his symptoms reduced to 2/10 fairly consistently and became more localized, core and scapular strengthening was started.

Releasing Shoulder Pain

Three things come to mind when I think about shoulder pain or dysfunction. The first is how much I used to dread getting a new referral for a patient with any shoulder diagnosis. Helping my patients regain full range of motion after a shoulder injury or surgery was something I found to be very difficult. By understanding the principles I have learned as a result of this exercise program, I now have much more confidence in my ability to help most shoulder pain to some extent.

Secondly, I have noticed there are usually abnormalities both in the neck and *the lower back* affecting the shoulder. It is very common to assume the neck is involved in most shoulder conditions because the innervation for the shoulder is found in the neck. The influence of the lower back, however, is not usually factored into the problem or the solution.

This seems a bit odd when you think about it. It has long been recognized that anyone with neck pain will soon have lower back pain because of the compensatory nature of the spine. Or if the pain begins in the lower back, the person will eventually develop neck pain. I don't know how the shoulder can keep from being affected by this since it is situated in between the two. Also, when you consider the water balloon illustration, the involvement of the neck and the low back makes perfect sense. If you squeeze a water balloon at both ends, the pressure increase occurs somewhere in the middle. In the human body, this shows up as shoulder pain or dysfunction. Granted, the person may have been specifically throwing, pushing, or pulling when the shoulder injury occurred, but I would bet the injury was preceded by abnormalities above and below the shoulder. The best rehab results will be achieved if improved flexibility above and below the shoulder is included as part of the treatment plan.

Finally, the abnormalities or restrictions in the neck and/or lower back may or may not have been noticed by the patient. Just like the woman in the case study I cited for the acute cervical strain who had not noticed any lower back restrictions, the same thing frequently holds true for the shoulder patients I have met.

I evaluated a young twenty-year-old man about one week after a motor vehicle accident who illustrated this triad of involvement. His primary complaint was lower back pain with neck pain being his secondary complaint. He had not noticed any pain or restrictions in either shoulder. When I evaluated the movement of his shoulders *separately* in supine, his range of motion for shoulder abduction was easily within the normal limits of 180 degrees. When I instructed him in the upper body series of exercises, both shoulders were abducted simultaneously to complete the "angel" exercise. When he tried to abduct the arms *at the same time*, he demonstrated only 120 degrees bilaterally. After completing three sets of the angels and the pullovers, his abduction was the full 180 degrees on both sides during simultaneous motion.

This patient was not experiencing any upper back or shoulder pain or tightness, but his obvious decreased range of motion clearly exposed an area of asymptomatic neuromuscular dysfunction. I believe the tension in this area would have eventually become problematic. It also could have hindered the quality of his rehab results for his neck and lower back; instead, we were able to *thoroughly* address his problems in three to four weeks.

I can only speculate, but it seems reasonable to assume his chances of experiencing future upper back or shoulder pain, or some form of milder, but more chronic lower back and neck pain will be less because we addressed his whole body after his trauma. The discrepancy he demonstrated during unilateral and bilateral movement of his shoulders validates the need to *at least* exercise both sides of our body during the rehabilitation process.

Another helpful hint to consider to improve your tolerance for shoulder motion is the position of the eyes and the head. Moving your eyes *in the opposite direction of the affected shoulder* will often decrease the pain experienced during flexion or abduction. Sometimes this helps internal or external rotation. Rotating the head also in the opposite direction of the shoulder in combination with the lateral eye movement can further reduce the pain or improve the range of motion. I have seen this help one or two directions of motion on many occasions, but I remember only one patient where it helped all four directions.

Think about any limitations you may continue to experience after an injury. Did you only rehab the affected part? If so, see if you can identify with any of my patients in these case examples. They all achieved great results through this more comprehensive approach. Hopefully, you can too.

Shoulder Pain of Insidious Onset

The first case example I would like to share with you represents a fairly common history I hear from many of my shoulder patients. The particulars of their injuries will vary from patient to patient, but the areas of involvement stay the same.

This forty-nine-year-old female had been diagnosed with arthritis in her lower back in the past year. On other occasions, she confessed her neck had been painful. Considering her traumatic history, this was no surprise. At age thirteen, she fractured her tailbone on a slip and slide. She injured the same area a second time at age twenty-nine when she fell in the back of a truck bed. At age twenty-four, she sustained a severe whiplash injury in a motor vehicle accident and suffered from sciatica in her right leg for the next twelve to eighteen months. She could not remember ever injuring her left shoulder, however, but that was why she was being sent to physical therapy.

A very sharp pain occurred in her left upper trapezius one night while she was sleeping. Sharp, throbbing pains soon followed down the arm and into the left hand. The entire left arm and hand felt like the circulation was being cut off. The pain was constant from the onset. Her physician prescribed Celebrex, which reduced her pain to 0/10 while sedentary, but lifting her arm, turning her steering wheel, or sitting with the arm immobile in any position for one hour would provoke pain in the left shoulder, arm, and hand at 5–7/10. Her sleep continued to be interrupted by pain three to four times per week.

Upon initial evaluation, the obvious tension in her cervical spine and the pressure she felt in her head required ten centimeters of support to correct her cervical posture in supine and alleviate the symptoms in her head. She became even more comfortable when her upper body was elevated approximately 10 degrees. Interestingly enough, the additional discomfort she felt in her body while in supine was not in her left shoulder, but she noticed a tension of 5/10 in her left hip. Her range-of-motion measurements revealed restrictions in bilateral shoulder abduction of 130 degrees, internal rotation on the right of 30 degrees and the left of 13 degrees, and external rotation restrictions to 70 degrees only on the right. Not surprisingly, she demonstrated extreme range-of-motion deficits in both hips as well. Hip flexion on the right was only 82 degrees and on the left 94 degrees. Internal and external rotation were both 20 degrees on the right and 25 degrees on the left. Not only was the soft tissue of her neck and shoulder girdle extremely tender to palpation, but her psoas and adductor muscle groups of her thighs were equally as tender as well. After we completed her evaluation at her first appointment, I instructed her in the supine isometrics as well as the Seated Worker series of exercises.

When she returned for her second appointment, her left shoulder pain persisted in spite of the fact that she had done her seated exercises once a day and the supine isometrics three times. I proceeded with her exercise instruction and gave her the supine lower body, cervical, and eye exercises. We quickly discovered she needed to increase her upper body wedge to twenty-five degrees and her cervical support to ten centimeters to prevent excessive pressure in her head during lower body movement. She had never particularly noticed the tension and pressure in her head but was amazed at how pronounced it became with specific positioning or during lower body movement. Her eye and neck motions were all noticeably more restricted while in supine as opposed to sitting.

At her third appointment, she reported that she continued to perform the lower body exercises while on a twenty-five-degree upper body wedge, but she now tolerated a flat upper body position and four centimeters of support only under her head and neck while doing the eye and neck exercises. Lifting the left arm and turning her steering wheel were noticeably less painful, but sitting with the arm abducted and resting on the arm of a chair would still provoke shoulder and arm pain of 5/10. I instructed her in the supine upper body exercises. She was able to demonstrate a full range of motion but could only do so if we allowed her to bend her hips and knees.

At her fourth appointment, she was instructed in the progressive positioning. While her body was in this more challenging position, *she required eight centimeters of cervical support to accommodate the tension above the shoulder and one pillow under her knees to accommodate the tension below the shoulder.*

She was finally able to report at her sixth visit that she had experienced very minimal pain during the week she was doing her exercises on the pillows. She had even ridden eight hours in her car without any increased left shoulder and arm pain, even though the arm became somewhat stiff. At this appointment, I massaged her full back, bilateral shoulder girdle, and full neck and face. She left that day with left shoulder flexion of 160 degrees, abduction of 155 degrees, internal rotation of 70 degrees, and external rotation of 95 degrees *while her lower body was fully extended.*

She did her exercises daily between her sixth and seventh appointments. She had "felt wonderful" until she went camping and boating that weekend. Her pain returned in the form of a "knot" in the side of her neck at 8/10, but it was on the right side instead of the left. I once again treated her with massage to all her neck and fascial muscles. Plus, I addressed the tension in her inner thighs bilaterally, which was quite involved. She left slightly sore but looser and generally more flexible and relaxed throughout.

Our plan from here was to begin her strengthening program, but she was called out of town for a family emergency. Unfortunately, I never saw her again. It would be nice if we could pick up where we left off some day, but unfortunately, it is not uncommon for patients to reach a certain level in their improvement and not quite see it through to the end. The important concept to take away from her treatments, however, is that restrictions above and below her shoulder were influencing her condition. I believe she will enjoy greater longevity from the success she achieved in this method of therapy because of the thoroughness of the approach. I also believe she is in a better position to be less affected by lower back and neck pain in the future.

Shoulder Pain after Electrocution

The subject of workers' compensation can stir up strong emotions among employers and health-care providers. For those who possibly are not familiar with "workers' comp," it is the insurance employers provide their employees to cover the medical expenses they incur if they are injured on the job. This insurance operates like many other insurances and covers a variety of services. If the patient does not respond well to treatment, he/she will be reassessed by the medical provider coordinating the patient's care, who has the authority to decide if the patient has reached their maximum medical potential. At that time, the employee may be offered a certain amount of money by the employer to settle their case. Unfortunately, there have been cases where the patient does not cooperate in their care because they would rather opt for the cash settlement. The fact that money can be a variable in the patient's care leaves room for the system to be abused. In my experience, however, I have found this to be the exception rather than the rule. Most of my patients value their health and want to get back to work.

My next patient is a seventy-three-year-old male whose medical care was being covered by workers' compensation. He had done all the physical work required of an electrician since his late teens, and then he was electrocuted in October of 2006. He was working on a circuit breaker panel when a bolt of electricity entered his right arm at the elbow. The current traveled up the right arm, across his chest, and into the left arm where it then exited his body at the level of the left elbow. His left rotator cuff required surgical repair by April 2008. He underwent double bypass surgery to treat damage done to his heart by January 2009.

When we met in March of 2009, the persistent pain in his right shoulder and right hip was disabling. He had been advised to walk one mile per day for cardiac rehab, but walking this distance would provoke so much pain throughout his entire body he was forced to spend the next two to three days in bed. He described the pain across the top of his right pelvis and buttock, inner thigh, and groin as a burning tension of 8/10. This limited normal standing and walking with a cane around his house to ten minutes. He had received two series of epidural steroid injections in his lower back and hip that provided no significant pain relief. A constant achiness in his neck of 7–8/10 made it very difficult for him to hold his head up to look straight forward.

In spite of receiving previous therapy, his left shoulder continued to ache at 5/10 with any movement, and his range of motion was extremely limited. Forward flexion was 85 degrees, abduction 58 degrees, internal rotation 44 degrees, and external rotation 62 degrees. Left side lying would provoke a numbness throughout the left arm at 6–7/10. He was specifically unable to lift ten pounds with the left arm, but his whole body felt very weak and without energy.

Even though he was very reluctant to come to therapy, he was glad he did after I instructed him in modified supine positioning. The pain across his iliac crest reduced from 8/10 to 2/10 when his head was properly aligned and stabilized on ten centimeters of support, his upper body elevated on a fifteen-degree wedge, and one pillow was placed under his knees. When he returned for his first follow-up visit, he reported he was using the positioning to sleep every night. He was feeling much better every day upon waking. His energy level was noticeable better until noon, and then he was still "whopped" for the rest of the day. I instructed him in the Seated Worker series of exercises to add to his treatment protocol.

At his second follow-up, he told me he was doing his exercises once a day. Following his exercises, he required a couple of hours of bedrest as the exercises made him extremely tired and short of breath. His neck was feeling more flexible, but the tension in his right groin returned with activity at 8/10. I then took him through the supine lower body, head, and neck exercises in his modified supine position and the prone lower body exercises. For the first time in a very long time, the pain in his right groin reduced from 8/10 to 0/10.

At his third follow-up visit, he was able to lie flat with only six centimeters of support under his head. His right hip and lower back pain were now 5/10 most of the time instead of 8/10. He demonstrated the supine and prone lower body exercises as well as the cervical and upper extremity exercises in his newly tolerated supine position. Once again, the pain in his right lower back and hip reduced to 0/10. We discussed how he should increase his exercise at home up to three or four times per day.

He reported several new developments at his next appointment. He had been going to the gym to walk on the treadmill and ride the bike to get his heart rate up to at least one hundred beats per minute for his cardiac rehab. He was also doing fifty crunches on the ab machine with seventy pounds. His left shoulder pain was only 1/10, but now his right shoulder was painful at 9/10. He also required ten centimeters to support his head and neck as opposed to the six centimeters he required at his last visit.

I massaged his face, his eyes, and all his intraoral TMJ muscles and instructed him in self-massage of his jaw as well as craniofacial mobilization. He demonstrated the eye exercises while seated but with his arms propped up on two pillows to eliminate any strain the arms might have on the neck and/or shoulders. His shoulder pain decreased from 9/10 to 4/10. We were both astounded when the massage to his face and exercise for his eyes, instead of his shoulder, had such a positive effect on his shoulder.

He continued the self-massage during the next week, and both shoulders continued to improve. An additional unexpected bonus for him during the next week was a reduction in his right hip pain. The pain would now come and go. For the last two to three days, he had no pain at all in his right hip. He no longer required the assistance of his cane to feel safe while walking. At this point, he started to verbalize the possibility of returning to work with more hope and enthusiasm. So far, he had only been seen for evaluation and four follow-up visits.

This was when his progress began to fluctuate. While he was at his fourth follow-up appointment, I instructed him in the method of progressive positioning with ten centimeters added under his head and neck to correct his cervical positioning. When he returned for his fifth follow-up appointment, he was pleased to report he now experienced minimal pain in either shoulder or the right hip. He was able to maintain 3–4/10 pain level in the right hip by taking 500 mg of Aleve. The bigger concern for him was his *breathing*. It was obvious during his appointment that his breathing was more labored than usual. I was able to treat his upper body, head, and neck manually and release the increased tension the pillow progression had obviously provoked. By the end of the treatment, he was breathing normally again. I instructed him to position himself on a thirty- to forty-five-degree wedge while on the pillows in addition to stabilizing the position of his head and neck to soften the effect of the progressive positioning.

His response to the pillow positioning over the next several visits was a mixed bag. While his range of motion was improving (left shoulder abduction increased from 70 degrees to 160 degrees), his pain level would reduce temporarily with exercise but overall was becoming more constant again in the left shoulder and more intense in the right shoulder. He started wearing a lumbar corset to help manage his hip pain. Without the corset, his hip pain could range from 4/10 to 9/10. We shifted our focus from progressive flexibility to *light strengthening* for his upper and lower body. He continued his home exercise program, but in a flat position with the appropriate amount of cervical support rather than on the pillows. In addition, I did more manual treatments to his upper body to further release stubborn soft tissue restrictions. I also implemented the use of taping to his calves and abdominals to continue the myofascial release process between his visits.

He completed his treatment with full range of motion for shoulder flexion, abduction, and external rotation. Internal rotation was slightly limited but not functionally restrictive. He had no shoulder pain for the two weeks prior to his discharge but continued to wear his lumbar corset to prevent hip pain if he knew he would be doing some forward bending. His upper body strengthening was improving slowly, so he had plans to continue to progress his strengthening as tolerated at a local community center.

I rarely have a patient I don't enjoy meeting, but it was a real pleasure getting to know this patient and his family. His first impression of me was understandably a little shaky, but it was all good in the end as you will read.

> *Dear Nancy,*
>
> *I was skeptical of therapy when my doctors sent me to you. Therapy I had before for my left shoulder made me hurt worse! The injections in my back didn't help. As you explained your approach to my problems, I could relate to what you were saying. After spending my entire life working as an electrician, it was easy for me to visualize my brain as the breaker box in my body, my spine was the main panel, and all of my nerves were like the small breakers. Any breakdown in these connections would damage the efficiency of the system. I realized my therapy before had not worked because we had been working the wrong end of the system!*
>
> *I could see your methods were completely different from what had not helped me in the past. I would tell me wife, "I don't know about Nancy. She seems like a nice girl and all, but do you think she knows what she is doing?" I came to the conclusion that either that was the case or you were going to help me.*
>
> *As time went on and you gave me more exercises, I must admit, your theories made sense, but I asked myself several times, "Is this kosher?" Your therapy was 180° different from what I had before. Your exercises were crazy!*
>
> *The treatments were out of the ordinary, but they definitely worked. I've been to all kinds of doctors and therapists. For the first time, I'm feeling great. I'm finally sleeping in my own bed again. I have more energy throughout the day. My motion has improved in my left shoulder and is pain-free. My right shoulder will hurt at 5/10 at end range, but no longer hurts me at a 9/10 constantly.*

My wife and I have enjoyed knowing you. It has been good to work with someone who could see I wanted to get better. I've made a lot of money in my life and was not interested in some measly settlement check. I wanted to get better so I can make my own money!

Thank you for all your help!

Acute Shoulder Pain after Recent Motor Vehicle Accident

This patient is a good example of someone who was not improving with therapy in spite of the fact that she started treatment within two months of her accident. She was rear-ended and hit the back of her head on her headrest at the time of impact. Her head specifically hurt her the night of the accident, but within two days, her right upper arm and right knee began to hurt. Like most others who have been in her situation, she was sure her initial symptoms "would go away in their own in time."

Six weeks later, she decided to consult with her doctor because she was now feeling anxious, and she could not eat or sleep. The initial pain she experienced in her right knee had resolved on its own, but the arm pain had spread up into the right shoulder and right side of her neck. Her right shoulder was stiff, making it difficult for her to reach into the back seat of her car or to wash her hair. It was becoming increasingly more difficult to carry her groceries into her house. Her sleep was interrupted multiple times each night by pain in spite of careful positioning.

She started physical therapy approximately two months after her accident. She was seen two to four times per month for the next three months. The approach her therapist took toward treating her problems involved manual techniques specifically applied to the muscles of the shoulder girdle. She also used ultrasound locally to her shoulder to help reduce pain and inflammation. She gave my patient very few exercises to do at home. Unfortunately, these modalities were not helping my patient improve. In fact, it was during the time she was going to therapy regularly she began to consider she might be getting worse because she was beginning to experience stiffness and achiness in her left shoulder as well.

When we met, she was unable to hold her thirty-three-pound daughter for longer than five minutes. She was still unable to lift or lower light objects from overhead without provoking a cramping in the side of her neck of 7/10. Her right shoulder flexion was limited to 145 degrees, and her abduction was 153 degrees. Internal and external rotation were within normal limits, but she demonstrated mild to moderate strength deficits in the stabilizing muscle groups of her right shoulder. Hip flexion on the right was limited to 92 degrees in comparison to the 105 degrees she had on the left, but internal and external hip rotation on the right were within normal limits. Her cervical posture in supine only required four centimeters for stabilization. By the end of my evaluation, she told me she had very little faith in the benefits of therapy, but I'm glad she decided to give therapy one more try.

Before she left her evaluation appointment, I instructed her in the supine lower body exercises and the Seated Worker series. At her second appointment, I instructed her in the supine head, neck, and eye exercises. It was interesting for us to note that movement of her eyes provoked the same type of cramping in the side of her neck she had been experiencing with reaching or when she was stressed. At her third appointment, she reported the pain in her right shoulder, arm, and neck was no longer constant but noticeable only when she was stressed at 5/10. I instructed her in the upper extremity exercises and the pillow progression at this appointment. By the end of our session, she was able to demonstrate 180 degrees of flexion and abduction with her right shoulder.

At her fourth appointment, she began to report a noticeable correlation between spasms in her upper trapezius and prolonged standing. The assessment of her lower body postural muscles and core stabilizing muscles revealed significant strength and endurance deficits. I started her on squats and modified crunches to begin lower body reconditioning. At her fifth appointment, the tension in her upper trapezius and the pain in the right arm were much better. We started light resistive strengthening for her upper extremities.

At her sixth appointment, she was glad to report that she "was getting better." She was no longer aware of constant cervical tension. Her sleep was no longer interrupted. She was able to lift and lower three pounds overhead but still had some difficulty with five pounds. She had a better tolerance for holding her daughter but preferred not to extend the time much greater than five minutes. I instructed her in additional exercises for lower body strengthening that included a variety of lumbar stabilization exercises as well as planks and a few balance activities. She felt like she was ready for discharge and planned to integrate her exercises with running and swimming. These are some of her thoughts regarding a different approach to her therapy:

> *Dear Nancy,*
>
> *When I decided to make a switch in my therapy provider, I was discouraged and felt like crying most of the time. I was so relieved when I experienced almost* **immediate relief** *in my neck and right arm after I did the lower body active range-of-motion exercises! I did not understand what had just happened, but I was encouraged even though I thought it was odd. I was more hopeful that I would continue to make further improvements after you explained to me how the exercises were releasing fascial restrictions.*
>
> *Your treatment approach also helped me understand the weakness I had felt in my eyes. It was becoming very difficult for me to keep my eyes open while I was watching TV. I wondered if this had anything to do with my accident. The eye exercises validated my suspicions that my eyes were "weak" even though I had never thought of something like that happening before. Halfway through my treatment, I was no longer having problems with my eyes. After four treatments, I was experiencing relief from my constant neck and shoulder pain and I was sleeping better.*
>
> *You have made me more aware of the stress throughout my body and how I can alleviate the stress by doing my stretches. I appreciate having a tool to use that works for me to either prevent pain or correct it when and if it does occur.*
>
> *Thanks so much for your help!*

Chronic Shoulder Pain Secondary to Multiple Traumas

I had the opportunity to meet some wonderful people coordinating care for our elderly in Albuquerque during the time I worked at a local skilled nursing facility. One woman I met works as a family advisor for those whose parents are no longer able to live in their home. We had the opportunity to discuss my approach to therapy one day after she saw the improvement of one of her clients.

This energetic and vivacious woman had chronic pain in her right shoulder, so I invited her to come over for a complimentary treatment. Sometime after our meeting, she was gracious enough to write a reference letter for me for business purposes. I was able to follow up with her when I recently saw her again at a community function. It has been eighteen months since she first did the exercises, but she was pleased to tell me her shoulder was still doing great. Here is a portion of her reference letter:

> *I first met Nancy when she was on staff at a local nursing home. I was so excited when I found out she was the one responsible for a miraculous recovery from a stroke that one of my clients experienced! When I first visited this gentleman and saw what it took to get him up, I seriously doubted his ability to recover enough to leave the nursing home and move to assisted living. Then after a period of therapy, I could not believe his improvement. Happily for all of us, I proceeded to help him and his wife move to assisted living where they now live comfortably and fairly independently.*
>
> *The next thing that happened with Nancy has to do with my personal situation. I, as an athlete and person having been in several car accidents, have tried for years through physical therapists, chiropractors, acupuncture, and massage therapy to attain neck, back and shoulder pain relief. Nancy took me through her exercises around eighteen months ago. I followed the program daily for about three weeks and then reduced it to several times a week. I have not been back to my chiropractor or received an acupuncture or massage therapy treatment since my appointment with her!!!*

> *I told Nancy my goal was to be independent from all these treatments and to do things for myself that helped me. That's exactly what happened. Nancy has a program that works. She does something that gets people better and not so dependent on continuous treatment.*
>
> *With warm regards,*

Shoulder Pain and the Computer

One very common complaint in our world of computers is shoulder pain provoked by moving the mouse. Such was the case with another woman I had the opportunity to work with only one time. When I met my sister-in-law's coworker while I was visiting my mom for the weekend, she had suffered from chronic jaw, neck, and shoulder pain for one year. She hit the right side of her head, face, jaw, neck, and shoulder when she accidentally fell into her desk at work. Her workers' compensation physician had deemed her to be at her maximum level of improvement. This meant he had exhausted his resources to help her and did not expect any further improvement in her condition. Thankfully, she went from "hopeless" to "hopeful" in a matter of hours.

> *Good Morning Nancy,*
>
> *On August 2, 2006, I fell and injured my neck and jaw. I was sent to a doctor who sent me through the usual X-rays, MRIs, and therapy sessions. Everything that was tried made me feel a little better for a while and then I would go downhill again. Each time I tried something new, I would hopefully expect I was finally finding out what I needed to do to feel good again. I was disappointed a little bit more every time some treatment turned out to be ineffective. I was afraid I was never going to function normally again. I found myself getting more and more depressed to the point I didn't even want to leave my house. I had a constant headache, my neck hurt, I couldn't chew very well, and I wasn't sleeping.*
>
> *I stayed off work for about two months. Then my doctor told me it would be good for me to get back to work two hours a day, but I was having a hard time leaving the house each morning!*

I had a burning nerve-type pain in my left shoulder, arm, and hand at an 8/10 that kept me from even brushing my own hair. My husband had to help me get ready for work each morning. Once I got to work, walking in from the parking lot was hard. Because I am left-handed, I had a very hard time working the mouse to my computer. My left side was already hurting even before I tried to use it to do anything! After work each day, I came home, propped my head up on some pillows, and hoped I could get some sleep.

Then I was introduced to you. Your exercise regimen gave me immediate relief! By the time I met you, I was working six hours a day. Doing your exercises helped me get through the day so much easier. I gradually built up to where I am able to work full time. I do the sitting exercises in the afternoon to help me make it to the end of the day.

My left arm still aches most of the time at a 4/10, but I am able to control it and continue to work by taking Tylenol. I only have to take a pain pill two or three times a week after doing something continuous or repetitious with my left arm, like playing bingo. But at least I feel like getting out of the house! I know I need to progress your program if I am going to get any better. Maybe we can get together again sometime soon!

Thanks for all of your help!

Shoulder Pain with Pulling and Throwing

This case study involves a thirty-nine-year-old female who had always enjoyed playing several different sports. She had previous surgery to repair her left knee meniscus and ACL after suffering softball injuries but had never noticed any trouble with her shoulders, lower back, or neck. Then one day she was holding onto the back end of a pickup truck when it suddenly pulled forward. She felt a slight strain around her left shoulder but did not notice any functional restrictions in the shoulder during the next week.

The following weekend, she was throwing a football for distance when she felt another significant strain in the back of her shoulder. Over the course of the next several months, she developed a constant pain in the left shoulder at 6–8/10. Rolling over onto her left side at night or moving the left shoulder suddenly would provoke a sharp pain of 9–10/10. Upper body dressing, lifting, and carrying anything with the left arm became very difficult for her. She was finding it hard to even hold a cup of coffee with her left hand. She had decreased the fifty pounds she was lifting during her workout at the gym for the lat pull to five pounds.

Her postural evaluation in supine revealed the tension in her cervical spine and how it was affecting her left shoulder. The improvement in her range of motion after four centimeters of support was provided to correct her cervical posture validated the influence of her neck on her condition.

	Before Correction	After
Flexion	110°	143°
Abduction	35°	120°
Internal rotation	20°	70°
External rotation	90°	70°

When she demonstrated the head, neck, and eye exercises in the seated position, her pain level decreased from 6/10 to 2/10. After completing the lower body exercises, her pain level decreased to 0/10. Her pain was completely gone on the day of her evaluation, and she had not done a single exercise for her shoulder. Of course, her pain was not gone for good yet, but it was clear for her to see how much her neck and lower body were contributing to her shoulder pain.

When she came to her next appointment a week later, she was happy to report her pain level had reduced to 3/10 by doing the seated exercises. Only her pain at night would peak to 6/10. Within two more treatments, she was doing the full program in the flat position. She was dressing with very minimal difficulty, and her pain had further reduced to 1/10.

Her only significant residual deficits were regarding her strength and the pain she experienced in her left deltoid during the angel exercise. Progressing her exercises to the number 1 position on full pillows helped her regain most of her strength, but she found she could not progress beyond the number 1 position secondary to *lower back strain*. The progression also did not help improve her tolerance for strengthening her shoulder abduction. When she followed up with her orthopedist, he was able to completely resolve her deltoid pain with a steroid injection. This enabled her to once again tolerate strengthening with her left shoulder.

The most surprising thing for this patient to learn about her recovery was how much her neck and lower back were contributing to her problem. She had never noticed any pain or restrictions in her lower back, but the progressive positioning revealed her lack of flexibility in that area. Her plan at the time of discharge was to be more intentional about stretching her whole body.

Shoulder Pain Prior to Rotator Cuff Repair

The pain this fifty-six year old male experienced in both shoulders forced him to retire from his position as an auto mechanic thirteen months prior to his therapy evaluation. His job required frequent lifting overhead and carrying, but he could not recall any specific injury to either shoulder. His shoulder pain was first noticed about five years ago when he would lift objects at any angle. His pain progressed to a constant 5/10 at its least, which restricted his ability to even lift a coffee cup. Dressing his upper body or combing his hair was very difficult to complete unless he made compensations for his lack of motion. His sleep was interrupted by 10/10 pain whenever he rolled over, so he was only getting a few hours of sleep each night.

As with many of my shoulder patients, he had not noticed any pain in his neck or his lower back. His supine evaluation revealed extreme deficits, however. The tension and choking sensation he experienced in his throat was still quite noticeable at 6/10 even when his cervical posture was corrected with six centimeters of support. He was most comfortable with an additional 30-degree wedge placed under his upper body. His range of motion demonstrated in supine revealed a full 180 degrees of shoulder flexion, 70 degrees of abduction out of 180 degrees, 40 degrees of the normal 80 degrees of shoulder internal rotation, and only 30 degrees of 90 degrees for shoulder external rotation. It did not matter how much he would twist his trunk or lean backward in standing, however; he was unable to lift his right arm above shoulder height.

Significant medical history for this patient included a heart attack and mild stroke five years ago and ruptured appendix thirty years ago. More recently, he was bothered by chronic tension and popping in his left TMJ and chronic tearing of both eyes. Significant traumatic injury included a fourteen-day hospitalization for a fractured skull as a ten-year-old boy during which time he spent most of his time unconscious.

At his first follow-up appointment, I instructed him in the Seated Worker series minus the eye exercises. He rated the pain in the front of his shoulder at 9/10 before we started. After we completed the exercises, he rated his pain at 6/10. At his next visit, he was pleased to report the intensity of his pain was significantly reduced in response to daily completing his exercises. I then instructed him in the eye exercises in the seated position and the lower body exercises while he was positioned on a thirty-degree wedge. When we assessed his range of motion at the end of his treatment, he shocked me, his wife, and himself when he pushed his right hand straight to the ceiling with very little hesitation or guarding.

Within ten days of his evaluation, he was sleeping through the night and experienced pain with only certain movements at 5/10. Just a week before he underwent surgery to repair the tear in his rotator cuff muscle, he had a full range of motion for all shoulder motions, except internal rotation for which he had fifty-five degrees of the normal range of eighty degrees. He was strengthening his arms with a twenty-pound weight. He was able to lie flat supine with five to six centimeters of support under his head and neck.

His recovery from surgery also went very well. Even though he was unable to exercise the arm for six weeks, he did not require any pain medications after the second day into his recovery. He was kind enough to give me his impression of my treatment method.

> *Dear Nancy,*
>
> *I have been amazed with the results I have seen since I have been with you in therapy. When I first went in, I was not able to hold a cup of coffee much less pour it. The exercises you gave me gradually helped me gain strength. You can work wonders with your treatment! I have to say I am totally relaxed now all day. Your method has relaxed my shoulder, my mind, and my overall physical condition.*

I was doing well before my surgery and look forward to continuing therapy with you afterwards as I recover. My wife and I thank you. We are very proud to know your caring concern. Thank you!

Shoulder Pain after Rotator Cuff Repair

Another patient demonstrated restrictions above and below the shoulder as well as the benefits of releasing lower body tension, in particular, to help regain shoulder motion after surgery. This lovable fifty-six-year-old male had survived a series of strokes over the last several years. Even though weakness on the left side of his body did little to affect his daily routine, it hindered his ability to move through a full range of motion. He also experienced left lower back and left hip pain that forced him to use a cane on the right side of his body to ambulate. Over the years, weight bearing on the right hand took its toll on his right shoulder. When right shoulder pain almost completely prevented his ability to sleep, he was diagnosed with a full tear of his supraspinatus muscle, which was then surgically repaired.

His medical history was significant for arthritis in his low back and left hip, high blood pressure since high school, and diabetes. He wore a CPAP machine to improve his breathing and ability to sleep, which required him to sleep sitting up at a thirty-degree angle. His traumatic history was significant for a rollover MVA in the late 1980s during which he was struck in the head by an unrestrained boom box. In addition, he had played high school and college football.

The restrictions for cervical rotation were moderately limited to forty-five degrees bilaterally. Cervical extension was mildly limited to forty degrees. Extreme deficits in motion were identified more in the lower body. Hip flexion for a man his size in supine should have been at least ninety degrees; instead, his hip flexion on the right was seventy-five degrees and only twenty-five degrees on the left. The left hip could be flexed at fifty degrees passively, but the patient had no strength beyond twenty-five degrees to help make this happen. In addition, hip internal rotation was limited to twenty-two degrees on the right and twenty-five degrees on the left. External rotation was thirty-five degrees on the right and thirty-two degrees on the left. The norm for all hip rotation is forty-five degrees.

Most orthopedic surgeons have a rehab protocol for their post surgical patients to follow to help them regain their strength, movement, and function. While this patient's specific protocol was followed as designed, I initially complemented the protocol with active motion for the neck and the lower body. This patient, in particular, desperately needed to improve his ability to extend his trunk (lean back at the waist) and bend at his hips, especially on the left. Anyone who sleeps sitting up thirty degrees for any reason needs to do something throughout the day to offset the fact that he or she have been bent at the hips so much throughout the night. Prolonged flexion makes the body resistant to lengthening or stretching out. Sitting for long periods or sleeping in the fetal position are detrimental for the same reason.

By the time the patient came to his third follow-up visit, he continued to experience shoulder pain of 5/10 with exercise. In addition, the pain in his left hip was 3/10 on a good day but often as much as 8/10. His shoulder flexion in supine steadily progressed from 130 degrees when evaluated to 165 degrees at his sixth follow-up visit. He was able to strengthen in supine with a medium weight theraband through his full available range of motion without difficulty. The problem he was having was that he was unable to lift his arm in sitting beyond 60 degrees and in standing 65 degrees. It wasn't until he reached this roadblock in his improvement that I implemented some different ideas.

I use kinesiotape frequently to relieve fascial tension. For this patient, I applied the tape in supine to both of his psoas muscles that flex his hips. Immediately after the application of the tape, he was able to lift his right arm to 105 degrees in standing. After completing the lower body exercises in supine and prone, he was able to lift his arm to 115 degrees of shoulder flexion in standing without difficulty.

At his next visit, he reported that the kinesiotape stayed on for forty-eight hours. He had done the lower body exercises in supine and prone every other day. His active shoulder flexion in standing at this appointment was 130 degrees without difficulty. The kinesiotape was reapplied to his psoas and the paraspinal muscles along his spine bilaterally at this visit. When he returned for his final appointment, his shoulder flexion in standing was 150 degrees, scaption 145 degrees, supine shoulder internal rotation 80 degrees, and external rotation 90 degrees. He had no shoulder pain and no functional restrictions. In addition, his left hip flexion improved to 55 degrees actively.

This patient's inability to lift his arm was not due to lack of strength or joint capsule restrictions. The fact that he was able to strengthen his shoulder with a medium resistance band in supine exemplifies the fact that more than sufficient strength was available for him to lift his arm. *His immediate response to the kinesiotape clearly demonstrates it was fascial restrictions in his lower body that restricted his ability to move his arm.*

Chronic Shoulder Dislocations

I have had only a few patients with chronic instability of their shoulder, but each of these patients reported multiple head traumas previously. This twenty-seven-year-old female serves as a good example. She recalled her first concussion at age seven or eight when she had a bicycle accident. During her teenage years, she remembers voluntarily dislocating her left shoulder on several occasions to "gross out my friends." At age sixteen or seventeen, she fractured her tailbone in a motor vehicle accident. Then at nineteen, she lifted a case of beer into her car after painting a three-thousand-square-foot room in one day. Her left shoulder popped out of place, and her left arm went completely numb. She was afraid to confess to her parents how she had injured herself, so she repositioned her shoulder by herself.

That was the beginning of many experiences with involuntary shoulder dislocations and self-correction. Her neck would become very stiff and sore each time her left shoulder "went out." At one point in her early to mid-twenties, she worked in the seafood department of a grocery store. She was required to lift a forty to fifty pound marble slab in and out of the display case. After work, she was often unable to turn her head for driving and used her legs and right upper extremity to steer her car.

Two years before we met, she sustained a very serious frontal concussion when she raised underneath a large pizza stone as it was being brought out of the oven. She slept twenty hours per day for the next seven months. She was unable to work for the next six months secondary to anger issues and poor memory. She found it very difficult to read and concentrate on her school assignments. An increased sensitivity to light and noise often provoked nausea. Headaches persisted at 3–4/10 and could escalate to 6–7/10 on occasion. In addition, for the past two years, her hips popped in and out of joint when she changed position while sleeping or "if she stepped wrong" while walking.

By the time we met, she often found it difficult to sleep on her left side, wash her hair, dress herself, drive her car, or even hold a paperback book with her left hand. Sneezing or being startled would easily provoke a dislocation of her shoulder. Even wearing a sweater beneath her favorite jacket would cause a dislocation of her shoulder. She finally gave the jacket away. She rated her left shoulder pain as *severe* three to four times per month with each episode lasting three to four days. Sometimes her pain persisted for a full week. When the pain reached 9/10, it referred down the left arm and into her pinky and felt like it would explode her collarbone.

Her standing postural evaluation revealed bilateral forward shoulders of six centimeters on the right and three centimeters on the left. She required eight centimeters of support under her head and neck in supine to correct her posture and reduce the pain in her suboccipitals and left jaw. Left shoulder flexion was 150 degrees, abduction 120 degrees, internal rotation 55 degrees, and external rotation 60 degrees. The strength in her left rhomboids and full trapezius was noticeably impaired. In spite of a long history of miserable complaints, this patient surprisingly progressed very *quickly*.

After I completed her evaluation, I instructed her in the supine isometrics and rows 1–3 of the seated worker series. She returned two and a half weeks later with reports of feeling more relaxed in her neck but no change yet in her shoulder. I instructed her in rows 4–5 of the Seated Worker series and gently stretched her cranial fascia. I suspected the muscles of her TMJ would be very involved because of her recurrent head trauma, so I massaged this area bilaterally. Much to her surprise, she was exquisitely tender on both sides.

Even though she thought the eye exercises would be very easy, she was surprised again at how difficult it was to isolate her motion. I also taught her how to massage her ocular muscles. By the end of the treatment, her left shoulder subjectively felt more stable during motion. Her requirement for cervical stabilization in supine improved from eight centimeters to four centimeters.

By her third visit ten days later, she had not experienced any shoulder pain or dislocation since her last visit. She continued to position her head and neck correctly in supine for twenty to thirty minutes daily and did the seated exercises every other day. I instructed her in the lower body supine and prone exercises as well as the supine head, neck, and eye exercises. She tolerated only the angels and the pullovers in the upper body exercises, so she was instructed to do those as tolerated. The elbow winging and overhead lift exercises gave her the strange feeling of instability; instead, I gave her some light strengthening with an exercise band to use while keeping her elbow tucked into her sides.

Her shoulder pain continued at 0/10 by her fourth appointment, even though range of motion in the left shoulder was not improving and even feeling stiffer since she had started the band exercises. She also developed a very uncomfortable tension across her upper trapezius, which she rated 6/10. I decided to massage her left anterior/lateral neck, full trapezius, and pectorals as well as her gluts, posterior adductors of her thigh, and left calf. Her shoulder tension decreased to 2/10. Her range of motion was within a full limits in all planes. Her homework for the week included isometric exercises for the shoulder as tolerated and to continue to treat the soft tissue of her jaw and left side.

At her fifth follow-up appointment, she was able to report that she was less tender in the muscles of her jaw and eyes during self-massage. In addition to feeling stable in her left shoulder, her hips were no longer popping in and out of joint. I decided at this time to approach her shoulder strengthening a little differently. I asked her to stand to perform active shoulder flexion, scaption (lifting the arm at a forty-five-degree angle from the body), extension, internal and external rotation, as well as pushing and pulling with her eyes focused straight forward. After each exercise, I asked her to repeat the exercise with her eyes laterally shifted to the left side. *Most of the exercises were noticeably more difficult with the eyes shifted in the lateral position towards the affected shoulder.*

At her sixth and final follow-up appointment, she told me doing the exercises with the eyes shifted continued to make her left shoulder sore temporarily. That was her only semi-negative report. She was now able to use the yellow band without any pain. She resumed a tai chi class she had dropped because of her unstable shoulder. She was able to tolerate the full class cautiously. Side lying on either side was nonrestricted. She had lifted ten pounds overhead without any discomfort or instability. She had even transferred a one hundred sixty pound patient without any pain or apprehension. Another bonus was the pressure and headache behind her eyes previously at 2/10 constantly with increases to 6–7/10 under stress were now 0–1/10 constantly and no more than 2–4/10 under stress. I added wall push-ups and quadruped (on all fours) exercises to her home exercise program and sent her on her way.

I met with this patient two months after her last appointment. As she reflected on her therapy, she told me she was most surprised by how "off" her body was. During her standing postural exam, it was obvious her torso was significantly rotated to the right. She felt like she was facing perfectly straight. During her supine exam, her eyes were noticeably up and to the left of the center of her orbit. She recalled how correction of her trunk rotation made her "feel weird and off-balance." The correction of her gaze made her feel very dizzy and a little nauseated. She also remembered how difficult it was for her to isolate her eye motion. "How can something you have taken for granted your entire life be so hard? I thought it would be easy! It was the hardest thing you asked me to do!" She told me in the week prior to our meeting she had been turning compost in her yard, hauling manure, and pitchforking hay to the top of her chicken coop. As we departed, she said, "Thanks, Nancy. You've given me back my life!"

One of the interesting things I have learned over the years working with shoulder patients of different diagnoses is how the shoulder can be further challenged by repositioning the eyes. This clinical observation clearly demonstrates the neural and/or fascial continuum that spans from the eyes to the upper extremity. The arm acts as a lever to gently pull on the soft tissue restrictions at the eyes that make it more difficult to move the arm. As movement is repeated, the restriction in the head is addressed more completely than it would be by only doing the routine eye exercises. Typically, moving the eyes laterally in the direction of the affected shoulder makes shoulder movement more difficult. Most of the time, this will be true for one or two directions of movement. For this particular patient, it increased the difficulty of flexion, abduction, and internal and external rotation.

Shoulder Pain after Tumor Removal

The removal of cancerous tumors is a common procedure in today's world. On several occasions, I have treated patients whose pain complaint can be directly traced to adhesions, or scar tissue, that has developed where the tumor was removed.

A sixty-year-old female patient of mine had lived comfortably in her body for the past twenty-one years since a large portion of a meningioma, or nonmalignant, tumor was removed from the right occipital lobe of her brain. Unfortunately, the tumor returned eight years ago, so the procedure was repeated a second time. Even though she experienced no pain in the surgical area, she developed some facial paralysis on the right side of her face and became deaf in her right ear. She also told me "her eyes had never worked together correctly," and her right eye was typically rather dry.

She had not associated any of these aspects of her eye health with the left shoulder pain she was now experiencing. The front of her shoulder ached very mildly at 1/10 while she was sedentary, but reaching out to her left side provoked a sharp jab in her shoulder at 5/10. She felt a 10/10 sharp, burning pain if she tried to reach overhead. Cervical rotation was limited to 60 degrees to the right and 30 degrees to the left. Bilateral shoulder flexion was 146 degrees, abduction on the right was 150 and 108 on the left, internal rotation on the right was 80 degrees and on the left was 56, and external rotation was 90 degrees on the right and 25 on the left. She required a 20-degree upper body wedge with four centimeters of cervical stabilization while in supine to accommodate the difficulty she had swallowing. She had been told the nerve to her esophagus was paralyzed during surgery.

One of the first things I noticed during her postural exam was the position of her head. She had unconsciously developed the habit of turning her head to the right. There were a couple of reasons for this. The scar tissue on the right side of her neck surely influenced her position, but even more importantly, she favored her left eye and ear. Whenever a person has a distinctly dominant eye, he or she tends to position the eye so it is more centered regarding their field of vision. I have seen this on numerous occasions when a person is blind in one eye for one reason or another. This not only distorts the alignment of all the eye muscles but affects the tension of the neck muscles as well.

This patient had unknowingly developed this deviation in her posture over several years. She decided the day of her evaluation to make a conscious effort to be more aware of her head position. I took her through the third and fourth rows of the seated exercises and said goodbye until the next week.

At her first follow-up visit, she was pleased to report the jabbing pain she experienced with "cautious" overhead reaching had decreased from 10/10 to 3–4/10. She had been doing her exercises two to three times a day and corrected the position of her head throughout the day. She felt like this was making a big contribution to her improvement. I took her through the full seated program and massaged the muscles inside her mouth by the end of her session.

She was a very devoted to her exercises and massage each day of the next week. She was even more improved at her second follow-up visit, reporting pain of 1/10 now with overhead reaching and 3/10 when reaching out to the side. I progressed her lower body and cervical exercises to the supine position. A week later, she returned with 0/10 pain in her left shoulder while reaching overhead or out to the side. She had strained her left elbow carrying firewood, however, so I gave her arm and shoulder "a good once over" massage, along with some beginning strengthening exercises for the left scapula, shoulder, and elbow.

At her fourth follow-up visit, she stated she was experiencing left shoulder pain of 5/10 again with sudden reaching movements to the side, even though most movements throughout the day continued to be 1/10. To address this complaint, I expanded her exercise program at her fourth and fifth follow-up visits to include torso and general lower body strengthening.

She uncharacteristically canceled her next two appointments but returned the third week to tell me of a very bad fall she had taken on asphalt while walking her dog. She landed on both knees and elbows and blackened her left eye. She spent much time at home nursing her wounds with frequent ice and over-the-counter pain medications. She resumed her exercises one week prior to her therapy return. In spite of her setback, her left shoulder pain was never more than 2–3/10 and 0/10 if she was cautious.

She completed her course of treatment with 160 degrees of left shoulder flexion, 120 degrees of abduction, 80 degrees of internal rotation, and 56 degrees of external rotation. She was also able to lie flat with only eight centimeters of cervical stabilization while doing her exercises with minimal difficulty swallowing. This very delightful patient was eager to share her experiences with this different approach to exercise.

> Dear Nancy,
> Thank you for wanting to talk to me about your book. I am so excited for you and that you feel I can be of help to others. I am so grateful my doctor suggested a referral to physical therapy for me. I feel very fortunate to have been assigned to you.
>
> I am skeptical of anything that "smacks of exercise"! Starting me out with the eye exercises was the right thing for me, even though I was a bit skeptical of their purpose initially. They have shown me that exercise need not be strenuous to be powerful! After doing them for only a few short days, I began to experience some very noticeable, but gentle, changes in the left side of my head, neck and upper shoulder area. Within one week, I was reaching up to the second shelf of my cupboards! I was amazed at how well my shoulder began to feel. I had never considered the link between muscles in one's head and neck to the other muscles throughout the body.
>
> Over the ten weeks we spent together in therapy, you built on the eye exercises with other exercises for the arms, legs, and full body that one would associate with PT. The most effective exercises (and easiest to do) are still the eye exercises. I find myself doing them as I stand in front of the mirror in the morning, during stops at traffic lights, and while watching television at night. The gentle stretch that runs down my neck into my left shoulder is still the most effective.
>
> Thanks for giving me a gentle, easy way to maintain flexibility and strength without the burden of the dreaded "e" word ... exercise!!

Shoulder Pain and Dysfunction after CVA

After spending eighteen months in the acute care setting of the hospital, I changed my place of employment to an inpatient rehabilitation center. This was the final facility type I needed to work in to validate the benefits of this treatment approach in the most commonly used areas of health care. Inpatient rehab centers provide care for patients who are medically stable enough to leave the hospital but are not yet strong enough and/or functionally safe enough to discharge from the hospital to home. To qualify for admission to an inpatient facility, the patient must be able to tolerate as much as three hours of therapy a day. Physical therapists work closely together with occupational therapists, speech therapists, and nursing on a daily basis to provide comprehensive care to patients in this setting. My hope was that I would finally be in a setting where multiple providers could work together to reinforce the principles of this program.

The realization of my hopes began on my very first day on the job. I was fortunate to meet a very special seventy-eight-year-old female who had spent the last twelve weeks at our facility following a CVA, a cerebral vascular accident, or stroke. A stroke is a devastating vascular event that damages the nervous system in the brain secondary to a disruption of blood flow. This damage then manifests itself in weakness on one complete side of the body. The amount of damage created by a CVA can vary greatly. The weakness may be minimal, and the lost strength may be fully recovered with exercise, leaving no functional deficits. Or the damage can be extensive, resulting in complete paralysis of one side of the body, changing the stroke survivor's life, and life for their families, on many different levels.

When I met this patient, her chief complaint involved the pain she was suffering in her affected shoulder. The pain limited 99 percent of her movement in the left shoulder. *Any movement* of her shoulder, or even lightly touching the arm or hand, provoked excruciating pain. This, of course, made showering or getting dressed torturous for her every day. Pain limited her ability to fully straighten her left elbow, even with assistance. She was unable to straighten her wrist to a neutral position; instead, her wrist flexed down, and her fingers curled into a loose fist.

Her sleep the night before we met was interrupted by 10+/10 pain every sixty to ninety minutes. Her husband was up with her every night, trying ineffectively to help her manage her pain. When we met, rigid stiffness in her left arm and leg prevented any movement of either limb. I proposed the option to her to try some new treatment ideas to help her on the first day we met. I explained the anatomy of fascial planes and how traumatic injury can significantly damage the tissue, resulting in pain and dysfunction. My explanation resonated with her as she recalled an old ankle injury. She went on to tell me how she had twisted her left ankle in a staircase banister twenty years ago. She sustained multiple spiral fractures in her left lower leg and ankle when she fell on the stairs. Her left leg and ankle were never the same after the accident. She had also taken several significant falls since.

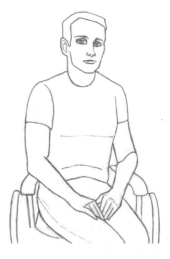

Before any exercise could be done, several postural errors were in need of correction. She was sitting in her wheelchair with the left side of her pelvis very posterior, or back, in her wheelchair. This distortion was easily recognized by looking at the position of the pelvis but also by looking at her knees. When the pelvis is rotated in the seated position, one knee will come forward more than the other. This, in turn, caused her torso and left shoulder to be rotated back as well. Her head was slightly rotated and side bent to the left. Her head position caused the position of her gaze to be to the right of the center. The importance of her eye position will be clearly demonstrated as I walk you through her first day of treatment.

This patient's response to the seated eye exercises the first day of her treatment was like a miracle for her. We did not begin the exercises until the alignment of her body, neck, and head was correctly repositioned. In addition, her left arm was supported on a pillow for comfort with her elbow bent and her forearm resting across her abdomen. When we began the eye exercises, it was no surprise that her eyes pulled to the right each time she looked up. Her eyes were accustomed to being positioned to the right of the midline because of how they were positioned while she sat in her wheelchair all day long. After tracking with me to complete two sets of two to three repetitions with her eyes through all planes of motion from a position of correct alignment, the pain in her left shoulder reduced from 6/10 to 0/10 for the first time in more than three months. *In less than five minutes, her shoulder pain was gone.* Even though her eye motion was poorly coordinated and she fatigued very quickly, the movement still effectively helped decrease her pain. We continued her exercise instruction for the neck and upper extremities before completing our morning session together.

Later that afternoon, I had the opportunity to work with this patient again during her session with the occupational therapist. The use of modified supine positioning was explained to the patient and the OT. The patient had been sleeping almost completely flat with both of her legs fully stretched out. I recommended she raise the head of her bed twenty or thirty degrees and put a slight amount of flexion in her hips and knees while she slept. I also suggested she use the same position to stretch out in bed for about an hour after lunch each day instead of staying up in her wheelchair the entire day.

These two suggestions proved to be very beneficial. Based on the "water balloon theory," it was important for her to reduce the amount of pressure she pushed into her head and neck during the day and night. It is often recommended that patients recovering from almost anything to be out of bed as much as possible, so this patient was sitting up in her wheelchair from first thing in the morning to bedtime. By mid to late afternoon, her left shoulder pain was beginning to become significantly more intense. Then as she lay flat in bed, the pain was excruciating. I explained the effects of positioning to her in this way: It is normal for pressure to increase in the lower back during sitting. This effect naturally occurs even in a perfectly healthy body that has no abnormal pathology and has never been injured. This increased pressure will redistribute up the spine during sitting.

In the case of this patient, the pressure was being pushed up into an area that was too tense to accommodate it. The result was increased pain. The same explanation applies to lying flat. Considering the fact that our bodies are largely water, the fluid in our body redistributes when we lie flat. Again, the extra tension in this patient's head did not accommodate the redistribution of fluid. The increased volume in her already tense head and neck produced increased pressure, which provoked increased pain. Elevating the head of the bed hindered the increased pressure from reaching up into her head. Slightly bending her hips and knees also reduced the tension on her lower back that further reduced the amount of pressure in her spine.

Following her time of being stretched out in bed, the patient was able to transfer back to her wheelchair with moderate assistance of one person. Previously, her transfers required maximum assistance of one person and, occasionally, the assistance of two people. While she was sitting, I assessed her tolerance to more fully straighten her left knee. To our surprise, *this additional lengthening of her left leg provoked her left shoulder pain.* What we had done was increase the stretch on her left hamstring, the posterior thigh muscle that crosses the hip and knee joint. This provoked pain in her left bicep tendon, where she experienced her left shoulder pain. The bicep is the muscle in the upper arm that crosses the shoulder and the elbow. The two muscle groups are complements of each other. *Over stretching one muscle complement provoked pain in the other muscle.* The principle of shoulder pain resulting from tension and pressure above and below the site of pain, in this case, her eyes and hamstring, proved to be true once again. Understanding the effects of complementary muscles also further explained her constant left shoulder pain.

I was so pleased, as was she, to tell me the next morning she had slept until four o'clock without pain. Even then, it was left leg pain, and not left shoulder pain, that woke her up. Her entire left arm was much less sensitive, which made getting dressed much more tolerable. On this second day of treatment, she repeated three sets of three repetitions of the seated eye, neck, jaw, and bilateral upper extremity exercises. In addition, she was able to complete the trunk and lower extremity exercises. The previous day, her eyes absolutely did not tolerate three sets of the exercises. Either they were unable to initiate movement for tracking or the coordination of movement was so poor that I chose not to continue with a third set. On this particular day, eye motion almost made her fall asleep in her chair. She went straight to bed after our session to nap for about an hour before lunch.

On her third day of treatment, she told me she continued to be so tired after yesterday's session that she took another one-hour nap of very sound sleep after lunch. It was good to hear she slept through the night without any left arm or left leg pain; instead, she woke up with increased pain and tension on the right posterior side of her neck.

Friday, the fourth day of our treatment together, began with more good news. She had slept throughout the night and woke up with no pain or unusual tension anywhere. The nursing assistant commented on how easy it was to handle her left arm during showering and dressing—all without any pain. The only complaint the patient had was of feeling somewhat tired even though she had slept all night long. This is understandable considering all the changes her body was going through. I decided to progress her exercises to the modified supine position. Her husband asked if he could skip her session that morning to go play racket ball. He was also starting to feel better since he was now sleeping better. So away he went as I transferred the patient from her wheelchair back to bed. Even though she was now able to independently move her bottom forward to the edge of her chair, which was an improvement, her fatigue was apparent in her transfer, which required maximum assistance on my part. This is an example of how progress can wax and wane a bit during the process of recovery. After the patient and a nursing aide helped me position her in the same modified position she had been using for sleep, we completed all the eye, jaw, neck, and lower body exercises 3 sets x 2 repetitions. I left the patient that Friday afternoon feeling very good following her exercises. She had 0/10 left arm pain.

This patient was on my mind the entire weekend. When I returned to work on Monday, I was disappointed to learn she had suffered through the entire weekend. Sometime during the night on Friday, she began to experience left "upper quadrant" pain. The location of her pain was now on her ribs underneath her left arm instead of in her bicep tendon. Frequent muscle spasms in that area provoked excruciating pain. In addition, she was experiencing spasms in all four extremities, not just her left leg. Thankfully, these spasms were uncomfortable but not painful.

I cannot be completely sure what prompted this agonizing change in status but made an assumption based on my experience with this program. The pain she was experiencing was in her left serratus anterior muscle, which interdigitates with the oblique abdominal muscles. This area can be stretched during the lower trunk rotation exercise, which was extremely limited by the patient. She possibly overstretched the area under her arm by doing the lower trunk rotation movement to both sides. She also had a huge knot that covered her right cervical spine. That problem led me to believe the exercises had been too strenuous for her, even though they did not appear to be at the time they were done.

If the lower body exercises we did in supine had provoked this painful episode, might it have been avoided if she started the exercises with the head of the bed at forty-five or sixty degrees instead of thirty and put more bend in her hips and knees than just a slight amount? I can't know for sure, but for any patient I see in the future with increased neurological tone already, I will be sure to begin the supine exercises with the head of the bed elevated to at least forty-five and probably sixty degrees.

It took the next two days to calm down her pain. She required strong pain medication that made her sleep much more than usual. The spasms stopped while she slept. By the third day, she no longer required pain meds. We were finally back to where we had left off the Friday before. She was sleeping through the night again without pain. Her left arm was easy to manage for showering and dressing again. She discharged to home the following day, so I can only hope that she has continued to do as well.

This patient exemplifies the importance for all of us to maintain good sitting posture. The posture of our head will dictate where our eyes sit in the orbit. In the case of the patient I am currently discussing, turning her head to the left caused her eyes to shift to the right whenever she looked straight forward from her body. If the head is rotated to the right, the eyes will shift to the left. This not only happens with a stroke survivor, but I have also noticed it occurs whenever there is blindness in one eye. The person will rotate the head to center the position of the eye with vision. In the case of hearing loss, the rotation of the head may occur so the ear with better hearing capability will be rotated toward the front to face the person being listened to.

Releasing Headaches

There are various types of headaches, but the types most commonly referred to are sinus headaches, tension headaches, and migraine headaches. Sinus headaches usually occur in the lower portion of the forehead and around the eyes in response to some type of irritation inside the head like a sinus infection or overuse of the eyes. Tension, or stress, headaches are associated with the tightening of the muscles at the base of the skull secondary to emotional strain, fatigue, overuse, poor posture, or bad body mechanics. Migraine headaches are presumed to be the result of obstructions to or spasms of the blood vessels that supply the intracranial tissues. It is unfortunately true, however, that most of the understanding we have for the cause of headaches is based upon hypothetical reasoning and largely not understood.

Interestingly enough, the first time I experienced overwhelming success in reducing a migraine headache I was actually treating a woman for sciatica. My patient was a forty-one-year old nurse's aide who had injured her lower back as she fell during a patient transfer. To make a long story short, the treatment efforts I directed toward decreasing the tension in her lower back and lower body helped her sciatica *partially and temporarily*. What responded more *consistently and dramatically* to the treatments were her migraine headaches.

On one specific occasion, her headache had lasted over a five-day period during which time she had visited the emergency room because the headache had exacerbated to "12/10." The injections she received reduced her headache to only 8–9/10. This was the level of her headache when she arrived at her next appointment with me. I cannot remember how much her sciatica was affecting her that day, but within twenty to thirty minutes of treating her lower back and abdomen, her headache reduced to 2–3/10.

As a result of this incident, I began to instruct each patient suffering from headaches in the complete exercise program, but always started with the lower body. I often direct much of my manual assistance to the lower back and the abdomen. By using this treatment protocol, I have successfully treated tension headaches as well as migraines, premenstrual headaches, and headaches following MVAs. The patient usually does not complain of lower back pain, but it is often *lower body activity*, such as running, hiking, or sitting, that provokes the headaches. My palpation exam will always expose tension of some degree within the soft tissue of the abdomen, the lower back, and the lower extremities.

I have found the treatment of muscle complements to be particularly helpful in the treatment of headaches. For example, I was able to relieve the temporal headaches of a woman post CVA by releasing tension in her gluteus medius. Another eighty-four-year-old patient had suffered from headaches at the crown of her head since she was eleven years old. In an effort to understand her headaches, I referred to trigger point charts to see which muscles are known to refer pain to the crown of the head. The splenius capitis muscle specifically refers pain to the top of the head, while the upper trapezius and clavicular head of the sternocleidomastoid also refer pain up into the head. Direct treatment of these particular muscles did very little to help my patient. Her body responded much better when I directed my treatment to the complements of these muscles at the pelvis and the torso by treating her gluteus medius, oblique abdominals, and adductors of her thigh.

I should also mention these exercises have been known to provoke an extreme exacerbation of a headache. On two separate occasions several years ago, I was sorry to learn from two different patients that beginning the lower body exercises had caused them to experience a bout with a very painful headache. At the time, I supposed this was a natural response to beginning new exercises. I now understand these headaches could have been avoided by beginning the exercises in the seated or modified supine position. In both cases, I instructed the patients to begin all the exercises in supine with their head correctly positioned in neutral.

These were unfortunate experiences, but they have taught me to gradually progress people from the seated position to the supine position. If you suspect you have extreme restrictions in your upper body, head, or neck, begin the exercises in the seated position. Then gradually lower your upper body incrementally toward flat supine by using modified supine positioning.

A few things can alert you to possible difficulties. If a choking sensation in your throat restricts swallowing, breathing, or speaking when your cervical spine is correctly positioned, you should begin the exercises in a seated or semi-reclined position. Extreme pressure or fullness in the head as well as the sensation of lying with the head tilted down lower than the rest of the body are other indications of extreme tension in the head and neck. These feelings typically go away completely once the necessary amount of compensation is provided to help correct the cervical posture and elevate the body. Regardless, I now recommend my patients begin in the seated position or in a modified supine position on a wedge to avoid the possible exacerbation of a headache.

Chronic Migraine Headache

One patient in particular responded surprisingly fast to this treatment method. Her response was even more significant considering the severity of her symptoms. She was still doing very well when I contacted her one year after her discharge from therapy.

The patient is a thirty-year-old phlebotomist, or a medical technician who draws blood for lab tests. She had experienced a constant migraine headache on a daily basis for the past four years. She rated her headache at 7/10 with nausea and vomiting about two times each month. Her headache ran from the base of her head to the crown of her head. The pain would exacerbate to 9–10/10 with any type of forward bending. Additional symptoms included a constant tingling on both sides of her face. Her sitting and standing tolerance was limited to sixty to ninety minutes by hot flashes in her face, which caused her to grind her teeth. Her sleep was interrupted six to seven times every night by head pain.

Interestingly enough, this patient was not referred to me for her migraines. Her referral was for neck pain she developed three weeks prior to our meeting. The tension at the base of her head occurred very suddenly one day at 8–9/10. Trigger point injections to the area decreased her symptoms for only two days. She was hoping to relieve her neck pain with therapy but had given up on ever being rid of her headache.

Over the course of the last four years, she had explored every treatment possibility currently available to find relief from her headache. Modifying her diet gave her no relief. She spent four months evaluating her hormones to learn they were completely normal. Finally, a neurologist ordered multiple MRIs and CAT scans of her head. A "spot" showed up on one of these tests indicating a possible tumor, but no further testing could be done based on the location of the spot.

At this point, she hopelessly concluded she was stuck with her headache for the rest of her life. She tried numbing the pain with painkillers, only to find the medication made her headaches *worse* after a couple of months. Her head would throb with pain, and blood vessels in her eyes would burst. One day out of desperation, she withdrew thirty vials of her own blood. This tactic successfully decreased the pressure in her body enough to give her one to two days of relief from her headache. She continued this practice every two weeks to keep her sanity.

Following her evaluation, I instructed her in the flare-up positioning I recommend for pain exacerbations. We were both pleasantly surprised when this positioning alone immediately decreased her head pain to 3/10.

Her next appointment was four days later. She was thrilled to report she had managed to keep her pain at 3–4/10 by positioning herself in the flare-up position three to four times each day for ten to twenty minutes. During her appointment, I instructed her in the lower body exercises and the side-lying exercises for her torso. It was interesting to note her head was in a very minimal amount of cervical extension in supine, but active correction of this position resulted in a thickness of 8/10 in her throat. With only one centimeter of support, this thick feeling reduced to 2/10. After doing the lower body portion of the exercises, the thickness in her throat without any support decreased to 1/10. Her head felt very "light," and her headache was gone.

Three days later, the thickness in her throat had decreased to 1/10 with correct cervical positioning, and her neck was much more flexible. She also mentioned she was able to *maintain her increased lower body flexibility* from day to day, which was something she had never experienced with her regular daily stretches. During this visit, I completed her exercise instruction while noting the eye exercises were especially difficult for her. I also evaluated her for the first level of the lower body progressive positioning. This was initially challenging for her neck. Even though she normally did not experience lower back pain, within sixty to ninety seconds, her low back was achy at 6/10.

During her re-evaluation one month later, she was thrilled to report she was sleeping through the night without pain. She had experienced only one headache since her evaluation. She attributed her headache, which did not exceed 5–6/10, to stress-related issues. She was able to sit for two hours without any increased head pain. Even forward bending provoked head pain of only 2/10.

She was doing the lower body exercises daily and was now at position no. 3 in the progressive positioning. I was so surprised when she told me she had lost her handouts so the only portion of the program she had been doing was the lower body exercises, which she had committed to memory. She had a better tolerance for more intense workouts on the treadmill with less fatigue, enabling her to lose weight she had been unable to lose by walking six miles per day.

Objectively, her hip flexion and straight leg raise on the right improved by twenty-five percent and was now symmetrical with her left leg. Her cervical range of motion increased by twenty to thirty percent and became symmetrical in all planes of motion. *The significant point to remember is she had not even been exercising her neck.* It was the reevaluation of this patient that convinced me in several objective ways of the influence of the lower back on the rest of the body, especially the head and the neck.

Significant past trauma for this patient included a head-on collision three years ago, "but no one was injured." Four years ago, she sustained multiple blows to her head during altercations with inmates while she was employed at a juvenile detention center. Five to fifteen years ago, she had taken multiple hard falls either flat onto her back or her tailbone while skiing or snowboarding. She also had a C-section done eleven years ago and had noticed more scar tissue on the right side of her abdomen than the left. I do not believe it is coincidental that deficits in her range of motion were all also on the right side of her body. This unforgettable patient also agreed to share her experiences with you in a letter.

Dear Nancy,

My experience with migraine headaches started about 4 years ago. After exhausting all of my treatment options, I was convinced I was cursed to live with these awful headaches for the rest of my life. About one year ago I moved to New Mexico from Washington and my migraines proceeded to get worse. It was at this time I started drawing my own blood to relieve some of the pressure in my body and decrease the pain temporarily. About 2 months ago I developed painful knots in the back of my neck that were so bad I finally went to see my doctor for help. After looking at my neck, she suggested I see you.

After seeing you for only 2 visits my headaches went from being so painful I could hardly function to being barely noticeable! After 3 visits I noticed I had not had a headache in days! Now it's been about 2 months and I haven't had a headache in about 6–7 weeks.

If it had not been for you I am certain my headaches would have eventually gotten worse. I am scared to even think about what I might have resorted to. But thanks to you, I will never have to find out. I don't know how to thank you enough. All I can say is thank you. I hope your book and your wonderful stretches get all the recognition they deserve.

Thanks again,

I should mention most people I have treated who suffer from headaches do not respond as quickly as this patient. I am finding people who exercise regularly in spite of chronic irritations respond more quickly to the right treatment once it is provided. This is not true 100 percent of the time, but it is a true general statement. But there are many people who do not exercise regularly. These people improve eventually, but it takes a little longer before they experience the results from their efforts than a person who exercises regularly.

This patient also serves as a good illustration for a hunch I have. She did not complain of lower back pain, but my palpation exam uncovered tenderness in her psoas on the right of 6/10 and on the left at 8/10. I have found the psoas to be tight in other patients who complain of nausea on a regular basis. Massage therapists and other types of bodyworkers have long associated tightness of the psoas with constipation and stomachaches.

I wonder if the tension in the psoas is also the possible precursor to the abdominal pain many of my patients have told me they experienced prior to the onset of a migraine.

Acute Neck Pain with Headache Secondary to Recent MVA

I would like to share a letter written by a patient who had no previous history with headaches before he was in a MVA. He had the advantage of being evaluated only three weeks after his accident. I would like to believe his example of success with this program justifies the need for an early comprehensive intervention after a MVA.

> *Dear Nancy,*
>
> *As you know, I am an attorney here in Albuquerque. A portion of my civil litigation practice includes Plaintiff's Personal Injury cases. This past October I was the victim of an automobile collision and I experienced firsthand the pain and discomfort my client's experience as a result of traumatic injuries. I suffered from back and neck pain and strain that my primary care physician treated with painkillers, muscle relaxants and rest. Unfortunately, after two weeks my symptoms worsened and I developed constant low-grade headaches. My physician then prescribed N-Rich Physical Therapy.*
>
> *I was skeptical. Stretching and exercise conjured up images of high school football hamstring stretches and other painful tortures. I grew up on the mantra "No pain - No gain." After all, I was hurting already. The last thing I wanted to do was aggravate my aching neck and back! During my first session I was even more skeptical. The exercise movements were too simple, too easy, and most of all, they didn't hurt. So I figured they must not be effective.*
>
> *I gave it a shot and followed my instructions at home. I did my sets twice a day, in the morning and in the evening. The results were almost immediate. My headaches were substantially reduced and the neck and back pain were diminished. By the third physical therapy session, my headaches were gone and I began to regain my prior range of motion in my neck.*

> *I am confident I will soon achieve not only my pre-accident condition, but "an even better than before" condition as a result of this exercise program. I am now a believer despite the simple movements. These are powerful exercises that produce results. I am now convinced the only way to go is "No Pain - Only Gain." Thank you, Nancy, for restoring my well-being.*
>
> *Sincerely,*

Releasing TMJ Pain

My own experience with TMJ pain confirmed to me once again that treating pain at the opposite end of the body gets the best result. I was attending a conference where I had the opportunity to meet all types of health-care providers from all over the world. One evening I sat next to a structural integration therapist who told me about a manual technique that involved pulling quickly on the tongue to relieve pressure and discomfort under the sternum or breast bone. She mentioned the technique was very uncomfortable, but the few seconds of discomfort were well worth the effective result.

I had been experiencing very painful chest discomfort for about two years, so I attempted to treat myself with this technique. I did not execute the technique exactly as she had explained because I was *afraid of the pain*, so I stuck my tongue out as far as I could and applied a sustained stretch on my tongue by gently pulling on it for fifteen to twenty seconds. What I did was not painful, but I could tell there was uncovered tension in the left side of my tongue I had not addressed by doing the exercises in my program.

The next morning I woke up to an incredible amount of left jaw pain. My heart goes out to anyone who has suffered with this type of pain. Normal talking was even painful at times. Any amount of opening was painful. I had to be protective of my jaw whenever I chewed anything firmer than a banana. Sometimes even that was difficult. I was acutely aware of the tenderness in my jaw at all times.

I completely understand the natural instinct to directly treat the painful area because that is exactly what I did with my jaw pain! I massaged my jaw plus stretched and iced it and my neck for several days. My symptoms were relieved only partially and temporarily.

Finally, it occurred to me to take my own advice and move my lower body. The external rotators of my right hip were the most restricted area, so I actively exercised them and followed up with some static stretching. My jaw pain was not completely gone the next morning, but the constant tenderness was gone. Opening was much better but still restricted by tenderness when I reached the end range of motion. I did the same lower body exercises that night.

The next morning, my symptoms were completely gone. It is now four months later and, I'm glad to say, never to come back. My brief encounter with TMJ pain made me feel like a real wimp after I heard this next story.

Chronic TMJ Pain

A twenty-six-year-old colleague of mine had been told by her mother that her jaw had clicked since she was a toddler of four years old. It was assumed this was a "genetic condition" in her family because her mother had suffered with a painful clicking jaw since she was a teenager. By the time my friend was in elementary school, the right side of her jaw was locked most mornings upon waking. She would pop it like she popped her fingers and did not think about it much throughout the rest of the day. At age twelve, she started a four-year plan to wear braces to straighten her mouthful of very crooked teeth.

During her freshman year of high school, the pain suddenly switched to the left side of her jaw. Throughout her high school years, the left side of her jaw did not pop but was painful at 5/10 constantly. In addition, it was now "stuck" and would not open greater than a half inch each morning. As the day progressed, her pain would reduce to 3/10, and her jaw would loosen up to allow more opening but never quite opened all the way.

During her freshman and sophomore years in college, she developed Crohn's disease, celiac disease, and irritable bowel syndrome that distracted her away from her jaw for once in many years. As these conditions began to subside, her TMJ pain became significantly worse. The pain on the left side of her jaw was now 10/10 each morning. Eating any kind of meat was difficult. Chewing gum was "a nightmare." She had noticed the muscle inside her left cheek was tight, ropey, and thick.

By this time, she had consulted with several different TMJ specialists, dentists, and therapists. Their advice was to eat soft foods and to provide her with a night splint. Within two months, each splint would be useless from grinding her teeth all night. No one could ever identify specifically what was wrong with her jaw, but at one point, she even agreed to undergo surgery. She got cold feet a few days prior to her scheduled operation and canceled the procedure. On another occasion, she was told the pain was there because "she was too much into her own head."

These types of comments made her begin to wonder if *she was crazy*. How could she be making up such a severe pain? Why would she want to fabricate a pain that made her so grouchy, irritable, and sleep-deprived? She tried yoga and inverted traction, but being head down was excruciating. Searching for a solution to a problem that did not seem to be real to those she consulted with was maddening. At times, she thought she was literally losing her mind.

Approximately five years ago, she started taking eight hundred milligrams of ibuprofen four times each day. Two years ago, she stopped trying to find any kind of help. She resigned herself to waking up twice each night with jaw pain so bad she cried herself back to sleep.

When she attended one of my continuing education classes, her partner during the practical portion of the class noticed that any movement in her body provoked movement at her jaw. This surprising observation confirmed to her that other parts of her body must be affecting her jaw. She was encouraged when her jaw pain each night reduced to 7/10 as she continued to do the seated version of the exercises throughout the next week.

One week after she started the seated exercises, she came to my house for some individual instruction with 7/10 jaw pain. As I worked with her in sitting, I noticed that her jaw now remained still as she moved every other part of her body. What was startling was how poorly coordinated her eye movement was. She often had difficulty moving her eyes correctly even with tracking. The best surprise came when I suggested she do a static stretch of her external hip rotators on the right. Within seconds of placing her hip on a static stretch, her jaw pain was gone but would return when she released the stretch.

After completing the supine and prone lower body exercises and the supine eyes, neck, and upper body exercises on a twenty-degree wedge, again, she had no jaw pain, and this time it did not come back. On Monday morning at work, she told me she was in tears *again* that morning because of her jaw, but this time *it was because she had slept undisturbed all night and woke up to 0/10 jaw pain.*

It is worth mentioning that she woke up feeling congested Monday morning, even though she was pain-free. The congestion progressed to a full-blown cold that kept her home from work on Tuesday and Wednesday. Side effects like this do not mean she had done anything wrong to herself but that her body was changing and "purging." She returned to work on Thursday feeling 50 percent over her cold and 60 percent by Friday. She did not exercise Monday night and did only the lower body exercises only Tuesday and Wednesday night and the full program again by Thursday night. In spite of the fact that she was under the weather and doing limited exercise, she still slept through the night all week long with jaw pain at 0/10.

She estimates her ability to open her mouth was previously limited to 60 percent of complete opening by painful popping of her left jaw. She now opens her mouth 80 to 90 percent without pain or popping but is restricted by a "stiffness." Her jaw will pop at the end range when her mouth is fully open, but the pop is not painful.

You may have wondered what would cause such a small child of only four years old to develop jaw symptoms. I believe her trouble probably started when she broke her nose at age three on a carnival ride. The problem was complicated by a fall out of a tree at age four that fractured her left ulna, a bone in the forearm. She broke her nose again in first grade playing soccer and took a very hard hit to her nose in judo the same year. Later in life at age twenty-four, she slipped on a step, landing directly on her tailbone.

This is how she explains her story:

> *Dear Nancy,*
> *I have to thank you, from the bottom of my heart, for everything you have done for me through your wonderful* **Rapid Release** *program! At the time I am writing this letter, I haven't had jaw pain for over three weeks now. If you told me a month*

ago that someday I would be able to live my life without pain, there's no way I would have believed you.

Growing up is quite a challenge when you constantly have 10/10 pain. "Why are you in such a bad mood?" "What's wrong with you?" "Why can't you focus?" Just a few of the questions that my family, friends, and teachers would ask me on what seemed like a daily basis. Life at that time was difficult, and it turns out it was only going to get harder from there.

When I started college, I began to have multiple health problems. Jaw pain, headaches, and disabling gastrointestinal issues (to name a few) plagued me every day. I saw numerous specialists to find a solution for my pain. Dentists, orthodontists, craniofacial experts, chiropractors, physical therapists all tried to help me with my pain. Simultaneously, I was seeing numerous gastroenterologists who were desperately searching for a diagnosis.

In the span of just a few years, I had numerous procedures, scans, a surgery, and multiple biopsies. I almost had my jaw broken and rewired. No one could give me an answer for any of my pain. I tried splints and mouth guards for my jaw, and was gluten-free for over five years in an attempt to control my intestinal problems. I took pain medication every day. Nothing was helping me. No one could find an answer or figure out how to help me. "My gosh," I would think to myself. "I'm going crazy. I'm losing my mind." One day, my doctor told me what I feared the most. "It's probably all in your head," she stated.

There's only so much pain a person can take before they just break down physically, mentally, and emotionally. What should have been the best years of my life, were turning into empty, lonely, painful days which dragged on for eternity. On some of those days, I could not get out of bed. I cried multiple times during the night, and almost every morning because the pain was so intense. It was literally torture.

On the day I went to your class, I did not know what to expect. To be honest, I was a little apprehensive. I had tried so many things that never succeeded in eliminating my pain. However, seeing the success you were having with so many other patients at our hospital, I was willing to give it a try. Once I understood the foundation, anatomy/physiology, and premise *behind the program, it started to make sense. Your* **Rapid Release** *program is easy to follow, and can be modified to enable anyone to be successful with it. I felt instant relief after that initial attempt. After our second session together, I felt even better. The next day when I woke up, I sobbed, as I had so many other mornings. On this morning, however, it was so different. I had slept through the night, I had no indications of pain. I could hear the birds outside my window. For the first time in years, I felt relief.*

I never knew that this was how life was supposed to be. I've had no traces of jaw pain, headaches, and even my intestinal issues are resolving. I can focus and function in daily life. So far, I haven't had to take multiple pain pills to be able to function during the day. Perhaps most importantly, I am happy. I can get out of bed, and I can live and enjoy my life.

Thank you Nancy, for all you have done. Thank you for developing this program, and for sharing it with everyone. This program is absolutely amazing. I will continue to complete it every day.

Thank you for giving me my life back!

It is now eight months since my colleague learned the exercises. She told me, "I am doing great! My jaw rarely clicks or gets stuck anymore." She continues to do the exercises two to three times a week. She was even in a MVA one month after her pain initially resolved, but that did not set her back. It was good news to learn she used the exercises to keep her on track.

The bad news is wondering how many kids are suffering like she did. Her letter brought me to tears. Children are typically seen in pediatric clinics, so I have not had the opportunity to work with many kids. I now pray for the opportunity to teach this method to those who care for children in public and private schools as well as pediatric therapy clinics anywhere and everywhere. Growing up is hard enough without being in constant pain. It would be great if we could start screening kids in school and provide them with help they might not receive otherwise.

Releasing the Elderly

"Hindsight is always 20/20."

Several years ago, I worked at a skilled nursing facility (SNF) with geriatric or elderly patients with a variety of diagnoses. The time I spent with that population has given me the opportunity to come even closer to validating my hunches and theories regarding the long-term effects of trauma with "living proof." As I collected histories from patients in this unique setting, I was keenly aware of the previous trauma included in each one. *If we are wise, we will consider the course of those who have gone before us to minimize or eliminate our own pain, suffering, and loss of function in the future.*

The purpose of a SNF is to bridge the gap between a hospitalization and discharge to home. These patients no longer require the medical help of an acute care hospital, but they are not yet strong enough or functionally independent enough to go home. The admitting diagnosis for some of the patients I worked with was as diverse as cardiac insufficiency, hip fractures or total joint replacements, respiratory failure, general weakness, low back pain, dementia, sciatica, and the inability to urinate.

At some time in their lives, however, they could all identify a specific time they were previously injured in a MVA or a fall. Many times, the trauma included a blow to the head. The side effects these patients suffered at the time of their accident varied in duration and intensity. The course of treatment provided ranges from nothing at all to surgery. The two consistencies in every case, however, include *what was not done.*

Never was treatment considered for the person's entire body. Never was there a plan of care given to specifically address the damaged soft tissue. This observation is offered for consideration as constructive criticism. In many instances, medical care was never sought out by the patient. They assumed their injuries "would heal on their own in time." These are common mistakes that continue to be made today.

The argument can be made that anti-inflammatory medications and muscle relaxers are now being prescribed to address soft tissue damage. I am being told all too often how medications are not helpful. In addition, most people prefer not to take medication for a variety of reasons. *I propose there is no substitute for an early comprehensive intervention and the correct use of cold packs, massage, and gentle movement to address soft tissue damage.* Again, I cannot help but wonder what these elderly patients' lives would be like today if a more comprehensive approach had been taken to rehabilitate them after their accidents or injuries.

It is a misconception on our part to assume poor health and declining function are a natural part of growing older. The first two ladies you will read about were both leading very full, independent lives, even though they had already reached their "golden years." They thought their current problems began "out of the blue because they were wearing out." I, on the other hand, suspect their problems began the day one was involved in a MVA, and the other one took a fall.

Another misconception we have about the elderly is that their ability to rehabilitate is severely hindered because they are older. I understand age can influence our expectations in some ways or to a certain extent, but we should not underestimate someone's potential solely on the basis of their age. The third woman I will discuss in this section was kind enough to write a letter expressing her appreciation for these exercises. She serves as a very good example of someone who had more potential for improvement than initially seemed possible in spite of her age.

The final case example involves a man who had been negatively tested for multiple neurologic conditions. For anyone living with an undiagnosed debilitating rigidity throughout their body, his remarkable recovery will give you hope for improvement. I, also, wanted to include his story so I would have a "really cool person" in my book. I have been careful not to include identifying information about the patients I have written about in my case examples. This man gave me his permission to share some personal information about him because I knew my grandchildren would find this information to be "very cool." Fifty-five years ago, this patient and his close friend and professor at the University of Michigan developed non-linear optic technologies, the single largest classification of applications in lasers. The development of the concept of nonlinear optics established a new field of physics. Concurrently, my patient had also developed a laser capable of intercepting and destroying another airborne laser. This was the beginning of the so called "Star Wars" program. For my grandchildren and myself, we are now reminded of my patient as they play with their Star Wars light sabers!

Case Study #1

This woman came to our facility at ninety years and seven months of age for extended rehabilitation of a hip fracture she sustained secondary to a fall. Two months prior to her eighty-ninth birthday, she was living independently without any physical restrictions. She was doing all her own driving, shopping, housecleaning, and yard work, except for the heavier jobs. It was at this time she was broadsided in a MVA. Her seat belt tightly engaged across her chest and abdomen while the airbag inflated in her face, leaving her significantly bruised for several weeks after the accident. The most obvious injury she sustained was a fractured right shoulder. She went to physical therapy for her limited shoulder motion but never regained her normal range of motion.

Approximately ten to eleven months after the accident, she noticed a pain in her lower back radiating into her right buttock. This pain made it difficult for her to get out of bed. Within three to four more weeks, the pain was so severe she literally *could not* get out of bed. She was taken by ambulance to the hospital, where she spent the next three to four days. She was then transferred to a skilled nursing facility for extended therapy to treat this functionally restrictive pain. In spite of receiving daily ultrasound, electrical stimulation, and exercises, she was still taking pain meds and muscle relaxers regularly. She continued to rely on her walker for ambulation when she was discharged two to three weeks later. She was able to walk around her house without her walker within two weeks of returning home, but she still relied on medication to manage her pain.

She had no history of high blood pressure or cardiac problems, but it was at this time she very unexpectedly experienced a severe, gripping chest pain, leaving her extremely short of breath. All the necessary tests were run to screen her for a heart attack, but all the tests were negative for any type of abnormality. Shortly after this episode, she lost her balance at home and fell. The result was a fractured hip.

My objective findings were consistent with all post-MVA patients. The range of motion at her hips was very asymmetrical. This could be expected because of the fracture on one side, but I am inclined to believe this was the case even prior to the fall. In fact, it is highly probable this imbalance partially precipitated the fall. She also held her head in significant extension in supine. Her ability to isolate her eye motion was virtually absent. I have no doubt these same objective findings were present to some degree soon after her motor vehicle accident when she only received physical therapy to her right shoulder.

This is another example where active trigger points in the pectoral muscles of the chest mimicked a heart attack as previously mentioned on p. 164. If a random episode of chest pain is experienced, I would never discourage anyone from utilizing whatever tests are available to objectively rule out problems or expose a potentially dangerous situation or condition. But what are we to think when the objective tests say "nothing is wrong"? What are we supposed to do then? Could this woman's experience with chest pain been avoided if she had received early treatment to the damaged soft tissues of her chest soon after her MVA?

The force exerted on a body by a seat belt and/or airbag is certainly capable of inflicting its own form of injury even as it protects the passenger from more serious injuries or potentially even death. Persistent bruising following an accident should always alert us to the magnitude of the trauma inflicted upon the soft tissues. The trigger points in the muscles of her face and chest were still very active and tender when I met this patient fourteen months after her accident. The potential fear of a heart attack could have been quenched long before it had the opportunity to be provoked if the damaged soft tissue of the chest had been treated with cold packs, massage, and gentle exercise.

My list of additional questions regarding this patient is quite long. Could the sciatica, the loss of balance, and the fall that resulted in a fractured hip been prevented if a *more thorough approach* had been taken to her rehab following her MVA? Could two trips in the ambulance, two hospitalizations, one surgery, two admissions to a skilled nursing facility for a total of six to seven weeks with daily physical therapy, one walker, plus multiple medications for several months *all been avoided*? If her initial therapy after her MVA had been more comprehensive, yes, I do think so. Even if this list could not be completely eliminated, I believe it could have been substantially reduced. *In a day of ever-increasing health-care costs, this is an area where a little bit of prevention might well have gone a very long way.*

Case Study #2

The next woman I will share with you was eighty-six years old when she came to our facility to prepare for a right total hip replacement. When she was seventy-eight years old, she was still enjoying a very full and independent life, free of any health problems. In fact, she was so active it was during her seventy-eighth year she fell a short distance down a hill onto her right side while she was out hiking. She, of course, did not correlate her current condition with that fall. In fact, she had almost forgotten about it. After all, "she did not break any bones when she fell, and she was only sore for about a week or so."

By reviewing her progression of symptoms since her fall, I am inclined to believe her fall was the precipitating factor triggering the following series of events. Six years ago, she suddenly developed a pain throughout the entire right side of her body. She could not recall ever injuring herself, so there was no apparent explanation for her pain. Five years ago, she was unable to sleep unless she propped herself up on one or two pillows. Strangely enough, she had developed asthma later in life. She now had zero tolerance for sleeping on her right side, and sleeping on her left side was not much better. Three years ago, she developed a constant pain in her lower back and neck. She has required pain medication twice a day ever since to keep her pain at 6–7/10. Even when she would lie down on her back with two pillows under her head, her pain never dropped below 4–5/10. Two years ago, she was given the diagnosis of osteoporosis as the explanation for her right arm and leg pain. One year ago, she randomly fell onto her right side while attending a funeral. Then two months later, she sustained a second fall onto her right side while walking on a level surface. Neither fall was provoked by tripping or by a position change.

The crepitus, or creaky, noisy joint sounds throughout this woman's body with movement were quite severe. All her joints sounded like they needed a good shot of WD-40. What was amazing was how quickly she responded to just the lower body and neck exercises. The day following her instruction, her crepitus was gone everywhere, except in her right shoulder. Plus, she was surprised when she caught herself using her right hand to feed herself. She had not been able to do that for at least eighteen months. The pain originally covering her entire back was now localized to her right shoulder blade during movement. Her right hip pain was prominent only during sit-to-stand activities.

What is worth noting is how the past six years of this woman's life had become progressively more complicated, painful, and debilitating. I personally do not blame "old age" for her problems. I clearly see her condition as her body's response to neglected soft tissue damage and/or dysfunction following the trauma of her fall. Again, my question is, "How much of her pain, suffering, and loss of function could have been prevented if her full body had been considered and treated with conservative methods like cold packs, massage, and gentle exercises immediately after her fall?"

Words of Precaution

This woman soon left our facility to proceed with her right total hip replacement, so I lost track of her. Before she left, however, some of her aches and pains had returned. Looking back, I wonder if her increased pain was a response to the eye and upper extremity exercises I gave her after the lower body and neck exercises. Or was it from increasing her activity level too quickly when her pain initially subsided?

I mention this part of her experience to serve as an example and a warning, especially for the elderly whose bodies can be more sensitive to change or something new. This is why it is good to learn the exercise program one part at a time. For some elderly patients, it might even be wise to do only one section for two or three days before you add the next section. This will give you the opportunity to monitor your response to each section before you add more exercises. It is also best to gradually increase your activity level. This woman's tolerance for walking with her walker was only twenty to thirty feet prior to her admission. After she learned the back and neck exercises, she was able to walk one hundred feet with her walker. This may have been a case of "too much, too soon" regarding her activity level.

Another response I noticed more frequently among the elderly is a more generalized soreness or flu-like symptoms after progressing the exercises on top of the pillows. If there was significant tension in the chest, bronchial symptoms might even develop. One woman even suffered from bronchial-type symptoms the day after she first did the tongue and eye exercises *in the seated position*. These occurrences are the exception and not the rule, but I mention them so you can be aware of different possibilities. Don't be alarmed by such responses but definitely modify or eliminate whatever you need to until these symptoms subside. Responses to the exercises can vary from person to person but be aware they can be more pronounced and more easily provoked among the elderly.

Case Study #3

I met this last patient about one week before her discharge from our facility. She had fallen two months earlier and broken her right hip. A few days after her surgery, she was transferred from her surgical hospital to another rehab hospital. There, she became very ill with pneumonia and a flare-up of gout. Of course, her illness hindered her progress to a certain extent, but because she was making such minimal improvement in therapy, she made arrangements to transfer to our facility after six to seven weeks. Much to her disappointment, she still required the assistance of another person to help her with all her transfers, even after working ten to fourteen days with our staff. It was at this time one of my coworkers asked me to see her.

This patient was very sweet and pleasant and genuinely concerned about her inability to get out of a chair or out of bed by herself. Even walking very short distances alone with her walker felt unsafe for her. She was seventy-eight years old and would soon be going home to be with her eighty-year-old husband. She did not want to be a hardship on him or be dependent on him or anyone else for that matter.

This woman was also very interesting because she had no recollection of ever being involved in a MVA or of taking a fall. She did tell me, however, the right side of her body had been slightly smaller and weaker than her left side her entire life. The discrepancies had never hindered her function, so she never sought out medical help or even had the problem diagnosed. Her letter expressed her appreciation for these exercises.

> *Dear Nancy,*
> *After I fell and broke my right hip, I did well in therapy for the next two to three days. Then I had a flare-up of gout and a bout of pneumonia. I continued to go to therapy while I was hospitalized in a couple of different places. All of my therapists*

were very kind and caring, but the exercises they gave me for my legs did not help me gain enough strength to get out of bed or up from a chair by myself. By the time I met you I felt like I was only getting worse instead of better. I still needed help to do everything, plus my arms were shaking uncontrollably most of the time.

The first exercises you gave me for my legs were helpful, but when you gave me the exercises for my neck, it felt like "my whole body came back to life again." Every part of my body loosened up! My right foot no longer felt "stuck to the ground" when I tried to move it. Within two to three days I was standing up and completing my transfers with someone nearby for moral support and as a precaution.

The improvement in my strength has helped me overcome the fear I have had to go home. I thank God for sending you to me.

Sincerely,

Case Study #4

This 78-year-old man began to notice his legs were feeling weaker going up and down stairs four years ago. Then it became more difficult to get up from a chair. Eventually, he and his wife were no longer able to take their daily walk outside because he was unable to make it up the hill outside their home. The weakness further progressed until he was unable to even walk through his home without holding onto furniture and the walls. Finally, six months prior to our meeting, his primary care physician suggested he go to physical therapy for six weeks. It became obvious to his therapist he was becoming much worse after only three weeks of treatment. She instructed him in the use of a walker to ambulate more safely and suggested he schedule a neurology consultation as soon as possible.

The neurologist first suspected he was having recurrent TIA's, *transient ischemic attacks*, or small strokes, but none of the testing that was done confirmed this. MS, multiple sclerosis, was ruled out. The patient himself suspected he had myasthenia gravis. His father had died from this condition and now he had all the same symptoms including muscle weakness, difficulty swallowing and chewing, fatigue, slurred, slow speech and worsening symptoms in response to exercise which had happened with physical therapy. Test results for this condition returned negative. The extreme stiffness in his neck and hand tremors also made Parkinson's disease a likely diagnosis, but this, too, proved not to be the case.

He finally was hospitalized following a fall at home. The high levels of calcium detected in his blood were stabilized during this ten day hospitalization. Initial testing was done on his parathyroid gland to consider its potential contribution to his symptoms because of his high calcium levels. He was then sent to rehab for six weeks. His leg strength did not improve in response to the exercises he was given during that admission. He was using his wheelchair more than his front wheeled walker to get around the house following his discharge from the rehab facility. The physical therapist that came to his house did a good job progressing his ambulation to a front wheeled walker, but within two months, his wife was noticing a decline in his condition again. They decided then to follow-up on more testing of the parathyroid with a specialist in the field. It was then they learned of the tumor in his parathyroid gland. Within two weeks, the gland was removed. As soon as he became medically stable, he was admitted to the facility where I was working.

His presentation at the time of his evaluation was very concerning. His wife described him as "a petrified person after surgery. He was unable to move his head or feed himself." His head dropped down and forward. He was unable to lift his chin off his chest without difficulty and required assistance to lift his head to a neutral position. He had zero degrees of cervical extension, or the ability to tilt his head backwards, actively or passively. He was barely able to lift either arm above shoulder height with assistance. Neither elbow straightened out completely. He demonstrated frequent tremors in his right hand. He lacked forty-five degrees of knee extension on the left and thirty degrees on the right. He required the maximum assistance of one to two people to help transfer him from the bed to a chair and back to bed. His hips and knees remained significantly flexed when he stood or laid down. He no longer appeared to be the six foot tall man he was for most of his life. His slow speech made it difficult to participate in routine conversation. His appetite had been diminished for more than a year.

I explained the importance of postural correction to the patient and his wife on the day of his evaluation. I also explained how I would help him do that by using the supine position. He preferred to sleep on his left side, but I taught him how to improve his tolerance for supine by elevating the head of the bed forty-five degrees and using the bed controls to bend his hips and knees as much as possible. He required two pillows underneath his head to correct his cervical alignment, or about sixteen centimeters. I also explained that I would be using eye and tongue exercises to help him loosen up his extremely tense neck.

I was glad his wife was present to observe his lack of eye movement the day I started the eye exercises. I had never seen anything quite like it. While I held his head facing forward in correct alignment, I asked the patient to look up. His eyes remained fixed in the center of the orbit. He truly thought he was moving his eyes, but they were *not budging*. The same thing happened when I asked him to look down and to the left. The only direction he was able to move his eyes was to the right through a very limited range of motion. He had slightly more movement with tracking, but not much. I did not attempt any diagonal motions that first day. Just attempting to move his eyes, however, allowed me to passively move his neck into three to five degrees of cervical extension. I also encouraged him to slouch some in his chair while sitting up. Scooting down on his pelvis while sitting helped him keep his head up and back in a more upright position.

The change in this patient the very next day was remarkable. He was noticeably more alert and holding his head up in better alignment. He was able to actively move his eyes through all planes of motion. He only tolerated two or three repetitions in each direction and only one set in most directions, but this was his place to start. I was happy to see movement! I was able to passively move his neck into ten degrees of cervical extension. Within two more days, he was napping in the modified supine position for up to three hours after lunch as opposed to being in poor alignment on his side. After only four more days, he had thirty degrees of active assistive cervical extension while sitting. In standing, his cervical extension was five to ten degrees. By the end of the first week in rehab, he was using a front wheeled walker to ambulate thirty feet. Within ten days of treatment, he was lying flat on his back with eight centimeters of support under his head and neck with his hips out straight. His knee extension had improved to minus ten degrees on the right and minus twenty degrees on the left.

I used the principle of "Give a Little, Take a Little" to improve his tolerance for lying more flat in supine. I continued to use that principle throughout his three week stay with us. Up until the very end, he tolerated lower body movement best when his head and neck were elevated some. His tongue, jaw, neck and eyes moved much more easily when he was slightly bent at his hips and knees. By the time of his discharge, he was transferring himself in and out of bed, off and on a variety of seated surfaces, and ambulating up to three hundred feet with his four wheeled walker.

There were a couple of muscle compliments I used repeatedly with this patient that effectively progressed his outcomes. He was lacking cervical extension and knee extension. Alternating active motion between these two areas gradually released the tension in both of them. Adding mildly resistive elbow extension also helped. The most interesting association we discovered was how actively moving his hips into internal rotation relaxed his jaw. This enabled him to more naturally *keep his mouth closed.* His ability to slide his bottom jaw forward noticeably improved. This did not surprise me as I recalled how much hip rotation previously helped to alleviate another patient's jaw pain (see page 354-359).

I asked this patient if he would be willing to submit a letter for the book. His wife chimed in as she smiled at me, "If we can say how crazy we thought you were!" I told them their reaction was nothing new. Of course, they were to feel free in stating what best explained their experience with me in therapy.

> *Dear Nancy,*
>
> *When I first met you, we had been through an ordeal with my health. My wife was concerned that some of your suggestions sounded "crazy." She spoke with our son about your ideas to move my eyes and stick out my tongue as part of my therapy. She was surprised and relieved to learn they did not seem crazy to him at all. His wife is a psychologist and familiar with how the eyes can be used to help many different problems. I have been an experimental physicist my entire career. I perceived your ideas as "very unconventional," but was not opposed to participating in "experimental physical therapy."*

What I have enjoyed the most about our sessions is how the crazy correlations you made always made me feel better. You would explain to me why you were doing what you were doing and what to expect. It was amusing when things always worked out the way you said they would. Your treatments seems to be very much like acupuncture in that you treat one area to make another area feel better.

If we had only heard about your methods, we might not have believed what we were hearing. But we have seen your methods work. "Seeing is believing."

Thanks so much for all you have done to help me improve. I have the mobility I needed to go home with confidence.

Sincerely,

Releasing Pain during Hospitalization

After working twenty-plus years in outpatient rehab clinics, home health, skilled nursing, and private practice, I transitioned to the acute care hospital setting. Since traumatic injury is a prevalent part of most people's medical history, I wondered how much more effective this approach would be if it was implemented at the time the trauma occurred. My initial idea was to work with patients admitted to the hospital following a traumatic injury sustained specifically from a motor vehicle accident or fall. The way things worked out was so much better.

I had the opportunity to spend time with patients who had suffered a recent trauma but even more fortunate to be "floated" all over the hospital. The patients I saw had been admitted to all different types of service, including oncology, cardiology, general surgery, general medicine, orthopedics, and the emergency room. I learned that, regardless of their admitting diagnosis or how their condition was categorized, every patient I met in the hospital *also had a history of previous trauma. The patients in the hospital were not so different from the patients in the outpatient clinics.* The main difference I saw was the severity of the inpatient's complications after their trauma had become significant enough to land them in the hospital.

I did not have the opportunity to follow patient improvement in the hospital like I could in the outpatient setting. Most of the time, the patient was not in the hospital for weeks at a time. I may have seen a patient to complete his or her initial evaluation and then never see them again. On other occasions, I was able to follow the patient for a couple of days.

The following list exemplifies how a previous trauma may have influenced a person's condition during hospitalization. The examples I cite show snapshots of deficits that can be addressed with the principles from **Rapid Release**. The admitting diagnosis and traumatic history is in **bold lettering**. Regardless of their diagnosis, **Rapid Release** was an appropriate treatment strategy for these hospitalized patients. *In a setting of medical complexity, implementing the simple principles of improved posture and flexibility still made a significant contribution to a more complete recovery.*

1. **Forty years ago,** a seventy-nine-year-old male **was assaulted with a cue stick to his right frontal lobe.** He was hospitalized at that time for five to seven days for a concussion and brain bleed. Twenty years ago, he suffered a stroke, affecting the left side of his body. He had been caring for himself independently until the last couple of weeks until **both lower legs started to swell.** The side affected by the stroke was becoming increasingly more tense, provoking **near falls.** Transferring and dressing himself were becoming increasingly more difficult. He was losing his ability to take care of himself.

   This patient spent all day every day sitting in his wheelchair. When he slept, he was C-shaped with his upper body and head to the left, his pelvis was shifted to the right, and his legs then shifted back to the left again. His body was never fully lengthened, and his alignment was never corrected.

   When his cervical motion was assessed, he demonstrated forty-five degrees of cervical rotation to the left but only ten degrees to the right, which is the opposite for a stroke survivor with left-sided weakness. When his eye motion was assessed, we found it was very difficult to stabilize his eyes in the center and turn his head to the left; it was impossible to stabilize his eyes and turn his head to the right. It is probable his left side was becoming more tense as the tension in his eyes and neck was increasing.

This patient's daughter was taught how to help her dad with his positioning and exercises. My hope is for him to regain the independence he was slowly losing.

2. A fifty-four-year-old male was hospitalized for **chest pain**. In flat supine, his upper body was centered on the bed, but both legs were shifted to the right lower corner of the bed. When his legs were brought directly beneath his pelvis, his whole body "felt off 10/10." Interestingly, his eyes had been stinging constantly, and his left eye had been swelling daily for the past three weeks. When the head of the bed was elevated at thirty degrees and his legs were positioned straight underneath his pelvis, it was difficult to move his eyes in any direction at 8/10. When he was allowed to bend at his hips and knees, it became only 2/10 difficult to move his eyes. **The traumatic history for this patient included four rollover MVAs in his twenties to thirties. He was unrestrained in each one. He sustained a concussion from each accident.**

3. A twenty-six-year-old female was admitted for a **thoracic strain after a three hundred pound patient fell on her.** She underwent **emergency surgery for a herniated disc** in the center of her upper back. Her back pain resolved with surgery, but she continued to complain of excruciating pain in her left oblique abdominals. She had been sitting up at sixty degrees in bed constantly since her surgery to avoid increased pain. I decided to assess how sitting at different angles might effect her pain. When the head of her bed was lowered to twenty degrees, her abdominal pain increased to 7–8/10; as the head of the bed was raised to thirty-five degrees, her pain reduced to 5/10. When the head was raised to forty-five degrees, her pain reduced to 0/10.

Her eyes were very droopy when I arrived in the room, slightly more so on the right. Her eyes fatigued with only two repetitions of movement in each direction. When she attempted to stick her tongue out straight, her eyes crossed. **Her traumatic history included a dog bite to the crown of her head at age two.** Her eyes have been sensitive to the light as long as she could remember. She has required drops in both eyes several times each day for the past ten years. She has suffered from migraine headaches six to seven times a year for the past six years.

4. A fifty-three-year-old female was admitted for **lower back pain**. She had suffered from LBP 3–5/10 constantly for the past five years after being struck as a pedestrian by a moving car. Suddenly, her pain increased to 10/10 for no reason she could identify. Her pain also expanded into her left hip and left leg. She was unable to sit or stand without provoking 10+/10 pain. She was brought to the hospital by ambulance.

After being hospitalized for three days, she was still unable to sit on the edge of the bed. Within one hour of teaching the patient how to correct the alignment of her head and neck, and completing the eye, head and neck, and arm exercises, she was able to sit on the edge of the bed with pain of only 4–5/10. **The traumatic history for this patient, in addition to being struck by the car, included a fall from a fence, hitting her head on a concrete slab at age eleven.**

5. A twenty-nine-year-old female was admitted for **bilateral lower extremity weakness**. Within twenty-four hours of her admission, she had lost the strength in both upper extremities also. The day I evaluated her, all motion in all four extremities was completed *passively. She did not have enough strength to even assist with the movement of her extremities.* Passive range of motion in her arms was restricted to fifty percent, but passive motion in her hips and knees was limited by eighty to ninety percent. Both ankles were rigidly positioned with her toes fully pointing down. *There was zero passive movement at her ankles.*

For the past six months, this patient had suffered with neck pain 10/10 and the inability to lift her chin off her chest. Taking her gabapentin regularly reduced her pain to 6/10 and enabled her to lift her head normally. At night, she slept with two pillows to alleviate the intense pressure she felt in her head.

On the Monday of this patient's evaluation, we learned she was able to tolerate correct alignment of her head and neck without the two pillows if the head of her bed was raised to thirty degrees. Within ten minutes of sustaining this position with her head and neck, her ankles tolerated passive movement to the neutral position for her ankles. *In other words, she gained sixty to seventy degrees of passive motion.*

This young woman's improvement was beyond remarkable. Without recounting her daily improvement, I will say by Friday, or with only four follow-up visits with myself and three additional treatments with an occupational therapist, she walked 150' x 1 with a FWW (front-wheeled walker)—pain-free without medications.

The traumatic history for this patient included **a fracture to the frontal bone of her head when she fell over a fence as a child onto a concrete slab.** The laceration to her forehead required seven to eight stitches to close. She also **fell out of a tree at age eleven.** One leg was jerked during the fall especially hard when it got tangled up in a rope as she fell. And what the patient forgot to mention, but her mother told me about when she came to take the patient home, was that **she was born cross-eyed.** The alignment of her eyes was not surgically corrected until she was four years old.

6. A forty-year-old male was **found down** at a local business establishment. He was hospitalized for testing secondary to the fact that he had **recently suffered a mild heart attack.** The patient's biggest concern, however, was a five-year history of sciatica. While he sat in a bedside chair, we learned looking up with his eyes, tucking his chin, or looking over his right shoulder all provoked stabbing pains in his left lower back or left leg. **Past trauma for this patient included having the side of his face slammed into a concrete slab as a teenager. Ten years ago, he fractured his nose on a dashboard in a MVA.** His nose continued to bleed off and on for the next five days after the accident.

7. A similar example is a forty-two-year-old female hospitalized for **lower back pain and right leg pain.** She was unable to stand straight at the waist. Any amount of weight bearing on her right leg provoked sharp, stabbing pains in her leg and lower back 10+/10. After sixty minutes of instruction regarding positioning and exercise for her eyes, neck,

and full body with the head of the bed elevated to thirty degrees, she effortlessly stood straight from the edge of her bed. She was even able to shift her weight onto her right leg without pain. She did not stand for long so as not to push her luck but understood she could expect more lasting results as she progressed to doing the exercises flat on her back. **The traumatic history for this patient included landing wrong on her left arm when she jumped off the arm of the sofa, fracturing her humerus, or upper arm, at age six.**

8. A fifty-six-year-old male was hospitalized for a **cervical fusion**. The patient's neck pain and arm pain improved considerably after surgery. The problem he was having now was the inability to stand straight without immediately collapsing in response to severe muscle spasms around his right shoulder blade. The only way he was able to walk ten feet to the restroom was by putting both hands on the back of his head.

This patient had not lowered the head of his bed any lower than forty degrees since surgery. Completing a simple heel slide in this position with either leg pulled in the back of his neck. *Completing very poorly coordinated large eye circles provoked cramping in between his shoulder blades.* After doing the seated exercises for two days and the supine program once with the head of the bed at thirty degrees, the patient was able to ambulate 300' x 1 without spasms at his shoulder blade. **The traumatic history for this patient included numerous MVAs, some with his seat belt on and some not, and many times being hit in the head with fists, bottles, bats, or other objects.**

9. A forty-seven-year-old male was admitted for **the sudden onset of unstoppable coughing, shortness of breath, and bilateral lower extremity weakness.** Interestingly, this patient was born with his right eye crossed into the middle. This same eye hurts constantly 7–8/10. Prior to doing any exercise, the patient attempted to ambulate ten feet to the door of his room. He was coughing so severely, even while on three liters of oxygen, he had to turn around and go back to bed. After doing the full seated exercises, with and without covering his good eye, he was able to ambulate 150' x 1. He felt a little shaky

in his legs, but he did not cough a single time while being on only two liters of oxygen. **The traumatic history for this patient included a motor vehicle accident eight years ago. The patient was told he fractured his neck, but surgical intervention was not required.** He now suffered daily with chronic neck pain at 8–9/10.

10. Another sixty-two-year-old female was admitted for **bilateral leg weakness and two recent episodes of fainting**. Interestingly, but unfortunately for her, she had suffered ten TIAs (trans ischemic attacks or small strokes) in the last four years. When she attempted to ambulate twenty feet in the hallway of the hospital, her coughing was so severe and restrictive we turned around and went back to her room. In the seated position, she completed the exercises for her eyes, neck, jaw, and both arms. Immediately following the exercises, she was able to ambulate 125' x 1 with a brief rest stop for her right leg. Then she walked 150' x 1 back to her room. Not only was she able to demonstrate an improved gait pattern while walking, but she did not cough a single time as well. **Her traumatic history included a MVA five years prior.** She did not think she was injured in the accident, but the next day, she curiously passed out for no reason that could be determined.

11. A sixty-four-year-old male was hospitalized for **DKA (diabetic ketoacidosis)**. This is a life-threatening complication for diabetics that occurs when the body produces high levels of blood acids called ketones. The condition develops when the body does not produce enough insulin or when the patient is noncompliant in taking their insulin as directed.

After the patient was stabilized medically, PT was ordered to help him mobilize. On the day of his evaluation, it took three people to help him roll over in bed. His right arm and leg felt like they were covered in road rash with 10+/10 pain, so he was initially not enthused about having anyone even touch him. When he was asked to center his eyes in the orbit, he positioned his pupils in the bottom of the orbits. His son explained it was normal for his father to tilt his head back and look at others from the bottom of his eyes while he talked to them.

After instructing this patient how to center his eyes in the anatomically correct position, completing active movement of his eyes from that position, and completing the neck exercises, the pain in his right arm and leg reduced to 2–4/10. He was able to active assistively participate in the range of motion for the rest of his body. **The traumatic history for this man included two motor cycle accidents in his twenties. Plus, he fell headfirst into the siding of his house fifteen years ago, leaving a permanent dent in the side of his house.**

12. A ninety-year-old female was admitted to the hospital for **frequent falls, UTIs (urinary tract infections), respiratory distress, and hyponatremia, or low sodium, in the blood.** Sodium is an electrolyte that regulates the amount of water in and around the cells. Low sodium can result in nausea, vomiting, headache, confusion, loss of energy or fatigue, restlessness, irritability, muscle weakness, cramps or spasms, seizures, and even coma. This sweet little lady could not anticipate when she was going to fall. She said, "My legs just get twisted up, and I fall!"

When this woman stood, her posture spoke volumes. She demonstrated an upper thoracic kyphosis, or "humpback" in her upper back, a forward head of approximately six to eight centimeters (her ear was in front of her shoulder by six to eight centimeters), and her face was parallel with the floor. Past traumatic history for this patient included **a fall onto her back ten to twelve years ago with a lower back spinal fracture. She also stated, "My neck is bad all the time. I may have broken it once when I was little."**

13. **NSTEMI, or "non-ST segment elevation myocardial infarction,"** is a diagnosis frequently seen among cardiac patients. Simply put, a specific segment of the electrocardiogram does not show a change in elevation, which indicates a milder form of a heart attack. A fifty-two-year-old male had the classic signs of a heart attack with tightness and pressure in his chest, pain radiating down his left arm, and elevated troponins in his blood. Troponins are a type of protein released by the heart muscle into the blood when it is damaged. He

also smoked two packs of cigarettes a day (which I didn't know anyone could still afford to do). His symptoms resolved with the medications he was given in the hospital, but the pressure in his chest would return mildly after eating. The pressure in his chest improved when he was instructed how to correctly align the posture of his head and neck while his upper body was elevated thirty degrees.

This patient **seriously injured his neck in a MVA twenty years ago, requiring him to wear a hard collar for six weeks after the accident.** He continued to experience neck pain in cold weather, but his sleeping posture was more of his problem. He used five or so pillows under his head each night to sleep, pushing the position of his neck into full flexion, or with his chin tucked all the way to his chest. If he did not have as many pillows as he needed or they were too soft, he would hold his head in that position with the muscles of his neck while his head was unsupported. He also read news articles on his cell phone all day.

An additional complaint of his was constipation. Gentle soft tissue mobilization to exquisitely tender psoas muscles on both sides and to the muscles of his TMJ bilaterally produced very effective relief of his constipation within a few minutes after the conclusion of his treatment.

14. Heart involvement was ruled out for another fifty-six-year-old male admitted with **progressively worsening chest pain, abdominal pain with nausea, and lower extremity swelling.** Persistent nausea was this patient's primary complaint once his chest pain improved, so the focus of his testing was directed toward various gastrointestinal disorders. This patient sustained **a very direct blow to the left side of his head by a quickly lowered truck ramp** five years prior to this admission. He had "a very large lump" on the side of his head for two weeks. His very poor tolerance for the seated exercises was surprising. Interestingly, isolated eye motion in all directions, especially looking up, *provoked nausea*. Gently twisting his trunk *provoked nausea*. Dropping his knees apart to do seated fallouts *provoked nausea*. Even straightening his knee and pumping his ankle on the right side *provoked nausea*.

I mention these last two patients particularly to suggest conventional aerobic cardiac rehab might be enhanced by postural correction and improved general flexibility. The next two patients provide examples of how balance and sitting posture can improve in a radical way in ten to fifteen minutes by completing the eye exercises. I have not worked with a patient population that regularly treats altered sitting balance, but I would guess that recovery time might be accelerated by days, or maybe even weeks, by implementing the eye exercises in conjunction with standard treatment.

15. A fifty-seven-year-old male came to the emergency room after experiencing **increased shortness of breath, increased swelling in both of his legs, and orthopnea or the inability to breathe while lying down flat.** This patient typically slept on one side or the other but was forced to sleep in a propped-up position and finally sitting up in a chair for the past ten nights because he could not breathe when he was lying down. In addition to the problems he was admitted to the hospital for, the patient explained to me he had been completely exhausted and found it very difficult to even keep his eyes open for the past ten days. His noticed that his eyes started feeling very heavy at the same time the shortness of breath started.

This patient had been in multiple MVAs as a teenager and young adult. He had also suffered multiple concussions. The amount of tension and pressure he experienced in his head was obvious when his tolerance for supine positioning was assessed. When the head of the bed was lowered to thirty degrees, his breathing became significantly hindered. When the head of the bed was lowered to twenty degrees, the patient stated that he felt like his body was now perfectly flat. As I lowered the bed below twenty degrees, he began to feel as if he was standing on his head.

On the day of his evaluation, I instructed this patient in the eye and neck exercises. In these situations where there is so much tension and pressure in the head, it is best for the patient to sit up as much as possible. *The seated exercises should then be done from the feet up.* (After stabilizing his eyes during cervical movement, he became extremely tired and requested to return to bed. In less than one minute, his heart rate increased significantly for twenty seconds, which explained his extreme fatigue.)

16. **A thirty-four-year-old female was ejected from her vehicle during a motor vehicle accident** one month prior to our meeting. She suffered a (+) loss of consciousness, a non-displaced fracture of her second thoracic vertebra, a sacral fracture, and an ankle fracture. Her nurse requested my help because her own body was so tired and sore from moving this patient in bed for the past three days. The patient was not following commands, so it had been up to the nurse and another helper to roll the patient or pull her up in bed with no assistance from the patient. **The patient's ability to mobilize herself was virtually nonexistent.**

When I entered the room, the patient's head was over to the right of the bed, and her feet were in the lower left corner. Her head was strongly rotated to the left. It took a moderate amount of assistance from myself and the nurse to sit this patient up on the edge of the bed from the flat supine position. She then required moderate assistance from the nurse to maintain her sitting balance. Without the help of the nurse, she would have fallen backward on the bed. The patient attempted to stand from the edge of the bed three separate times but was unable to initiate the task.

While the nurse supported the patient's sitting balance, I corrected the position of her head to neutral. I held her head in correct alignment while I led her through the eye exercises through all planes of motion. To the amazement of her nurse and myself, the patient was able to independently sit on the edge of the bed for the next ten minutes while I led her through the neck exercises. During the time the patient sat on the edge of the bed, she was able to correct her slouched sitting posture with verbal cues. After the exercises, the patient was able to stand from the edge of the bed on her first attempt with only "contact guard assistance." (Contact guard assistance = help from another to assist with some unsteadiness, but the patient used all their own strength to rise from the seated position). The patient was able to step to her left four times and then get herself back into bed. She was able to center herself on the bed and bridge up on the bed three times to push herself up in bed completely independently.

17. The final patient I will share demonstrated this same improvement in sitting balance while being hospitalized in the medical intensive care

unit. This patient was a fifty-six-year-old male who was rushed to the hospital early one morning when his wife found him unresponsive in his recliner at four o'clock in the morning. He became **hypoxic after aspirating some food** while sitting in his recliner, passing out and losing consciousness. His life was threatened by the incident, and he spent the next two days on a ventilator to keep him alive and breathing.

I spoke with the nurse prior to my evaluation of the patient. He informed me the patient had sat up earlier in the day with an occupational therapist. The patient required maximum assistance of two people to hold him in the seated position for one minute. At the end of that time, the patient was completely exhausted and requested he be returned to the supine position in bed. I told the nurse about my exercises and how I hoped they would improve the patient's sitting tolerance. The nurse was eager to observe and assist with the treatment session to see if the patient's ability to sit upright improved after completing such simple exercises.

The traumatic history for this patient included **many motor vehicle accidents and falls. On one occasion, he struck his forehead on the windshield. In another accident, he hit the left side of his head on the driver's side window.** He suffered with degenerative disc disease in his upper back that he attributed to a **fall from a slide in elementary school**. This particular patient had an especially difficult time stabilizing his head in neutral. He had a very strong tendency to keep his head tilted backward. I chose to instruct this patient in the exercises while he was long sitting in bed with the head of the bed elevated at forty-five degrees. Looking up and down with his eyes was especially uncoordinated, but movement of his eyes in all directions was impaired or sluggish. He was able to complete the range-of-motion exercises for his neck without any difficulty.

To the amazement of the patient, his wife, daughter, granddaughter, and the nurse, the patient *independently moved himself* from long sitting in bed to the edge of the bed. He required no assistance making the transfer and even sat independently on the edge of the bed for two minutes without a trace of imbalance in his trunk. The nurse was eager for more by this time and asked the patient if he would be willing to attempt standing. To the pleasure of everyone in the room, the patient stood to his feet on his first attempt and easily maintained his upright standing posture for one minute without any assistance from myself or the nurse. He returned to sitting independently and then stood to his feet again two more times and maintained his standing position for one minute again each time without assistance. He took three lateral steps to his right before putting himself back to bed. Once in bed, he independently moved himself over to his left to center himself in the bed. What the nurse and this patient's spouse witnessed was not what they were expecting. His nurse was kind enough to share his impression of our session.

> *Dear Nancy,*
>
> *This letter is written in response to your treatment session with a patient we used your **Rapid Release** therapy with. My medical opinion as a medical cardiac intensive care nurse is that your treatment method is extremely effective. Your **Rapid Release** method restored my patient's equilibrium and calibrated his movements to progress him from a deconditioned, weakened state to standing in one session! The patient was post intubation secondary to aspiration with neurological defects and had been sedated in bed for approximately seven days.*
>
> *The patient had done a traditional rehab session six hours prior to your therapy. He was unable to hold himself in an upright seated position for one minute with the assistance of two people. He could follow commands, but did not have the strength or the gross motor skills to initiate sitting or standing. Your **Rapid Release** therapy lasted one hour. At the end of the session, we stood the patient for the first time in seven days. He was able to stand on his own with only supervision for safety a total of three times. His posture, coordination, and pain level all improved. The patient also showed clinical signs of mentation improvement with increased lucidity in his sentence formation.*
>
> *In my opinion, the therapy worked to calibrate the spatial awareness of his brain which in turn improved all aspects of his dexterity and movement. I will be using aspects of this therapy in my daily work to help my patients recover from deconditioned states. Thank you so much for the work you are doing.*

These few examples of different diagnoses represent a small portion of what any person might be admitted to the hospital for. The list could easily go on and on. I trust you can see that past trauma and/or pre-existing asymmetries are affecting these patients' current conditions. I believe treating these findings would provide more thorough care and, hopefully, better recovery from each one's current diagnosis and less chance of a hospital readmission.

Consider one of the last patients I saw in the hospital before I ended my time there. An eighty-year-old woman came to the emergency room with severe abdominal pain. Four days later when I arrived in her room, she was packed up and ready to go home. She had been effectively treated by surgically removing gallstones, was getting in and out of bed by herself, and was able to walk three hundred feet in the hall by herself. By most standards, her case was straight forward, her problem had been resolved, and she was functioning independently, so there was nothing more to do. Or was there?

Her traumatic history did not include any MVAs, but she confessed to two very bad falls in the last two years. During this time, she was the primary caregiver for her terminally ill husband. She assumes she was very tired when she accidentally tripped in her home the first time, falling to the right, hitting her right leg, torso, and arm on some boxes. Unfortunately, she hit the right side of her temple, jaw, and face on a small amplifier. She had dark bruises along the whole right side of her body but did not have the opportunity to rest since she was caring for her husband.

Her second fall occurred six months ago. She still wasn't sure what happened. She thinks she may have fainted. She fell hard onto the left side of her body and, again, bruised the entire side of her body and face with dark-black and purple bruises. Her grandson told her that her whole body was shaking and shivering uncontrollably for a short time after she hit the ground. Her husband had passed away one year prior, so this time she was able to "take better care of herself and rest more." She barely got out of bed for the next week. Even though she did not associate the falls with the current weakness in her neck, she had not been able to lift her head from her pillow for the last year. She complained her head "felt very heavy." She *literally* pulled her head up by the hair to lift her head off the pillow.

When I assessed the posture of her head and neck in supine, she needed six to eight centimeters of support to stabilize her head and neck in correct alignment. Her torso laterally bent to the right while she lay on her bed in supine. When her shoulders were lined up over her pelvis, she felt "very off." She tolerated the eye exercises with minimal deviations in sitting, but in supine with her legs extended, it was difficult at 7–8/10 to stabilize her eyes forward while she turned her head to the right. When she bent her hips and knees, the difficulty to do the same thing decreased to 2–3/10. In addition, she had noticed she was cold most of the time in the last year.

This patient's nurse knew nothing about the falls this woman had taken. That is not to fault the nurse. When the patient was asked if she had taken any recent falls, she said no because she did not think her falls were recent and did not see how they could be contributing to her current problems.

When a patient is asked about his or her fall history and the answer is no, maybe the patient needs more information to answer more correctly. Like this patient, if the fall was a long time ago or did not directly involve the current painful area or diagnosis, the patient will answer no to the questions about fall history. He or she does not understand a trauma from any time could be influencing his or her current situation. While it may be impossible to reach everyone with the message of how damaging car accidents and falls can be, we should seize the opportunity to promote wellness and prevention whenever we have the chance.

This woman did not know what provoked her last fall. The fact that her body "shivered uncontrollably" at the time she fell suggests something neurological was happening. By addressing the deficits found during her hospitalization, it may be possible to prevent future falls, which could lead to "who knows where" for a woman in her *eighties*.

Closing Thoughts

I never get tired of seeing all the different ways this program helps people overcome their challenges. I have approached every patient I have seen for the last eighteen years with this method. You would think I would be sick of it. But instead, *every patient is different,* which keeps my work interesting and rewarding. It's fun to know I helped them uncover some far removed glitch in their body that could have prevented them from reaching their full recovery potential. I frequently remind myself about the patients years ago who lost their lives to unsanitary health practices prior to the acknowledgment of the importance of good hand hygiene. It seems odd now, but the suggestion to implement hand washing between surgical patients at the time it was first introduced was met with hostile resistance. It is encouraging to know the best practice for the patient eventually prevailed. As it turns out, I have experienced resistance as well for implementing this simple exercise program to help my patients.

My hope and prayer is that the time and the attention required to restore the basic qualities of correct posture and improved flexibility to restore overall health and function will soon be granted their rightful place of importance in mainstream health care and rehabilitation. *Doing what is best for the patient needs to once again prevail.*

Chapter 6

Why Does It Work?

If you purchased this book solely for the purpose of learning some exercises for pain management, you can skip this chapter if you'd like. You can be successful with these exercises even if you never understand the theory behind "why" they work. If you are curious about what may be changing in your body, I hope to present as much of the information as I can in a way for you to get a basic idea of what might be happening. If you are a therapist, I hope my theories help you understand what this method may be facilitating in your patients to help them accomplish their goals.

This program provides a method of movement to gradually restore correct posture and maximum flexibility. Posture is something so fundamental to how we feel and function it's easy to forget how important it is. Flexibility often takes the back seat to strengthening whenever we consider "being in shape" because strong muscles *look* good. Flexible muscles *feel* good. Ideally, muscles should be strong *and* flexible. When the basics are corrected, many other things fall into place.

Think of it this way. If you intended to flip a house with multiple problems like crooked doors, windows, and cabinets, the faulty foundation probably contributing to all these problems should be corrected first. If you were asked to drive down any random street in a residential area to report what the homes have in common, you might be hard-pressed to come up with an answer. Each house would have a front door, but one might be wooden, the next one metal. Some would have panes on the windows, others would not. One might have a shingled roof, while another would have tile. The details of these houses could vary in hundreds of ways. Regardless of the many ways these houses can be different, the one thing they all have in common is the foundation. The most important structure in the house is never seen. The foundation must be level to provide integrity and balance to every other part of the house. If the foundation is faulty, the entire structure will be also. Our posture is the "foundation" of our body. The unfortunate thing about a foundation is it is taken for granted and rarely acknowledged.

This is what I have noticed when it comes to illness and injury. Health problems can manifest in a *multitude of different ways*. The issue may be headaches, neck pain, decreased movement of the shoulder, chest pain, shortness of breath, decreased mobility, lower back pain, sciatica, decreased leg strength, etc. Regardless of the manifesting problem, the fascial system, which greatly influences our postural foundation, is not symmetrical or relaxed. Restoring symmetry and flexibility to this very important system is at least part of what needs to be accomplished as maximum recovery is pursued. Maintaining good posture and flexibility throughout our lives will help us enjoy our later years more fully.

The Importance of Posture and Flexibility

By definition, posture is "the alignment of the body parts whether upright, sitting, or recumbent. It is described by the positions of the joints and body segments and also in terms of the balance between the muscles crossing the joints. Impairments in the joints, muscles, or connective tissues may lead to faulty postures; or, conversely, faulty postures may lead to impairments in the joints, muscles, or connective tissues as well as symptoms of discomfort and pain. Many musculoskeletal complaints can be attributed to stresses that occur from repetitive or sustained activities when in a habitually faulty postural alignment."[6] According to Florence Kendall, PT, whose muscle testing and function book is a standard reference for physical therapists, good posture is demonstrated from the lateral, or side, view when a plumb line drops from the ceiling "through the lobe of the ear, . . . through the bodies of the cervical vertebrae, through the shoulder joint, . . . approximately midway through the trunk, through the bodies of the lumbar vertebrae, . . . slightly posterior to the center of the hip joint, slightly anterior to the center of the knee joint, and slightly anterior to the lateral malleolus of the ankle."[7]

CHAPTER 6

[6] Kisner, Carolyn and Colby, Lynn Allen, *Therapeutic Exercise Foundations and Techniques*, Fifth Edition (F. A. Davis Company, 2007), p. 383.
[7] Peterson Kendall, PT, Florence, Kendall, and McCreary, Elizabeth, *Muscle Testing and Function*, Third Edition (Williams and Wilkins, 1983), p. 278.

Evaluating the posture of my patient is the foundation of this program. *Doing something* about the discrepancies I find is the next step. *Restoring correct movement from a position of correct alignment is how the body returns to a position of balance and symmetry.* Posture cannot be in a category of its own where observations are made and filed away. The information must be integrated into the treatment plan so postural abnormalities are corrected.

Asymmetrical fascial tension in our body has the potential to "unlevel" the foundation. The fascia has been described as "a continuous tensional network throughout the human body, covering and connecting every single organ, every muscle and even every nerve or tiny muscle fiber."[8] The fascia has also been described as a functionally integrated body-wide continuum of webbing or connective tissue fabric. Understanding that fascia exists as a whole body system "will lead to a more three-dimensional feel for musculoskeletal anatomy and an appreciation of whole-body patterns of compensation and strain distribution. Clinically, it leads to a directly applicable understanding of how painful problems in one area of the body can be linked to a totally 'silent' area at some remove from the problem."[9] These definitions resonate with the osteopathic concept of the global lesion mentioned in chapter 1. Many osteopaths would probably agree the mechanism driving the global lesion is tension variations via fascial aponeuroses or sheets of fascia that bind muscles and organs together.

Assessing the body for fascial restrictions in supine is how postural discrepancies are revealed and corrected with this program. As fascial restrictions in the connective tissue are released with movement and the body becomes more relaxed and flexible, the foundation is "leveled" again. The body is able to move and function from a position of correct alignment more comfortably.

The far-reaching effects of posture are being recognized and validated in the world of neuromuscular dentistry. One of their textbooks states, "When a patient presents with several complaints of pain and dysfunction in the neck, shoulder, and back, this should be an indication for a complete

---

[8] Schleip, R., Findley, Thomas W., Chaitow, Leon, Huijing, Peter, A, *Fascia - The Tensional Network of the Human Body* (Churchill Livingston Elsevier, 2012), p. xv.

[9] Thomas W. Myers, *Anatomy Trains* (Churchill Livingstone Elsevier, 2001), p. 1.

whole body postural evaluation. It is a fact there is no way to separate the head from the shoulder girdle and the cervical spine, the dorsal and lumbar spine, or the pelvis from the upper and lower limbs. To make an adequate diagnosis, a neuromuscular dentist should be able to find postural abnormalities at every level of the body, so they can properly understand if the presenting symptoms can be directly treated alone. Otherwise, other health care specialist should be involved in order to achieve a proper and complete treatment which will restore the musculoskeletal system to its normal function."[10] "Quite often there is a close relationship between the molar classification and the body posture."[11]

In normal occlusion, or how the teeth make contact with one another, the last molar of the maxilla, or upper teeth, should rest in the grove of the last molar of the mandible or lower teeth. This is molar classification I. If the top teeth are positioned forward on the bottom teeth, or overbite, it has been noted the head will also come forward in a "forward head" posture. This is referred to as retral shift of the mandible or molar classification II. The plumb line will shift to the front of each landmark all the way down the body to the ankles and the feet. In molar classification III, the top teeth shift back onto the bottom teeth or underbite. The plumb line falls behind the postural landmarks all the way to the ankles and the feet.

---

[10] *The Application of the Principles of Neuromuscular Dentistry to Clinical Practice, Anthology IX*, The International College of Cranio-Mandibular Orthopedics (The International College of Cranio-Mandibular Orthopedics, 2010), p. 20.

[11] *The Application of the Principles of Neuromuscular Dentistry to Clinical Practice, Anthology IX*, The International College of Cranio-Mandibular Orthopedics (The International College of Cranio-Mandibular Orthopedics, 2010), p. 22.

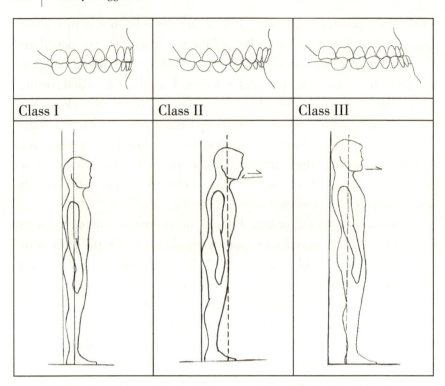

| Class I | Class II | Class III |

"The influence of either craniocervical (head/neck) and/or craniomandibular (head/jaw) dysfunctions onto fascia and postural muscles (as far down as the lower extremities) can be easily and reliably assessed by doing the tests described by Marx."[12] These tests objectify the imbalance in the lower body and legs prior to any intervention from the jaw.

1. The Variable Leg Length Discrepancy: Patient is standing. Clinician puts their thumbs on the medial malleolus (or inside ankle bone). A pelvic rotation will functionally shorten one leg by 1–2 cm.
2. The "Leg-turn-in Test": Patient is standing. Increased fascial tension in the leg is indicated when one foot turns in less than the other foot.

---

[12] *The Application of the Principles of Neuromuscular Dentistry to Clinical Practice, Anthology IX*, The International College of Cranio-Mandibular Orthopedics (The International College of Cranio-Mandibular Orthopedics, 2010), p. 31.

3. Rotation of the Thoracolumbar Junction: Patient is sitting. Rotation of the trunk to one side will be limited when there is craniocervical or craniomandibular dysfunction.
4. Priener Abduction Test: Patient lies down on their back with one leg stretched out flat on the surface. The other leg is bent 90° at the hip with the foot resting on the surface. The knee is then dropped down and out to the surface. The distance between the lateral side of the thigh and the surface is measured. For example, the thigh may be resting on the plinth 0° or elevated off the surface 30°.

The initial measurements of these leg positions are taken on both sides of the body while the jaw is first in its resting position without any contact being made by the teeth. They are remeasured when the back teeth are maximally loaded by biting down. They are measured a last time when the patient bites down on 1-2-4-6-8 pieces of paper which is the Mersemann test. (Any before and after changes in the measurements for tests #1–4 objectively indicate the influence that biting down has on the lower extremities).

One dental group performed these tests on 555 TMJ patients. Improved symmetry in the lower extremities and trunk after maximally loading the teeth demonstrated the influence of the TMJ on the lower extremities. The most significant change came in response to the Mersemann test where the average improvement in hip motion increased by 21°! This measurement clearly demonstrates the effects of jaw position and occlusion onto the peripheral body parts.

These results validate the effect the cranial end of the body can have on the other end. I have also seen this principle work reciprocally, where the release of peripheral fascial restrictions at the hip reduced jaw pain. Refer to case example on pages 354-359.

My Theory of the Program's Effectiveness

Three intentionally different characteristics set this exercise program apart from others. First, positioning the head and neck in correct alignment improves outcomes on final range of motion and pain levels. Second, movement of the eyes and the tongue facilitates results you would not expect. Lastly, global exercises completed from a position of correct alignment thoroughly address soft tissue restrictions. These distinctions facilitate the opportunity for the body to respond differently to exercise.

1. The Position of the Neck

The area of cervical correction most targeted with this program is the upper cervical spine. The *suboccipital muscles* in this area attach to the bottom of the skull and to the top two vertebrae of the spine. When the head falls backward into cervical extension, these muscles are shortened and the tension increases in a very localized area.

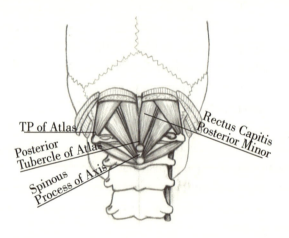

"The *atlas* (Cervical Vertebrae 1 = C1) is the most superior, or upper, cervical vertebra of the spine. It is named for the Atlas of Greek mythology, because it supports the globe of the head. The atlas and the *axis* (C2) form the joint connecting the skull and the spine. The atlas and axis are specialized to allow a greater range of motion than normal vertebra. The atlanto-occipital joint allows the head to nod up and down on the vertebral column. A specific section of C2, the *dens,* acts as a pivot that allows the atlas and the attached head to rotate on the axis, side to side. **The atlas**

and axis are important neurologically because the brainstem extends down to the axis."[13]

This area where the brainstem transitions into the spine is already tight quarters as the canal area for the spinal cord is quite small in the cervical spine. When the head falls backward, the potential for this small area to create a negative impact on some very important structures is clinically significant. "The normal diameter of the cervical spinal canal is between 17mm and 18mm.[14] "The diameter of the normal lumbar spinal canal varies from 15 to 27 mm."[15] "The spinal cord extends from the foramen magnum where it is continuous with the medulla to the level of the first or second lumbar vertebrae. It is a vital link between the brain and the body, and from the body to the brain. The spinal cord is 40-50 cm long and 1cm to 1.5 cm in diameter." [16] In other words, the spinal cord is consistently 10 to 15mm in diameter from the medulla to the lumbar spine. The extra space available for housing the spinal cord in the cervical spine is significantly less than in the lumbar spine, for example, based upon the diameter of the spinal canal.

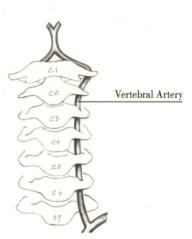

Positioning the head and neck in correct alignment is one of the most important aspects of this exercise program. One reason that maintaining correct alignment of the upper cervical spine is so important is because of

---

[13] Wikipedia - Atlas anatomy.
[14] Coughlin, T.A. BM BS BMedSci MRCS, and Klezl, Z. MD PhD (c) 2012 British Editorial Society, Bone and Joint Surgery, Spine: Focus on Cervical Myelopathy.
[15] Nadalo MD FACR, Lennard A., Chief Editor Smirniotopoulos MD, James G. Medscape. emedicine Spinal Stenosis Imaging.
[16] Dafny, PhD, Nachum, Department of Neurobiology and Anatomy, The UT Medical School at Houston. *Neuroscience Online*: an electronic textbook for neurosciences provided by the Department of Neurobiology and Anatomy at the University of Texas Medical School at Houston. Section 2, Chapter 3 Anatomy of the Spinal Cord.

its relationship to the *vertebral artery* which literally runs through the transverse process of every cervical vertebrae. The vertebral artery will be further discussed later in the chapter.

While the exercises themselves affect specific muscles and soft tissue, correctly positioning the neck maximizes the body's response to the exercises. To validate this point, I evaluated the range of motion at the knee and the shoulder when the neck was incorrectly and correctly positioned. The difference in the measurements clearly shows the direct effect the position of the neck has on movement. Thus, achieving and maintaining the head and neck correctly in neutral is crucial to achieve maximum success with this exercise program. Also, the neck is rarely, if ever, included in knee rehab. These following case examples demonstrate the need for us to make this correction in our rehabilitation processes:

Patient 1 was referred to physical therapy following surgical reconstruction of the ACL, or anterior cruciate ligament, of the knee. When the patient was positioned in supine to measure the available range of motion in the knee, the initial range of motion (ROM) measured was zero degrees (fully straightened) to eighty-two degrees of flexion or bend. During this measurement, the neck was left in whatever position the patient naturally lay down in. When the cervical spine was corrected to the "neutral" position, the patient's ROM increased from zero degrees to ninety-five degrees. It is significant to note these measurements were taken within *seconds* of each other. The only thing that changed was *the position of the neck*.

Patient 2 was also referred to therapy post-ACL reconstruction. Correcting the position of the cervical spine had minimal effect on her ROM. The pain she experienced during the motion, however, decreased from 8/10 to 2/10.

Patient 3 was evaluated post-arthroscopic knee surgery. This procedure is done to repair torn cartilage without making a large incision. The initial ROM measurement was 0 degrees to 90 degrees. When the head was correctly positioned in neutral, the new ROM measurement was 0 degrees to 108 degrees.

These examples suggest that the position of the neck significantly affects the performance of the knee. Because the majority of ACL tears occur during a sporting event, such as being hit and falling while playing football or soccer, etc., it is not unreasonable to assume the neck may have been strained at the same time the knee was injured. Or, the condition of the neck may be the result of a completely separate and unrelated incident.

It is worth mentioning these patients did not notice any significant problems with their necks. The neck does not have to be noticeably painful or restricted to be a contributing factor to the problem. The changes within the soft tissues of the neck can be detrimental to the health and function of multiple areas of the body *even when the neck itself is asymptomatic* or without symptoms.

Now consider **patient 4** who came to physical therapy with a suspected tear of his right rotator cuff or shoulder muscles. Look at the changes in his shoulder motion when the head was incorrectly and correctly positioned in the supine position.

Direction of Motion	Incorrect	Correct
Flexion	140°	153°
Abduction	116°	148°
Internal rotation	53°	68°
External rotation	64°	55°

Remember, these measurements were literally taken within seconds of one another. The only thing that changed was the position of the neck. For the three knee examples, the patient was able to maintain the corrected position without any extra support or assistance. The patient in the shoulder example required four centimeters of support under his head and neck to maintain neutral.

The importance of the cervical spine for pain control and comfortable movement has been previously recognized by F. M. Alexander (1869–1955). Alexander was performing as a Shakespearean actor when chronic hoarseness resulted in a loss of his voice. Through nine years of self-observation and experiment, he solved his problem and regained his full, rich voice. He developed a technique of movement based upon the premise of *the primary control.* By definition, "The primary control is the relationship between the head, neck, and the spine. The quality of that relationship—compressed or free—determines the quality of our overall movement and functioning. When the neck is not overworking, the head balances lightly atop the spine, the torso expands and breath comes more easily. We restore the efficacy of the postural reflex."[17] This approach to self-care teaches people of all ages how to relieve pain and stress by stripping away incorrect movement habits and tension patterns to improve movement efficiency. The success of the program has been attributed to the fact that it addresses the complete body, not just segments, to improve overall functioning.

Upper cervical spine chiropractic is a branch of chiropractic whose focus is on understanding and correcting the relationship between the skull and the first cervical vertebra, the atlas. This one particular joint is considered by many as the most critical point of communication among the central processing unit, the brain, and the system under its control, the body. Those who specialize in upper cervical chiropractic believe "any compression and/or traction on the nerves and blood vessels in this area will most definitely inhibit the body's ability to maintain bodily specifications at their optimum."[18]

Because the cervical spine holds a position of great influence, we should strive to maximize this influence. As I demonstrated, one way to do this is through proper alignment. For many people, however, it is either very difficult or impossible to correctly position their head in neutral while in supine. More often than not, I have witnessed my patient's inability to achieve the position of cervical neutral without extra help and support for stabilization.

Another way to maximize the influence of the neck is by releasing the tension below it. I have seen tension in the neck reduce by as much as fifty percent after completing the lower body active range-of-motion exercises. By reducing the tension or pressure in the lower back with active range of motion, the flexibility of the cervical spine improves.

Research articles written by Brieg and Marions in 1963[19] and Brieg in 1978[20] provide an explanation for these results. Radiographic studies were

---

[17] www.alexandertech.org.

[18] www.upcspine.com/chiropractic3.htm.

[19] Breig A. Marions O. *Biomechanics of the Lumbosacral Nerve Roots.* Acta Radiologica. Diagnosis I (1963), pp. 1141–1160.

[20] Breig A. *Adverse Mechanical Tension in the Central Nervous System* (Stockholm: Almqvist and Wiksell, 1978).

performed on actual neural tissues of the spine to determine the response of the tissues to movement. Prior to testing, a horizontal incision was made in the neural tissues of the lumbar spine. Images were then taken of the lumbar region in response to cervical motion. The images clearly show how flexion of the cervical spine separates, or distracts, the lumbar tissue; cervical extension approximates the lumbar tissues.

Movement at one end of the spine creates a tension within the nervous system that can be translated to the other end of the spine. What I have seen clinically demonstrates the opposite effect is true also. Relaxation at one end of the spine facilitates relaxation at the opposite end. These examples demonstrate the concept of *neural tension*.

2. The Effects of the Eye and Tongue Exercises

Addressing adverse, or unwanted, tension in the nervous system through positioning and movement for pain management has been a treatment modality used in therapy clinics for decades. David Butler, PT, and Michael Shacklock, PT, have published books to explain the mechanics and the science behind this treatment strategy. Dozens of illustrations are included in their books to show the reader how to correctly position and move the body to engage *spinal and peripheral nerves.*

"The peripheral nervous system consists of all parts of the nervous system that are not encased in the vertebral column or the skull."[21] This includes all neural structures distal to the spinal nerves that innervate the viscera, skin, subcutaneous tissues, muscle, tendon, joints, sweat glands, and arterioles. The strategy premise behind neural tension is to lengthen the body part (arms, legs, trunk, and neck) as much as comfortably tolerated and then specifically position the part so the nerve can best be tensioned. Active or passive motion is then used to "glide" the nerve to release the unwanted neural tension believed to be contributing to the person's pain and/or symptoms.

---

[21] Lundy-Ekman, Laurie, PT, PhD, *Neuroscience: Fundamentals for Rehabilitation*, Fourth Edition (Saunders, an imprint of Elsevier, Inc., 2013), pp. 5, 268–269.

Rapid Release uses these same principles of positioning and movement to release neural tension beyond the spine and the peripheral nerves of the extremities. The eyes, the tongue, and the muscles of mastication, or chewing, are used like "handles" or "levers" to reach into the head to address more of the peripheral nervous system, the *cranial nerves*. Even though the cranial nerves originate from the brain, they are considered as part of the peripheral nervous system.

The cranial nerves are "twelve pairs of nerves that connect to the undersurface of the brain, mostly on the brain stem. Cranial nerves pass through small foramina (holes) in the cranial cavity of the skull, allowing them to extend to or from their peripheral destinations."[22] "All cranial nerves innervate structures in the head and neck. In addition, the vagus n., cranial nerve X, descends through the neck into the thorax and abdomen where it innervates viscera."[23]

The cranial nerves this exercise program most involves are the following:

CN II, the optic nerve, travels from the retina of the eye to the midbrain.

CN III, the oculomotor nerve, originates in the midbrain and innervates four of the six external muscles of the eye: the inferior, superior, and medial rectus and the inferior oblique.

CN IV, the trochlear nerve, also originates in the midbrain to innervate the superior oblique muscle of the eyes.

CN V, the trigeminal nerve, originates in the pons to innervate the muscles of mastication or the chewing muscles.

CN VI, the abducens nerve, originates in the pons to innervate the muscle that moves the eye from side to side, the lateral rectus.

CN XII, the hypoglossal nerve, originates in the medulla to innervate the muscles of the tongue and some of the muscles of the throat.

These cranial nerves originate from all three sections of the brain stem: the midbrain, the pons, and the medulla.

---

[22] Patton, Kevin T., PhD, and Thibodeau, Gary A., PhD, *Anatomy and Physiology*, Seventh Edition (Mosby Elsevier, 2010), p. 464.

[23] Drake, Richard L., Vogl, A. Wayne, and Mitchell, Adam W. M., *Gray's Anatomy for Students*, Second Edition (Churchill Livingstone, Elsevier, Inc., 2010), p. 807.

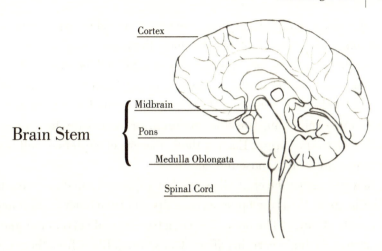

Brain Stem { Cortex, Midbrain, Pons, Medulla Oblongata, Spinal Cord

The brainstem is positioned in between the spinal cord and the cortex of the brain. Each area of the brainstem is responsible for controlling various functions of the body. When the cranial nerve is tensioned by moving the muscles where the nerve inserts, it is theoretically possible to produce tension and/or stimulate the functions of the brainstem in the areas where the nerve originates.

Consider the specific functions of each area. "The *medulla oblongata* is the part of the brain that attaches to the spinal cord. It is, in fact, an enlarged extension of the spinal cord located just above the foramen magnum. Located in the medulla are various *nuclei,* or clusters of neuron cell bodies. Some nuclei are called control centers for the cardiac, respiratory, and vasomotor (vessel muscle) control centers. Other centers present in the medulla are for various nonvital reflexes such as vomiting, coughing, sneezing, hiccupping, and swallowing."[24]

"In Latin, the word *pons* literally means bridge. The pons is a portion of the hindbrain that connects the cerebral cortex with the medulla. It serves as a communication and coordination center between the two hemispheres of the brain. As a part of the brain stem, the pons helps transfer messages between various parts of the brain and the spinal cord. The pons contain nuclei that relay signals from the cerebrum to the cerebellum, along with nuclei that deal primarily with sleep, respiration, swallowing, bladder

---

[24] Patton, Kevin T., PhD, and Thibodeau, Gary A., PhD, *Anatomy and Physiology*, Seventh Edition (Mosby Elsevier, 2010), pp. 421–424.

control, hearing, equilibrium, taste, eye movement, facial expression, facial sensation, and posture. Without the pons, the brain would not be able to function because messages would not be transmitted, or passed along."[25]

"The *midbrain* forms the midsection of the brain as it lies above the pons and below the cerebrum. Certain auditory and visual centers are located in the midbrain. Two other midbrain structures are the *red nucleus* and the *substantial nigra*. Each of these consists of clusters of cell bodies of neurons involved in muscular control."[26]

Now reconsider the cranial nerves that originate from these sections of the brain stem. First, the optic nerve is distinct from other cranial nerves in a couple of ways. "The optic n. is not a true cranial nerve, but rather an extension of the brain carrying afferent, or sensory, fibers from the retina of the eyeball to the visual centers of the brain"[27] in the midbrain. The optic nerve is the only cranial nerve that connects brain tissue to brain tissue. By connecting directly to the retina, the optic nerve theoretically "glides" with each position change of the eye. The tension along the optic nerve created by eye movement would then, in turn, stimulate the midbrain at the other end of the nerve where it inserts into the midbrain.

The oculomotor nerve also originates from cells in the midbrain. As previously mentioned, this nerve innervates all but two of the external eye muscles that move the eye. The autonomic fibers of this nerve "extend to the intrinsic muscles of the eye, which regulate the amount of light entering the eye and aid in focusing on near objects."[28] The oculomotor nerve regulates the amount of light allowed to enter the eye by controlling the size of the pupil. Tensioning this nerve with eye movement also has the potential to theoretically stimulate the midbrain.

One of the eye muscles not innervated by the oculomotor nerve is the superior oblique muscle. This muscle is innervated by the trochlear nerve, which also arises from the midbrain. The superior oblique muscle directs

---

[25] biology.about.com, answers.com, the brain made simple.com.
[26] Patton, Kevin T., PhD, and Thibodeau, Gary A., PhD, *Anatomy and Physiology*, Seventh Edition (Mosby Elsevier, 2010), p. 423.
[27] Drake, Richard L., Vogl, A. Wayne, and Mitchell, Adam W. M., *Gray's Anatomy for Students*, Second Edition (Churchill Livingstone, Elsevier, Inc., 2010), p. 894.
[28] Patton, Kevin T., PhD, and Thibodeau, Gary A., PhD, *Anatomy and Physiology*, Seventh Edition (Mosby Elsevier, 2010), p. 466

the pupil of the eye down and out. It has been my clinical observation that deficits in the oblique eye muscles will be duplicated by deficits in the oblique muscles of the trunk. I assume the reason for this is these muscles are "muscle complements," which will be discussed later in this chapter.

The final muscle of the eye is the lateral rectus, which is innervated by the abducens nerve, which originates in the pons. The lateral rectus muscle is the prime mover of the eye to the right or the left. I have noticed clinically that restrictions in this motion most commonly occur when the patient has symptoms in the lower extremity or the leg. Not only will lateral eye movement help address symptoms in the leg, but it will also theoretically stimulate functions of the pons.

It is most interesting to notice the relationships between the structures in the following illustration of a cross section of the midbrain in the brainstem. The dotted lines indicate the pathway of the oculomotor nerve from its cells of origin through the brain toward the muscles it innervates. The pathway directly passes through the red nucleus and the substantia nigra, areas specifically dedicated to muscular control.

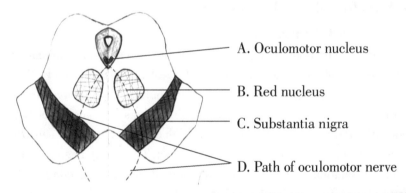

A. Oculomotor nucleus

B. Red nucleus

C. Substantia nigra

D. Path of oculomotor nerve

It is possible eye movements have a calming or stimulating effect on all three areas of the brainstem. This is evidenced by the improved range of motion throughout the body in previously restricted areas. As the eyes are moved through all planes of motion, the external eye muscles directly glide the oculomotor, trochlear, and abducens nerves and indirectly glide the optic nerve. By stabilizing the head during eye movement, or stabilizing the eyes during head movement, the optic nerve theoretically "glides" within the brain as the movement occurs.

The trigeminal nerve arises from the pons to innervate the muscles of mastication or chewing. Because the pons is a relay station among many areas of the body with the potential to influence much of the brain, this may explain why the Mersemann's test on page 393 created such a change in the range of motion of the hips. The muscles of mastication are engaged by the controlled opening exercise. These muscles are also engaged whenever the teeth are clenched.

The hypoglossal nerve exits the anterior side of the brainstem from the lower section, the medulla. The hypoglossal nerve innervates the tongue and a few muscles under the tongue. When the tongue is protracted, or stuck out of the mouth, the same type of nerve glide theoretically occurs. The movement of the tongue potentially stimulates the medulla as the tension changes within the area. This may explain why the tongue exercises sometimes provoke increased heart rate, respiratory rate and/or nausea. I have been told by a few patients that their nausea progressed to vomiting several hours after completing the exercises, but this has literally happened five times in eighteen years.

The Far-Reaching Effects of the Eyes and Neural Tension

Sciatica is a condition typically thought to be the result of inflammation or impingement of the sciatic nerve, the largest nerve in the body. The sciatic nerve accepts peripheral nerve contributions from spinal levels L4-S3 in the lower back or lumbosacral spine. The symptoms of sciatica include pain or weakness in the posterior thigh or lower leg and/or sensory changes in the lateral leg or in the skin of the foot. There have been reports, however, of sciatica resulting from anatomical changes in completely different places from the lumbar spine.

An article in *Spine* (1995) cites a case where right sciatica was the direct result of a C2-3 tumor in the neck. Tumors were also present and directly resected first from the right sciatic nerve and the right retroperitoneal region. *The removal of these two tumors did nothing to resolve the patient's symptoms.* It was not until the tumor at C2-3 was removed that the patient experienced immediate relief of the sciatica symptoms in the right leg. Refer to p. 184-185 for a case example illustrating the effect of the neck on the leg.

Another patient experienced sciatica in the right leg for ten months after experiencing lower back pain for two years. Radiographs of the lumbar spine were normal, but a kyphosis in the thoracic spine from C7 to T7 severely compressed the spinal cord in the thoracic spine. The kyphotic deformity developed when the patient suffered from tuberculosis of the spine at age five. Even though it seemed unlikely the cause of the sciatica was the long-standing thoracic kyphosis, anterior cord decompression surgery of the thoracic spine resolved the patient's symptoms immediately.[29]

Even though this next paper is from 1955, I felt it is worth mentioning. The paper was presented at the eleventh meeting of the Scandinavian Neurosurgical Society. Two patients, one male and one female, who suffered with shoulder and arm symptoms as well as sciatica were discussed. In both cases, the arm pain and, surprisingly, the leg pain resolved with decompression of C4–T1.[30] It was humorous to read that *marriage* had been suggested to the woman as a possible remedy for her pain after many different interventions failed. At one point, her condition was considered to be psychologically provoked. The report states she refused the suggestion of marriage therapy. She was surely glad she did when the cervical procedure succeeded.

In addition to obvious anatomical blockages, Michael Shacklock, PT, validates the mechanical effect positioning and movement has on the nervous system. He notes yet another area to consider as a possible influence on the sciatic nerve. In his book *Clinical Neurodynamics—A New System of Musculoskeletal Treatment*, he refers to a personal communication that I quote: "Macnab (1988, personal communication) has stated that, at surgery, the lumbosacral nerve roots can be seen to move with dorsiflexion of the foot whilst the lower limb is held in the straight leg raise position. *Another example of this mechanical continuum is the inward movement of the eyes with a bilateral straight leg raise* (emphasis mine). It is possible the eye movement is induced by tension that passes along the spinal cord and brain to the optic nerves."[31] This statement, in particular, shows how far-

---

[29] Hack, Gary D., DDS, Koritzer, Richard T., DDS, PhD+, Bobinson, Walker L., MD, Hallgren, Richard C., PhD[S], Greenman, Philip E., DO, FAAO, *Spine Magazine*, 1995, Volume 20, Number 23, pp. 2484–2485.
[30] ActaPsych.etNeurol.Scand.XXXI, 3 p. 337.
[31] Michael Shacklock, *Clinical Neurodynamics - A New System of Musculoskeletal Treatment* (Elsevier Butterworth Heinemann, 2005), pp. 13.

reaching forces can be transmitted along the nervous system in response to movement.

Assuming this force can be transmitted in either direction, then increased neural tension created by eye motion can be used to affect the lower extremities. *This mechanical effect is frequently manifested by the resolution of sciatica in the legs in response to the eye and/or neck exercises.* See pages 182-184 for case examples.

While advocates of neural tension therapy might credit the release of neural tension for the improvement of sciatica in response to the eye movement, I believe it's a combination of neural tension and connective tissue release. The nervous system is one continuous system, but the connective tissue can be traced continuously as well. The connective tissue follows the nervous system so closely it seems impossible to mobilize one without mobilizing the other.

3. The Effect of the Exercises on the Soft Tissue

I have identified three ways these exercises affect the soft tissue. First, it thoroughly mobilizes the fascia. Next, it exposes and treats what I call muscle complements. Finally, it addresses a unilateral, or one-sided, pathway of pain and dysfunction regardless of where the primary complaint of pain is reported.

The Superficial and Deep Fascia

As previously mentioned, the fascia is a pervasive sheath of connective tissue running throughout the body. The most important characteristic to note about fascia as it pertains to this exercise program is that it is a continuous three-dimensional membrane. Anytime the body is bent, the fascia is on slack in one area while it is stretched in another. A stretch to the fascia is not synonymous with a release. Most motion is too forceful to facilitate a release, or relaxation, of the restricted fascial tissue.

To understand how **Rapid Release** addresses the fascia differently from other forms of exercise, it helps to know something about fascial anatomy. "There are four primary layers of fascia. The *pannicular, or superficial fascia,* surrounds the entire body, with the exception of a very few places, like the orbits of the eyes and the nasal passages. Superficial fascia attaches to the under surface of the skin, is loosely knit, fibroelastic, and an areolar tissue. Within the superficial fascia are fat and vascular structures, including capillary networks and lymphatic channels, and nervous tissues. Within the superficial fascia is potential space for the accumulation of fluid and metabolites.

The *axial, or deep, fascia* is tough, tight, and compact. It is composed of two, parallel connective tissue tubes that course anterior and posterior to the vertebral column just beneath the superficial layer and is fused to it. Deep fascia compartmentalizes the body. It envelops and separates muscles, surrounds and separates internal visceral organs, and contributes greatly to the contour and function of the body. The peritoneum, or the abdominal and pelvic lining, the pericardium, or the sac enclosing the heart, and the pleura, the pair of linings in the thorax and envelopes of the lungs, are specialized elements of the deep fascia. Axial fascia is referred to as *appendicular fascia* as it extends into the extremities investing in individual muscles and as the intermuscular septum, dividing the anterior side of the extremity from the posterior side.

The third fascial layer is the *meningeal fascia*, which surrounds the central nervous system. The fourth fascial layer is the loose, areolar tissue that covers the internal visceral organs, *visceral fascia*. This fascial layer is the most complex of the four main layers of fascia. . . and surrounds the body cavities."[32,33] A closer look at meningeal fascia will help us better understand the effectiveness of this program.

It is obvious full body movement is needed to address the superficial fascia, which covers the whole body. What is not so obvious is the fact that the appendicular fascia in the extremities extends from a portion of axial fascia regionally termed the prevertebral fascia. "The arrangement of fascia on the body wall is made very complex by the attachment of the limbs. The muscles of the upper extremity, such as the pectoralis,

---

[32] Schleip, R., Findley, Thomas W., Chaitow, Leon, Huijing, Peter, A, *Fascia - The Tensional Network of the Human Body* (Churchill Livingston Elsevier, 2012), pp. 12–14.

[33] DeStefano DO, Lisa, *Greenman's Principles of Manual Medicine*, Fourth Edition (Lippincott Williams and Wilkins, a Wolters Kluwer business, 2011), p.155.

trapezius, serratus anterior, and latissimus dorsi muscles, form long wing-like expansions that wrap over the torso to attach to the spinous processes on the midline of the body or to structures that ultimately attach to the midline such as the thoracolumbar fascia."[34] The fascia at the distal end of the previously mentioned muscles then continues down the arm to the hand and fingers.

In other words, the fascia in the arms can be traced back to the spine, *even to the thoracolumbar fascia in the lower back.* It is possible, because of this anatomical fact, that some upper extremity and hand restrictions cannot be thoroughly resolved unless the fascia in the thoracolumbar spine is released as well. This is one explanation for how the low back can be involved in problems with the shoulders and upper extremities and vice versa.

The Meningeal Fascia

Understanding the location of the *meningeal fascia* helps further explain the effectiveness of the eye and tongue exercises. The two parts of the *central nervous system* (CNS) are the brain and the spinal cord. "Because the brain and spinal cord are both delicate and vital, nature has provided them with two protective coverings. The outer covering consists of bone: cranial bones encase the brain; vertebrae encase the spinal cord. The inner covering consists of membranes known as **meninges**. Three distinct layers compose the meninges:

1. Dura Mater
2. Arachnoid
3. Pia mater

The dura mater, made of strong white fibrous tissue, serves as the outer layer of the meninges and also as the inner periosteum of the cranial bones. The arachnoid mater, a delicate, cobweb-like layer, lies between the dura mater and the pia mater, or the innermost layer of the meninges. The transparent pia mater adheres to the outer surface of the brain and the

---

[34] Schleip, R., Findley, Thomas W., Chaitow, Leon, Huijing, Peter, A, *Fascia - The Tensional Network of the Human Body* (Churchill Livingston Elsevier, 2012), pp. 13–14.

spinal cord and contains blood vessels... A number of spaces lie between and around the meninges. Three of these spaces are the following:

1. **Epidural Space.** The epidural ("on the dura") space is immediately outside the dura mater but inside the bony coverings of the spinal cord. It contains a supporting cushion of fat and other connective tissues. Around the brain, because the dura mater is continuous with the periosteum on the inside face of the cranial bones, no epidural space is normally present.
2. **Subdural space.** The subdural ("under the dura") spaces between the dura mater and arachnoid mater. The subdural space contains a small amount of lubricating serous fluid.
3. **Subarachnoid space.** As its name suggests, the subarachnoid space is under the arachnoid and outside the pia mater. This space contains a significant amount of cerebrospinal fluid."[35] The serous fluid on the dura and the arachnoid fluid between the arachnoid and the pia mater serve as a supportive, protective cushion for the brain and the spinal cord. This is the fluid that theoretically changes its distribution in response to tension and pressure created by the water balloon theory.

Meningeal fascia is the connective tissue treated by craniosacral therapists. To intentionally engage these fascial restrictions inside the head and spine with a specific series of exercises adds a new dimension to myofascial release treatment techniques. The exercises can be used to enhance the release facilitated by the manual therapist. By engaging meningeal tension inside the cranium, **Rapid Release** more thoroughly addresses myofascial restrictions. The dural layer of the meninges seems to be the fascial component linking this exercise program together in several places.

Consider the eye itself. The eyeball also consists of three layers. "The outer *sclera* is a heavy collagenous bulb which gives the globe shape to the eyeball, protects its contents, and receives the attachment of the ocular muscles. The middle layer, the *choroid*, is a vascular layer which nourishes

---

[35] Patton, Kevin T., PhD, and Thibodeau, Gary A., PhD, *Anatomy and Physiology*, Seventh Edition (Mosby Elsevier, 2010), p. 413-415.

the eyeball and is heavily pigmented to reduce internal reflections. The innermost layer, the *retina*, is actually a part of the brain which grew out of the forebrain to become incorporated into the other components of the eye."[36]

The first unique characteristic previously mentioned about the optic nerve is that it connects the brain tissue of the retina to the brain tissue of the midbrain. The other cranial nerves arise from the brainstem but travel to peripheral destinations that are not neural tissue.

There is another significant difference between the optic nerve and the other cranial nerves. Peripheral nerves are covered by *epineurium*, which I will explain more in the next paragraph. The optic nerve is not covered with epineurium but "is surrounded by the cranial meninges"[37] from the midbrain to the posterior eye and, ultimately, the retina. In addition, "a fascial sheath encloses a major part of the eyeball. Posteriorly, this fascial sheath is firmly attached to the sclera at the point of entrance of the optic nerve into the eyeball; as the muscles approach the eyeball, the investing fascia surrounding each muscle blends with the fascial sheath of the eyeball as the muscles continue to their point of attachment."[38] In summary, the fascial covering of the eye, the fascial covering of the muscles of the eye, and the meninges (the dura, pia, and arachnoid) of the optic nerve converge together as they attach to the posterior sclera of the eye. Changing the position of the sclera can potentially affect all these different fascial structures because of their union.

The dura mater is most commonly associated with the central nervous system, but the dura continues as the epineurium of efferent, or motor, nerves that leave the skull. "Meningeal fascia terminates with the development of the epineurium that surrounds the peripheral nerve."[39] "As spinal nerves

---

[36] Weston D. Gardner, M.D., and William A. Osburn, MMA. *Structure of the Human Body* (W. B. Saunders Co., 1973), p 302.

[37] Drake, Richard L., Vogl, A. Wayne, and Mitchell, Adam W. M., *Gray's Anatomy for Students*, Second Edition (Churchill Livingstone, Elsevier, Inc., 2010), p. 894.

[38] Drake, Richard L., Vogl, A. Wayne, and Mitchell, Adam W. M., *Gray's Anatomy for Students*, Second Edition (Churchill Livingstone, Elsevier, Inc., 2010), p. 886.

[39] Schleip, R., Findley, Thomas W., Chaitow, Leon, Huijing, Peter, A, *Fascia - The Tensional Network of the Human Body* (Churchill Livingston Elsevier, 2012), p. 15.

and their roots pass laterally, they are surrounded by tubular sleeves of dura mater, which merge with and become part of the outer covering, the epineurium, of the nerve."[40]

Theoretically, if force can be translated along a nerve by increasing the tension with movement, eye movement has the potential to change the tension of the optic nerve based upon the posterior attachment of the optic nerve to the sclera and the fascial covering of the eye. The tension translated through the meninges covering the optic nerve during movement has the potential to affect the meninges of the central nervous system and the continuation of the dura as the epineurium lining the peripheral nervous system.

Even though dura is generally found as a protective lining for the nervous system, it has also been found to attach to two different muscles directly. A connective tissue bridge from the rectus capitis posterior minor muscle (page 394) at the cranial base was identified to project to the spinal dura in eleven cadavers. The article "supports the previous speculation that skeletal muscle and dura mater may be related via fascial continuity."[41] "The dura has also been found to attach to the inferior oblique muscle of the eye."[42] Moving these muscles is one more way to specifically engage the dura and potentially affect whatever restrictions may be just beyond that connection. This is a possible explanation for why eye movement can sometimes be felt as far down the spine as the lumbar region.

How does *Rapid Release* address these restrictions?

The purpose of this exercise program is to release restrictions in as much connective tissue as possible through positioning and movement. Meningeal restrictions within the cranium are highly suspect in individuals

---

[40] Drake, Richard L., Vogl, A. Wayne, and Mitchell, Adam W. M., *Gray's Anatomy for Students*, Second Edition (Churchill Livingstone, Elsevier, Inc., 2010), p. 104.

[41] Hack, Gary D., DDS, Koritzer, Richard T., DDS, PhD+, Bobinson, Walker L., MD, Hallgren, Richard C., PhD[S], Greenman, Philip E., DO, FAAO, "Anatomic Relationship Between the Rectus Capitis Posterior Minor Muscle and the Dura Mater," *Spine Magazine*, 1995, Volume 20, Number 23.

[42] Schleip, R., Findley, Thomas W., Chaitow, Leon, Huijing, Peter, A, *Fascia - The Tensional Network of the Human Body* (Churchill Livingston Elsevier, 2012), p. 61.

who require extreme amounts of cervical correction to achieve correct alignment. Using the eyes and the tongue "as handles to reach into the head" provides a way to access these tissues. The tension inside the cranium can contribute to increased cervical extension just like increased lower back tension can.

Extreme superficial and deep fascial restrictions in the body are manifested most clearly by those who require modifications to the supine position. The "positions of ease" alleviate the strain on specific areas of fascia in the upper body, neck, and head to promote relaxation in the tissue. The positioning optimizes conditions for gentle movement to facilitate the release of fascial restrictions and lengthening of the connective tissue. The fascial "playing field" is made even when the body finally tolerates flat supine while positioned in correct alignment. There are no areas on slack or on a stretch.

When the body is elevated on top of the pillows with the arms unsupported, the fascia is placed on a gentle stretch to expose areas of greatest restriction. What else could explain the variety of responses people experience in this position ranging from mild to intense changes in low back pain, knee pain, headaches, shoulder pain, swallowing or speech difficulties, dizziness, etc.? There has been no change made to the body, except it is now elevated one inch or less. The only thing conceivably "on a stretch" is the muscles in the front of the shoulder. In most people, a one- to two-inch change in position is not enough variation to stretch the muscle.

As gentle active exercise is combined with a light stretch, a release in the fascia occurs. This theoretically relieves the tension and the "squeeze from the water balloon." By thoroughly addressing the *complete myofascial system, including the meningeal fascia*, the pressure within the system is relieved.

Muscle Complements

When I first applied my neuromuscular skills to my practice, I would thoroughly assess all the soft tissue in the localized area of the patient's complaints. I noticed consistencies in my findings for each area of the body regardless of the different patients' diagnoses. For example, the results of my palpation exam for a patient diagnosed with a rotator cuff strain were not so different from those of a person diagnosed with a bicipital tendonitis. Both are shoulder problems but distinctively different. It became clear to me I needed to address specific muscles in each area regardless of how the pain was manifesting itself. The foundation of the rehab program was similar, even though the treatment for the pain would be patient-specific.

As I noticed the exercises in each area of the four body quadrants helping release tension in another area of the body, I wondered why this was happening. As I analyzed the anatomy, I drew this conclusion. The muscles of the upper and lower body are positioned with great similarity, as if they are a reflection of one another. I noticed these muscles with similar appearance were affecting each other. More often than not, if a muscle was tender in the lower body, the muscle "complement" similarly positioned and shaped in the upper body would be tender as well, even if the diagnosis was in the lower body. This principle goes both ways. Diagnoses in the upper body displayed tender muscles in the upper body, but the complement to the muscle would also be tender in the lower body. The patients usually were unaware of the localized tenderness in the other area until it was revealed to them. It is my hypothesis neither muscle will become completely restored to its maximum health and potential as long as its complement remains dysfunctional.

Consider the psoas muscle again, for example, and the muscle "complement" for it in the neck, the scalenes. Note how each muscle has several points of origin on the transverse processes, or side appendages, of several vertebral bodies. They 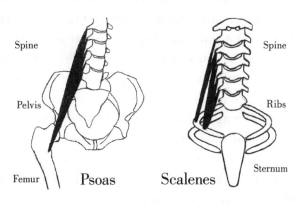 both insert at an anterior location after traveling through the body at a similar angle.

It was a personal experience with my hip rotators and the muscles in the floor of my mouth that first demonstrated these relationships to me. Several hours after receiving a manual treatment to the rotators of my left hip, the muscles in the floor of my mouth on the left side spasmed so severely I was unable to speak for two hours and was completely exhausted during that time. This was utterly confusing to me.

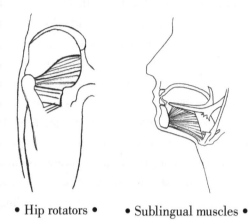

• Hip rotators •   • Sublingual muscles •

Taking a look at my anatomy book in search of an explanation opened my eyes to a new way of understanding painful muscular relationships.

This type of similar muscular relationship has been written about by Frank R. Wilson in his book *The Hand*. Wilson recognized an interesting muscular parallel between the muscles that control the orb of the eye and the muscles that control the rounded head of the humerus. Wilson states, "In the orbit and at the shoulder, the eye and the humerus are free to rotate (or swing) in front-to-back or side-to-side planes, and also around their long axes. In both cases there is a precise arrangement of muscles aligned and attached to power each of these movements."[43]

A colleague of mine sent me a blog written by Dr. Cedrick Noel, DC, that explains this principle. The title of his article, *"Could Your Eyes Be the Cause of Your Back Pain?"* validates the muscular relationships I have seen on a different anatomical level. "The connection between the muscles of the eyes and stabilizing muscles of the spine is undeniable. They have been connected since the embryonic development phase when the muscles of the eyes and spine differentiated at the same time, which makes them part of what is known as a *homologous column*. A weakness in an ocular muscle can cause a change in the alignment of the eyes resulting in a

---

[43] Wilson, Frank R., *The Hand* (Pantheon Books, a division of Random House, Inc., 1998), p. 88.

spinal compensation over time as the brain strives to maintain function in the body and seek normal gaze. A shift in angulation of spinal joints alters the mechanics leading to painful wear and tear which can often become debilitating over time. Essentially, it would be very difficult to have a problem in the ocular muscles without affecting the spine and vice versa."[44] The definition of homologous is "the structures which are similar in their morphology, anatomy, genetics and embryology but dissimilar in their functions." This provides a scientific explanation for why the eye exercises in this program have such a direct effect on the cervical, thoracic, and lumbar spine in particular. The fact that the eye muscles are also "complements" to other muscles around the shoulder, hips, and abdominals may explain their effect on other joints as well.

My clinical experience causes me to believe muscle imbalance at the eyes has far-reaching effects. First, there is the issue of muscle complements. I have recognized the effects of the eye muscles on the abdominal trunk muscles on many occasions. Strength and flexibility in the "core" muscles improve as the eye muscles move more freely. As motion and strength improve at the core, the eyes continue to improve. The two areas help each other. I've seen poor core strength improve in individuals as the tension relaxes in their eyes and neck.

I've also seen how dysfunction in eye motion and the jaw contributes to dysfunction in the rotators of the shoulders and hips. As movement at the eyes and jaw improves, the condition at the peripheral joint improves as well. The most dramatic improvement has been with patients who suffer with chronically dislocating shoulders. The case example on pages 334-337 is a good illustration of this relationship. The case examples on pages 354-359, 370-371 illustrates the relationship between the hips and the lateral pterygoid of the temporal mandibular joint.

The muscle complements I have recognized are usually on the same side of the body, either on the right or the left, but sometimes they "balance" each other out from front to back. I have seen muscles of the *upper body* release tension and become less tender as soft tissue mobilization, or massage, is administered to its complement in the *lower body*. This type

---

[44] *HealthJobs Nationwide.com*, "Could your eyes be the cause of your back pain?"

of response has further convinced me that the condition of one has a direct effect on the other.

I have identified and listed fifteen pairs of complements with a fair amount of certainty. While this list has not been scientifically validated, I have verified these muscular relationships on numerous occasions clinically. My current list of muscle complements is not conclusive, but it is a start to illustrate this principle. The anatomy of the forearm and the lower leg replicates each other in many ways, but because I do not have much personal experience with muscles of the forearm, I did not include them in my list. In my opinion, the intrinsic muscles of the larynx and the pharyngeal muscles of the throat greatly resemble the abdominals. This consideration might be helpful if applied to speech therapy. If you are dealing with a problematic muscle not on the list, consider the anatomy to help you find the complementary muscle to co-treat.

Releasing Pain | 417

LOWER BODY	UPPER BODY	HEAD AND NECK
1. Gluteus maximus	1. Pectoralis major	1.
2. Gluteus medius	2. Pectoralis minor	2. Splenius capitus
3. Gluteus minimus Vastus medialis	3. Pectoralis minor	3. Splenius capitus
4. Superior rectus abdominus and Diaphragm	4. Latisimus dorsi	4. Infrahyoids, Frontalis, Inferior and Superior Rectus of the Eye
5. Inferior rectus abdominus	5.	5. Suprahyoids, Inferior and Superior Rectus of the Eye
6. Oblique abdominals	6. Serratus anterior	6. Sternocleidomastoid Oblique eye muscles
7. Psoas	7. Anterior and Medial Scalenes	7. Medial pterygoid
8. Quadratus lumborum	8. Posterior scalene	8.
9. Small hip rotators	9. Rotator cuff	9. Pharyngeal muscles
10. Piriformis and Plantaris	10. Infraspinatus, Brachioradialis	10. Lateral pterygoid
11. Hip adductors	11. Trapezius and Rhomboids	11. Masseter and Hypoglossus
12. Gracilis	12. Coracobrachialis	12.
13. Hamstring	13. Biceps	13.
14. Quadricep	14. Tricep	14. Cervical retractors
15. Transverse abdominals	15.	15. Inferior and Superior Pharyngeal

Compensation for pain in our bodies is a well-accepted fact. I believe this compensation can be traced directly to complementary muscles. I also believe this is why *flexibility improves more effectively* by *doing this program in its entirety instead of stretching isolated muscles individually.*

I have been simultaneously treating complementary muscles since I first recognized this principle. The idea of massaging the jaw or the eyes to help reduce hip pain sounds pretty "out there," so I asked a patient to share her firsthand experience with muscle complements in a letter.

She is also a good example of a patient who did not initially tolerate progressive positioning on top of the pillows. When the time came to progress her exercises, the stretch she perceived in her lower back, right hip, and thigh while lying on top of the pillows was so painful she was unable to maintain the position; instead, we folded a blanket for her to lie on top of that was half an inch thick. The difference this made in her flexibility helped her reach a significant functional goal. Her letter describes how her response to this program has helped her achieve more daily independence.

> *Dear Nancy,*
>
> *I have learned the hard way that an eighty-three-year-old woman should not try to move her heavy furniture alone! That's how I broke my right hip. The extreme pain I experienced afterward was not a surprise, but the benefit I gained of it being such a positive learning experience came as quite a surprise.*
>
> *By the time I met you, my abilities to function independently were so limited and the pain was so bad, I was willing to try anything that might help me. My previous experience with yoga taught me about the importance of spinal flexibility. This, in turn, helped me to relate with the suggestions you were making to me. It was through your methods I learned to relieve the pain in my hip and legs by massaging my head! I was also amazed that such small movements of my eyes and my head could bring so much benefit to other areas of my body.*
>
> *Another surprise came when I started doing my exercises on such a shallow amount of support under my body. It was at this point my flexibility improved enough so I could finally bend over to feed my cat. And most importantly to me, I can now easily get in and out of my van on the driver's side!*

The progress I've seen so far gives me the confidence to believe I will soon fully regain my independence. Thanks for all of your instructions and your efforts to help me in my recovery!
Wishing you the best,

Unilateral Pathway of Pain

Prior to my corrective surgery in 2004, I experienced minor problems dispersed throughout *the entire left side of my body*. I noticed I would position myself in ways to accommodate this tension *if I allowed myself to*. For example, if I sat to watch a movie, I preferred to bend my left hip and knee by putting my foot up in my chair. I even liked to put my left leg out my car window when I drove. When I finally noticed I was repeating the same positions over and over, I realized I was accommodating a *pattern of dysfunctional tension*.

You might be able to relate to this. For example, you may tend to weight bear more on one leg while standing. The opposite leg might bend at the knee and rotate out at the hip. Or you may be most comfortable sitting Indian style or with just one foot underneath you, and it will usually be the same foot. Others repeatedly rotate their trunk in one direction while sitting or cross their legs or their ankles in the same way. Frequently rotation of the trunk occurs simultaneously with crossing of the legs or ankles. And finally, more people than not sleep in the fetal position to one extent or another.

I have observed this same pattern of unilateral dysfunction repeatedly in the overwhelming majority of my patients. There are a fair amount of people already aware of problems in more than one area along one side of their body. Others admit one or more areas on the side of their current complaint have previously been a significant problem. More times than I can count, I have heard people say, "There is something wrong with the right (or left) side of my body."

Interestingly enough, the problematic muscles I find to be tender in different people's bodies are the same ones all the way down one complete side of each person's body regardless of their current complaint. There are many muscle complements simultaneously active along the unilateral pathway of pain. The connection among these muscle groups forms a vertical chain of pain. The pattern of the dysfunction is predictable.

The good news about this pattern is it is *reversible*. As with any problem, recognizing the problem is the biggest part of the solution. Bodyworkers speak of "body memory," or how the body holds on to a previous trauma in the soft tissues. Identifying this pattern is a way to *physically see the memory*. I no longer allow myself to bend my left knee and hip just because it feels more comfortable. When I have a choice, I choose a position that encourages hip and knee extension instead of flexion. Doing this exercise program helps release the tension in the pattern, so it is no longer a problem or is, at least, counteracted.

One day it occurred to me this vertical finding is nothing new. In fact, it's ancient. There are many alternative medicine practices that treat the body along pathways, or *meridians*, that run up and down the full length of the body. The most commonly known of these therapies is *acupuncture*. Chinese philosophy and medical science believes this meridian system provides a continuous flow of vital energy to all parts of the body. Each meridian is named for a body organ it is associated with. Most of the meridians connect the upper and lower body together. The exceptions to this are the meridians originating somewhere on the torso and travel down either the arms or the legs. In many other instances, the meridians of the upper and lower body are also connected with the head and neck.

I spoke with an acupuncturist to see if the effectiveness of this program could be the result of acupuncture meridians being mobilized through movement. I learned several meridians could be specifically mobilized with a full body systematic exercise approach. It was not surprising for me to learn two of the most commonly treated acupuncture meridians, the stomach and the urinary bladder, extend all the way to the eye.

Thomas W. Myers describes *the myofascial meridian* in his book *Anatomy Trains*. He distinguishes acupuncture meridians from myofascial meridians by stating "the word 'meridian' is usually used in the context of the energetic lines of transmission in the domain of acupuncture. Let there be no confusion: the myofascial meridian lines are not acupuncture meridians, but lines of pull, based on standard Western anatomy, lines which transmit strain and movement through the body's myofascia around the skeleton. They have, perhaps, some overlap with the meridians of acupuncture, but the two are not equivalent."[45] I agree when he says the recognition of this meridian system "fills a current need for a global view of human structure and movement."[46] His book includes diagrams of eleven distinctly different patterns of traceable fascia. Six of the eleven meridians extend either from the toes or the fingers in a continuous fascial sheet to different locations on the outside of the cranium. "A grasp of the Anatomy Trains scheme will lead to a more three-dimensional feel for musculoskeletal anatomy and an appreciation of whole-body patterns of compensation and strain distribution. Clinically, it leads to a directly applicable understanding of how painful problems in one area of the body can be linked to a totally 'silent' area at some remove from the problem."[47]

The function of the human body as a linked system has been described by others in different ways. "In 1955, A. Steindler suggested the human body be thought of as a chain consisting of the rigid overlapping segments of the limbs connected by a series of joints. He defined a *kinetic chain* as "a combination of several successfully arranged joints constituting a complex motor unit."[48] The word "kinetic" refers to the motion of a material body and the force and energy associated with the motion. What he was describing was a chain of motion where forces and energy are translated from one joint to the next, or the concept that the body functions as a linked structure based upon the skeleton. To assume the muscles attaching to these joints are also part of this chain is a reasonable conclusion. Whether energetically, fascially, or skeletally, others have recognized our bodies have different parts but function as an integrated system.

The body's accommodation for this dysfunctional pattern of tension manifests itself in postural abnormalities. Remember, posture is posture regardless of our activity. Sleeping incorrectly for six to eight hours is as detrimental as sitting or standing with slouched shoulders for prolonged periods. Anytime we repeat a posture or a position that deviates from correct postural alignment, we reinforce an abnormal pattern of tension

---

[45] Myers, Thomas T., *Anatomy Trains* (Churchill Livingstone Elsevier, 2001), p. 5.
[46] Myers, Thomas T., *Anatomy Trains* (Churchill Livingstone Elsevier, 2001), p. 4.
[47] Myers, Thomas T., *Anatomy Trains* (Churchill Livingstone Elsevier, 2001), p. 1.
[48] William D. Bandy and Barbara Sanders, *Therapeutic Exercise - Techniques for Intervention* (Lippincott Williams and Wilkins, 2001), p. 179.

and dysfunction. If respiratory or digestive issues force you to sleep on a wedge, be sure to make time each day to either lie out flat or do some prone or standing exercises to lengthen the front of your legs, trunk, neck, and eyes.

Be aware this can be an ongoing process, especially if you have a permanent structural change in your body. I once attended a two-day course that required prolonged periods of sitting. I know I have a tendency to rotate my head to the right, so I sat on the right side of the room. This forced me to rotate my head to the left to focus on the speaker. My intentions were good, but as I became more interested in the program, I unconsciously made position changes with my chair and body to make myself more comfortable. I was surprised to find after two hours of sitting I had repositioned my chair to face to the left, which allowed my head to rotate to the right after all.

If you recognize asymmetrical positional patterns in your posture distracting you from a balanced alignment, decide how you can correct them today. Take the initiative to disrupt potentially harmful tension in your body. Use **Rapid Release** to help. By completing the full exercise program, you can address current problems and prevent potential problems along this vertical unilateral pathway of pain.

Other Possibilities

I doubt if many of you reading this book have ever done exercises for your eyes. Prior to this exercise program, I was only aware of eye exercises being included in rehab programs prescribed for vertigo or balance disorders. We tend to forget "it takes muscles" to change the position of the eye every time it moves.

The ocular muscles are no different from the other striated muscles in the body. Striated muscles are attached to the skeleton by tendons and are under voluntary control. *Any* striated muscle can be sprained, strained, and overused. When a person crochets for two to three hours at a time, the eyes must isometrically contract or change their focus through a very small range of motion for prolonged periods. Whenever fifty, one hundred, or five hundred pages are read in a book, the eye muscles are asked to move the eyeball from the center to the right *thousands of times*. If these muscles have been strained by a previous trauma or are not pulling from their optimal position of leverage, they will not hold up well under these demands. I equate the response of the eye muscles to these activities to repetitive motion syndrome commonly found in the shoulder, elbow, wrist, and/or hands of assembly line workers who must complete the same task hundreds or thousands of time each day. Instead of becoming stronger with repetitive use, the muscles and soft tissues of the shoulder, elbow, wrist, or hand begin to break down and become inflamed. When a person spends hours on a computer stabilizing their gaze or reading from left to right most of the day, time should be taken to move the eyes from the center to the left, up and down, diagonally, or in circles to restore proper balance around the eye. The focus of the eye should to be changed from short to long range several times.

Observing my patients as they demonstrate these exercises has shown me how "out of balance" tension around the eyes can become. When I ask patients to simply move their eyes up or down, the vast majority are unable to move in a straight line. The eyes pull either to the right or the left, especially when looking up. Sometimes the eyes roll around in the orbit a bit before finally getting on course. Lateral motions typically pull more down toward the lower lid of the eye. Oblique motion is difficult to coordinate in at least one or two of the four directions. Sometimes a full range of motion is lacking. Active movement of the eyes may appear very sluggish or "ratchety." Poor endurance for isolated eye motion is surprisingly common. I have had a few patients who are unable to open and close their eyes more than two to three times in succession. The majority of the time, the patients are unable to center one, or both, of their eyes in the orbits or their head in the midline without assistance. When the position of the eyes, head, and neck is corrected, the patient *then* feels off-centered.

The question is can lack of range, coordination, and endurance of the eye muscles really contribute to other problems? An even better question may be can the rehabilitation of these eye deficits facilitate improvements in other areas of the body besides the eyes?

Vision - a Bimodal System

"Seventy percent of all sensory processing in the entire body is directly affected by information coming from the two eyes. These visual influences are directed to the midbrain and the majority extend themselves to the occipital cortex for the purpose of seeing. Normal vision requires the accurate function of two modes of visual processing. The *focal process* delivers information via eighty percent of the sensory nerve fibers from the retina of the eye directly to the occipital cortex for the purpose of seeing detail. The focal system enables us to concentrate and attend to the task at hand. If we had only the focal process, the world we see would break apart into a mosaic of fragments. We would see only lines, shadows and shapes on a person's face. Even though we would be able to see clearly, we would not be able to recognize the inter-relationship of the individual parts. We would not recognize that those parts come together to make one face.

The other twenty percent of the sensory nerve fibers from the retina travel to the midbrain via the *ambient process* before reaching the occipital lobe where the ambient process provides spatial boundaries for other detailed information. This visual process matches information from the kinesthetic, proprioceptive, tactile, and vestibular systems in the midbrain to organize spatial information about balance, movement, and orientation in space. This function has been labeled the sensory-motor feedback loop. Without the ambient visual process, an individual would experience fragmented vision as well as difficulty organizing posture and movement. If there is a mismatch between the ambient and other systems, *the body's concept of visual midline will shift.* (emphasis mine). If the visual midline shifts, it will reinforce and/or cause postural imbalances.. While balance between the spatial (ambient) and detail (focal) visual processing systems provides a means by which organization of time and space become a normal process for humans, injury as a result of a TBI, traumatic brain injury, can affect the balance between the systems . . . Metabolic imbalances and changes in cell membrane permeability have been noted even after minor whiplash accidents."[49]

In other words, direct injury to the head or whiplash can provoke imbalances in the visual system and the eyes. While we cannot "see" the imbalance in the midbrain or occipital cortex, *we are able to see* when the head does not sit in correct alignment on the neck, which then means the eyes are not in correct alignment with the neck. *We are able to see* when the

---

[49] Zasler, Nathan D., Katz, Douglas I., and Zafonte, Ross D. *Brain Injury Medicine Principles and Practice* (Damos Medical Publishing, LLC, 2007), p. 513.

eyes do not move in a smooth, coordinated manner. *We can appreciate the fact* that most people do not feel centered when the posture of their head and neck is corrected to the midline. *Could the imbalanced way the eyes move be an outward manifestation of imbalance in the brain we cannot see?*

By requiring movement of the eyes to occur from a position of correct alignment and by stopping each movement of the eyes in the midline, the concept of "being centered" is reinforced to the brain and the body. The information contributed from the eyes into the ambient system is now more correct information. As strength and range of motion become more symmetrical around the eye, postural imbalances are more likely to improve.

The Vestibulo-Ocular Reflex (VOR)

Correcting reflex deficiencies in the eyes also seems to be another component contributing to the success of this program. "Vestibulo-ocular reflexes (VORs) stabilize visual images during head movements. This stabilizing prevents the visual world from appearing to bounce or jump around when the head moves, especially during walking . . . In daily life, lack of image stability can be disabling because the ability to use vision for orientation is lost . . . All VORs move the eyes in the direction opposite to the head movement to maintain stability of the visual field and visual fixation on objects."[50] When the head turns to the right, the eyes should shift to the left. When the head turns to the left, the eyes should shift to the right. Vertical VORs can be elicited by flexion and extension of the head.

"VOR cancellation reflects the ability to synchronize simultaneous eye and head movements in the same direction and is associated with the ability of the brain to suppress the VOR. This function allows an individual to track an object while moving the head at the same speed. Testing results are reported as normal if the eye can remain in the center of the orbit as the head and eyes track an object as it moves across the visual field. If the central integration capabilities are abnormal, the client will not be able to

---

[50] Lundy-Ekman, Laurie, PT, PhD, *Neuroscience: Fundamentals for Rehabilitation*, Fourth Edition (Saunders, an imprint of Elsevier, Inc., 2013), p. 381.

override the reflex activity and cannot keep the eye and head moving at the same rate in the same direction."[51]

In my practice, the majority of my patients demonstrate the ability to cancel the VOR very well. Turning the head and the eyes in unison is easily accomplished by most people. What is commonly difficult is stabilizing the eyes during head movement, which is to engage the VOR. This task has been easily regained by even some of my more restricted patients. Mastering this activity seems to be most helpful to releasing tension within the cranium and the neck.

A small percentage of my patients have demonstrated even greater deficits when they must initiate head movement with their eyes. In other words, when the patients are asked to turn the head to the right, the eyes move laterally to the right first, and then the head begins to rotate. These patients are typically in extreme pain and experience excessive tension throughout their body. In a discussion I had with a chiropractic neurologist, he mentioned to me that the loss of the VOR results in stiffness throughout the body. These patients validate that point to the extreme since the sequence of their eye movement is especially dysfunctional. Even this abnormality can be corrected with time and practice.

The Unique Eye

The eye is the only organ in our body that functions for the purpose of vision. This is the most obvious way the eye is unique from any and every other part of the body. The eye is also the only organ in the body in which both voluntary and involuntary muscles are found. "The extrinsic muscles of the eye are skeletal muscles that attach to the outside of the eyeball and to the bones of the orbit. They move the eyeball in any desired direction and are, of course, voluntary, striated muscles . . . The intrinsic eye muscles of the eye are smooth, or involuntary, muscles located within the eye. These muscles are called the *iris* and the *ciliary muscles*. The iris

---

[51] Umphred, Darcy A., Lararo, Rolando T., Roller, Margaret L., and Burton, Gordon U. *Neurological Rehabilitation* (Mosby, an imprint of Elsevier, Inc., 2013), p. 699.

regulates the size of the pupil. The ciliary muscle controls the shape of the lens."[52]

The eye is also the only place in the body that consists of all three types of developmental tissue. Muscles, for example, are made from only mesoderm. The lungs are endoderm. The nervous system is all neuroectoderm. "In fetal development, the eye is created from endoderm, mesoderm, and neuroectoderm. Of importance is the fact that neuroectoderm also develops the cortex which allows for recognition that the eyeball is neurologically the result in part of developing brain tissue. The eyeball is richly endowed with nerve fibers that feed all aspects of the cortex as well as relaying information to midbrain structures."[53] Could it be possible that these shared cell types provide another way for the eyes to influence areas in the body not directly attached or connected with it?

Unexpected Benefits of Anatomical Relationships

Before I learned how to ease my patients into supine by using modified positioning, I heard reports from them of some extreme side effects. Thankfully, none of the side effects were damaging and did not last very long. It was puzzling to me how such gentle movements could provoke such extreme reactions. These side effects were evidence that something was physically and physiologically changing in response to the exercises. The majority of the time, the changes occurred in response to the eye, tongue, and neck exercises.

The first and most common side effect I heard about was increased urination and increased perspiration. Feeling pleasantly relaxed, sleepy, or extremely exhausted were other common responses. At times, I noticed visible changes in my patient's rate of breathing. Other patients told me about feeling changes in their heart rate. Occasionally, patients would notice changes in anxiety levels or appetite. Looking at the anatomy again helped me understand the responses I was seeing and hearing about involved changes in the *autonomic nervous system*.

---

[52] Patton, Kevin T., PhD and Thibodeau, Gary, A., PhD, *Anatomy and Physiology*, Seventh Edition (Mosby Elsevier, 2010), pp. 513–514.

[53] Zasler, Nathan D., Katz, Douglas I., and Zafonte, Ross D., *Brain Injury Medicine Principles and Practice* (Damos Medical Publishing, LLC, 2007), p. 513.

"The autonomic nervous system maintains homeostasis by regulating the activity of internal organs and vasculature. Thus, the ANS regulates circulation, respiration, digestion, metabolism, secretions, body temperature, and reproduction."[54] "Pathways of the ANS carry information to the *autonomic*, or *visceral* effectors, which are the smooth muscles, cardiac muscle, glands, adipose tissue, and other 'involuntary' tissue. As its name implies, the ANS seems autonomous of voluntary control—it usually appears to govern itself without our conscious knowledge"[55] and "can be exerted by hormones."[56] What I learned even more specifically was the side effects were indicative of stimulation occurring at the *hypothalamus*.

What is the Hypothalamus?

"The hypothalamus (from Greek 'under' thalamus) is a portion of the brain that contains a number of functions. One of the most important functions of the hypothalamus is to link the nervous system to the endocrine system via the pituitary gland . . . All vertebrate brains contain a hypothalamus. In humans, it is the size of an almond.

The hypothalamus is responsible for the regulation of certain metabolic processes and other activities of the autonomic nervous system. It synthesizes and secretes certain *neurohormones*, called *releasing hormones* or hypothalamic hormones, and these in turn stimulate or inhibit the secretion of *pituitary hormones*. The hypothalamus controls body temperature, hunger, important aspects of parenting and attachment behavior, thirst, fatigue, sleep, and circadian rhythm." [57]

The Effect of *Rapid Release* on the Hypothalamus

"The *diencephalon* (literally, "between brain") is the part of the brain located between the cerebrum and the midbrain (mesencephalon). The

---

[54] Lundy-Ekman, Laurie, PT, PhD, *Neuroscience: Fundamentals for Rehabilitation*, Fourth Edition (Saunders, an imprint of Elsevier, Inc., 2013), p. 168.
[55] Patton, Kevin T., PhD and Thibodeau, Gary, A., PhD, *Anatomy and Physiology*, Seventh Edition (Mosby Elsevier, 2010), p. 375.
[56] Lundy-Ekman, Laurie, PT, PhD, *Neuroscience: Fundamentals for Rehabilitation*, Fourth Edition (Saunders, an imprint of Elsevier, Inc., 2013), p. 170.
[57] wikipedia.com

main structures of the diencephalon are *the thalamus, the hypothalamus, the optic chiasm, and the pineal gland.*"[58]

A. Thalamus
B. Pineal Body   } Diencephalon
C. Hypothalamus

D. Midbrain
E. Pons   } Brainstem
F. Medulla

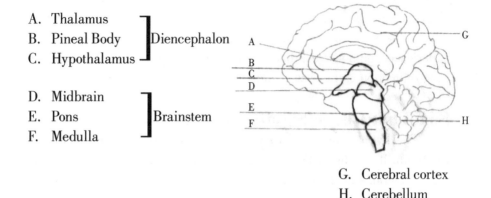

G. Cerebral cortex
H. Cerebellum

The focus of our next discussion will be about the **hypothalamus** and the **optic chiasm**. By taking a closer look at the anatomy, you will see how the potential "gliding of the optic nerve" has the ability to stimulate *even more* of the nervous system, specifically the hypothalamus.

To understand the simple illustration to the right, imagine the top of the brain has been removed. You are looking down on the inside center of the brain. You can see both eyes and the optic nerves as they travel back toward the center of the brain. The *optic chiasm* is the area where the two nerves cross. The optic nerves are identified as the

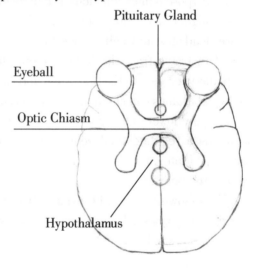

• Superior view •

---

[58] Patton, Kevin T., PhD and Thibodeau, Gary, A., PhD, *Anatomy and Physiology*, Seventh Edition (Mosby Elsevier, 2010), pp. 426.

optic tracts as they continue toward the back of the brain to attach to the midbrain.

Notice the proximity of the pituitary gland in the front of the optic chiasma and the hypothalamus in the back. In photographs of actual brains, the structures appear to be touching one another. My clinical experience would suggest that movement of the optic nerve during active range of motion of the eyes is stimulating the hypothalamus.

Small but Oh, so Significant . . .

"The hypothalamus is a small but functionally important area of the brain. It weighs little more than 1/4 oz., or 7 grams, yet it performs many functions of the greatest importance both for survival and for the enjoyment of life. For instance, it functions as a link between the psyche (mind) and the soma (body). It also links the nervous system to the endocrine system. Certain areas of the hypothalamus function as pleasure centers or reward centers for the primary drives such as eating, drinking, and sex.

The hypothalamus functions as a higher autonomic center or, rather, as several higher autonomic centers. By this we mean that axons of neurons whose dendrites and cell bodies lie in the nuclei of the hypothalamus extend in tracts from the hypothalamus to both parasympathetic and sympathetic centers in the brainstem and spinal cord. Thus impulses from the hypothalamus can simultaneously and successively stimulate or inhibit few or many lower autonomic centers. In other words, the hypothalamus serves as a regulator and coordinator of autonomic activities. It helps control and integrate the responses made by autonomic (visceral) effectors all over the body."[59]

The following is an abbreviated list of hypothalamic functions that describe responses I have witnessed in my patients in response to this exercise program. I have italicized the responses I have seen in my patients.

"1. Neurons in the supraoptic nuclei of the hypothalamus (which is brain matter just above and on either side of the optic chiasm) synthesize

---

[59] Patton, Kevin T., PhD and Thibodeau, Gary, A., PhD, *Anatomy and Physiology*, Seventh Edition (Mosby Elsevier, 2010), pp. 426–427.

the hormones released by the posterior pituitary gland. *Because one of these hormones affects the volume of urine excreted,* the hypothalamus plays an indirect but essential role in maintaining water balance.

2. The hypothalamus functions as a crucial part of the mechanism for *maintaining normal body temperature.* Hypothalamus neurons whose fibers connect with autonomic centers for vasoconstriction, dilation, and *sweating,* and with somatic centers for shivering, constitute *heat-regulating centers. Marked elevation of body temperature* often characterizes injuries or other abnormalities of the hypothalamus.

3. The hypothalamus plays an essential role in maintaining *the waking state.* Presumably it functions as part of an arousal or alerting mechanism. Clinical evidence of this is that somnolence (sleepiness) characterizes some hypothalamic disorders.

4. The hypothalamus functions as a crucial part of the mechanism for *regulating appetite* and therefore the amount of food intake.

5. The hypothalamus functions as several higher autonomic centers. *Nuclei in the hypothalamus extend in tracts from the hypothalamus to parasympathetic and sympathetic centers in the brain stem and spinal cord.* Thus impulses from the hypothalamus can simultaneously or successively stimulate or inhibit few or many lower autonomic centers. In other words, the hypothalamus serves as a regulator and coordinator of autonomic activities. It helps control and integrate the responses made by autonomic (visceral) effectors *all over the body.*

6. Some neurons in the hypothalamus have endocrine functions. Their axons secrete chemicals, *releasing hormones,* into blood which circulates to the anterior pituitary gland. These hormones control the release of certain anterior pituitary hormones, specifically growth hormone and hormones that control hormone secretion by sex glands, the thyroid gland, and the adrenal cortex. *Thus indirectly, the hypothalamus helps control the functioning of every cell in the body.*"[60]

Characteristics 5 and 6 indicate the hypothalamus has the potential to "control and integrate the responses made by autonomic (visceral) effectors *all over the body*" and "helps control the functioning of *every cell in the*

---

[60] Patton, Kevin T., PhD and Thibodeau, Gary, A., PhD, *Anatomy and Physiology*, Seventh Edition (Mosby Elsevier, 2010), pp. 427–428.

body." This may offer some insight into how this exercise program typically has such a widespread positive effect on almost everyone who does it regardless of their current diagnosis.

The Eyes and the Endocrine System

The chain of events and reactions to eye movement continues beyond the hypothalamus. As stated previously, some neurons of the hypothalamus have endocrine functions. In addition, because the hypothalamus has the ability to stimulate the pituitary gland, another complete system within the body also stands to be affected by eye movement, *the endocrine system*.

"The endocrine system refers to the collection of glands of an organism that secrete hormones directly into the circulatory system to be carried towards distant target organs. The endocrine system is an information signal system like the nervous system, yet its effects and mechanism are classifiably different. The endocrine system's effects are slow to initiate, and prolonged in their response, lasting from a few hours up to weeks. The nervous system sends information very quickly and responses are generally short lived. In vertebrates, the hypothalamus is the neural control center for all endocrine systems. The major endocrine glands include the pineal gland, the pituitary gland, pancreas, ovaries, testes, thyroid gland, parathyroid gland, salivary gland, sweat glands, mammary glands, the hypothalamus, gastrointestinal tract, and the adrenal glands"[61] as well as "the thymus and the placenta in a pregnant uterus."[62] Of these glands, this exercise program seems to have the greatest effect on the *pituitary gland*.

A lateral, or side view, of the hypothalamus and the pituitary gland shows how the two structures are, not surprisingly, separated by the optic nerve. The hypothalamus is just superior and slightly posterior to the optic nerve. The pituitary gland is just inferior and slightly anterior to the optic nerve.

---

[61] Wikipedia en.m.wikipedia.org Endocrine System.
[62] Patton, Kevin T., PhD and Thibodeau, Gary, A., PhD, *Anatomy and Physiology*, Seventh Edition (Mosby Elsevier, 2010), p. 535.

"The pituitary gland is a small but mighty structure. It measures only 1.2 to 1.5 cm, or 1/2 inch across. By weight, it is even less impressive— only about 0.5 grams or 1/60 of an ounce. And yet so crucial are the functions of the anterior lobe of the pituitary gland that, in past centuries, it was referred to as the 'master gland.'

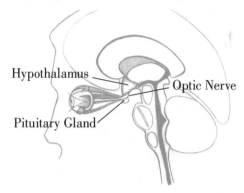

• Lateral view •

The pituitary gland has a well-protected location within the skull on the ventral surface of the brain. It lies in the *pituitary fossa* and is covered by a portion of the dura mater called the *pituitary diaphragm*. The gland has a stem-like stalk, *the infundibulum*, which connects it to the hypothalamus of the brain.

Although the pituitary looks like one gland, it actually consists of two separate glands, the *adenohypophysis*, or anterior pituitary gland, and the *neurohypophysis*, or posterior pituitary gland. In the embryo, the anterior pituitary develops from an upward projection of the pharynx and is composed of regular endocrine tissue. The posterior pituitary, on the other hand, develops from a downward projection of the brain and is composed of neurosecretory tissue. . . As you may suspect, the hormones secreted by the adenohypophysis serve very different functions from those released by the neurohypophysis."[63]

The anterior pituitary secretes five different hormones that have to do with growth and reproduction. Because "the hypothalamus directly regulates the secretion of the anterior pituitary gland, you can see that the supposed 'master gland' really has a master of its own—the hypothalamus."[64] "The posterior pituitary serves as a storage and release site for two hormones, ADH, antidiuretic hormone, and OT, oxytocin. The

---

[63] Patton, Kevin T., PhD and Thibodeau, Gary, A., PhD, *Anatomy and Physiology*, Seventh Edition (Mosby Elsevier, 2010), p. 546.

[64] Patton, Kevin T., PhD and Thibodeau, Gary, A., PhD, *Anatomy and Physiology*, Seventh Edition (Mosby Elsevier, 2010), p. 549.

cells of the posterior pituitary do not themselves make these hormones. Instead, nuclei of the hypothalamus synthesize them . . .

The term *antidiuresis* literally means 'opposing the production of a large urine volume.' And this is exactly what ADH does—it prevents the formation of a large volume of urine. In preventing large losses of fluid through the excretion of dilute urine, ADH helps the body conserve water. In other words, ADH maintains water balance in the body. . .

ADH has many other effects in the body as well. One of the most well known is that ADH stimulates contraction of muscles in the walls of small arteries, thus increasing blood pressure."[65]

In my experience, it seems the posterior pituitary is "overactive" in this regard. It appears increased tension and/or pressure within the cranium overstimulates this gland to erroneously restrict urine output. As the optic nerve theoretically glides in the area in between the hypothalamus and the posterior pituitary, the gland relaxes to allow for urination. Less frequently, I have worked with patients with urinary incontinence, but even these patients have improved urinary control in response to the exercises. Also, on a few occasions, I've witnessed reductions in blood pressure.

In the early years of teaching this program, patient reports of *excessive* increased urine output were easily the most frequent, unexpected side effect I heard about. I never asked my patients from the outpatient setting to measure their urine output, but working in the hospital setting has given me the opportunity to discuss these objective measurements with the nursing staff. I will give you one example that hopefully represents previous patients' experiences to some extent.

A fifty-six-year-old male was admitted to the hospital from the emergency room with complaints of progressive generalized weakness, difficulty breathing, fatigue, productive cough, abdominal dissension, swelling of both legs, and extreme discoloration of both calves and feet with flaky skin on both calves. In addition, this patient was unable to sleep greater than one hour at a time. Three years prior, he was treated for the same symptoms and diagnosed with heart failure.

---

[65] Patton, Kevin T., PhD and Thibodeau, Gary, A., PhD, *Anatomy and Physiology*, Seventh Edition (Mosby Elsevier, 2010), p. 552.

The traumatic history for this patient included one concussion playing high school football, one time being hit in the head with a two-by-four while working as a bouncer, and exposure to multiple explosions and altercations during ten years in the military. He required thirty-five degrees of elevation at the head of his bed to relieve 10/10 pressure in his head when I attempted to lay him flat in supine.

He had been on the same dosage of Lasix for the past two days in an effort to "diurese," or excrete more fluid, to reduce the swelling, especially in his legs. The largest measured output of urine this patient excreted in a three-hour period was a total of 300 cc. On one occasion, he voided 125 cc; on the second occasion, he voided 175 cc. Many times over the last two days, he voided *either* 125 cc total *or* 175 cc total in a three-hour period.

The head of the bed was kept at thirty-five degrees of elevation while I instructed him in the eye and neck exercises. He was able to fully participate with all the exercises three sets of three repetitions. Ten minutes after completing the exercises, the patient voided 500 cc of urine with a faster, easier flow rate as well. One hour later, he voided another 400 cc. Three hours later, he voided another 450 cc. In addition, he was able to report the next morning he had slept for three and a half hours, woken up for ten minutes, and then went back to sleep for another three and a half hours. This patient suggests the hypothalamus and the pituitary gland are being stimulated by the exercises.

Another common response I witnessed in the early years was *change in body temperature accompanied by changes in perspiration*. For some patients, the perspiration was provoked only while doing the exercises, but for most people who experienced this side effect, random episodes of perspiration occurred throughout the day for no apparent reason. The intensity of this response varied from patient to patient. One woman literally kept a high-speed fan directly on her while she did the eye exercises to manage the perspiration. Others commonly reported waking up with wet hair and/or pajamas. For some, only the hands and feet would sweat. Conversely, I have had a couple of patients who could not stop sweating prior to doing the exercises. For one of these patients, a twenty-six-year-old male, the sweating stopped immediately after the alignment of his cervical spine was corrected in supine. He had been struck by a moving vehicle while riding his bicycle at age five.

A patient who injured her lower back eight years prior to our meeting specifically noticed her body's ability to sweat had "shut off" sometime after her injury. She unsuccessfully took sauna baths in an attempt to illicit some type of perspiration response from her body. After doing her home exercise program for about two weeks, she noticed she was sweating during a time of *non-exertion*. In addition, her frequency of urination increased to once an hour. This, in turn, was surely a contributing factor to the *weight loss* experienced by this patient and others. This sounds similar to the remarks made by the patient I discussed on pages 260-263.

Even though I would never advocate these exercises specifically for weight loss, they have helped a few of my patients in this way. I would like to share a testimonial with you from a woman who lost weight as a result of consistently doing these exercises. I don't usually share the names of my patients, but I can make an exception for this person. I can conceal her identity but still call her what I always have—it's my mom.

> *Dear Nancy,*
>
> *At the age of seventy-two, I decided it was about time to do something regularly for my general health and well-being. I have struggled with my weight ever since I had my three children over forty years ago. I have been discouraged over the years as I have tried many different diets, thyroid medications, and "water pills" to no avail. Little did I know that someday my own daughter would be the one to finally help me with this long-standing problem!*
>
> *I started going to my local gym five days a week to ride the stationary bike and lift light weights. After six months I noticed some improved tone, but no weight loss. At this point I started doing the* **Rapid Release** *program every morning before breakfast.* **Making up my mind to commit to a certain time of the day to do my exercises has been one of the keys to my success.** *Even though I never anticipated any weight loss because the exercises are not aerobic, it is now six to seven months later and I've lost twelve pounds! I have gone down two sizes in my pants and one size in my shirts!*

Plus, I am experiencing an increased level of energy and vitality immediately after doing my exercises that lasts throughout the day.

The most fun and rewarding experience is being on the receiving end of compliments from friends who have known me for decades. I am frequently asked, "What have you been doing? You look so good!" My favorite question has come from those friends who have been brave enough to ask, "Have you had a face lift?" My immediate response each and every time is, "I'm doing Nancy's exercises—and they work!"

Keep up the good work, hon!
With love,
Mom

I do not typically hear reports of *extreme* responses to the exercises any longer like I did during the first few years of my experience with this program. Using the *seated program* and the *positions of ease* to gradually progress my patients toward an improved tolerance for the supine position has reduced these side effects. Just as muscle soreness can be controlled by easing into the intensity of a regular workout, these physiologic responses can be better controlled by easing into this program with modified positioning.

How Does *Rapid Release* Reduce Pain?

The ability to experience decreased pain in response to doing these exercises was a mystery to me for years. Studying the locations of the cranial nerves engaged by eye movement and the body's "natural painkillers" has given me what seems to be a possible explanation.

"When a person is injured, pain impulses travel up the spinal cord to the brain which releases endorphins and enkephalins. *Endorphins* are thought to block pain principally at the brainstem. *Enkephalins* block pain signals in the spinal cord. Both are morphine like substances whose functions are similar to those of opium-based drugs."[66]

---

[66] Medical discoveries.com, endorphin and enkephalin.

More specifically, "endorphins can be found in the pituitary gland, in other parts of the brain, or distributed throughout the nervous system. Stress and pain are the two most common factors leading to the release of endorphins. Endorphins interact with the opiate receptors in the brain to reduce our perception of pain. Endorphins act similarly to drugs such as morphine and codeine. In contrast to opiate drugs, however, activation of the opiate receptors by the body's endorphins does not lead to addiction or dependence."[67] It is possible the pituitary gland is stimulated to release endorphins during eye movement.

"Enkephalin producing cells for pain suppression have been found in the *periaqueductal gray area* (PGA) located within the midbrain. The periaqueductal gray is the primary control center for descending pain modulation. This region has been used as the target area for brain stimulating implants in patients with chronic pain. The *oculomotor nuclei* of the oculomotor nerve arise from the area of the PAG."[68]

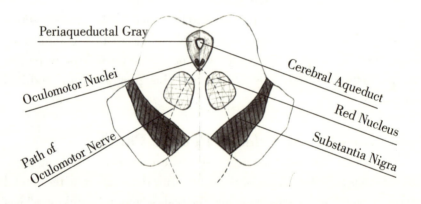

Since the oculomotor nerve innervates four of the six external ocular muscles, it is possible movement of the eyes stimulates the area of the PAG to release enkephalins to reduce pain. Also, notice the pathway of the oculomotor nerve passes through *the red nucleus and the substantia nigra*. These are the two areas mentioned on page 403 as being areas of the brain involved with muscular control. This may

---

[67] Medicinenet.com, "Where are endorphins produced?"
[68] Wikipedia Periductal Gray Area.

explain the relaxation of muscle tone that occurs and allows for the improved range of motion.

The modality that continues to confuse me pertains to my patients' response to massage for the muscles of the TMJ joint in the jaw or the muscles of mastication. There have been many times over the past eighteen years that patients with shoulder, hip, or knee pain have experienced partial or complete relief from their joint pain in response to this specific treatment. It is such a dependable treatment I rarely exclude it from the therapy I provide to my patients regardless of their diagnosis.

And Finally . . . the Circulatory System

We have seen how eye movement affects the fascia and the autonomic, central, and peripheral nervous systems and the endocrine system. The vascular system is the last system to consider. The following illustration shows how the major branches of the vascular system are one continuous system. Might there be potential for the eyes or the position of the neck to affect this system as well? Following the anatomy again helps answer this question.

If it were possible to identify a place in the body where the circulation begins, the heart would be the most likely choice. The *abdominal aorta* descends from the heart to the lower abdomen, where it divides to form

• The circulatory system •

the right and left common iliac artery (CIA). The CIA divides into the internal and external iliac arteries. The external iliac continues down the anterior aspect of each leg as the *femoral artery*. Any other circulation in the leg is a branch of the femoral artery anteriorly or the internal iliac artery posteriorly.

The vasculature above the heart is of most importance as it pertains to the **Rapid Release** method of movement. The aortic arch comes out

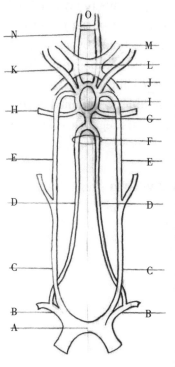

A. Aortic arch
B. Right and left subclavian arteries
C. Right and left common carotid arteries
D. Right and left vertebral arteries
E. Right and left internal carotid arteries
F. Foramen magnum
G. Basilar artery
H. Posterior cerebral artery
I. Posterior communicating artery
J. Optic tract
K. Middle cerebral artery
L. Optic chiasm
M. Optic nerve
N. Anterior cerebral artery
O. Anterior communicating artery

• **Blood Supply to the Cerebrum** •

the top of the heart. The *brachiocephalic artery* (BCA) leaves the aortic arch on the right and then divides into the *right subclavian artery* (RSCA), which proceeds down the right arm, and the *right common carotid artery* (RCCA), which proceeds up the side of the neck. The arteries on the left side of the heart are laid out a little differently but involve the same structures minus the BCA. In the absence of the BCA, the *left subclavian artery* (LSCA) and the *left common carotid* (LCCA) branch directly off the aortic arch. The right and left SCA and all the circulation that branches off from it inferiorly provides circulation down both arms all the way to the hands. The right and left *vertebral arteries* arise superiorly from the right and left subclavian arteries. The *vertebral arteries and the carotid* arteries, *more specifically the internal carotid artery*, are the two large arteries that ascend from the aortic arch to supply blood to the head and neck.

"The brainstem and the cerebellum are supplied with blood by branches of the vertebral arteries and branches of the *basilar artery.* The basilar artery is formed by the union of the vertebral arteries."[69] By referring back to the illustration of the vertebral artery on page 395, it is easy to understand how the alignment and position of the cervical spine can influence the vertebral artery. The vertebral artery literally runs through a notch in the transverse process of each cervical vertebrae. Restrictions of blood flow in the neck can potentially affect the blood flow to the brainstem and the cerebellum.

"The two internal carotid arteries arise as one of the two terminal branches of the common carotid arteries. They proceed superiorly to the base of the skull where they enter the carotid canal. Entering the cranial cavity each carotid artery gives off the *ophthalmic artery, the posterior communicating artery, the middle cerebral artery and the anterior cerebral artery.*

The cerebral arterial 'Circle of Willis' is formed at the base of the brain by:

1. an anterior communicating artery connecting the left and right anterior cerebral arteries to each other;
2. two posterior communicating arteries, one on each side, connecting the internal carotid artery with the posterior cerebral artery."[70]

The optic chiasm and the hypothalamus are surrounded by the circle of Willis, the anastomotic ring of nine arteries which supply all the blood to the cerebral hemispheres, or the cerebrum.

The area most of us identify as "the brain" is the *cerebrum.* "The cerebrum is entirely supplied by the internal carotid and posterior cerebral arteries. The internal carotid arteries enter the skull through the temporal bones; small branches from each internal carotid become posterior

---

[69] Lundy-Ekman, Laurie, PT, PhD, *Neuroscience: Fundamentals for Rehabilitation,* Fourth Edition (Saunders, an imprint of Elsevier, Inc., 2013), p. 15.

[70] Drake, Richard L., Vogl, A. Wayne, and Mitchell, Adam W. M., *Gray's Anatomy for Students,* Second Edition (Churchill Livingstone, Elsevier, Inc., 2010), p. 837.

communicating arteries that join the internal carotid with the posterior cerebral artery. *Near the optic chiasm, the internal carotid divides into the anterior and middle cerebral arteries.*(emphasis mine)"[71]

The *middle cerebral artery* (MCA) lies slightly posterior and lateral to the optic chiasm. "The MCA is the largest branch of the internal carotid. This artery supplies a portion of the frontal lobe and the lateral surface of the temporal and parietal lobes, including the primary motor and sensory areas of the face, throat, hand and arm and in the dominant hemisphere, the areas for speech. *The MCA is the artery most often occluded in stroke.*"[72](emphasis mine)

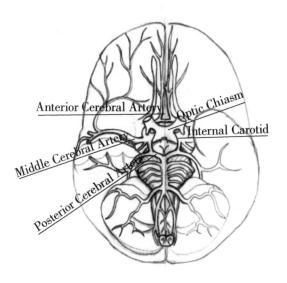

Compromised circulation may be the underlying cause for the neuromuscular pattern of dysfunction I see in the "unilateral pathway of pain." It has been my clinical observation this pattern of soft tissue dysfunction and abnormal movement that can develop along the unilateral pathway of pain resembles the dysfunctional movement patterns created by a stroke, even though a literal stroke has not occurred. *I have also watched these symptoms subside as my patients complete the exercises.* It is as if

---

[71] Lundy-Ekman, Laurie, PT, PhD, *Neuroscience: Fundamentals for Rehabilitation*, Fourth Edition (Saunders, an imprint of Elsevier, Inc., 2013), p. 16.

[72] Medscape.com Middle Cerebral Artery stroke. Daniel Slater MD, chief editor, Denise Campagnolo MD.

movement of the eyes relieves tension in the area of restricted cerebral vasculature. As blood flow improves, symptoms subside.

Consider the abnormal movement patterns presented by two patients on the day of their physical therapy evaluation. These patients were discussed on pages 271-277 in "Lifelong Lower Back Pain" and pages 304-308 in "Neck Pain after Cervical Fusion." In spite of their differing diagnoses, they demonstrated very similar dysfunctional movement. I chose to refer to them because the abnormal pattern of movement was more developed and easily recognized in each of their cases. Both of these patients were dragging their left leg behind them while their trunk rotated to the left and the left arm was bent at the elbow with the forearm either across the chest or tucked closely into the side of the torso. (More about this pattern will be discussed in the next chapter.) **The good news is they both were walking normally by the end of their therapy sessions.**

In Conclusion

Traumatic injury distorts posture. By doing so, every system in the body can be affected to some extent. I have observed that the effects of trauma to the head and the cervical spine, in particular, have far-reaching effects. Consider the fact that quadriplegia is paralysis of all four limbs and the entire body below the neck following an injury that severs the spinal cord in that area. Anyone who has suffered the effects of a "broken neck" has *no doubt* their neck affects their torso, arms and hands, legs and feet, and numerous bodily functions. Apparently, the right amount of abnormal tension in the neck due to incorrect alignment or soft tissue dysfunction can also have varying degrees of effect on these same areas.

The idea the body functions as a mechanical continuum is clear whether it be skeletal, muscular, fascial, neural, or circulatory. Even though each system can be traced individually, they obviously function collectively. Fascial patterns have been identified and are treated from the most distal ends of all four extremities and from the body to several different locations on the external surface of the cranium and face. Craniosacral therapists address meningeal fascial restrictions inside the spine and the skull with their manual techniques. The neural tension tests and treatments I have reviewed address the complete spine and all four extremities.

The documentation compiled in previous articles, manuscripts, and books about each system is thorough and extensive, but I have observed an interesting omission as I have reviewed each one. The fascial connections of the eye and the optic nerve as being directly connected to the peripheral facial system are not mentioned. The eye and the optic nerve are not included in neural tension treatment techniques. Chiropractors and osteopaths use repositioning of the eyes to create a specific response to cervical adjustments, but I'm not sure to what extent this maneuver is applied throughout these professions.

My clinical observations have shown me gentle mobilization of the eyes affects everything. The anatomical relationship of the optic nerve to critical arteries in the brain seems to be significant. Physiological responses to the eye exercises suggest that eye movement provokes change within the autonomic and endocrine systems. The extensive influence of the eyes should be acknowledged and integrated into our treatments however we can to improve outcomes for our patients and for ourselves.

The results I see in my patients in response to doing these simple exercises are enough to keep me using this program to help nearly every patient I encounter. Conventional Western medicine requires evidence-based explanations, however, for their practice. Satisfying the research requirements for the delivery system so many people depend on for help is needed.

My hope is to someday soon validate my theories to satisfy this requirement and encourage widespread acceptance of this treatment method. Embracing the need for and implementing holistic health-care treatment strategies should help improve patient outcomes now. Ideally, this type of intervention should be implemented as soon as possible following any type of injury, but **it's never too late to do so.** Reducing future health-care costs and personal disability by preventing the unseen complications of traumatic injury could also be an attainable reality.

Chapter 7

Putting It All Together

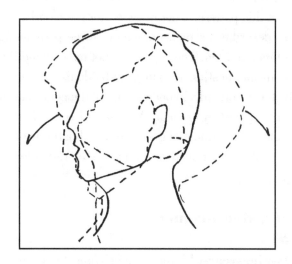

I specifically noticed a couple of things about two women I treated years ago that caught my attention. One came to outpatient therapy for knee pain and the other for hip pain. Both told me their sleep was being interrupted in the middle of the night by a severe headache accompanied by a nosebleed. Both demonstrated decreased dorsiflexion while walking, or an inability to strike their heel on the ground before bearing weight on the foot. This provoked a poor tolerance for weight bearing on the affected leg. Both were showing range-of-motion deficits in their arm as well as their leg, even though they did not complain of arm pain. The pattern of dysfunction they demonstrated in their arm and leg was not extreme, but components along the unilateral pathway of pain had been activated.

The good news about their conditions is that the headaches, nosebleeds, and arm deficits all resolved as their hip and knee pain improved. What I observed with these patients and others caused me to seriously ponder what I was seeing.

Both of these women were in their seventies, but I began to notice the manifestation of this pattern is not reserved for the elderly. The following case examples describe the presentations of three patients ages twenty-nine, twenty-three, and ten. These patients not only exemplify the effects of trauma already manifesting in younger individuals, but they also further exemplify why I have formed a hypothesis about the neuromuscular pattern of dysfunction triggered by trauma. As you will see, I have highlighted specific characteristics found along the unilateral pathway of pain for each patient. Unfortunately, the effects of trauma are no respecter of persons or a person's age.

Age Is Not a Requirement
- **Patient #1**

A twenty-nine-year-old young man came to see me because of chronic tension in his lower back and lower extremities. In spite of rigorous training, stretching, and conditioning, the tightness he experienced had only gotten worse over the last several years. It was now more intense, more easily provoked, and more difficult to relax. His passion was jet ski racing. He had noticed this chronic tension was having a negative effect on his racing speed.

His history contains two significant traumas to his head. At the age of two, he pulled an anvil off his father's workbench. As it fell, it hit him in the forehead. Then at age ten, he took a very serious fall on his bicycle. He was retained for observation in the emergency room all day because of a continuous bleed from his ears. A suspected fractured jaw was ruled out by a negative X-ray. He also separated his right shoulder fifteen years ago snow skiing and separated it again four years ago when he crashed a motorbike. I guess "boys will be boys." Points of interest in his history included frequent episodes of a bloody nose during his adolescence, a noticeable weakness on his left side compared to his right during weight lifting, and a chronic tension in his lower back since his early twenties.

As we spoke, there was an obvious difference between the left and right side of his face. The right side looked more flushed even while he was sitting up. When I laid him in supine, the redness in the **right** side of his face and head became even more pronounced. He could feel a pressure of 6–7/10 building in the **right** side of his head. His first reaction in his lower extremities was to **cross his left leg over his right**. We had to create a twenty- to thirty-degree wedge for his upper body, head, and neck plus put an additional six centimeters of support under his head just to make him comfortable in supine. He had been having headaches on the **right** side of his head and noticed significant crepitus in his **left** shoulder during weight lifting. As previously mentioned, he had noticed the **entire left side of his body** seemed to be weaker than the right. Range-of-motion measurements revealed deficits in the **left shoulder** as well as the **left hip**.

This young man looked like the picture of health. He was very disciplined to comply with his strengthening and cardiovascular training as well as his diet to keep him a viable jet ski racing competitor. Simple, isolated trunk and hip extension exercises, however, were almost impossible for him to do. The eye exercises were very challenging and immediately fatiguing. When he attempted any form of antigravity range of motion exercise in supine for his cervical spine, his lower back immediately cramped.

- **Patient #2**

This **twenty-three-year-old** young lady had always been very active. In high school, she kept busy with volleyball, basketball, and tennis. Most recently, she participated in yoga classes several times each week. She had no chronic illnesses, allergies, or physical restrictions. Then one day she was hit from behind while she was stopped in her car. The impact forced her car underneath the car in front of her. She noticed a severe burning in her neck at the time of impact. Two days later, her lower back began to ache and spasm.

She received physical therapy daily for one month consisting of ultrasound, electrical stimulation, and hot packs to her neck. Her therapy then dropped to three times a week for several weeks. She was improving somewhat but only temporarily. She was having so much residual pain in her neck she was forced to quit her job in Los Angeles and move back to Albuquerque to be near family support.

At the time of her evaluation, her neck pain was circumferential, and her lower back pain was constant at 5–6/10. Her pain would exacerbate to 8–10/10 with prolonged sitting or upon waking each morning. In addition, she was surprised when the pain started interrupting her sleep three to four times each night because she had always considered herself to be a very deep sleeper. She was no longer able to stretch out and relax while she slept. In fact, she was now sleeping in the craziest position I have ever seen anyone demonstrate. She was most comfortable with her head rotated to the right while she held it so far back her chin was pointing straight to the ceiling. If she wanted to get really comfortable, she would side bend her neck to the left, in addition to the right rotation, and slide her jaw to the left. She would then bend at the hips and knees and let her knees drop over to her right. She was about as deviated as you can get from good posture.

To make this even more interesting, she would wake up each morning in the reversed position. Her head would be rotated to the left, side bent to the right; her jaw would be over to the right; and her knees would be bent up but be rotated to the left.

Her pain had also spread into her jaw. Chewing was difficult on the left, and she noticed a "shearing" sound on the left each time she yawned. Her cervical flexion, or chin-tuck position, was limited to eight degrees of the normal range of motion, which is fifty-five degrees. This limited her tolerance for reading to only ten minutes. She was also complaining of veering off to the right while she was walking. Sinus infections had become such a chronic problem for her she recently had a CAT scan done of her head. Before her accident, she had suffered from only one sinus infection in her life.

What I found in my evaluation was a combination of the pattern I will soon discuss on both sides of her body. The most dominant component of the pattern, however, was her tendency to adduct, or cross, her **right leg across the midline** and **rotate her head to the left**. Her right shoulder was rotated forward four centimeters in front of her ear. She preferred to keep both elbows bent with her forearms and hands supported on her abdomen. When her arms were positioned alongside her body, **the right elbow would automatically bend, and the forearm would simultaneously pull up across her abdomen while she completed the right heel slide exercise.**

Interestingly enough, she was not positioned very long in supine with her legs directly underneath her when she put her left foot on top of the right foot. She did not cross the whole left leg over the right, but she crossed at the ankles as she **pointed her foot down and in at the left ankle**. One of my more troubling findings was her inability to move her head in any direction without initiating the movement with her eyes. She was not showing any specific limitation in one direction or another. She was limited in all directions.

- **Patient #3**

    A ten-year-old girl came to see me after being hit in the right side of her face with a soccer ball. This blow to her head made her neck especially sore on the right, and turning her head was becoming increasingly more difficult. She was also complaining of an earache in her right ear.

    I've known this young girl her whole life and have informally massaged her neck a time or two when she would complain of her neck feeling tense. I had never discussed a complete history with her or her mom until I laid her down this time in supine. It became obvious something else had been going on in her body long before she got hit in the face with a soccer ball two days ago. The most obvious alarm sounded from her head and neck. She was literally **lying on the crown of her head**. Her chin was almost pointing straight up toward the ceiling. Her **lower back was arched** up a good three inches off my treatment table. She immediately **crossed her left leg over her right** as soon as she hit the table. Even though she never experienced lower back pain, her psoas was incredibly tight and tender on both sides, especially on the left. In fact, she was incredibly **tender throughout her entire left side** from her adductors to her psoas and onto her serratus anterior. The tension continued superiorly into her pectoralis major and pectoralis minor, scalenes, and sternocleidomastoid, as well as her levator scapulae. Interestingly enough, her right sternocleidomastoid (SCM) was the muscle most *noticeably* sore and painful from her recent injury, but she was surprised at **how much more tender her left SCM was when it was palpated.**

This young girl had sustained three specific head traumas in the past. One of them was especially bad. When she was four years old, another little girl jumped down from a top bunk and accidentally pushed my patient into the corner of a dresser. My patient's parents were at the other end of the house when they heard a noise that sounded like someone had just hit a baseball inside their home. When they reached the bedroom, their daughter was unconscious with a sizable laceration on her forehead. The second trauma occurred when she fell face-first onto an asphalt surface. The final incident occurred when she ran quickly around a corner in her home and ran into an opened oven door.

For the most part, this little girl felt pretty good. She is very active and does very well in school. She has, however, recently noticed a burning pain in the left posterior aspect of her neck when she wakes up. The specific muscle she is complaining of is her levator scapulae.

At ten years of age, she is already beginning to experience recurrent pain in one specific location of the unilateral pathway of pain. She has not noticed any other pain along this pattern, but the entire length of the pattern is tense and activated.

The component of this pattern I would most like to consider is the way her head tended to always turn to her right side **or to the side opposite from all her symptoms.** This characteristic was not only demonstrated by her and the two other case examples I just reviewed. I have noticed it is overwhelmingly present to some degree in almost everyone I evaluate.

"Denial" Posturing

When the position of the head is turned away from the side of the body manifesting dysfunction, the head is said to be in "denial." This posture is commonly associated with those people who have suffered a CVA or "stroke." The explanation given for denial posturing is the stroke victim is so detached from the affected side of their body they literally turn their head away from the affected side to disassociate from it. I now have a different understanding and perception of "denial" posturing.

The *sternocleidomastoid* (SCM) muscle of the neck turns the head to the opposite side. For example, when the *left* SCM contracts, the head turns to the *right*. I have noticed the tone of the SCM is often more pronounced on one side of my patient's bodies regardless of his or her diagnosis because it is one of the muscles involved in the unilateral pathway of pain and neuromuscular dysfunction. As the tone of the SCM increases, the head is more inclined to rotate to the opposite side. Abnormal activity in the SCM can be detected in patients where the tone of the SCM is just beginning to change, even though it has not yet become so excessive it literally repositions the head in a noticeable way. The dysfunction can be recognized when the head does not or will not return to the midline during the neck rotation exercises. Or if the patient is passively positioned in neutral, they will complain of feeling off-centered. Most of the time, these patients do not hold their head so their face is looking straight forward; instead, the head will be rotated slightly or significantly to one side or the other. In a stroke victim, the tone can increase so much the muscle literally pulls the head to the opposite side so strongly the head is unable to even return to the midline, much less to the opposite side.

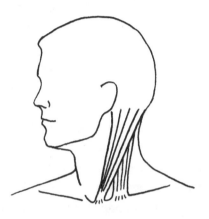

• Left SCM contracts. •
• Head turns to the right. •

What I have come to realize is that this same neuromuscular pattern of dysfunction is present in trauma victims regardless of their current diagnosis. Many times, it is so subtle it is unrecognizable unless you know what to look for. Or if the pattern has not been in place long enough, one section of the pattern may not be active yet, even though two or three other sections are. The symptomatic site just happens to be the location where the pain is currently manifesting itself. *The point is there is a very wide spectrum of how and when this pattern of dysfunction displays itself in individuals following traumatic injury.*

This explains why so many of my patients tell me *they always have trouble on one side of their body*. If their right shoulder, for example, is hurting them now, they may have previously had right hip or right knee pain. Or maybe the shoulder pain is now *in addition to* the original pain that never went away on the right side. **This is why I stated in the beginning of this book that patients suffering from a diverse list of problems or diagnoses have far more in common than I would have ever suspected.**

The Best Defense Is a Good Offense

My goal in identifying this pattern is not to provoke fear and panic. **Taking a fall or being in a car accident does not guarantee you will suffer a stroke.** If it did, most of us could anticipate having a stroke sometime in our lives. I do believe we can use the knowledge of this concept, however, to identify an abnormal pattern of dysfunction much earlier than we currently think. Identifying the presence of this pattern could provide us with an additional treatable risk factor for stroke. Education and understanding empower us to make better decisions and take confident steps toward better management of our health.

Consider the "hindsight" perspective I gained from the patient who first opened my eyes to this idea. This particular sixty-five-year-old patient had already suffered a stroke and developed a very painful left shoulder on the side of her body affected by the stroke. She was referred to physical therapy for her shoulder pain. I had already recognized that treating the lower body was helpful in some of my other patients with shoulder pain. I wondered if this approach would help a stroke survivor with a *neurological diagnosis* as well as it had for someone with a *musculoskeletal or orthopedic diagnosis*.

As I took this woman's history, I was hopeful some of my ideas would help. As it turned out, she had been in a very serious "pile up" accident four years ago. She was thrown into the floorboard of her car and stuck underneath her steering wheel for two hours. She had suffered with low back pain ever since the accident. Two years later, she noticed she was limping because of left hip and left knee pain. Then one year later, she developed neck pain and headaches on the left side that interrupted her sleep. During the last six months, she experienced frequent nosebleeds. Then one day she experienced a stroke significantly affecting the left side of her body. Her ability to walk and care for herself independently was gone in an instant.

As I listened to her history, I began to question if there was more to consider regarding the events leading up to a stroke. *But as this woman told her story, I saw her problem unfolding the opposite way.* I visualized her as a water balloon being squeezed so much from below that the top of the balloon literally did burst. The tension from one side of her body progressed from her lower back up into her neck and head on the same side. The tension on one side of her head created an increase in the pressure on the opposite side. When the pressure became too much, a traumatic incident finally occurred on that side of her head. *Then the neuromuscular pattern of dysfunction already present on the opposite side of her body was intensified.*

After working with this patient, I began to pick up on the widespread display of this pattern. Almost all my patients were either reporting components of this pattern to me and/or actually demonstrating parts of it. Recognizing the presence of this pattern might be a step toward preventing more serious problems.

So what does this pattern look like? For the sake of example, I will trace the muscles of the pattern and note presentation characteristics about the patient from the head down to the feet for **right-sided pain.**

MUSCLES OF DYSFUNCTION	PRESENTATION CHARACTERISTICS
1. The oblique muscles along the medial aspect of the right eye.	1. The eye on the affected side is usually smaller.
2. The left splenius capitis and left posterior cervical paraspinals on the back side of the neck.	2. The posterior muscles on the opposite side of the neck are tight in an effort to balance out the increased tone on the anterior side of the neck on the affected side.
3. The right rectus capitis posterior major and right splenius capitis also on the back side of the neck.	3. The back of the neck is often very tight and tender all the way across the back of the neck, but it may be *less so* on the affected side of the body than it is on the opposite or nonaffected side.
4. The right SCM and scalenes on the front side of the neck.	4. The increased tone in the right SCM rotates the head to the left or away from the affected side of the body.
5. The right pectoralis major and minor and the serratus anterior of the chest.	5. The pectoral muscles pull the upper arm into the trunk of the body; the increased tone in the serratus anterior inhibits the ability to reach forward.
6. The right coracobrachialis, the anterior deltoid of the shoulder, and the long head of the bicep.	6. The coracobrachialis and anterior deltoid also pull the upper arm into the body; the long head of the bicep flexes, or bends, the elbow.
7. The right teres major and subscapularis of the scapula or rotator cuff; the infraspinatus and teres minor.	7. The subscapularis and teres major contract to internally rotate or roll the shoulder in toward the center; increased but lesser tone in the infraspinatus and teres minor attempts to offset.
8. The right psoas and external obliques of the abdomen.	8. The right psoas flexes the hip; the external oblique rotates the torso forward on the right toward the left side of the body.
9. The right quadratus lumborum of the low back.	9. The right quadrus lumborum elevates the pelvis, making it difficult to weight bear on the affected leg.
10. The gluteus medius and/or minimus of the pelvis or hip.	10. The gluteus medius and minimus roll the leg *in* at the hip and fail to stabilize the pelvis on the opposite side of the body.
11. The adductors of the thigh, particularly the adductor magnus and gracilis.	11. The adductors pull the thigh across the midline in the "scissoring" position.
12. The semimembranosus and semitendinosus of the hamstring.	12. The semimembranosus and semitendinosus of the hamstring slightly bend the knee; the gracilis also can slightly contribute to knee flexion.
13. The vastus lateralis and vastus intermedius of the quadricep.	13. The tone of the lateral quadriceps increases to balance out the increased tone of the medial hamstring and adductors; increased tone resists knee flexion.
14. The gastrocnemius, soleus, tibialis posterior, and plantaris.	14. The gastrocnemius, soleus, and plantaris pull the foot down while the tibialis posterior and medial head of the gastroc pull the foot in to create a "drop foot."
15. The popliteus of the knee.	15. In weight bearing, laterally rotates femur on tibia creating medial knee pain.

Curious Again

My curiosity about the medical histories of stroke victims compelled me to interview fifty different stroke survivors very informally. My goal was to identify what types of previous injuries each one had sustained and what kinds of neuromuscular problems they were having prior to the onset of their stroke. I would like to do a larger survey someday, but this information has given me a start to validate some of my theories.

As I had expected, all but three of these survivors, or 94%, had suffered some form of previous trauma. Of the three non-trauma victims, one woman's stroke occurred at the time of a motorcycle accident. The two other men could not recall any specific trauma. This does not necessarily mean a trauma never occurred, however. Sometimes it takes a while for people to recall previous incidents. For example, one man I interviewed initially denied ever being hit in the head until he remembered his nose had been broken fifteen times while working as a police officer in Chicago. I guess being punched in the face was so common for him he did not classify it as head trauma. In my book, it counts. Another young man did not think he had ever sustained any injury to his head, even though his very crooked nose was broken and all his bottom teeth were knocked out when his face was beaten with brace knuckles. He did not consider trauma to his face as head trauma.

The most significant finding from my survey was that 87% of those surveyed had experienced some form of head trauma, 52% had taken a fall, and 36% had been involved in a motor vehicle accident. The second most significant finding was 60% of those surveyed had experienced previous pain or had current pain in at least one area of the side affected by the stroke. These areas of pain included the hip, knee, shoulder, or sciatica in the affected leg. Even though 60% is a fairly high percentage, I must admit I had expected it to be much higher. Thirty percent had experienced pain in two sites prior to their stroke. Several people mentioned they had so much trouble with their back, hip, or knee or any combination of the three they were forced to take an early retirement from their chosen profession.

It was interesting to note 52% had experienced lower back pain, and 38% had experienced headaches. Not all the lower back pain patients experienced headaches, but all the headache victims also complained of lower back pain. I found it interesting that more people complained of lower back pain than headaches. I would have assumed headaches would be very high on the list since a stroke happens in the head. This finding, however, is consistent with the water balloon theory.

Do not assume that the passing of much time in between different problems you experience negates them from being a part of the neuromuscular pattern of dysfunction. Symptoms occurring even several years apart are worth noting. Particular attention should be paid if the problems all fall on the same side of the body. The exception is a shoulder/knee or shoulder/hip problem on the opposite sides of the body. For example, pain will be sited in the right hip and the left shoulder. Or pay more attention when the pain is combined with a noticeable loss of strength altering function. The best example is hip pain that causes the leg to drag while walking. These characteristics are indications you would benefit from this program.

Another piece of surprising information caught my attention as I spoke with these stroke survivors. The age when their strokes occurred was often much younger than I would have expected. The eldest person I surveyed was eighty-eight at the time of her stroke, but the youngest person was twenty-one. At one survivors' meetings I attended, over half of the members suffered their stroke in their early forties. I was aware stroke can occur during surgery or childbirth, for example, so the potential for stroke to affect people of all different ages through these avenues is there, but I thought these incidents were the exception, not the rule. And those types of situations probably are the exception. But based on the examples of the three younger patients I gave at the end of the previous chapter, I believe past traumatic injury can play a crucial role in our predisposition for neurologic calamity or dysfunction.

Of course, everyone who suffers from lower back pain or knee pain is not a stroke waiting to happen. But if several parts of the puzzle are in place, it is only wise to become proactive in an effort to disrupt this pattern. This is not a puzzle you want to complete. The majority of the stroke survivors I interviewed never connected their head trauma, motor vehicle accident, or fall to their current condition. They assumed each problem was an isolated incident. My clinical experience has caused me to think differently. If you have suffered a concussion, head trauma, or facial trauma, do not necessarily disassociate it from your present experience. It may be contributing to your current condition.

Anyone who has a history of trauma should be on the alert regarding the occurrence of other problems possibly related to the previous trauma. If there has been head trauma, a fall, or a motor vehicle accident in your past, particularly if you sustained a whiplash injury, be aware of what else occurs in your body after the incident. *By rehabilitating this complete pattern instead of the isolated problem, better results may be achieved and many other problems may be prevented.* Could stroke possibly be one of them? Please refer to the final case example in the shoulder pain section of chapter 5 on pages 341-347 to more specifically see how this program was used to help a woman who had suffered a recent stroke.

Using Our Heads about Head Trauma

I would like to consider head trauma more closely since it was by far the one thing most of these stroke survivors had in common. Of course, the mechanism of injury when the head trauma occurred was quite diverse. Most of the time, it was nothing unusual. It was "normal accidental stuff." Several people had fallen out of trees onto their heads. Others fell on the ice. Quite a few hit their heads on windshields as children. Some of the men confessed to participating in many fistfights growing up as young boys or while they were in the military. Unfortunately, a handful of the women had been battered. And, interestingly enough, there were several who had accidentally run into a pole for one reason or another.

Some other similarities came out of my conversations with this group of people. Those who had hit their head very hard on concrete or the ice as children remembered frequent nosebleeds as children. By adolescence, most of the nosebleeds stopped, but then some kind of chronic lower back problem started in their twenties or thirties. If you remember, this is what my twenty-nine-year-old patient reported to me on pages 446-447. Several who had been in car accidents remembered having the distinct experience of a numbness, tingling, or electric shock going down one complete side of their body at the time of impact. One woman who had fallen off a stair banister onto a concrete slab headfirst at the age of four later experienced a tingling in her complete right side throughout her pregnancy in her thirties. The survivors who suffered a brain stem or cerebellar stroke had all taken a hard fall previously onto their tailbone.

Concussions also fall into the category of trauma. I wish I had kept track of how many people have told me about having *at least one concussion in their life*. I have not kept track of that information, but to conservatively say fifty percent of the patients I saw as inpatients in the hospital, with varied diagnoses, had previously suffered a concussion would certainly be a low estimate. I have not used this program to directly treat concussion at the time of the incident, but I suspect the principles of my method and the exercises could be used as a helpful form of treatment for concussion.

Early in my practice I met a woman suffering from severe vertigo, headaches, and neck pain. She lost consciousness when she went headfirst through the back windshield in a MVA twenty years before we met. She commented to me that she did not think she had hurt her head because "there was very little bleeding." Of course she traumatized her head. I am inclined to believe that any significant blow to the head is not benign and will eventually manifest in other problems. We would all be wise to seek out forms of holistic, following a traumatic injury, especially if the head and neck are directly involved.

Hope for Change

"The number of people in the United States alone affected by stroke each year is approximately 795,000. Each year 130,000 Americans die from stroke related causes making it the third leading cause of death in our country. On average, one person dies of stroke every 4 minutes. That's 1 out of every 20 deaths in the U.S. Based upon these numbers, at least 665,000 people each year experience this catastrophic event that has the potential to change their lives forever. Stroke is the leading cause of adult disability. The impact this has on individuals, families, and society as a whole reaches into the mental and emotional areas of life in addition to the physical losses of the stroke survivor. Financially, stroke costs the United States an estimated $34 billion each year. This total includes the cost of health care services, medications to treat stroke, and missed days of work."[73] If you google the top 10 leading causes of death in the United

---

CHAPTER 7

[73] Stroke Facts.gov.

States, you will find stroke listed as number 5 after heart disease, cancer, chronic lower respiratory disease, and accidents or unintentional injuries.[74]

Medical providers have recognized the importance of educating their patients and the general public about the effects of stroke and how to best prevent its occurrence. Stroke prevention education includes the identification of stroke **risk factors** and stroke **warning signs**. High blood pressure, heart disease, high cholesterol, and diabetes have currently been identified as "risk factors" for stroke. Managing these conditions well with diet, exercise, and medication is an offensive strategy used by health-care providers to help their patients avoid stroke. Smoking has also been found to increase the chance of stroke, so smoking cessation is always encouraged.

The current list of "warning signs" for a stroke can be remembered by using the acronym FAST:

- **F**ace drooping: Does one side of the face droop, or is it numb?
- **A**rm weakness: Is one arm weak or numb? Ask the person to lift both arms. Does one arm drift downward?
- **S**peech difficulty: Is speech slurred? Is the person unable to speak, or are they hard to understand?
- **T**ime to call 911: If the person shows any of these symptoms, even if the symptoms go away, call 911 and get them to the hospital immediately.

Beyond **FAST**, there are other symptoms that you should know:

- sudden onset of numbness or weakness of the face, arms, or legs, particularly on one side of the body
- sudden confusion and trouble speaking or understanding speech
- sudden trouble seeing in one eye or both eyes
- sudden trouble walking, dizziness, or loss of balance or coordination
- sudden severe headache with no known cause[75]

---

[74] Google, Leading Causes of Death.
[75] American Heart Association website.

Of the fifty people I interviewed who suffered a stroke, no one said they experienced anything prior to their stroke they would have considered as a "warning"; *instead, they reported experiencing these symptoms as their stroke occurred.*

Based upon what people told me, the label given to this list is somewhat misleading. If you experience any of these symptoms, or warning signs, be aware **you are experiencing a medical emergency.** Call 911 immediately or get to the nearest emergency room as safely and as quickly as possible. Many communities now have designated stroke centers. If you suffer from any of the stroke risk factors, it would be a good idea to familiarize yourself with the location of such centers.

Managing current risk factors is one way to avoid a possible catastrophic event. I propose identification of this neuromuscular pattern of dysfunction, *or improved body awareness,* could be another valuable way to maintain good health. The best thing about this suggestion is you do not have to wait for an appointment for someone else to test you. And it's absolutely free. Being aware of your traumatic history and assessing yourself for components of this abnormal pattern can give you information you can start doing something about today.

In the case of my three patients, who are all under thirty years of age, all three have had episodes of significant trauma in their lives. They were all manifesting pain somewhere along the unilateral pathway of pain. They were all making postural accommodations for the pain. None of them smokes. None of them has high blood pressure, heart disease, high cholesterol, or diabetes, but all three were demonstrating abnormal patterns of movement. They have also been educated about how to reverse this pattern by following through with exercises to "back them out of" their condition.

I wonder if the lingering effects of unresolved trauma in our bodies can contribute to or predispose us to the development of other medical conditions later in life. Since this pattern of neuromuscular dysfunction is already present in my patients at twenty-nine, twenty-three, and ten years of age, what symptoms could this pattern provoke if it persists into their forties, fifties, or sixties? Or the better question may be "What conditions might they avoid by restoring healthy flexibility to their soft tissues and improving their overall posture today?"

Exercise is always part of the treatment protocol for diabetes or heart disease. Aerobic conditioning is always valuable, but I believe postural correction and improved myofascial flexibility are just as important. In fact, clearance of postural deficits and myofascial restrictions may be "a must" before other forms of exercise can be tolerated. For those who do not tolerate walking or aerobic conditioning, the exercises proposed in this text offer a stepping-stone to help you get there. For those who have had a poor tolerance for exercise, **Rapid Release** provides a form of movement most anyone will potentially tolerate.

In Conclusion

The current burden on medical professionals to relieve the ailments of the American population is overwhelming. It is not uncommon to wait several weeks or longer to get an appointment to see a physician for a routine check-up. Scheduling an appointment to see a specialist is often even more difficult. Waiting rooms are full of people needing help.

Unfortunately, I've listened to *hundreds* of people tell me their stories of persistent pain, missed work, lost sleep, multiple doctor appointments and tests, and one failed medication after another. After "being through the entire system," they still have the same complaint they started with. The "pain" of missed work, strained relationships, and mounting medical and pharmaceutical bills are separate but very real aspects of this pain. The frustration felt and the discouragement lived with is real and valid. Sadly, living with chronic pain is becoming "the American way."

If you see what I do based upon the examples I have given, hopefully, you will agree the effects of unresolved trauma are largely responsible for the magnitude of this problem. You are probably asking yourself, "But, how can I avoid trauma?" Short of living in a bubble, you can't. There are probably very few of us who have not taken at least one serious fall. There are probably very few who will make it through life without being in some sort of motor vehicle accident. With sports now being so highly competitive at younger and younger ages, I fear the upcoming generations are in store for some pretty rough times in the years ahead.

But the future need not look so bleak. We do not have to give up everything we love doing today for fear of destroying our futures. *But we should be more reasonable about the way we maintain our bodies.* If you play hard or make great demands on your body through hard physical labor or fun or have suffered some form of direct trauma, making a deliberate effort to offset the damages done would be a wise choice. Be smart and intentional in the way you take care of your body.

Hopefully, the information I have provided in this book will give you some direction to do just that. *Maybe you should begin by correcting your posture.* The solution to improving and maintaining your health can be quite simple, even though it may not be easy to carry out. If the ideas put forth in this book do not provide you with "the cure" you are looking for, improving your posture and flexibility should, at least, contribute to your improvement.

The notion that injuries from a fall or a MVA "will heal on their own in time" needs to go. *Early intervention* to treat damaged soft tissue with ice and gentle comprehensive movement following any form of trauma is critical. Achieving and maintaining improved posture and flexibility throughout life should be the goal. **The main thing is to start moving and keep moving.** A flexible body is a more pain-free, comfortable, and functional body. Follow up your improved flexibility with reasonable strengthening and aerobic conditioning.

But what if you already suffer from lingering pain? Your opportunity to address your problem early has already passed you by. Begin by identifying the root of the problem. I am sure if you think about it, you will remember a time when your body sustained a trauma. I am also sure you will find evidence of increased fascial tension already in your body as you assess your posture in supine. Then as you follow the instructions put forth in this book, you will begin to see a positive change and improvement in your condition. You will not only improve your current situation, but you will be taking steps today to assure yourself of a much healthier and richer quality of life for many years to come.

It's never too late to begin this process.

Consider the history of a seventy-one-year-old woman who recently went through a very stressful time in her life. Her mode of escape was to spend eight or nine hours each day reading. After keeping this schedule for one week, she developed constant bilateral (right slightly greater than the left) sacral pain of 6/10 and right groin pain and tightness of 8/10. The groin pain would decrease slightly with walking to 6/10 but would return to 8/10 immediately with sitting and reading.

The traumatic history for this patient included a fractured tailbone at age thirty-one when she fell on a loose brick on a concrete sidewalk. She was unable to sit for four to six weeks as the fracture healed. At age forty-one, she sustained a moderate whiplash injury when she was rear-ended. She has had bilateral shoulder bursitis ever since, making it very difficult to do any type of overhead work. She cannot wear a bra without cutting off the circulation to her hands, creating a noticeable numbness.

Approximately ten years ago when her shoulder pain reached constant pain levels of 8/10 restricting more of her motion, she tried physical therapy. The modalities helped reduce her pain to a constant 5/10, but the exercises actually made her range of motion worse. She discontinued the exercises, accepted her movement deficits, and has learned to tolerate her persistent pain. She has not been able to identify the cause, but her shoulder pain will increase at times to 8/10. This pain usually occurs at night, disturbing her sleep.

The last trauma she sustained affected her right hip and leg. Twenty years ago, she hurriedly went over an eight-foot wall. She fell five or six feet onto her right shoulder and hip, causing her old tailbone injury to flare-up. The pain of 2–9/10 she has experienced in her right hip and thigh, gluts, and lower back since this injury has restricted her ability to forward bend at the waist. Simple tasks like loading and unloading her dishwasher provoke severe right thigh pain. She was unable to go to sleep each night until complete exhaustion finally ushered her into sleep. She finally resorted to using either pain or sleeping medications each night to sleep. Lastly, about twelve years ago, she used her right leg to help move a grandfather clock. This injury exacerbated her right thigh pain. At times, the pain still limits her stride so severely she can barely walk.

Her response to this complete exercise program was remarkable. After two weeks of daily completion of the exercises, her right groin pain decreased to 3/10—if it occurs. It no longer is provoked every time she sits. Her sacral pain is still constant but only at 1/10. Prior to beginning the exercises, she could not run her vacuum. She now vacuums as much as she needs to with very minimal sacral pain. Because she loves to work in her yard, she would spend every other day for up to four hours planting, raking, or digging with the assistance of painkillers. Now she tolerates the same routine yard work for up to six hours daily without painkillers. She uses her pain meds to help her tolerate only especially heavy physical activities.

This has all made her very happy, but she has been the most pleased to report that she no longer is experiencing the shoulder pain she has suffered with for the past thirty years. Part of the joy she feels is because this relief came as a total surprise. She was not expecting to see any change in such a long-standing problem. But her shoulder pain is completely gone. Her range of motion is no longer restricted overhead. She continues to experience the numbness in both hands with overhead work, but digging in her yard, pulling weeds, or scrubbing walls no longer provokes any type of shoulder pain. She has been reluctant to sleep without her medications, but we are both hopeful sleeping will improve as she works through the exercise progression.

She has always pushed herself to do the kind of work that has confused people about her age. It's nice for her to be able to do some of those things now without the constant pain she has grown accustomed to.

It is never too late to improve your health. These are the words she wrote about these exercises at the completion of her therapy:

> *Dearest Nancy,*
>
> *Thank you for your gift of healing.*
>
> *As you know, I have coped with several painful problems over the course of the past thirty years. I have always sought help at different times for each specific one. When my response was either partial or temporary, I was convinced some things just can't be fixed.*
>
> *I never would have guessed all of my aches and pains could be helped with one exercise program! What a wonderful surprise it was for me to begin the exercises to help relieve my lower back pain, but I improved in my lower back and in my shoulders! Plus, my endurance and stamina for working outside in my yard has noticeably improved.*
>
> *I have only been doing your complete program within this last month, but I am encouraged by the improvement I am already seeing. I still need to take my painkillers if I plan to do really heavy physical labor and will experience some returned*

pain if I skip my exercises. I am hoping to see improvement even in these areas as I progress the exercises in the way we discussed.

I do your exercises nightly. This is a "lifetime program" I plan to use for the rest of my life. Thank you, Nancy, for your creative healing exercises.

With love,

This patient had lived with shoulder pain for thirty years. Now it's gone. I must say it is sometimes still hard for me to believe what I am hearing, even though I have heard things like this from my patients over and over for the past eighteen-plus years. It is now nine years since this patient learned the exercises. I just met her for dinner a few nights ago. She told me her shoulder pain has never returned in spite of the fact that she has not continued to do the exercises on a daily basis.

One of the most recent patients I treated made so many positive comments to me about this program, you would have thought I had given her a list of compliments and observations to read back to me! She came to my current place of employment following a total hip replacement, but had an extensive history of dental complications throughout her lifetime. These complications were influencing her recovery from surgery. I will use her letter as the closing comments from my patients.

Dear Nancy:

It was a pleasure working with you after total hip replacement surgery. The exercises you have given me will go a long way in helping me. Perhaps this letter will encourage others to give them a try.

The exercises are designed to reduce pain, increase range of motion, and provide relaxation. They have done all of this for me. In addition to the positive results, I like them because:

- *They are easy to learn.*
- *They are non-invasive (I don't need another medication)*
- *They do not violate any of the surgical hip precautions.*
- *They require no special equipment.*
- *They are flexible as to time commitment, whether I have 10 minutes or an hour.*

- They are progressively challenging and build post-op confidence while remaining tailored to individual needs and limitations.

I think these exercises would have been useful and helpful for me as pre-operation physical therapy. They could be taught to patients and caregivers in small groups.

Perhaps most of all, these exercises have shown me that individual, small changes can make a big difference. I'm not even sure how to communicate what such small movements with my eyes and tongue have done to help my leg and knee. The results are impressive!

Best wishes,

This patient could be the "poster child" for **Rapid Release.** I could not have summarized the benefits of this program any better than she did. Now that you have read what many of my patients have said to me, I would like to leave you with some thoughts of my own.

Dear Reader,

It's your turn to do the exercises!

If you are any type of therapist or medical provider, I hope my message of correcting postural imbalances and improving global flexibility as a forerunner or adjunct to other therapies resonates with you. I hope you will consider what part the eyes, jaw and cervical spine might be playing in the condition of your patient who is struggling to improve. I, also, hope the different case examples I have included help you understand how to apply the principles of this method to help patients on your current caseload.

If you are a "patient," my hope and prayer is for you to experience the pain relief you have been looking for. Consider how the rest of your body may be influencing your current area of pain or dysfunction. Make time to take care of yourself and get the help you need. Be patient with yourself. Taking "two steps forward and one step back" can happen to anyone attempting to recover from anything. Just don't give up!

Consider the following three questions as you begin to help yourself or your patient:

1. Has there been a previous trauma that could be complicating my current condition, or the condition of my patient?
2. What am I doing or is being done by my patient on a recurrent basis that causes deviation away from correct posture or bodily symmetry? Are there lifestyle changes that could be made to facilitate more improvement in my condition? Examples are interrupting prolonged use of my eyes for reading, time on the computer, or crafting as well as sitting with my computer or television off to one side of center, or poor posture while sleeping.
3. How much time will I ask my patient to designate or can I designate each day towards correcting my posture in the modified supine position or by lying down flat on my back with the position of my head and neck in correct alignment? When will I begin to implement the exercises in this book to improve my posture and general flexibility?

I wish I could be there personally to help each one of you. I've tried to be clear and thorough in my instructions so you can successfully help yourself. I hope I accomplished what I set out to do.

God bless you in your journey to improved health and healing!

Sincerely,
Nancy

Made in United States
Troutdale, OR
02/17/2024

17754285R00300